WILLIAMS, Peter F. The organ music of J.S. Bach. v.2: Works based on chorales (BWV 599-771 etc). Cambridge, 1980 357p (Cambridge studies in music) bibl index 77-71431. 47.50 ISBN 0-521-21517-X. CIP

An important and excellent reference work for organists and students of music. Volume 2 (the first to be published) is very clearly organized. Each composition is studied via sources and their relationship; chorale melody is printed in full; one or more stanzas of the text are given in German and literal English translation. There are, in addition, a description of the chorale's place in the life of Bach's church, analysis of the form and style of the organ setting with comments on motif structure, and a valuable synthesis of other commentators' views, citing both standard books and less available sources. Williams is editor of *The Organ Yearbook* and author of the volumes in the "BBC music guides" series, *Bach organ music* (1972), *The European organ* (1966), and *Figured bass accompaniment* (CHOICE, May 1973). For graduate, undergraduate, and public libraries.

Cambridge Studies in Music
General Editors: John Stevens and Peter le Huray

The Organ Music of J. S. Bach

I

The Organ Music of J. S. Bach

I

Preludes, Toccatas, Fantasias, Fugues, Sonatas, Concertos and Miscellaneous Pieces

(BWV 525–598, 802–805 etc)

by Peter Williams

CAMBRIDGE UNIVERSITY PRESS

CAMBRIDGE
LONDON NEW YORK NEW ROCHELLE
MELBOURNE SYDNEY

Published by the Press Syndicate of the University of Cambridge
The Pitt Building, Trumpington Street, Cambridge CB2 1RP
32 East 57th Street, New York, NY 10022, USA
296 Beaconsfield Parade, Middle Park, Melbourne 3206, Australia

First published 1980

Printed in Great Britain at the
University Press, Cambridge

Library of Congress Cataloguing in Publication Data
Williams, Peter F.
The organ music of J. S. Bach.
(Cambridge studies in music)
Includes indexes.
Bibliography: p.
1. Bach, Johann Sebastian, 1685–1750. Works, organ.
I. Title. II. Series.
MT145.B14W53 1978   786.6′22′4   77-71431

ISBN 0 521 21723 7

For Lucy and Daniel

Contents

Preface

Even were the *Neue Bach-Ausgabe* complete or near-complete, neither this nor any other book on Bach's organ music could claim to have the last word. Each generation must look anew at this incomparable body of music, re-examine it in the light of contemporary knowledge, view it in a way relevant to its own attitudes towards music and towards the task of the music scholar. Because it is now thirty years since this music last received a complete commentary, the need for one has grown as, too, the wider possibilities of contemporary musical research have made it possible.

One current attitude is to analyse the composer's creative method in general (i.e. what 'style' he is adopting) and in terms of the music theory contemporary with him (e.g. whether his attention was focused on the *Figurenlehre*). Another is to place each piece against a background of its own source-material, not only to establish (or question) its authenticity but to supply the present-day performer with evidence for the piece as it stands. This book aims at satisfying these two current attitudes, both of which centre on the notes themselves – *as composed* on the one hand and *as preserved in the sources* on the other. It frequently refers to other attitudes or approaches, most notably those of the composer's admirers in the first decades after his death (Marpurg, Kirnberger etc), of the scientific scholars a century later (Rust, Spitta etc) and of the more recent commentators (Schweitzer, Keller etc). But each of these, including the earliest, wrote in musical and church contexts far removed from, and in some cases alien to, those of the composer in Weimar and Leipzig. All such approaches are therefore based both on fact and on conjecture; at best they serve to show what 'facts' and what 'conjectures' any one period will accept. Some of the big issues, particularly the dating of the organ works, allow room only for conjecture, however careful it might be; in a piece-by-piece commentary of this kind, the context does not allow the expansive treatment which is really required by any such label as '*c*1710–12'. Thus some questions have been left without summary conclusion, many pieces have been commented on from only one or two angles, and only a wide reading of the book will give the reader an idea of the several possible analytical approaches to music by this most carefully reasoning of all organ composers.

The present volume concerns all works not based on chorales, including those of *Clavierübung III* and including transcriptions by J. S. Bach of other composers' music, as well as arrangements by other composers of J. S. Bach's music.

I wish to thank in particular the following for help and advice: Dr

Roger Bullivant (Sheffield), Mr Stephen Daw (Birmingham), Dr Alfred Dürr (Göttingen), Dr Dietrich Kilian (Göttingen), Professor Dr Hans Klotz (Cologne), Dr Peter le Huray (Cambridge), and the Rev. Theo Thermann (Freiberg). Amongst other kindnesses, Dr Dürr and Dr Kilian allowed me to use the source lists of *NBA* iv/5 *KB* before they were published. Mr Eric Van Tassel of the Cambridge University Press sifted the text and gave it whatever ease of expression it may have. As for the help of Dr Hans-Joachim Schulze (Leipzig), I do not think the book could have been written without it, although he has no responsibility for any opinion or mis-statement.

January 1977   Peter Williams

Errata in Volume II

p. 6, footnote † line 3: *for* L. P. Plantinga *read* L. B. Plantinga

p. 124, line 24: *for* nineteen *read* fifteen

p. 166, line 4: *for* (b37 etc) *read* (b27 etc)

p. 175, line 19: *for* Balthaser *read* Balthasar

p. 206, line 1: *for* used also in *read* used partly in

p. 207, line above Ex. 201: *for* second lines *read* second line

p. 269, last line: *for* repeated five times as bb53–102 *read* repeated four times as bb63–102

p. 280, last line: *for* (p 285, *read* (P 285,

p. 295, line 2: *for* (p 285) *read* (P 285)

p. 336, under 'Brussels II.3919': *the second line should read* MS probably once in Fétis's collection, corresponding in part to his

p. 337, line 1: *for* P 244 *read* P 224

p. 344, line 31: *for* Paretorius *read* Praetorius

p. 350, under 'Legrenzi': *for* 1636–90 *read* 1626–90

p. 351, under 'Plantinga': *for* L. P. *read* L. B.

p. 351, under 'Scheibe': *for* Naumburg 1736 *read* Hamburg 1736

p. 351, under 'Schmid(t)': *after* 175, *insert* 177,

p. 352, under 'Türk': *for* Halle from 1774 *read* Halle from 1776

Note on the Commentary

The commentary on each work is arranged in the following order:

Title. In the case of the present volume, the title is that accepted in most of the various editions of the last hundred years or so. However, as the listed titles from selected sources of certain pieces show (see 'Headings' below), a familiar title such as 'Fantasia' may not be that by which the work was first or always known; many pieces may well have had no title at all in the composer's or first copyists' MSS from which others were made; many may have had a more conventional title than 'Toccata and Fugue' or 'Prelude and Fugue', such as 'Praeludium'. Some titles, such as 'Aria in F', are of particularly uncertain or unverifiable origin and have been left in quotation marks.

All nicknames, including those familiar to half a dozen generations of English organists, have been omitted, as being either unwarranted (e.g. 'Dorian Toccata') or, in view of the BWV numbers, unnecessary (e.g. 'Wedge Fugue', 'Great G major'). The same applies to names not justified by the sources (e.g. 'Trio Sonatas').

Sources. The first reference is to any known Autograph MS, reputed autograph or printed edition ('published 1739'). Important 'copies' are then referred to, 'copy' being understood to mean 'written specimen' in general, not a reproduction of the autograph. The order implies only the approximate chronology and/or importance of the sources. No attempt is made to provide a full *Kritischer Bericht* or textual commentary, nor to borrow the as yet unpublished numbering system for the sources to be adopted by the *NBA* IV/5–6 *KB* volumes. Copies listed are those of particular importance to the 'genealogy' of the pieces, including any autograph, original engraving, early copy (perhaps of an earlier version or draft than the extant autograph), including lost or destroyed MSS. A name in brackets ( ) after the MS number is that of the previous owner or copyist. The term 'late sources' does not necessarily indicate poor, unauthorized or unimportant sources, since some may derive more directly from an early good source than older copies. Where the basic source is good, other copies are often summarized as belonging to such groups of copyists as the 'Kirnberger circle' or 'Kittel pupils'. For further details of the MSS, including fuller library references, see the List of Musical Sources. Typical abbreviations in the commentary are:

Autograph MS P 271 = autograph copy extant, listed as P 271 (for which see the List of Musical Sources)

P 1109 (Penzel) = copy in the hand of, or once in the possession of, C. F. Penzel (for whom see the Index and the List of Musical Sources)

Brief biographical details of the copyists etc are included in the Index.

Headings. Any subsidiary title or direction (e.g. 'a 2 clav. e ped.') is taken from a named source; these are not always the same as in *BG* and subsequent editions. For a note on the various titles, see above. Some good sources such as the *Andreas-Bach-Buch* use titles to suggest, with or without authorization, that the work concerned has a stylistic association or pretension.

That most pieces were copied on two staves only underlines the doubts that must occasionally arise about what if anything is to be played by pedals, what the composer originally expected, whether he or another copyist gave the work a different aspect later by specifying pedals, etc. The history of three-stave organ notation, as distinct from an open score, is a subject of its own and deserves fuller treatment in a more general study.

Commentary. The references to previous authors are selective and usually concern those who recently or formerly, worthy or unworthy, have had wide influence on players and writers. No attempt has been made to list the published views of all commentators on any one piece; rather, remarks have been included when typical of a particular period (e.g. Harvey Grace) or when particularly useful (e.g. Emery), even as examples of views or information no longer considered correct. Particularly selective have been the references to English authors.

The references are normally expressed in abbreviated form; thus 'Spitta 1 p595' = P. Spitta, *Johann Sebastian Bach*, vol. 1 (Leipzig, 1873), page 595. All the abbreviations are explained with full details in the List of References.

In this commentary, discussions of chronology, purpose, the organ, registration, manual-changing, performance practice etc are limited to questions arising from the stylistic nature of the piece concerned (e.g. the 'rhetoric' in BWV 538 or proportional tempos in BWV 572 or BWV 802–805) or from the reliability or meaning of the source material (e.g. the Concerto in D minor BWV 596). Such subjects require wider treatment in a separate volume, and emphasis here has rather been laid on two particular aspects of the music: form and figuration.

(*a*) *form*, i.e. the overall design behind the bar-by-bar composition.* Not only is the variety of shape from one prelude or fugue to another itself a matter for understanding and admiration, but it is instructive in the total view of a composer who, though unequalled in this particular field of organ music, worked also in several others which can

---

* In general, the bar-numbering in this volume ignores any repeat-marks. In most prelude-and-fugue pairs, sonatas, etc the movements are numbered separately, each starting afresh with 'b1'; but the bar-numbering is in one sequence through the whole of each of the following multi-sectional works: BWV 551, 553–560, 561, 563, 565, 566, 571, 572, 582, 588, 591.

hardly be thought isolated or irrelevant. Organists are perhaps not always aware of the great importance of Bach's organ music in the evolution of musical form and idioms; conversely, musicians attempting to understand (e.g.) sonata form are rarely aware of the appearance of development sections in some of Bach's organ music. Moreover, the form of a movement relates to various aspects of its performance – not so much when or whether to change stops but how to articulate, phrase, plan paragraphs and 'communicate the spirit' of the work, which is usually a question of specific musical details. All of these aspects could be misleadingly conveyed by a performer who, for example, misunderstood the nature of fugues with more than one subject, or who missed the fact that the final paragraph of the D minor Fugue BWV 538 begins not with the last pedal entry but a bar earlier with the manual stretto.

To limit the amount of commentary in this volume, particularly on smaller pieces, emphasis has often been laid exclusively on the *form* of the movement concerned. An example is the Four Duets BWV 802–805, where the carefully thought-out differences between the four pieces – amounting to a conscious repertory of formal, figurative (motivic) and other details – are demonstrated by the brief account of their differences in shape and in fugue form.

(*b*) *figuration* or use of *figurae* (see Glossary). In the commentary on the Six Sonatas BWV 525–530, for example, the concentration on the motifs and the way in which lines have been built up by the composer has led to an account of the works very different from the several kinds of commentary to which such faultless works could lead. However, apart from the instructiveness of this approach to the creative process of J. S. Bach, such an examination of the bar-by-bar detail has implications for the performer. In general, Bach performance can be considered to be still in its infancy as far as the harpsichord and organ music is concerned, since no more than a tiny minority of performers are yet able to convey the motivic inventiveness of this music. The precise relationship between a particular motif and the way it should be played is complex and certainly outside the scope of this book. One cannot show that a *messanza* or even a *figura corta* should always be played in a certain way, for example. But equally, the performer must be aware that a group of sixteen semiquavers is not merely a group of sixteenths-of-a-semibreve which happen to occupy the same amount of absolute time as a semibreve; they comprise specific shapes and motif types, sometimes listed and described as such in contemporary theory books, and they deserve as much liveliness of thought from the interpreter as they required inventiveness of creation from the composer in the first place. I think awareness of the compositional detail brings to the alert performer awareness of his role as 'interpreter' – a word much misused but essentially suggesting that the performer has his own understanding or 'interpretation' to convey, but only if or when he has understood how the composer reached the finished product. The preludes of Bk I of *Das Wohltemperirte Clavier* (*The 48*), for example, exploit a far-flung range of motifs which no player could hope to convey unless he has understood the details of that range, the distinction intended between the eight-semiquaver motif of the C major Prelude and that of the C minor Prelude, or the totally different purpose served by the triplet figure of the D minor from that of the G major Prelude, and so on. More subtly, the lines of the Six Sonatas for organ are constructed of figures or motifs not only as a means for the composer but as a vehicle for the performer. Insufficient attention is paid to this fact even by thoughtful performers – one of the beliefs which have governed the emphases and lines of approach in this book.

131a   Fugue in G minor

No Autograph MS; copies in P 320 (J. C. Kittel) and early-19th-century sources (P 313, P 319, P 557, Lpz MB III.8.22, Lpz Go.S.318a) perhaps directly or indirectly from Kittel (e.g. by way of a MS by Dröbs: Seiffert 1907 p 180).

Usual heading, 'Fuga'.

The 45 bars are a keyboard version of the final fugue of Cantata 131, 'Aus der Tiefe rufe ich, Herr, zu dir' (1707). It is uncertain whether the keyboard or choral version came first, who made the arrangement if the keyboard version came second, or whether it is for organ. It has been asked whether the cantata movement may be derived from the organ fugue (Seiffert 1907 p180), although the contrary is usually assumed; it has been suggested (Keller, in *BJ* 1937) that J. S. Bach was the arranger, although he is usually thought not to be (Spitta I p451; *MGG* I col.1014); and the fugue is assumed to be for organ, although the sources contain miscellaneous keyboard fugues.* The extant score of the cantata is a contemporary autograph, but both BWV 131 and 131a seem to have been known by certain later copyists (e.g. Anton Werner's copies of the cantata in P 442 and of the organ fugue in P 313). As a species of fugue, the movement is somewhat different from most of the organ fugues of more certain origin and raises important questions of style and form.

Ex. 1

a

b b2   *c* b5

The fugue is a permutation fugue in which the three subjects (Ex. 1) are invertible and are systematically inverted in different order. The themes, themselves clearly distinguished from each other in their character as archetypes or prototypes, can combine at points other than those shown in the opening bars; thus although it has no interludes (unlike such permutation fugues as that of the Passacaglia BWV 582) the movement is more complex than others in this genre. A particularly characteristic prototype theme is the chromatic tetrachord (*b*), unusual in this instance in that it is rising (but a further example is the subject of Pachelbel's C minor Ricercar). It seems to have been natural for one

---

* E.g., Lpz MB III.8.22 contains four fugues (BWV 549, 579, 131a, 546), only the last of which is headed '...con Pedale obligato'.

of the lines in a permutation fugue to be chromatic (cf. Buxtehude's D minor Praeludium BUXWV 140).*

Correspondences between the choral and organ fugues are as follows:

BWV 131	BWV 131a
SATB, oboe, violin, 2 violas and continuo	2-stave keyboard
bb313–25	bb1–13: opening chord added; continuo bass omitted in bb1–2, 5–7, 9 etc; confuses inner double subject in bb4–5 (b4 = tenor, b5 = alto); bass simplified for pedal in bb11–12
bb326–40	14–28: *c* subject from oboe omitted in bb14–15, 18–19; semiquaver lines of oboe and violin omitted in bb23–8; continuo bass omitted; inner parts omitted bb24, 27
bb341–53	29–41: *c* in bass simplified in bb29–30, soprano omitted ditto; continuo bass omitted; semiquaver and quaver lines of violin omitted bb31–41; bass simplified and altered for pedal in bb34–7; also simplified in bb36–7
bb354–8	42–5: last five bars of original (which began with an echo repeat of previous phrase) omitted, replaced by the four bars that preceded the fugue in BWV 131 (there in nine parts)

Other details in BWV 131, both thematic and non-thematic, are absent from BWV 131a. From the absence or omission of thematic material, it can be assumed that BWV 131a is taken from 131, for although the versatile motif shape of *c* could have been added by a skilled composer to a pre-existing texture – i.e., in this respect BWV 131 could be a more complex re-working of BWV 131a – the point of a permutation fugue would be its permutations, which always required *c*. The omission of lines impossible for two hands suggests that BWV 131a was made for performance on a keyboard, while the simplified bass line specifically suggests the organ. Although the simpler, more succinct ending of BWV 131a does not prove it to be an arrangement of the climactic and vocally conceived ending to BWV 131 – because the ending of BWV 131a is also vocal in origin – the gradual increase from two to five parts in the cantata version, with its increased complexity as the movement proceeds, does suggest that it was the original version. It is an interesting and unusual feature of the cantata itself that its opening and closing movements are cast as a prelude and fugue.

* Mattheson's treatment of three-part invertible counterpoint (1739 p442) included an example from J. Krieger's D minor Fugue, one of whose lines was also a descending chromatic tetrachord or *passus duriusculus*.

525–530   Six Sonatas

Autograph MS P 271. No autograph title-page; each sonata entitled 'Sonata à 2 Clav: et Pedal'. Title-page by G. Poelchau (1773–1836), who bought the MS after C. P. E. Bach's estate was sold in 1790 (*Dok* III p496): *Sechs Orgel-Trios für zwei Manuale mit dem obligaten Pedal* ('Six Organ Trios for two manuals with obbligato pedal').

Questions concerning the sources (date, purpose) and nature of the Six Sonatas (musical origins, style and form, influence) can be summarized as follows:

(i) **Sources.** Although it is a unified and single manuscript, P 271 as the first complete source of the Six Sonatas (Kilian 1978 p65) 'is a compilation, based partly on earlier material' (Emery 1957 p80) and is to be dated *c*1730 (Dadelsen 1958 p104); its watermark has long been thought to indicate a date not earlier than 1727 (Spitta II pp692, 797). For other music in this manuscript, see BWV 651–668, 769.

P 272 is a copy made by W. F. Bach (pp1–36, probably direct from P 271) and by Anna Magdalena Bach (pp37–86, certainly direct from P 271). The latter section, and perhaps both sections, may have been written during 1730–3 (Dadelsen 1957 p18); W. F. Bach's section may well have replaced more generously spaced pages written by Anna Magdalena (Emery *op cit*). P 271 may have been completed by the time W. F. Bach was admitted to the University of Leipzig as a law student (5 March 1729), and P 272 by the time he moved to Dresden as organist of the Sophienkirche, where his duties began on 1 August 1733. None of these speculations are certain, however. In addition to MS copies of single movements, of movements in other instrumental versions, and of earlier versions of the movements taken into P 271, the Six Sonatas were perhaps copied complete in at least four major sources: Am.B. 51 (copied indirectly from P 271 for Princess Anna Amalia of Prussia, by the same copyist as the chorales in Am.B. 46) and Am.B. 51a (copied from Am.B. 51 by an anonymous copyist once thought to have been J. F. Agricola (1720–74)); Vienna Cod. 15528 (J. C. Oley (1738–89)); P 840 (C. A. Klein (late eighteenth century)). Amongst other copies, some belong to the early nineteenth century (P 273, P 278, P 302, perhaps all directly or indirectly from P 272), by which time the sonatas had been published or were about to be published (Wesley & Horn, London 1809–10; Nägeli, Zürich 1827). Late copies of single sonatas or movements, now held in Leipzig, Berlin, Brussels, Darmstadt, Göttweig, Göttingen, and Bethlehem (Pennsylvania), will be collated in future *NBA* volumes.

(ii) Origin and purpose. While the date when P 271 is thought to have been compiled serves as an end-date for the sonatas as now known, the movements have various histories. A general survey gives the following picture of the movements (Eppstein 1969; Emery 1957 pp128, 194):

BWV	composed for compilation	as organ work	as transcription	uncertain	later adaptation
		composed previously			
525	ii	i?	iii?		
526	i iii			ii	
527			ii?	i iii	ii?
528		ii iii	i		
529	i iii?	ii		iii?	
530	i ii iii				

According to such surveys, only the last sonata was composed throughout as an organ trio or sonata. No significance in the choice of keys and of their order has yet been found (Eppstein 1976 p38), although it is possible that an original or intended order was C minor – D minor – E minor – C major – E flat major – G major (Kilian 1978 p66).

The purpose and even the period of the compilation were clear to Forkel (1802 ch.ix):

Sechs Sonaten oder Trio[s] für zwey Claviere mit dem obligaten Pedal. Bach hat sie für seinen ältesten Sohn, Wilh. Friedemann, aufgesetzt, welcher sich damit zu dem grossen Orgelspieler vorbereiten musste, der er nachher geworden ist. Man kann von ihrer Schönheit nicht genug sagen. Sie sind in dem reifsten Alter des Verfassers gemacht, und können als das Hauptwerk desselben in dieser Art angesehen werden.

Six Sonatas or Trios for two manuals with obbligato pedal. Bach drew them up for his eldest son Wilhelm Friedemann, who had to prepare [= must have prepared?] himself by this means to become the great organ-player that he was afterwards. One cannot say enough of their beauty. They were made during the composer's most mature age and can be looked upon as his chief work of this kind.

Whatever speculation may be thought justified about the term 'zwey Claviere' (organ? harpsichord? clavichord?), it should be noted that Forkel's paragraph is included in the section 'Organ Pieces'; he did not say 'composed' for W. F. Bach but 'aufgesetzt'.* Both the terms 'Trio' and 'for organ' were usual in references to the Six Sonatas. The Obituary of 1754 had referred to 'Sechs Trio für die Orgel mit dem obligaten Pedale' (*Dok* III p86); in a MS catalogue of 1783 they are called '6 Sonaten für die Orgel, mit 2 Clav. & Pedal' (*Dok* III p272), as they

---

* Forkel's usual words for 'composed' were 'componirt', 'gemacht', 'ausgearbeitet', etc; 'setzt' is also used in connection with other instrumental works (Violin Solos etc) which had been so composed 'that their players were able through them to progress on their instruments' (ch. ix). However, in a review of 1799 Forkel had already noted the 'sechs Trios, welche der Grosse Mann für seinen ältesten Sohn Wilhelm Friedemann einst gemacht hat' ('Six Trios which the great man once wrote for his eldest son' – *Dok* III p585).

are in other references of the period. Despite assertions still made, there is no clear indication that '2 Clav. & Pedal' suggested pedal harpsichord or pedal clavichord, as Kinsky has shown (Kinsky 1936). Moreover, since neither hand goes below tenor c, the pieces 'can be studied on organs of only one manual and pedal' with 4' registration and the left hand down an octave (Klotz 1975 p377).

Several early references are full of admiration:

Trios, sind 6. dergleichen für die Orgel von ihn übrig, für 2 Manuale und das Pedal, die so schön, so neu, erfindungsreich sind, dass sie nie veralten sondern alle Moderevolutionen in der Musik überleben werden (c1777, *Dok* III p313)

Trios: there still exist six of these by him for the organ, for 2 manuals and pedal, that are so beautiful, so new and rich in invention, that they will never age but will outlive all changes of fashion in music.

The terms of this praise, however, are so like those of the 1788 'Comparison between Handel and Bach' (*Dok* III p441) as to suggest plagiarism rather than intimate acquaintance with the music itself. More to the point was Kollmann's remark in 1799 that 'pieces of this kind, when properly executed, exceed everything else in the art of organ-playing' (*Dok* III p582), not least since such praise suggests the sonatas to belong to 'the art of organ-playing' rather than to the functional repertory of the church organist as such. No doubt several Bach pupils worked in the trio medium as players and composers. Examples are W. F. Bach himself in a lost Trio on 'Allein Gott' (Falck 1913 no. 38.2) and H. N. Gerber, whose autograph organ book dated 1727 (Princeton University Library) already includes an 'Inventio 4 in E a 2 Clav. & Ped'. Although the date of this 'Inventio' is unknown, Gerber wrote other sets in or before 1734 (six *Concert-trios für Zwey Claviere und Pedal*) and 1737 (*VI Inventiones für die Orgel mit 2 Klavier und Pedal*), according to E. L. Gerber's *Lexicon* (1790–2, under 'Gerber'). Four short anonymous 'Inventions' in the MS LM 4941 (which also contains a 'Trio a 2 Clav & Pedal' of J. J. Adlung) are composed more in the Telemann manner, i.e. partially imitative dialogues above a continuo bass. In addition, later-eighteenth-century arrangements of the Six Sonatas are not uncommon – by Mozart for string trio (see BWV 526, 527), by an unknown arranger for two harpsichords (all Six Sonatas in the MS St 401), by S. Wesley for three hands on one piano (published 1809–10). That the left hand does not descend below c may also have suggested to arrangers of these later periods that it could be put down an octave and both parts played on one manual.

The two traditions of the Six Sonatas, as music first to practise and secondly to admire, were enough to account for their origins and purpose in all known references to them before the nineteenth-century editors and commentators began to equate 'Clavier' with clavichord and thence to speculate on the purpose in domestic music-making of both the Sonatas and the Passacaglia (e.g. Griepenkerl, preface to Peters 1, 1844). While there is some evidence for instrumental trio sonatas being played in north German churches during Communion or on special occasions in which such composers as Buxtehude or Reincken took part

(Riedel 1960 p180), there is none for organ sonatas in any such context; nor are any details known of the organ trios said by Forkel in 1803 to have been composed by Handel while he was still at Halle (Kinsky 1936 p160). It was hardly sonatas of this kind that Mattheson had in mind when he suggested that preludes before cantatas ('Kirchen-Stücke') or hymns ('Choräle') could take the form of 'little sonatas or sonatinas' as distinct from fugues or variations (Mattheson 1739 p472).* Trio technique as a treatment for chorale melodies was of course familiar, and by the 1780s Türk used the term 'Orgeltrio' to describe them – three-part organ chorales, which were by then normally called 'Vorspiele' ('preludes' – *Dok* III p432). It is not known who told Forkel that the Six Sonatas were compiled for W. F. Bach – perhaps C. P. E. Bach, who corresponded with Forkel and who seems to have owned P 271 (*Dok* III p496). Nor is it certain that the compilation was made for the first time in P 271.

(iii) Trio types in organ music. While it remains true that no 'direct models for these Sonatas . . . have been discovered' (Emery 1957 p204), the various elements of form and texture were familiar to the composer by the time he had left Cöthen. Of the two, the texture was older.

Organ chorales in three parts are by nature more feasible as a texture than (e.g.) organ fugues in three parts, and they can be found in several different forms by the early eighteenth century. Parallel to such German chorales were the *trios, trios en dialogue* and *trios à trois claviers* of various 'good old French organists' evidently admired by J. S. Bach (*Dok* III p288). Most examples by Lebègue, de Grigny, Raison, Boyvin and Clérambault – i.e. from 1670 to 1710 – divide the texture into two manual parts above a bass-like pedal; sometimes the upper parts are imitative/fugal, but there is much movement in parallel thirds etc. Occasionally, all three parts have similar if simple imitative lines, producing mostly short movements, not binary or ritornello shapes as such. As is clear from the registrations given by the French composers, the various colour possibilities work towards clear but conventional timbres between the three parts of the trios: (1) manual with mutation colour (e.g. Cornet), (2) manual with 8′ (e.g. Cromorne) or 8′+4′ stops, (3) pedal 8′ Flûte.

That Bach had long known traditional three-part textures with cantus firmus is clear from (e.g.) Cantata 4; that at Weimar he also worked a chorale cantus firmus, a chorale paraphrase and an independent pedal part into a highly idiomatic movement of nearly a hundred bars is implied by the supposed history of the 'Trio super Allein Gott' BWV 664a. But the creative leap between Cantata 4.iv and BWV 664a cannot be matched by any known music written by other composers. If the trio 'Allein Gott' BWV 664a is to be dated to the middle or late Weimar years and the slow movement of Sonata IV to c1708, generalizations

---

* Mattheson speaks of preludes 'worunter aber eigentlich weder Fugen, noch variirte Sachen, obwol keine Sonaten oder Sonatinen gehören' ('amongst which, however, neither fugues nor variations really belong, although no sonatas or sonatinas do'); but 'keine' ('no') should presumably read 'kleine' ('little').

can be made about the way the trio technique developed. Sonata IV (BWV 528.ii) has a continuo bass line for the pedal part (like the trios of de Grigny etc) and two themes alternate and appear in various guises, the whole emphasizing two-bar phrases of immense charm but rather arbitrary continuity. On the other hand, BWV 664a has elements familiar in the developed sonata *allegro*: a thematic bass, subjects organized into a fully-fledged ritornello shape, episodes with broken-chord figures. Yet the distinction between the two trio techniques should not be overstated, for there is no single 'organ trio-sonata movement type'. Thus the octave imitation of BWV 528.ii is of itself no more an 'early' sign than the relatively homophonic style of the opening of BWV 526; on the contrary, the non-fugal openings to the C minor, C major and G major sonatas suggest a later date than the fugal opening of the others.

While it is generally true that the three-movement plan seems to resemble that of the organ concerto transcriptions, and the three-part texture that of trio sonatas by then familiar throughout Europe, the music itself is also in general very well suited to manuals and pedals. The upper parts would rarely be mistaken for violin or even flute lines, irrespective of compass. Moreover, as Emery observed (1957 p207), passages in the concertos that may resemble some of those in the sonatas (e.g. Concerto BWV 594.i b93ff and Sonata BWV 530.i b37ff) are typical of neither. If the organ concertos had any influence on the sonatas it would be a matter more of their form, and such details as their sequential episodes, than of their texture. Often the player may also feel that the two hands are not merely imitative or contrapuntal but are actually planned for the sake of the single player – in (e.g.) BWV 529.i syncopations dance from hand to hand in a manner not often familiar even to the two violinists of a trio sonata. Such syncopations are conceived specifically for the independence and balance of two hands in apposition and opposition. Similarly, the patent invertibility of two lines – e.g. the last eleven bars of the E minor Sonata – is not characteristic of the instrumental sonatas, despite their contrapuntal devices of stretto, canon or fugue. The question is one of degree: upper parts are exchangeable in music other than the Six Sonatas but rarely so patently as in the closing bars of the E minor Sonata.

(iv) Trio types in instrumental sonatas. Despite such details, the closest parallel to the Six Sonatas is clearly to be found in the works for solo instrument (violin or flute or gamba) and *cembalo* obbligato. This similarity is one of idiom and of the linear style. But although they all contain at least one fugal *allegro* movement, the instrumental sonatas differ in important details from the Six Sonatas for organ. Thus the manual compass of the latter – rh f♯–c‴ (mostly c′–c‴) and lh c–c‴ (mostly c–g″) – is obviously planned for the convenience of two hands and differs from that of the chamber sonatas. That the organ lines are not in fact easily adaptable is shown by the curious scoring by an anonymous later-eighteenth-century arranger of the E flat Sonata BWV 525 as a C major Sonata for Violin, Cello and Continuo (St 345). The two upper parts of the Six Sonatas for organ are always in dialogue, unlike those of the chamber sonatas, in which the harpsichord right hand sometimes accompanies in a kind of realized basso continuo.* The pedal lines at times resemble a continuo line (i.e. *cembalo* obbligato left hand in the case of the chamber sonatas), but only insofar as a continuo bass can be pedal-like, rather than vice versa. Whoever made the arrangement BWV 1027a certainly did not merely simplify the bass line of the Gamba Sonata BWV 1027; each version of the bass line has independent qualities. A common point is that in neither organ nor instrumental sonata does the bass part begin a movement thematically, though in both it sometimes starts a movement off (e.g. BWV 529.i and the E major Violin Sonata BWV 1016.iv).

Although various generalizations are often made about the Six Sonatas – e.g. that their first movements are more concerto-like in form than the violin sonatas (Eppstein 1969) – the variety between them precludes any easy summary. However, the final movements of both organ and instrumental sonatas usually have clear qualities in common. In form, texture and melody, the finale of the E major Violin Sonata is not unlike the first movement of the C major Organ Sonata; but the violin sonata has a more active bass line, and its rhythmic complexities would not be expected in an organ sonata. Together, the six organ sonatas and the eleven authentic instrumental sonatas present a repertory of trio techniques:

forms: slow first movements (not in organ sonatas)
        changes of tempo and form within a movement (BWV 528, 1030)
        ritornello movements of several lengths/sections, fast or slow
        ABA ritornello movements, fast or slow, with or without fugally answered subject, with clear or disguised return to A_2
        binary slow movements ⎱ ⎰ with or without full reprise
        binary fast movements ⎰ ⎱ of first theme
textures: in ritornello movements, subjects homophonic or imitative (at the octave or fifth), with or without subject in bass
        movements in four (or more) parts, keyboard homophonic or contrapuntal (not in organ sonatas)
        layout of the three parts in various areas of the compass (organ sonatas relatively consistent)
        bass line imitative *or* as a countersubject to fugal lines *or* ostinato *or* sparsely written (last two not in organ sonatas)

Particularly characteristic of the fast movements of the organ sonatas is the three-section plan (outer movements of BWV 527, 529, 530) in which the middle section modulates frequently and sequentially, forming an 'unstable' contrast to the framing sections. That in some cases the composer writes merely 'da capo' may suggest theoretical parallels with aria form (Schrammek 1954 p20), but only from the point of view of the overall plan; the parallel should not be overstressed, any more than the three-movement structure itself could have claimed to

---

* It is not always clear who added figures or harmonies to these bass lines; but the 'realized continuo' in the slow movement of the B minor Flute Sonata BWV 1030 (autograph MS) is certainly authentic.

'unveil the definitive form of the [later] classical sonata' (Dufourcq 1948 p286). The most important parallel between the Six Sonatas and classical sonata form is undoubtedly the development-like nature of the middle sections of some outer movements, or the manner in which (e.g.) the C minor Sonata first-movement subject is treated (see BWV 526 below).

In general, however, while few of the features listed above could not be found elsewhere in the various types of instrumental trio sonata common by c1720, the variety and comprehensive coverage of these features all within eighteen or nineteen organ trio-sonata movements seem to be deliberately planned. Not for the only time in the music of J. S. Bach, a set of pieces is planned as if to show the scope open to a composer working in a particular, restricted medium; similar points could be made about the sonatas/partitas for solo violin and the harpsichord partitas. Some close parallels can also be made between the organ and the instrumental sonatas: thus the finale of the E flat Organ Sonata resembles that of the C minor Violin Sonata in the details of its binary form (fugal imitation, inversion in the second half, type of episode material, etc). All such sonatas have common elements not normally found in the concertos; e.g., simple binary form is not known in the concertos.* On the other hand, the three-movement plan has common elements: the tutti/solo elements in the first movements of the organ sonatas in C, C minor and G, balanced with the fugues of their finales, produce much the same overall shape found in several keyboard and other concertos of J. S. Bach. Moreover, as in some concertos, the demarcation between 'tutti' ritornello theme and 'solo' sections is not always clear, quite apart from the fact that the organist does not distinguish the solo/tutti sections by stop changes. The first movement of the Fourth Brandenburg Concerto supplies a good example of the soloists having their own lines in the *ripieno* sections, suggesting parallels with the first movements of the C, G and D minor organ sonatas, though here on a smaller and more succinct scale.

Of the organ and instrumental sonatas as a whole, the organ movements seem usually more succinct, clearer in form and, because of limitations in the pedal, not as much involved in texture. Thus the inverted theme in the finale of the E flat Organ Sonata (second half) is clearer than that at the corresponding moment of the C minor Violin Sonata. But while the fast movements of the organ sonatas may exploit triple counterpoint less than those of the violin sonatas, it is striking that the imitative themes in the organ sonatas are sometimes so written as to be convenient for pedal (e.g. outer movements of the E flat Sonata). And while the finales of the organ and violin sonatas referred to include triple counterpoint, the violin sonata sustains it longer than the organ sonata. In general, the first movements of the organ sonatas employ the pedal as a supporting bass, motivic rather than thematic, while the third movements give the pedal the (fugue) theme complete.

* That in the Triple Concerto in A minor BWV 1044 is taken from an organ sonata (BWV 527), while that in the Triple Concerto in D minor BWV 1063 is written out in full with altered scoring.

Whether the Six Sonatas are indeed more succinct than the instrumental sonatas is difficult to say, since the textures of the violin, flute and gamba sonatas are so much more diffuse. It is rather that in certain movements the instrumental sonatas borrow or anticipate one particular characteristic of the organ sonata, namely identity between the two upper parts. This would accord with the theory that in the instrumental sonatas the composer moved gradually from the traditional trio and solo sonatas with continuo to the solo sonata with full obbligato harpsichord (Eppstein 1966 pp159–60); in concept and thus even in chronology, the organ sonatas may then be the last stage in this development. In that case, the opening unisons of the G major Organ Sonata would not be a sign of immaturity but of the opposite: a concerto-like tutti introduced by a composer who had already created over the years a wide repertory of trio effects and had found one more in the opening unison ritornello.

(v) **Contemporary and later trios.** If the organ sonatas are a late stage in the composer's development of trio techniques, their roots are to be found in the traditional trio sonatas for two violins and continuo rather than in earlier three-part organ music, whether German or French.* However, the French tradition is important in one particular respect: the choice of instruments that could be used for a *concert* or *sonate* was open. Telemann's *Six Concerts et Six Suites* (c1715–20?) could be played by harpsichord and flute (with or without cello), or violin, harpsichord and flute (with or without cello); Telemann thus allowed for the three parts to be played as trios or duos. The three parts are more imitative in the *concerts* than in the *suites* but are still not often fully fugal, complete with motivic stretto etc; nor is the figuration organ-like. Nevertheless, the second movement of *Concert IV* shows that the style at times approaches that familiar in BWV 525–530: Ex. 2. Coupled to this is the fact that the theme as it appears here is an inverted form of the main subject and opens the second of two binary sections; and it is then possible to see that both the texture and the form of certain organ-sonata movements were known elsewhere at this period. That is true of much chamber music in general, such as Telemann's published trios for two violins and continuo; the significance of the *concerts* lies in their variable scoring and hence the adaptability of the idiom. At times, Telemann slightly simplifies the bass when it becomes a cello part, though not as completely as the arranger of BWV 1027a (for organ pedal) did the bass line of the Gamba Sonata BWV 1027.

Unfortunately, it is not known whether Telemann's instrumental Sonata in E (*Essercizii musici*, Hamburg 1720) is the original version of a Sonata in D 'au 2 Clavier con Pedal' (Lpz MB MS 3) or vice versa;

* Though outside the scope of this study, it is also possible to relate French organ-trio movements to a particular Parisian tradition of wind trios (two recorders or flutes and bassoon) in theatre and church music from Lully onwards. Many details of idiom – compass, metre (lilting $^3/_4$, simple $^2/_2$), texture (two upper parts in thirds) etc – are features shared by trio sections in a motet of Lalande and an organ mass of Clérambault.

Ex. 2
Telemann, *Six Concerts*, IV.ii
b63

if the organ version is first, it is probably older than any complete sonata in BWV 525–530. The four movements frequently use the two upper parts in imitation (fugal or motivic), though not as consistently as BWV 525–530; nor, naturally, is the material itself on a comparable level. The bass line is throughout more in the manner of an instrumental basso continuo than is normal in the organ sonatas of Bach, and its general character suggests that the manuscript keyboard version is a direct transcription. The melodic idiom is distinctive and suggests a link with the organ trios of J. L. Krebs: Ex. 3. The organ-trio texture was indeed not unsuitable for the *galant* idioms popular amongst certain Bach pupils. For example, the repeated notes of such bass lines as in Ex. 4 could naturally become the characteristic throbbing basses of a later

Ex. 3   Telemann, Sonata in D

Ex. 4   BWV 527.iii

Ex. 5
J. L. Krebs, Trio in B flat
b27

period: Ex. 5. Similarly, the tendency for the upper parts of some Bach movements to become merely a duet above a continuo (e.g. first movement of BWV 529) could also allow for newer idioms – just as it itself was a reflection, a late flowering, of old idioms. Broken-chord episodes could also be simplified: Ex. 6. '*Galant*' was indeed a word

Ex. 6

J. L. Krebs, Trio in E flat ♭48

H. N. Gerber, Inventio in C ♭35

used in the later eighteenth century in connection with the organ sonatas of Bach:

ausser andern Trios für die Orgel sind besonders 6...welche so galant gesetzt sind, dass sie jetzt noch sehr gut klingen (1788 'Comparison between Handel and Bach': *Dok* III p441)

amongst other trios for the organ are in particular six...which are set so *galant* that they still sound very well.

Whatever the anonymous author (C. P. E. Bach?) meant by '*galant*', there are certain characteristics in the melodic turns of phrase of the Six Sonatas – particularly in the first movements – that belong to no part of the language of the organ chorales or fugues. Although the short-phrase, question-and-answer style of the opening of the C minor or C major sonatas, for example, may be different from the later *empfindsamer Stil* of C. P. E. Bach, its chamber-like, even concerto-like quality is unmistakable. That Telemann's chamber-like style can occasionally aspire to a similar idiom is clear from BWV 586, where it is the working-out and the sequences that betray its origin, not the opening contrapuntal melody itself. While the *galant* nature of the slow movement of the D minor Sonata BWV 527 might make it seem unsuitable as the prelude to a fugue from the *Art of Fugue* in Mozart's arrangement (Einstein 1936), it was no doubt this *galant* nature that appealed to Mozart in the first place: a pretty prelude to a learned fugue.

As 'sonatas', BWV 525–530 have a range of melody that can only be called chamber-like. Although the melodies may at times seem unlike flute or violin music, they are even less like most other organ music. Rarely if ever would such a melody be found suitable either for a chorale prelude or for any of the usual fugue types; only occasionally, as in the last movement of the G major Sonata BWV 530, do the lines resemble a chorale paraphrase of the kind known in the trios BWV 664 or 676. Rather, the chamber/keyboard quality of the melody suggests either a kind of sparkling, witty line or a somewhat plaintive melodiousness, both of them charming and curiously abstract, i.e. free of association. The slow movement of the E flat Sonata BWV 525, for example, either suggested or was typical of a species of melody admired by the younger composers – Ex. 7 – for which the clear lines of a keyboard trio were an admirable vehicle. However, for Bach such 'plaintive melodiousness' was more fitting for a slow middle movement and indeed replaced the more expressive melody-with-accompaniment Adagio known in the violin sonatas and elsewhere.

Ex. 7

J. T. Krebs, BWV Anh.46

---

525   Sonata No. 1 in E flat major

Autograph MS P 271; P 272 (W. F. Bach), MS formerly in Gorke Collection, whereabouts unknown (W. F. Bach), Am.B. 51 and Am.B. 51a (Kirnberger circle), Vienna Cod. 15528 (Oley), P 840 (late 18th century), LM 4842 (J. C. H. Rinck 1770–1846) and other late copies; published by A. F. C. Kollmann in *An Essay in Practical Musical Composition* (London, 1799), Pl. 58–67; first movement only in P 1115 (A. Kühnel c1770–1813) and Copenhagen Grönland MS, dated at end '1795' (Emery 1957 p31); St 345, arrangement in C major for violin, cello and basso continuo of movements 1 and 3 (unknown hand of 18th century, slow movement from Flute Sonata in A BWV 1032).

Headed in P 271 'J. J. Sonata 1. à 2 Clav: et Pedal'; second movement 'Adagio', third movement 'Allegro'. For 'J. J.' ('Jesu Juva', 'Jesus help') see also the first organ chorale in P 271 (BWV 651).

While the history of the three movements is unknown, it is just possible that the C major string version has a different middle movement because its direct or indirect source was too early to have contained the present slow movement (Eppstein 1969 p23); however, the title 'Concerto' in St 345 cannot be taken to imply that the outer movements are merely keyboard arrangements of instrumental works, for they have the same bass lines as those in P 271, which seem obviously conceived for organ pedals. The form of BWV 525.ii – binary, with a kind of recapitulation in the second half – has suggested that the movement is 'relatively late' (Eppstein 1969 p22). Details of form and figuration in the outer movements are so patently contrasted, yet their opening harmony and melody so nearly related, as to suggest that the composer carefully paired them for some didactic purpose. Either way, the three movements have all been seen as forms divisible into two halves (Schrammek 1954).

First Movement

The form may be expressed as:

A 1–11   Eb, lh opens
B 11–22   to Bb, rh opens
A 22–36   to F minor, rh opens; inverts parts from A_1 and extends to 15 bars (to include pedal entry b29)
B 36–51   to Eb, lh opens
A 51–8   pedal opens; b53(halfway)–b58(beginning) = bb6–11

The effect is that of a ritornello movement with a second half beginning clearly at b22, and the final A ending like the first A. However, there is no clear solo/tutti contrast in the movement, since motif a – Ex. 8(i) – runs through all sections, combining both with scale figures (ii) and

Ex. 8

(i)   **(ii) b3**   b5   **(iii) b11**

with arpeggio figures (iii), the latter of which has the function of a second theme (B above). Motif a is also presumably the source of subsidiary ideas, in manual or pedal (Ex. 9). The pedal has its own version of the

Ex. 9   **(i) b5**   **(ii) b4**

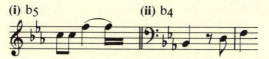

theme in bb29f and 51f, changing its second bar apparently more for reasons of three-part counterpoint than to make it suitable for pedals. The broken chord motif *a* also appears *inversus* and extended (Ex. 10(i)), and diminished both *rectus* and *inversus* (ii). This motif in its

Ex. 10

(i) b17   b18   (ii) b11

various shapes pervades the movement to a degree unusual even in the motif-dominated preludes of the *Orgelbüchlein*. Thus, section *B* makes play with three versions of the motif – Ex. 11(i) – while section *A* is characterized by more scale-like figures, at least in one part (ii).

Ex. 11   (i) b11

(ii) b6

Such emphasis on motif is rather more typical of the Two-part than the Three-part Inventions. The overall pattern *ABABA* can be seen in (e.g.) the three-part Invention in A major BWV 798, in which *B* is also a countersubject to a line derived from *A* (BWV 798 b9, b21). Moreover, some of the lines of BWV 798 are themselves somewhat like those of BWV 525.i in their kind of triple counterpoint (*a* bass line, *b* derived motif, *c* countersubject): Ex. 12. While such movements as BWV 525.i may be similar to the Inventions, there are important differences: the triple counterpoint of the Inventions can be more complete (bass line unaffected by pedal techniques), the forms of the sonata movements are usually clearer (because of textural variety), and as so often the composer tends to characterize a *genre* by giving it its own characteristic melody. Thus cadential pedal points, pauses or breaks before the final cadence are unknown in the Six Sonatas (except for the early Andante of BWV 528); there, cadences are very succinct even when, as is only rarely the case, they are 'homophonic' (BWV 525.iii).

Ex. 12

Invention BWV 798
b27

BWV 525.i
b27

That the final pedal bar quotes the opening motif is no sign that the composer is using motifs idly or superfluously. The pedal figure of b1, for example, is heard again only at A_2 (b22), and the main motif itself is continually used only in its varying shapes. The way it is often extended can be found in concerto movements of a kind already perfected by the composer. Thus the development of a pedal line from a simple motif – Ex. 13 – resembles the manner in which melodies are

Ex. 13   b6

derived from equally simple motifs in (e.g.) the Brandenburg Concertos – Ex. 14. While the length of the Brandenburg movements and their number of instruments allow the motifs to be treated on a bigger scale,

Ex. 14

Third Brandenburg Concerto BWV 1048.i
b74

the development in the Six Sonatas is comparable in two ways: (i) the line is extended until it reaches its own cadence, (ii) the motif in its original shape serves as counterpoint to another theme: Ex. 15.

Ex. 15
b9

BWV 1048.i
b77

Naturally, the simple texture of the Six Sonatas clarifies procedures. Thus BWV 525.i shows a subject working both *rectus* and *inversus* against two other subjects (bb11, 17), as does at least one of the Three-part Inventions (Sinfonia No. 7 in E minor, bb14, 25). Both concertos and Inventions, therefore, supply parallels to the form and conterpoint of 525.i.

Second Movement

The form may be expressed as:

binary, repeated halves (12, 16 bars); fugal first theme *A*, second 'theme' developing motifs from it, modulating to dominant; second half beginning with theme *inversus*, returning to tonic entry in b22* (quasi-recapitulation) and closing like the first half in the tonic, upper parts exchanged

Although this is a classic binary form – i.e. with partial recapitulation – the manner in which figures are developed gives a continuity the opposite of that for which such shapes could be used. While *a* frames the movement, the central sections either develop *a rectus* (pedal from b6) and *inversus* (all three parts from b13) or extend one of the little motifs taken from *a*: Ex. 16. The movement is thus essentially

Ex. 16

monothematic in that sections of the whole theme form the basis of long melodies and bass lines. As elsewhere, one motif appears in two different lengths or versions: Ex. 17(i). In fact, the whole of b2 is open to immense extension and inventive treatment: motif *c* is itself in sequence and can be heard to be related to such figures as Ex. 17(ii)

Ex. 17
(i) b2   **(ii) b6**

later on in the movement. Similarly, the head of the very lyrical fugue subject (*a* in Ex. 16) is open to development in the pedal. It is probably a mistake to see the pedal quotation in b6 as a subject entry; rather it is the point at which a bass sequence is begun, developing in its way as much from the main theme as do the long manual lines: Ex. 18. In the process, the pedal part gains a thorough logic and sense of melody of its own; even for such a composer in such a well-contrived *genre*, the bass line of BWV 525.ii throughout is unusually well motivated,

*Bar numbers not counting repeats.

Ex. 18
b6

etc

almost as if the whole movement were an embroidery upon a pre-composed bass line. It also contributes its themes to the tight binary shape. Not only can allusions to the theme be heard in bb6 – 9, 13f, 15f, 17–20 (sequence) and 25f, but the bass theme is part of the recurrent triple counterpoint. Thus bb6–10 are re-worked as bb17–21, and bb4–7, 10–12 are re-worked as bb23–6, 26–8. In the course of this, similar phrases reappear in different contexts. The beginning of the second half, with its quiet and incomplete inversion of the first theme, is thus the least tense moment in the movement, particularly as – uniquely in the Six Sonatas – the section begins without pedal.

The continuity of this slow movement tends to disguise the fact that at key junctures, other phrases could follow than those that actually do. The 'recapitulation' at b22 is not so much a C minor return as a dominant answer to the F minor entry of the previous bar, and in b23 it is grafted on to a passage from the original b4, not b2 as might be expected. The passage flows, but is less inevitable than appears at first. The constant development of motifs is such that any trochaic/iambic figure in the pedal seems to be developed from *a*, as any semiquaver group in the manuals seems to derive from *b*. Yet, probably because of the slow tempo, there are few of the sequential/episodic passages which sustain the motion and space out intricate thematic allusions in other binary movements, such as the finale to the C minor Violin Sonata BWV 1017. Similarly, the continuity means that there is a less clear distinction between 'first and second subject groups' than is often found in binary movements elsewhere, such as the first Allegro of the D major Gamba Sonata BWV 1028. Mature binary movements are often basically monothematic, e.g. the Gavotta of the E minor Partita BWV 830. All of these movements share characteristics of shape with BWV 525.ii, in particular the idea of binary form with partial recapitulation and with a common close to the two halves. The idea of an inverted subject opening the second half can also be found elsewhere, e.g. Gigue of the E minor Partita BWV 830, and Air of the E flat French Suite BWV 815. But the combination of these elements in the slow movement of this E flat Organ Sonata is particularly well organized. Moreover, the plaintive quality of the melody is preserved no matter what particular motifs the three parts happen to play. Remarkably little in the movement is in the major – most notably the first 3½ bars of the second half – and on these grounds alone the movement is a foil to the finale.

Third Movement

The form may be expressed as:

binary, repeated halves (32, 32 bars); fugal first theme *A*, second 'theme' developing motifs from it, modulating to dominant; second half beginning with inversion of subject, closing like the first half in the tonic, voices exchanged

Though this is similar in form to the second movement, there is here no recapitulation before the final pedal entry (b57), which is merely a tonic repeat of that at b25. Each half approaches its closing key only gradually. The two halves are indeed much alike, each presenting the material in such a way that the second can be seen at least in part as 'inverting and exchanging the parts' of the first (Schrammek 1954 p15). Thus the inversion of the subject in the second half is also accompanied by an exact inversion of its countersubject, an ideal not often achieved in such binary movements (cf. the Gigue of the E minor Partita BWV 830).

While the resemblances between the main subject and that of the chorale 'Jesus Christus unser Heiland' BWV 688 are superficial, the sonata subject is exposed to a faintly similar degree of variation: Ex. 19. The subject is thus developed* in a manner not unlike that of the

Ex. 19

first movement: the opening motif gives rise to various other ideas, different but derived. The semiquaver group Ex. 20 is also responsible for many a semiquaver line in the movement, while the countersubject

Ex. 20

Ex. 21(i) seems related to, if it is not the origin of, the later sequential figure Ex. 21(ii). Such 'derivation' is of a different order from the play with motifs in the first two movements; the *ton* of the sonata has changed, and the gaiety is unmistakable.

For all its *brio*, the movement is not unsubtle in form. The second half mirrors the first in several ways: literally (number of bars),

Ex. 21

---

* The bass motif of b41 is not a variant but an alteration made in the absence of pedal e♭'; the passage could not have been put down an octave as has been suggested (Emery 1957 p135) because of an unsatisfactory spacing and line.

contrapuntally (bb49–64 = bb17–32, upper parts exchanged) and thematically (bb33–49 = bb1–17 with inverted subject, countersubject and episode). The episode only partially inverts: b44 is as b12, but the contrary scales two bars later work cleverly in the second half towards a subdominant area and hence back to the tonic. The pedal version of the theme is also more complete than it appears, since the manuals take over its semiquavers (Ex. 22). Certainly BWV 525.iii is amongst the most tightly organized of all J. S. Bach's binary movements. Its simple harmonies convey charm to the listener but were the means of intricate cross-allusions for the composer.

Ex. 22   b25

526   Sonata No. 2 in C minor

Autograph MS P 271; P 272 (W. F. Bach), Am.B. 51 and Am.B. 51a (Kirnberger circle), Vienna Cod. 15528 (Oley), P 840 (late 18th century) and other late sources; P 228, P 298 early-19th-century copies of arrangements for string trio (said to be made by Mozart: Einstein 1936) of movements 2 and 3 paired as one trio, P 228 according to its title 'copied from the score to be found in the archive of the Österreichischer Musikverein' (i.e. MS IX/1061; cf. copy now at Göttweig, Stiftsbibliothek).

Headed in P 271 'Sonata 2. à 2 Clav: & Pedal'; first movement 'Vivace', second movement 'Largo', third movement 'Allegro' (Mozart: 'Moderato').

While no movement of the second sonata is preserved in early versions, the form and texture of the Largo may suggest that it alone is an arrangement or shortened transcription, so placed between two original sonata movements (Eppstein 1969 p23). This would accord with the theory that the first and last movements of the C minor, C major and G major sonatas form two groups of similarly conceived movements:

BWV 526.i, 529.i, 530.i:
concerto Allegro, beginning with tutti character (non-imitative), then 'solo' episodes; pedal = continuo only; movement closes with opening paragraph repeated

BWV 526.iii, 529.iii, 530.iii:
tutti fugue, with 'solo' sections, fugal middle section and final ritornello; pedal with fugal line; a movement type close to the fugal Allegro of the violin sonatas

Such three-movement sonatas suggest a concerto-like plan with a tutti/solo first movement and a fugal finale, rather than a chamber sonata of the various types known from the violin, flute or gamba sonatas.

First Movement

The form may be expressed as:

A	1–8	C minor
B	8–16	C minor
A	17–22	E♭
B	22–31	to G minor
A	31–8	G minor
B	38–71	to C minor; development section
A	71–8	first 8 bars

That such ritornello movements sustain continuity is undeniable, but the composer creates elements that could follow each other in various orders. Thus the passage built on sequential trills is followed on its first appearance by a statement of *B* (b22), and on its second by a statement of *A* (bb70–1). Both follow in a natural manner, the first slipping in 'unnoticed' and accompanied by a countersubject (right hand) that is itself smooth in continuity, the second approached more dramatically after a pedal lead-in and hence calling attention to the reprise. Thus in each case, between the sequential trills and what follows the composer has formed a link that suits the nature of the following material.

Continuity and contrast are also given the movement by the nature of the two main themes or theme groups. *A* is homophonic, *B* imitative/fugal; *A* begins on the beat with a conspicuous pedal bass, while *B* and the episode material in general emphasize figures beginning off the beat, all of which invite close or distant imitation: Ex. 23. It is probably because these figures are somewhat uniform that commentators have thought *d* to be derived from *a* (Schrammek 1954).

While the most general outlines of such a movement can be shown

Ex. 23

26

to correspond roughly to those elsewhere, such as the first movement of the B minor Flute Sonata BWV 1030 (Keller 1948 pp102–3), both the detail and conception are too different for real similarities to be found. The B minor Flute Sonata, for example, has a much less succinct and clear ritornello form, with a longer and thematically more complex final section. Remarkable in the organ sonata is the last-but-one section, a long development very original in idea:

38–46	G minor pedal point, first with concerto-like repetition of broken chords, secondly with reference to *A* (still basically in thirds, with lower voice coloured by semiquavers), thirdly with a quaver line dominated by pairs of semitones* (cf. concerto-movement pedal points in BWV 1064.iii from b169 and in BWV 1063.ii from b15)
46–54	ditto, C minor, upper parts exchanged
55–60	new imitation in upper parts above a pedal line developing a motif from *A*: Ex. 24
61–2	from *A* (bb3–4)
62–5	developing the opening motif of *B*, including its pedal counter-subject rhythm
66–70	developing the trills and countersubject of b20

Ex. 24

The 'development' of the main theme in b42 is by nature different from the usual 'motif-extension' found in the organ music of J. S. Bach, where a motif is applied to different chord contexts, which are in turn generated by the motif. The C minor Sonata shows instead a new move towards the kind of development section characteristic of classical sonata form. The theme heard in outline is both complete and easily recognizable; yet its intervals are altered to fit the pedal point, and in the process its character is changed to something much less forthright than the opening statement in b1. Also, the use to which the pedal part of bb55–60 puts one of the main motifs is different from the extensive and intensive play of motifs in such mature chorales as BWV 678: it is used in the sonata to spin out a sequence which requires new material to sustain it.

The tonic–dominant–tonic strategy of the movement is clear. The chromatic trills dispel the expectation of the tonic that is felt from at least b60 but also prepare it more spaciously than they do the new key heard at a similar moment in b22. Clearly the opening pedal point of the section beginning at b38 – serving at once as an interlude, a development section and a kind of cadenza – serves also to contrast with the shifting harmonies and bass line of section *B*, not least as its pedal motif is itself a more static reference to the opening pedal motif

* The phrase-marks at bb52–3 are more ambiguous in P 271 than modern editions make them appear: the composer seems to be implying a pairing-off of at least some of the melodic semitones.

Ex. 25
b1

of the movement: Ex. 25. There are probably other allusions to the theme: rising semiquavers, for instance, seem to refer back to parts of A (e.g. b4). The lines throughout are clearly designed for keyboard, both the broken-chord figures and such sweeping lines as bb44–6 (left hand). It is probably this fluidity of semiquavers that led to the sudden quoting in b61 of a passage from A and in b62 of a passage from B: Ex. 26.

Ex. 26
b60

Although belonging to the same ritornello family as in the first movement of the E flat Sonata BWV 525, such semiquavers produce quite different lines: between them, the two movements provide – in one key and its relative – a repertory of semiquaver figures characteristic of the ⁴/₄ concerto Allegro movement which otherwise does not appear in the Six Sonatas.

Second Movement

This is a unique movement:

1–8	subject (rh) and countersubject (lh) with quasi-codetta; the bass = basso continuo
9–16	ditto, dominant, upper parts exchanged
16–19	episode built on codetta theme from b8 (= sequence 1)
20–3	episode or new theme (= sequence 2)
24–6	episode or new theme, pedal line a simplified version of opening subject now in C minor (= sequence 3)
27–9	sequence 4

29–35   subject in G minor; for first 3 bars, pedal continues previous sequence, rh with new countersubject

35–8   sequence 2 in G minor, parts exchanged

39–45   subject (with countersubject from bb29–35) in C minor, serving as subdominant answer to bb29–35

45–8   cadential half-close to finale

The key-plan itself (E♭ closing in C minor at b45, then half-close on G) is unusual. A more traditional structure, such as the slow movement of the C minor Violin Sonata BWV 1017, would close on E♭ before the half-close to G; alternatively, the movement would begin and end on C minor before the half-close (e.g. BWV 537.i). The unusual key-plan, however, is hardly evidence that the movement is either a transcription or a shortened version of another movement, as has been suggested (Eppstein 1969 p21), nor can a short but highly involved movement of this kind be convincingly said to leave an 'improvisation-like impression' (Schrammek 1954). In thematic outline, the movement can be expressed:

A	1–16
B	16–29
A	29–35
B	35–9
A	39–45
Coda	45–8

In detail, the movement shows yet again a highly inventive treatment of several semiquaver and quaver motifs around the various statements of the main subject (itself in long notes). Key motifs are shown in Ex. 27: as elsewhere in the Six Sonatas, the exact order of their

Ex. 27

appearance seems to be laid down by on-the-spot decision rather than the 'demands of form'. The continuity means that the linking bars 19, 27–8 and 38 are assimilated and, indeed, that the shape of the movement is difficult to follow. At two points (bb32–3, 42–3) subject and (new) countersubject contrive to produce an off-beat stretto – Ex. 28(i) – and it is typical of the motivic ingenuity of such pieces that the composer then picks up the final motif for the coda: Ex. 28(ii).

The opening of the movement has an apparent simplicity not borne out by the rest of the movement; it may begin like a Telemann trio but by b5 is already developing lines of complicated semiquaver figures –

Ex. 28

(i) b42

(ii) b45

many of which appear both *rectus* and *inversus* – so that what follows is much more clearly characteristic of the Six Sonatas (e.g. bb5–7, 32–4).

Third Movement

For general comparisons between the last movements of the C minor and other sonatas, see above. The shape is as follows:

A	1–58	exposition, two episodes, two futher entries
B	58–82	new subject, then episode (b75); 4-bar link to:
A	86–102	unison stretto, answered at fifth below; to F minor
B	102–26	as bb58–82, fifth lower, parts exchanged; *ditto* 4-bar link
A	130–72	stretto at fifth, answered a futher fifth below; 137–72 = 23–58, parts exchanged

The form is clear and the details ingenious, chiefly in that the stretto possibilities of the main fugue subject allow A_2 and A_3 to expose the theme in its different facets before they lead on to and overlap the repeat of A_1. Moreover, the tail of the subject (Ex. 29) is developed as

Ex. 29   b6

sequential episode (from b18), as countersubject (from b30), as coda (from b51) and as the linking bars after *B* (bb82, 126). This unassuming quaver phrase is indeed found in various guises elsewhere: see notes to the C minor Fugue BWV 546.ii. In addition, the rising pedal fifth in semibreves is also useful in the linking bars, to anticipate the manual stretto that follows on each occasion. Particularly interesting is the running of B_2 into A_3, for not only does the overall form then become a kind of *da capo* fugue, but the stretto introduces elements of F minor foreign to the original passage in b23 but very relevant to the close of B_2 in A♭ major.

In view of such ingenuity, it becomes clear that the composer has carefully distinguished the two fugue themes in style and application as far as continuity (which is provided by the pedal) would allow. The second theme is short-breathed, with a distinct *stile moderno* character (rhythm, repetition), a continuo bass (not a third part), a lively countersubject vying with the subject, and a subsequent episode tending to *galant* simplicity. The first theme is long-phrased, has an *alla breve* character (with conventional subject-head or *caput*, dactyl rhythms etc), is answered in the pedal, and has 'correct' episodes and middle entries, and a classical countersubject with suspensions and a plain line. Despite its comparative length, the first subject also modulates far less than the second, and its episodes remain in the tonic, unlike those of the second subject. Moreover, on each occasion the second subject enters conspicuously, while the first slips in by way of a stretto: a more hidden reprise. There is thus a whole catalogue of differences between the two fugal themes, showing every sign of being systematically planned.

While the style and bar-by-bar character of the first two movements of the C minor Sonata depend largely on the composition and inventive treatment of motif – their highly organized forms notwithstanding – the final movement has little complexity of motif but rather manipulates two different fugue styles, dovetailing them in a manner that suits their styles. Such a conception and skill are unique to J. S. Bach. In this way too the movements present three musical idioms: concerto Vivace with lively rhythmic patterns, lyrical Largo more gentle throughout (the lines often rising only to fall again), and a fugal Allegro both with traditional *alla breve* elements and with fugal lines typical of chamber

Ex. 30

b11

b75

music. H. N. Gerber, J. L. Krebs, W. F. Bach and other pupils may have heard the newer styles they were themselves to achieve in such passages as that shown in Ex. 30.

---

527   Sonata No. 3 in D minor

Autograph MS P 271; P 272 (W. F. Bach), Am.B. 51 and Am.B. 51a (Kirnberger circle), Vienna Cod. 15528 (Oley), P 840 (late 18th century) and other late sources; 'early version' of sonata in P 1096 (H. A. Steffani, late 18th century?), Lpz MB MS 1, 5 (J. A. G. Wechmar, between 1740 and 1799), both MSS entitled 'Sonata 1 . . .'; 'early version' of first movement in P 1089 (anon. copyist) and Lpz MB MS 7, 16 (owned by J. N. Mempell, copied before 1747); P 228, P 298 early-19th-century copies of arrangement of middle movement for string trio (said to have been made by Mozart; see also BWV 526) serving as prelude to *Art of Fugue* Contrapunctus VIII (BWV 1080.viii); St 134 (J. H. Müthel?), parts for instrumental version of the middle movement, included in the Concerto for Flute, Violin and Harpsichord BWV 1044.

Headed in P 271 'Sonata 3 à 2 Clav. et Pedal'; first movement 'Andante' in P 271 (not in P 272, P 1089, P 1096), second movement 'Adagio e dolce' ('Adagio' in P 1096), third movement 'Vivace'.

'It can be assumed that P 1089 and P 1096 are derived from a lost autograph that was written before 1730, and was one of the sources from which P 271 was compiled' (Emery 1957 p90). However, the versions differ only in details, although the title 'Sonata 1 . . .' may suggest that the 'lost autograph' had such a title or began its compilation of the (six?) sonatas in a different order. Spitta dates the first movement c1722 (Spitta II p691), presumably because he supposed that the early versions of movements from *Das Wohltemperirte Clavier* (*The 48*) contained in P 1089 belonged to Book I and not (as is the case) Book II; in this he has been followed by some later authors (e.g. Keller 1948 p101). If the sonata as a whole 'originated as a compilation or/and transcription' (Eppstein 1969 p24), which is suggested by its 'general character' and 'details in the pedal bass line' (*ibid* p23), it may also be earlier than most of the others, affording a model for (e.g.) binary slow movements. Its outer movements are less usual in organization, though at no point and in no detail do they introduce elements outside the variety surveyed by the composer elsewhere in the Six Sonatas.

First Movement

The form may be expressed as:

> A   1–24   subject exposed fugally in upper parts above continuo bass,
>   followed by coda
>   24–32   subsidiary material, sequences

	33–48	as 9–24 now in tonic, upper parts exchanged
B	48–56	new theme in rising sequential imitation; but referring back to previous material (bars 51 and 55, see b21)
	56–60	second sequence, using previous motif (and bass) from b1
	61–4	third sequence, cf. b29
	65–8	fourth sequence, cf. b21
	68–72	fifth sequence; from b69, cf. b24
	73–6	sixth sequence, cf. b16
	76–88	opening section of B up a fourth, upper parts exchanged
	89–92	pedal point, lh reference to motif from b4
	92–6	seventh sequence, as bb4/36 but with closer imitation
	97–104	eighth sequence, corresponding to bb17–24 and hence to bb41–8
	104–8	ninth sequence; developed from b24, cf. fifth sequence
	109–12	Phrygian cadence decorated with previous motifs and leading to:
A	113–60	repeat of bb1–48

The chief point of interest in the *A B A* plan is the middle development section, which begins with new material but soon turns almost exclusively to previous ideas, running from one to the other in an apparently arbitrary way through nearby keys (F, G minor) which are not fully represented in the outer sections. Thus, while the *A B A* in such proportions (48:64:48 bars) may be exceptional and may even suggest to some a kind of inferiority to the other sonatas (Keller 1948 p105), the details of the development section obviously anticipate those of the (later?) C minor Sonata BWV 526. In this D minor Sonata, the 'development' is a matter of literal quotation and alternation of themes; the motifs are not so much 'developed' as displayed in different contexts. Such a technique is particularly apt – perhaps only apt – to organ trio textures, since one aim of these is to give the hands an equality of melody, interest and contrapuntal significance which is not standard even in Bach's instrumental sonatas.

While the movement as a whole does indeed suggest little if any tutti/solo contrast* (Eppstein 1969 p17), there are subtleties of bar-by-bar composition suggesting that the movement is no early work, though it is often described as being simple to play. Beginning both subjects on the mediant (b1, b48) is unusual; but more significant is the constantly varying lengths of phrase, from the long opening line down to the half-bar sequence of b29. Stretto within the first subject – Ex. 31 – is not so much conventional fugal imitation as a motivic device whereby *a* goes against *b* and vice versa. Also, the motif from b1 (Ex. 32) crops up in very different contexts (pedal b21, b22, b51, b52, b109 etc). The potential of such a motif as Ex. 33 for extension, sequence, imitation etc will be familiar from early preludes and fugues. The pedal seems to augment this motif in b16 etc, and indeed shows a high degree of

* Such contrast is in any case a formal matter and not one for the organist to make explicit with registration changes; that the clearer tutti/solo structure of the first movement of the C minor Sonata is hardly to be underlined by stop-changing on the part of the organist may bear on the arguments for and against manual-changing or stop-changing in other sectional works, in particular preludes and fugues in clear ritornello shapes.

Ex. 31
b92

Ex. 32

Ex. 33

b17

organization throughout, depending on only a handful of ideas: the detached quavers (b1 etc), the short scale-like line (b8 etc), the Italianate sequence (b24 etc) and so on. The most interestingly developed motif is that of b2 – Ex. 34(i) – since from it come the

Ex. 34

(i) b2   (ii) b24

subject codetta (b8), elements in the countersubject (b12), and a compressed form that appears throughout the *A B A* as a whole: Ex. 34(ii). The fact that *A* itself is a ternary structure:

bb1–24
24–32
33–48

gives the movement a round form matched by its constant back-reference.

Second Movement

The form may be expressed as:

binary, repeated halves (8, 24 bars); contrast between themes (one in thirds, the other more imitative); second half begins with first theme in dominant, then 'new' themes; reprise at b21, followed at b23 by two previous bars (= bb11–12 down a fifth, parts exchanged), then by a return to reprise of first section

The binary form thus has elements of ternary, a procedure not usually so clear-cut in the works of J. S. Bach (see BWV 525.ii), although both the E flat and G major sonatas have slow movements of a similar cast (Schrammek 1954 p24). The 'reprise' is not straightforward: two of the subjects appear in the tonic with exchanged parts (b21 = b1, b29 = b5), but between them appears material from elsewhere in the movement – conforming to the technique, common in the Six Sonatas, of juxtaposing themes in varying orders. Bar 26 is not a simple direct reprise of bar 3, since the right-hand line at b26 is an answer to the theme in the left hand; and the coincidence of pitch is of less moment than the chromatic complexity of bb25–8.

An unusual detail of the movement is that its continuity hangs on a succession of two-bar phrases. Every two bars necessarily demand a new theme or idea, and the returns of the opening melody are the more significant in pointing out the overall ternary plan. One result of this phraseology may be the nature of the 'new' themes in the second half. The two-bar structure means that different ideas occur at bb9, 11, 13, 15, 17 and 19. Of these, bb9, 13 and 19 have been heard previously; so perhaps, in different form, have those of bb11, 15 and 17. Is the descending line of b3, for example, to be heard decorated ('coloured') in b15 and b17?

The contrast between homophonic and imitative themes (b1; b3) was also known in the first movement: compare b1 of the Adagio with b21 or b51 of the first movement. The *galant* touch in the opening bars is rather belied by the rest, but the rubric 'e dolce' seems almost to invite flute stops, while the thirds and appoggiaturas would have seemed sufficiently *galant* to the copyist – whoever he was – of the 'Aria' BWV 587 for him to think that the two movements were the work of the same composer. As has been pointed out (Eppstein 1969 p24), the pedal line at b4 may suggest that the movement was taken originally from elsewhere, since it breaks the line and conforms less to b3 and b27 than might be expected; but whether it suggests that the movement had been a piece for other instruments or an organ movement in a different key can only be guessed. The version of the movement in the C major Triple Concerto BWV 1044 has a more continuo-like bass line at this and other points – Ex. 35. But it is 'reasonable to suppose that the concerto

Ex. 35
BWV 1044.ii
b2

version is the later of the two' not only because 'it is more highly organized' without repeats (Emery 1957 p122), but because the additional fourth part in the concerto version is a simple broken-chord figure with all the appearance of being added to a self-contained trio movement. Neither BWV 527.ii nor BWV 1044.ii can be shown to be the absolute 'original version' of this movement, though its form (binary–ternary) is typical of the Six Sonatas as a set of compiled works.

Third Movement

Like the last movements of the C minor, C major and G major sonatas, BWV 527.iii has elements of the *da capo* fugue, though here with basso continuo rather than thematic pedal:

A	1–16	subject exposed fugally in upper parts above continuo bass
	17–25	subsidiary material, sequences
	25–36	as 9–15 now in tonic, upper parts exchanged; short coda
B	37–60	series of six four-bar phrases employing invertible counterpoint, imitation and sequences
	61–72	main subject as in bb25–36 (still tonic), upper parts exchanged
	73–96	series of six four-bar phrases using similar motifs to previous episode but also referring to main subject (b73, b77) and countersubject (b81)
	97–108	main subject (decorated), as in 61–72 but now in dominant, upper parts exchanged
	108–44	series of nine phrases, mostly in four bars, very fluent and continuous, playing with motifs familiar from previous episodes and again directly quoting from the first episode: 117–28 = 45–56 now in tonic, upper parts exchanged; 133–40 same theme as 37–44 but new sequence; 141–4 = 57–60 in tonic, upper parts exchanged
A	145–80	repeat of 1–36

The parallel to the first movement of the sonata is striking, where however there is a conciseness not necessary in a finale. Here there is more scope for variety in the triplet figures. From the first episode (b17) on, figure after figure follows, clearly related but very varied and versatile. Some examples are shown in Ex. 36. Apart from the brief

Ex. 36

developments of the subject in b73 and b77, the triplets are absent from any exposition or entries of the main subject. Instructive for the bar-by-bar process are the two middle entries at b61 and b97, at which points the triplets from the previous episode spill over and for a moment colour the subject. Conversely, the episodes are almost entirely preoccupied with triplets.* It is characteristic of the movement that the

---

* In view of the significance of the triplets for the form or conception of the movement, it is a mistake to assume that any non-triplet rhythm (e.g. b73, b77) should be made to conform.

'countersubjects' to the triplet figures are usually leaping quavers or tied notes (sometimes both), while an unusual unifying factor is provided by the pedal, particularly its repeated notes which accompany more than the fugue subject. Such *Orgelbüchlein* preludes as BWV 624 and 635 show that the composer had long been practised in the treatment both of triplets and of repeated bass notes, though in both these cases the chorale melody itself governs their treatment (harmonically in BWV 624, thematically in BWV 635). In the way it uses these two important elements, the finale of the D minor Sonata is naturally much freer, and the formal plan of the whole allows the composer to introduce what figures he likes at any one point. Thus the motif labelled *b* in Ex. 36 appears in the middle of the passage developing the fugue subject (b82), although others would have been equally apt. Since the figures are related, each triplet may be exchanged for another if compass, spacing or harmony require it, while such cells as motif *f* serve to sustain the triplet motion between notes a third apart. Inevitably, the triplet figures are often reminiscent of Italian string sonatas or concertos, particularly when there is close imitation (e.g. b45, b108). As a whole, however, the movement shows the composer working in a highly individual manner with a group of little motifs which, though not exactly alien to chorales, achieve their potential only in such 'chamber' ternary forms as an organ trio-sonata movement.

---

528 Sonata No. 4 in E minor

Autograph MS P 271; P 272 (W. F. Bach first 15 bars only, then Anna Magdalena Bach), Am.B. 51 and Am.B. 51a (Kirnberger circle), Vienna Cod. 15528 (Oley), P 840 (late 18th century), Lpz MB MS 4, 17 and other late sources; 'early version' of first movement in Cantata 76 (see below); 'early versions' of the second movement in P 1115 (A. Kühnel? *c*1770–1813), Lpz Go . S . 311/2 (*c*1750?), Copenhagen Grönland MS and Peters 1, Appendix (Emery 1957 p96); first 13 bars of third movement in P 288 and P 319 (later 18th and early 19th centuries) as addition to the Prelude and Fugue in G major (see BWV 541).

Headed in P 271 'Sonata 4 a 2 Clav: et Pedal'; first movement 'Adagio', and 'Vivace' in P 271 (not in P 272) and P 67 (Cantata 76), second movement 'Andante', third movement 'Un poco allegro'.

The sonata 'is to all appearances a compilation of an instrumental sinfonia, an early but rewritten organ piece and a later piece written for the Weimar organ' (Eppstein 1969 p24). However, there is no evidence that the last movement was either composed or begun specifically for the Weimar organ – arguments based on (e.g.) compass are inconclusive – nor that at any stage it was meant by the composer himself to serve as an interlude or postlude to the Prelude and Fugue BWV 541. The middle movement exists in two early versions, both in D minor (Emery 1957 p95ff). From internal evidence the earliest appears to be the Peters I version (c1708? – Emery 1957 p101); the second is printed as appendix to Novello V. The first movement preserves the key and number of parts of the Sinfonia to Cantata 76 (P 67, autograph score dated 1723) where it serves 'nach der Predigt', i.e. to open Part II; the scoring is oboe d'amore, viola da gamba and continuo. Some figuration differs, but in general the pedal in BWV 528.i is of the basso-continuo kind common in the Six Sonatas. From the lines and nature of the texture, the cantata version is usually assumed to be the earlier, with allowance made later for trio compass – no left hand below c – and for the convenience of pedals when the composer arranged it for organ (Siegele 1975 p78ff). Since, unlike any other movement in the Six Sonatas, the Vivace begins with the left hand in the lower part of its compass, the texture will clearly have different emphasis than is usual; also, the slow introduction and the brevity of the Vivace are both exceptional in the Six Sonatas.

First Movement

The form is unique:

Adagio   4 bars, fugal exposition (with modified bass in b3) in three parts;
           b3, countersubject lh (not in BWV 76); apparent (but chance)
           similarity between subject and that of the middle movement
Vivace   imitatively treated material in concise ritornello form:
           5–13, 16–24, 31–9, subject answered at octave
               16–24 = 5–13 in dominant, parts exchanged
               31–9 = 5–13 in subdominant
           14–15, 25–30, derived episodes
           40–75, derived episode–coda

The unusual form of the Vivace is as striking as its having an Adagio prelude. Octave 'fugal' answers are not uncommon in the chamber sonatas but are normally found in slow movements (Sonatas in A major and G major for Violin and Harpsichord, Sonata in D for Viola da Gamba and Harpsichord) as here in the same organ sonata: see *Second Movement* below. Moreover, octave 'fugal' answers tend to continue through the movement once they have begun (e.g. G major Violin Sonata). While such movements in the chamber sonatas have a final imperfect cadence before a fast movement – i.e., they are both irregular and incomplete – the Vivace of the E minor Organ Sonata does not.* Yet from b61, an imperfect cadence looks feasible. Indeed, the final cadence is a simple Italianate formula complete with hemiola, rather out of place in such a movement. The Italianism of both this cadence and the four-bar Adagio prelude may have reached Cantata 76 through the sonatas prefacing Buxtehude cantatas, rather than direct from Corelli trios.

All three lines of the Vivace – subject, countersubject, bass – have

---

* It is doubtful whether the Vivace is so short because it also serves Cantata 76; instrumental movements are too few for generalization in the earlier cycles of Leipzig cantatas. But in any case, it is difficult to justify calling the movement a 'French overture' (Neumann 1967 p96).

a vividness of melody and line rarely surpassed in the Six Sonatas. The characteristic figures of both the subject and its contersubject may well be seen as arising from the special qualities of the viola da gamba: see Ex. 37, the second part of which implies the crescendo natural to so

Ex. 37

many passages in the Sonata in D for Viola da Gamba BWV 1028. All three lines also have a high potential for generating motifs. Thus the episode bb13–15 picks up the first bar of the countersubject (*b*), and bb25–9 the same motif plus the first bar of the subject (*a*). This first bar becomes a full entry at b31: Ex. 38. It is these same motifs that

Ex. 38
b25

dominate the long 'episode–coda' from b40 onwards, including the shortened entries emerging at b50 and b53. At the same time, the pedal line exploits two chief ideas, one in quavers and the other in crotchets. In the cantata version, such a bar as b5 relies on crotchets, with the result that the distinction between crotchet figure and quaver figure is the stronger: Ex. 39. The use of more notes in the organ pedal part than

Ex. 39
BWV 76.viii
b22

in the basso continuo of Cantata 76 suggests that the composer compensated for an 'inexpressive' organ tone lacking the natural tension of gamba phrases: Ex. 40. In the process, the pedal line gains at least one important motif (b5), of which the composer makes curiously little use: according to one editor (Emery 1957 p41), at the comparable point in b29 the motif is changed in the autograph MS P 271. Nevertheless, bass and subject produce two-part counterpoint that is typical of J. S. Bach but of almost nobody else, rich in accented passing-notes and appoggiaturas so that the final notes of many bars are momentary discords (e.g. throughout bb31–2). Such details of harmony, as well as melody, render the final cadence the more striking

Ex. 40 BWV 76.viii   BWV 528.i

in its conventionality, as is often the case with fugal movements in the chamber sonatas of Handel.

Second Movement

The form can be expressed:

A_1	1–11	subject *a* answered at the unison, against which is a countersubject *b*; two-bar episode based on *b*; subject *a* and its octave answer, both in dominant
B_1	11–23	imitative–sequential treatment of motifs probably derived from *b*; cadence in A major, then two linking bars to:
A_2	24–8	as 7–11 in E minor
B_2	28–38	as 11–21 beginning in E minor, changing to G (b31) and continuing as before, a fourth higher
Coda	38–45	modulation back to B minor (new material), then *a* answered in stretto before final entry with countersubject; interrupted cadence before close

The family likeness between the *b* motifs is a question of the opening notes only: Ex. 41. Equally striking and original is *a* itself. It remains

Ex. 41

unaltered even in imitation/stretto, and throughout its course the movement emphasizes to an unusual degree the two-bar phrase which *a* introduces right at the beginning. One result of this two-bar phraseology is that harmonic devices like the Neapolitan sixth become

Ex. 42   b8

very predictable – Ex. 42. The cadences in bb14, 21, 31 and 44 also gain
in significance since they break up the two bars; the 'rather large number
of perfect cadences' may then be not so much details 'reminiscent of
the Legrenzi Fugue [BWV 574] and certain other works' (Emery 1957
p101) as conspicuous elements skilfully introduced to underline the
phraseology.

Describing formal details cannot express the highly original charm
of this movement, though comparison with the so-called early versions
goes some way towards defining it. The figuration in the Peters I and
Novello V appendices is simpler, and although no certain chronology
or even authenticity has been established for these versions, it is
tempting to see them as showing the composer's maturing sense of
melody: Ex. 43. Certainly the last has an indefinably 'pleasing

Ex. 43
b3

Peters I   (transposed from D minor)

P 1115   (transposed from D minor)

P 271

angularity' (Emery 1957 p101); but it is not characteristic of organ music,
nor is it easy to see the 'final version' as transforming 'the stiff crudity
of the Peters version' (*ibid*) since the Peters version is rather more
smooth. 'Crudity' in the earlier versions is more a matter of cadences
and phraseology made less abrupt or cursory in the final sonata by some
subtle additions:

early version			in sonata version
b5 becomes	5+6		
b21 becomes	22+23		
b28 becomes	30+31 (first ½)		

The 'final version' thus emphasizes the two-bar structured referred to above.

The extra passing-notes in the 'final version' also have the effect both of relating some motifs more closely and of distancing others. Thus the *b* material seems less close when the lines are simpler, as they are in the source P 1115 – Ex. 44 – but the coda trills in b38 (or its counter-

Ex. 44

P 1115

b3

b12

cf. b3 in Ex. 43

subject semiquavers) are more clearly integrated in the earlier versions with what has gone before – Ex. 45. Consequently, the effect is more striking in the 'final version' (BWV 528.ii b38). But this version

Ex. 45

P 1115   (transposed from D minor)

b35

P 271

b38

has also lost some invertibility: from b31 to the stretto in the coda, the parts are in the same relationship as they are from b15, whereas in P 1115 in the later section the upper voice enters first and the counterpoint is therefore inverted. In BWV 528.ii, the parts stand as they did earlier in the movement, but in the 'early version', B_2 was not such an exact repeat of B_1; nor did the right hand descend so low as it does in b40 of BWV 528.ii. It does mean, however, that the left hand of P 1115 is unusually high, especially in the (inauthentic?) key of D minor, the key also found in Lpz Go . S . 311/2. Either way, the two hands are closer throughout the movement than is often the case in the Six Sonatas – e.g. the first movement of the same sonata – even to crossing parts at the final cadence.

Third Movement

The form can be expressed:

I	1–28	fugal exposition (subject *A*) complete with pedal subject
	28–36	episode, developing further triplet figures
	36–51	fugal entry and answer in relative major; similar counter-point to that in *A*
II	51–60	episode, developing triplet figures, including one from *A* (b16)
I	60–87	fugal exposition complete with pedal subject which is as b21 (upper parts exchanged); bb60–75 subdominant version of 1–16
Coda	87–97	coda, two five-bar sections (founded on episode bb28ff) of invertible counterpoint

As the left-hand column shows, the movement could be seen to have a ternary shape, the outer sections with a function similar to the tutti ritornello (Eppstein 1969 p19). The truncated quotation from this movement which in some sources is attached to the Prelude and Fugue in G major BWV 541 does not amount to a different version (see BWV 541); but the movement could be seen as an example of a rondo fugue in which the subject returns at regular intervals: clear, complete, without second subjects but following on regular episodes. To clarify the rondo shape would be to express the form as follows:

A	1–16	subject *A*, answered fugally
B	16–20	sequential episode
A	21–8	subject *A*, pedal
C	28–35	sequential episode
A	36–51	subject *A*, answered fugally
B	51–60	sequential episode
A	60–75	subject *A*, answered fugally
B	75–80	sequential episode
A	80–7	subject *A*, pedal
C	87–97	coda

The various triplet figures show the versatility and range already familiar in the finale of the D minor Sonata BWV 527, but here also characterizing the subject entries and throughout developed much more richly.* The versatility of such triplet figures can be seen by comparing two entries: Ex. 46. The latter of these takes on the shape of the former in the course of the melody, quite naturally and unobtrusively. Indeed, in the interests of invertible counterpoint the triplets accompany the subject and become its 'countersubject' (e.g. bb36–51) to a degree not common in, for example, the fugues of *The 48* Bk I. This does not reduce the variety of counterpoint, however; the aspect given the entry in b60 is new and unexpected, because of the dispersal of the triplets through the right hand and pedal – Ex. 47. Unlike most of the triplet figures in the finale of the D minor Sonata, several of those in the present

---

* Some of the same melodic elements can be seen in the *organo obbligato* part to the final aria 'Ich wünsche mir' of Cantata 35 (1726), although here the ³/₈ is presumably slower than in BWV 528.iii.

Ex. 46

b9

b36

movement suit the pedal, specifically the alternate-foot technique.* The pedal indeed has a versatile role: it is absent from the first episode, but has full triplets in the second, its own driving quavers in the third, staccato punctuation in the fourth, and so on; again the scope implies a development far more advanced than the finale of the D minor Sonata. The effect is of a continuous, unresting motion comparable to the finales of some chamber sonatas (e.g. G minor Sonata for Viola da Gamba BWV 1029).

Ex. 47

b60

---

529   Sonata No. 5 in C major

Autograph MS P 271; P 272 (Anna Magdalena Bach), Am.B. 51 and Am.B. 51a (Kirnberger circle), Vienna Cod. 15528 (Oley), P 840 (late 18th century), Lpz MB MS 1, 4 (J. A. G. Wechmar? late 18th century) entitled 'Sonata 4...', and late sources; 'early version' of second movement only in P 286 (J. P. Kellner), P 282 (19th century), LM 4718 (J. G. Walther? before 1717?), Lpz Go.S.306 (J. T. Krebs), P 1115

* The subject itself, however, is again without triplets save for b3. This probably suggests that bb7, 15, 42, 50, 66 and 74 should remain paired semiquavers while apparently comparable moments (bb27, 86) should be played in triplet rhythms.

(A. Kühnel?) and Copenhagen Grönland MS (Emery 1957 p31). In P 286, P 282 and LM 4718, associated with the Prelude and Fugue in C BWV 545.

Headed in P 271 'Sonata 5. a 2 Clav: et Ped.'; first movement 'Allegro', second movement 'Largo', third movement 'Allegro'.

For a general note on the outer movements, see also BWV 526. The C major Sonata too may have had its outer movements composed when the set of Six Sonatas was compiled (Eppstein 1969 p24), while the middle movement may be an earlier, Weimar work. However, as neither the date nor the scribe of LM 4718 is yet established, such speculation must still wait for external evidence. All five copies – and perhaps P 271 itself – of the 'early version' of the middle movement appear to have had an ultimate common source, probably the 'Moscheles autograph' described in *BG* 15, which may or may not have been autograph but which associates the sonata movement with BWV 545. The 'Moscheles autograph' and P 271 differ in points of detail only (slurs, a few notes); but any reasoning from the analogy of BWV 528.ii may suggest dating the 'Moscheles autograph' to c1715 or slightly earlier (Emery 1957 p113).

First Movement

The form may be expressed as:

A	1–17	tutti with question-and-answer phrases; scale sequences
	17–32	tutti now in dominant, parts exchanged; scale sequences altered to return to tonic for:
	32–46	'development' of several motifs from main tutti, including two pedal points (subdominant, tonic) with upper parts exchanged
	46–51	coda, using scale sequences from 12–17, now in tonic, upper parts exchanged
B	51–68	middle section beginning with own fugue subject (three entries answered in turn at fourth below, third below, octave below) and other scale material
	68–72	alternating motifs from both main themes
	72–84	ditto, fuller statement of first theme in F, then A minor
	84–105	as 51–72 now in A minor, upper parts exchanged; fugal answer (b87) altered to produce D minor and hence C (as distinct from G in b55 and hence F in b72)
A	105–55	repeat of 1–51

Section *B* in particular is continuous, and the bar numbers above do not imply clearly separated or even marked sections; *B* begins fugally but becomes a fully fledged development section, as in the first movement of the C minor Sonata BWV 526. Throughout the movement it is the main theme *A* whose appearance most clearly marks a new section (bb17, 32, 72, 80, 105). In its proportions, the movement shows a different emphasis from the first movement of the C minor Sonata.

For example, it already contains in its outer sections passages of 'development' of the kind reserved for the middle section of the C minor movement – in particular, the pedal points of dominant (b9), supertonic (b25), subdominant (b35) and tonic (b42), above which fragments of the main theme are heard. Moreover, there are important symmetries. Despite the *A B A* shape, the main theme returns conspicuously almost halfway through the movement (bb72–5), while *A* itself is highly symmetrical in subject matter if not in bar numbers:

b1 statement	b17 statement	b33 statement
b9 pedal point	b25 pedal point	b35, b42 pedal point
b12 scale sequence	b28 scale sequence	b39, b46 scale sequence

That *B* is symmetrical – itself a kind of *A B A* – is clear from the notes above.

Of the fast movements in the Six Sonatas, the first movement of this C major Sonata seems in its melody and rhythm to suit best the chamber idioms of instrumental sonatas. If it were not for the compass, the style would suggest a sonata for two flutes and continuo. However, the spacing is fully characteristic of the Six Sonatas, and the degree of motivic involvement is difficult to find outside the organ works. It is not the least remarkable feature of the movement that, despite its charming melody and its formal symmetries, the use of motifs is intricate and highly organized. The most suggestive of the motifs is the simple quavers marked *a* in Ex. 48(i), for not only do they lead to

Ex. 48   **(i)** b2   **(ii)** b9   **(iii)** b5

direct derivations (ii), but the quaver gesture can be heard in other figures: (iii). Clearly, the quavers also suit the pedal which, though like a harmonic continuo part, has its own motifs and indeed a highly varied idiom, both in figure and in sense of direction: Ex. 49. Counteracting

Ex. 49

b2   b9   b12   b39   b51

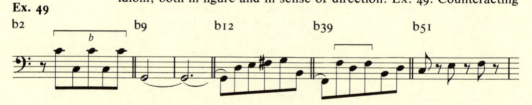

the various quaver figures are two semiquaver groups, clearly distinct and meant to contrast with each other: Ex. 50. The theme of the middle section falls somewhat between these two, derived from neither but seemingly related to both. In no sense is the reference to motifs rigid or arid. Both *a* and *c*, for example, are developed above the pedal points at bb35 and 42, but in a loose way more characteristic of classical development than of *Figurenlehre*. There is no over-use of motif. Thus

Ex. 50

at bb68ff, the alternation of *c* and *d* – Ex. 51 – could easily have been supplemented by the pedal taking *b* in one or another bar. Even the scale sequences (b12, b28, b54) are related only in general character.

Ex. 51
b68

But when two bars with the same bass line – e.g. b14 and b28 – are compared, it is clear that the motifs are versatile enough in the hands of an inventive composer. The literal concentration of *a*, *b* and *c* at b32 is in fact unusual in J. S. Bach and may have been intended more to create good organ lines than to create ingenious motif-complexes. This combination suits the organ quite as well as similar passages in the last movement of the E flat Sonata BWV 525.

Second Movement

The form of the movement may be expressed:

A	1–13	subject *a* answered at the fifth, against which a chromatic countersubject *b* (from b4 of subject); then five bars of sequential and cadential figures partly based on *a* and *b*; tonic cadence for:
B	13–21	second subject group beginning in tonic; 13/14, simple invertible counterpoint (cf. first subject of first movement); 17/18, sequential figures from b10
A	21–33	subject *a* answered at the fifth, upper parts exchanged; now in relative major (avoids chromatic countersubject); 24, 28 cf. b4; 29–32, sequence from second-subject group (15–18), upper parts exchanged
B	33–41	beginning with altered form of second subject (now in the dominant of D minor), but soon passing to D minor version (with exchanged upper parts) of previous cadence (35–8 = 9–12); two modulatory bars to:
A	41–52	repeat of 1–12 (except added countersubject *b* against first entry, 41–4)
	53–4	augmented sixth (Phrygian cadence) link

47

Since the three middle 'sections' alternate their components fairly freely, it is possible to see the movement as a *da capo* form:

A   1–13
B   13–41
A   41–52

Thus the middle section is one that begins independently but soon refers to previous material, though the 'development' features are not as clear as in the first movement of the C minor Sonata BWV 526. In effect, such a movement as the Largo of the C major Sonata could be said to contain elements of fugue (first subject), ritornello and *da capo*, achieved by two parts in dialogue above a basso continuo.

In the Six Sonatas, and elsewhere in the music of J. S. Bach, a theme returning later in a movement is often followed by material quite different from what originally came after it; it is as if themes can appear in any order, and the web of composition is consistent, whatever happens to be the theme at the time. A simple example is seen in this movement: already in b8* a bar is slipped in as if to separate b7 and b9:

bb1–3 subject	bb5–7 answer
	b8
b4 subject-codetta	b9 subject-codetta

During this last bar (b9) the opening motif also appears, as does a motif picked up from that codetta and developed at several points in the movement – Ex. 52(i). This motif is related closely to others (ii)

Ex. 52   **(i)** b9 (b4)   **(ii)** b11   b13

which are not only to be found in about half the bars of this movement but are typical motifs listed by J. G. Walther and other theorists and developed in many an organ chorale (see e.g. BWV 680). They themselves generate lines – Ex. 53 – much in the same way that triplet

Ex. 53
b10

b13

* The characteristic sequence bars 8 and 47 (diminished-fifth line) can also be heard in such contemporary works as the first movement of the A minor Partita for harpsichord (BWV 827.i bb66–70 lh).

figures in the finale of the E minor Sonata BWV 528 generate themselves by means of extension, continuation and mutation. Such 'composing by motifs' – i.e. composing a cell that grows into lines – is at work in at least all the slow movements of the Six Sonatas, a fact which becomes clear as they are examined in detail. Moreover, different movements employ different kinds of motif-composition. While the Largo of this C major Sonata can be seen as an example of 'generating cells', the first movement of the E flat Sonata BWV 525 can be seen more as a demonstration of a motif keeping its basic shape but bending to different contexts. In both, the motivic complexity of the music is very pronounced and goes much farther than mere 'thematic reference' or even 'thematic development'; and both techniques are an equivalent in the Six Sonatas to the motif-complexes typical of the *Orgelbüchlein* chorales.

A factor of importance in this Largo is that whether or not the lines are seen to be generated by such motif-cells, the main theme itself is without them. Its lyrical melody is not itself broken up or developed but returns each time as a simple statement. The similarly plaintive melody in the slow movement of the E flat Sonata is at least treated to sequences in the pedal, while the *galant* thirds of BWV 527.ii lead to a type of development typical of later binary movements. Also, despite a certain family resemblance between the slow movements of the D minor, C major and G major sonatas, they differ in two important respects: the lines themselves are clearly distinguishable from one to the other, and their figures do not arise from the same kind of 'composition by motifs'. While there may be some superficial resemblance between bars here and there – e.g. b20 of 529.ii and b34 of 528.ii – the similarity is no more than fortuitous.

Third Movement

Like the last movements of the C minor, E minor and G major sonatas, BWV 529.iii has a fugally treated theme in which the pedal also plays a part; as in the last movement of the E minor Sonata, only the opening notes of the theme are fit for pedal; like that of the C minor, the subject itself is very conventional in its fugal character (cf. subject and development of the A flat Fugue, *The 48* Bk II) and thus contrasted with the more 'modern' opening of the first movement. The form can be expressed:

A	1–29	fugally treated theme (subject in dominant b9) with counter-subject, above a continuo bass employing the opening notes (*caput*) of fugue subject (bb21f, 23f, 25f); b13 episode; b21 sequence founded on *caput* in bass
B	29–59	new subject in tonic answered at the octave (including entry in b39), followed by first subject in A minor (bb43/47) complete with countersubject; coda (b51) derived from combining both subjects (or their *capita*)
A	59–73	coda in dominant; stretto first subject, then episode from b13
A	73–119	development section passing through several minor keys:

73–89, fugal treatment of first subject now altered
after its first two bars (b73, b83)
89–97, strict first subject and octave answer in D minor
97–111, episode sequences
111–18, fugal first subject and answer, in subdominant

B   119–49   as 29–59 a fourth up, upper parts exchanged
A   149–63   coda as 59–73 (cadence altered), now in tonic, upper parts exchanged

This ingenious form serves as yet another example of modified binary structure:

bb1–73   *A*   *B*   coda (dominant)
bb73–163 A_2 B_2 coda$_2$ (tonic)

in which A_2 is a development, and B_2 and coda$_2$ are repeats towards (and in) the tonic. Thus although it shares fugal characteristics with the finales of the C minor and G major sonatas BWV 526 and 530, the movement can hardly be put in the same formal category (despite claims to the contrary: Eppstein 1969 p18). Rather, the C major Sonata serves as a complement to the C minor in *all* three movements, in particular the *da capo* movements (C minor last, C major first) and the movements which develop a first subject (C minor first, C major last).

Despite its conventional fugue subject, the movement develops its subject and motifs in a manner thoroughly characteristic of the Six Sonatas. The pedal line in particular supplies good examples of this. The sequential use of the *caput* in bb21–6 and bb51–9 anticipates that in the G major Sonata (see BWV 530.iii, bb8–13), while particularly effortless seems the way in which the *caput* is taken into a moving line – Ex. 54. The manual semiquaver figures are inventive and constantly

Ex. 54
b76

varied rather than re-derived from main motifs, while the second theme too is used rather sparingly (bb52, 54, 56, 58, and corresponding bars in B_2). In both cases – the pedal quavers of the first subject and the main motif of the second – special use is made of the opening notes (the subject-*capita*) and there is little free 'composing by motifs' of the kind found in the slow movement. The natural four-bar and two-bar character of the subjects is sometimes emphasized by the treatment: Ex. 55. It is also sometimes undermined, as in the three-part stretto (bb59–61) and the six-bar cadence phrases (bb67–73). The movement's

Ex. 55
b83

lively continuity is helped throughout by the tied notes and suspensions that characterize the first subject (though not the second) in each of the three parts.

---

530   Sonata No. 6 in G major

Autograph MS P 271; P 272 (Anna Magdalena Bach), Am.B. 51 and Am.B. 51a (Kirnberger circle), Vienna Cod. 15528 (Oley), P 840 (late 18th century) and other late sources.

Headed 'Sonata 6. à 2 Clav: e ped'; first movement 'Vivace' in P 272 (authority unknown; not in P 271), second movement 'Lente' in P 271, third movement 'Allegro' in P 271; at end of second movement in P 271 (bottom of a page) 'Volti', at end of last movement 'Il Fine dei Sonate'.

For a general note on the outer movements, see also BWV 526. The G major Sonata may well have had all three of its movement composed when the set of Six Sonatas was compiled, including a middle movement which conforms to the binary structure of other middle movements thought to have been newly composed (D minor and E flat sonatas BWV 527 and 525). It thus holds a unique place amongst the Six Sonatas, a fact perhaps reflected in its position as last of the six: last because specially composed for the set. This may also be the case with the autograph source of the Six Solos for Violin (Eppstein 1969 p25).

First Movement

A concerto-like arrangement of movements into 'tutti' and 'solo' passages is at its clearest in the opening movement of the G major Sonata; in structure, though not in registration or manual changes, it resembles the first movement of the Italian Concerto for Harpsichord (published 1735).

A	1–20	'tutti'; subject answered in dominant (i.e., the first eight bars are as fugue subject and answer)
B	20–57	'solo'; subject answered in dominant; episode of broken figuration; 'tutti' subject decorated b53
A	57–72	'tutti' subject decorated; abrupt turn to dominant for episode from A_1 (b60)
	73–85	'tutti' subject developed in sequence

B	85–101	'solo' episode = 37–53 down a fourth (motifs inverted, upper parts exchanged)
A	101–36	'tutti' subject further decorated, in sequence (101–9 = 53–61 down a fourth, parts exchanged); episode from bb8ff developed in sequence (109–14 = 117–22); stretto development of 'tutti' subject at fifth and unison
B	136–60	'solo' episode from 37/85, *rectus* and *inversus* motifs combined; minor-key development of first 'solo' subject (from b21) on dominant pedal point
A	161–80	repeat of 1–20 (penultimate lh figure altered for final chord*)

However, the so-called tutti–solo structure is no more than a framework or plan alluded to now and then; the movement is not a concerto with clearly marked sections. Thus, although in concertos the main theme may well be anticipated or hinted at in the solo episodes, such a passage as bb53–60 is more ambiguous than would be normal in a concerto; if the 'tutti' passage begins in b57 not b53, it does so by force of key (tonic in b57) rather than theme. In view of the invertible counterpoint over the whole passage, it might be more natural to regard b57 as a sequential answer to b53. Such formal 'ambiguities' are characteristic of so-called analogous forms, i.e. forms transferred from one medium (concerto) to another (organ sonata).

Further details in the writing seem to suggest concerto elements. The opening unison theme is unique in the Six Sonatas and certainly has this purpose. Moreover, when the first 'solo' passage appears, it does so above a pedal point (bb20–7) as is by no means unusual in the first movements of Bach concertos, e.g. D minor Harpsichord Concerto BWV 1052 and the Fourth Brandenburg. The ritornello structure itself is suggestive, though here too the composer brings in ideas perfectly typical of the Six Sonatas, for example the pedal point in b153 over which part of the first subject is treated in much the same way as those of the C minor and C major sonatas. Also characteristic is the minor chromaticism preparing a strong tonic entry (bb153–61); and indeed, the main subject loses its ritornello force if it is not so prepared (e.g. the ambiguous G major of b125).

The subjects are marked by different kinds of figure. The pedal line is particularly varied, and its figures are not so difficult to play as the semiquavers of the C major Sonata finale BWV 529.iii; in the development section, the pedal figures lend movement and tension to the strettos. Episodes and cadential phrases cross parts on the whole less than do passages in which the material is being developed. One particular motif serves as a link between phrases and subjects throughout the movement – Ex. 56(i) – and, taking various forms, it can be seen operating in bb4, 8, 20, 28, 56, 60, 72, 84, 104, 108, 160 etc and, by further derivation, elsewhere. At b56 it runs into a countersubject which first appears three bars earlier – Ex. 56(ii) – in which form it also appears in b104. The decorated version of the 'tutti' subject tends to disguise its entry (e.g. b101), unlike the only slightly modified head of

* The composer evidently had more than one thought on the last chord of the movement; see Emery 1957 p183.

Ex. 56

(i) b4   **(ii) b56**

the fugue subject in the finale of the C major Sonata (BWV 529.iii, e.g. b111).

Second Movement

Like the slow movements of the D minor and E flat sonatas, BWV 530.ii is a binary form whose second part contains a clear return to the opening theme of the movement. Its form may be expressed:

binary, repeated halves (16, 24 bars); one main theme, first half developing motifs from it; second half begins with new theme; b24 reprise, so that 25–40 = 1–16 down a fifth, upper parts exchanged

Further details are typical of the slow movements of the Six Sonatas: the bass below sequential episodes as in Ex. 57 (see also BWV 527.ii

Ex. 57   **b8**

b17 and 529.ii b15), the contrary-motion scales before the reprise (see also BWV 529.ii b40), and the many references in the pedal to the main subject as in Ex. 58.

Ex. 58

b10   b20

Ex. 59

The pedal takes a part in the development of material, of which a typical bar may yield several examples: Ex. 59. In this bar, *a* is the head of the subject and *b* a motif from it (b2); *c* and *d* are derived from the countersubject (bb5, 6). Such distinctions may be rather artificial, since the material is highly continuous and its evolution apparently natural; but such are the results of intense artistry. Thus, motif *e* can be picked up sequentially in the pedal at the close of each half, while the 'new' theme heard in the second half itself appears to be derived in much the same way – Ex. 60. After four bars this passes to yet another

Ex. 60

sequential figure above the derived bass, introducing alien notes before the reprise. Indeed the four bars 21–4 are amongst the most skilfully managed in the whole Six Sonatas from the point of view of strained harmonies worked logically above pedal motifs taken from the subject, and so worked as to delay an entry in a key already arrived at (A minor bb20f, b25).

Despite its binary form, the melodic style of the movement conforms more to that of an aria and its obbligato line (violin?) than to that of the chamber sonatas, where the melodic line is usually less cut up and varied. Although it has recognizable siciliano elements (the opening phrase, the $^6/_8$ dotted rhythms), the movement is marked 'slow' and hardly agrees with Quantz's directions concerning siciliano movements:

sehr simpel und fast ohne Triller auch nicht gar zu langsam gespielet werden muss (Finke-Hecklinger 1970 p83)

must be played very simply, almost without ornaments and not at all too slow.

It agrees with this even less than do the other ornate slow movements distantly related to the siciliano (Organ Sonata BWV 525, Violin Sonata BWV 1017, Gamba Sonata BWV 1028, Harpsichord Concerto BWV 1063). As is natural to the Six Sonatas, the countersubject has great independence of rhythm and melodic line, desirable in view of the need to exchange upper parts. Unusual even in the Six Sonatas, however, is this degree of independence throughout the movement: the voices never join together for a phrase in the way that they do in all the other slow movements of the set. Only the cadences unite them.

Third Movement

Like the finales of the C minor, E minor and C major sonatas, BWV 530.iii has a fugally treated theme in which the pedal also plays a part. As in the C major, it begins with a melody and counterpoint typical of the Three-part Inventions, as does the second subject (b19); each theme, however, soon passes to a simpler, more chordal passage – that in bb19–20 is almost *galant*. The form can be expressed:

A 1–18   subject answered in dominant, then broken-chord episode; pedal entry b8 used as basis for following sequence; coda with subject in stretto

B 19–31   second subject in relative minor, answered in its dominant (after four bars); sequential episode above a bass derived from b22

A 31–41   stretto development of first subject, then derived episode

B 42–51   second subject answered in its subdominant (after four bars); B_2 as B_1 in outline, but now filled in (pedal harmonies divided between feet and hands)

A 52–77   extended return to A_1 beginning in subdominant and including a second answer (dominant, b59); 67–77 = 8–18 without change

In particular details, the movement recalls several others. As in the first movement of this sonata, a broken-chord episode follows the initial subject and answer; as in the finale of the C major Sonata BWV 529.iii, the simplified version of the subject in the pedal (b8) is immediately taken up in sequence. In fact, the 'simplified pedal version' in both movements can only with caution be regarded as a pedal entry/answer, since the context and style are more in the nature of an episode (e.g., there is no original countersubject). The pedal cannot claim to be taking a fully equal part in the fugue, as it can in the finale of the C minor Sonata.

Despite the conventional fugal counterpoint of the subject and its bass, a more 'modern' relationship between subjects and their harmony can be sensed in the movement. The canonic imitation of bb14–18 leads to a somewhat circuitous harmonic sentence, while the tendency of the second subject to be harmonized in sixths clearly suggests a new approach to style. 'Almost *galant*' in this context suggests the style of Telemann trios. The broken chords or simple figuration of bb4, 50, 60 are more pronounced than is usual in the fugal movements of the Six Sonatas, and their pedal line is made to match; the episodes thus resemble those of the first movement of the same sonata. Bars 35–41 provide a fine demonstration of imitative writing over a continuo bass, but the actual sequences are more complex than anything in the first movement. The entry of the second subject is absorbed in a sequential figure which drops to become a countersubject, alas not taken further – Ex. 61. Several thematic entries are further hidden: although the stretto of b31/32 is made clearer by the return to G major, the episode semiquavers themselves disguise the entry, as they

Ex. 61

b40

do even more the decorated return in b52. The pedal often has an ungainly look which the variety of figure does not always help; that, as much as the wish to enrich the texture, may be the reason why the pedal line of bb21ff becomes distributed between pedal and manual in bb44ff.* This 'distribution', however, also aids the tension of the middle section, since it is picked up in sequential modulation a few bars later, and both in its subject and its sequences the whole middle section forms a clear contrast to the outer sections, modulating further and more often. This may be regarded as a standard characteristic of *A B A* form, as can be seen in the first movement of the C major Organ Sonata, finale of the E major Violin Sonata BWV 1016, etc.

* The C♮ of b44 is less problematic than some editors have suggested, since the parallel to this bar is b21 not b25: one function of the C♮ is to point to the ensuing subdominant answer (b46 lh).

531   Prelude and Fugue in C major

No Autograph MS; that once thought to be autograph (Washington Library of Congress ML 96.B.186) copied by unknown 18th-century hand; copies in Möller MS (BB 40644), P 274 (incomplete fugue; J. P. Kellner), P 286 (18th century, from P 274?), Württemberg Landesbib. Cod. mus II.288 (prelude only; owned by W. H. Pachelbel 1685–1764), two Scholz MSS, P 913 (Grasnick) and an unnumbered Oxford Bodleian MS (owned by Mendelssohn); *BG* 15 used a MS in the possession of Schubring ('Schubring MS') and Peters IV (which was based by Griepenkerl on two further MSS).

Two staves; title in Möller MS 'Praeludium pedaliter'.

That P 274, once thought to be autograph, is carelessly written (*BG* 15 p. xix) and as if by trial and error ('versuchsweise' – Spitta I p400) has suggested to some commentators that it is a first sketch; since it lacks bb26–54 of the fugue (the passage that contains the only fully thematic pedal entry), others have thought that the thematic pedal entry is a 'later addition' (Keller 1948 p50) contrasting with the 'more primitive' use of pedal in the Prelude. However, as P 274 also lacks the 'complete closing passage' of the fugure (*BG* 15 p. xix), no firm conclusion about the origin and history of the work can be based on it; BWV 531 was already complete in the Möller MS. Nevertheless, the fugue as it now exists does show signs of being some kind of patchwork.

It has become common to draw parallels between BWV 531 and the praeludia of Georg Böhm, even as far as supposing the work to date from the 'Böhmian' years before Bach travelled to hear Buxtehude in Lübeck (Schöneich 1947/8 p99); such qualities as 'the virtuoso brilliance of the closes and the freedom of the part-writing' also suggest the work to belong to an early period (Spitta I p401). Resemblances to Böhm's C major Praeludium are 'unmistakable' (Keller 1948 p50), while V. Lübeck's Praeludium in C major and various works of Buxtehude suggest other points of similarity to, and possible influences on, BWV 531. All such similarities concern first the overall form of Prelude–Fugue–Postlude, and secondly certain details of figuration (broken chords, scales, etc), texture, harmony and the use of the organ. As such, the basic similarities imply a common *genre* rather than specific influences or imitations, and it is notable that the Möller MS contains not the C major Praeludium of Böhm but his D minor and slighter works, no Lübeck but a fair amount of French music, and of Buxtehude only the less expansive A major Praeludium BUXWV 151 and G major Toccata BUXWV 165. Many useful parallels can be made with J. S. Bach's C minor Prelude and Fugue BWV 549 – also found in the Möller MS – almost suggesting that they were conceived as complements to each other: see notes to BWV 549.

Prelude

Opening pedal solos based on the same principles of alternate-foot pedalling, and thus related to each other, also tend to include rhetorical rests or *tmeses* (BWV 549, 564, Böhm in C major, Buxtehude in C major), though this is by no means a general rule (BWV 598, Lübeck in C major, Böhm in D minor). Such solos occasionally close with a pedal ornament (e.g. Lübeck in G major), and frequently the manual enters in octave imitation of the pedal or vice versa (e.g. Buxtehude in E minor, Bruhns in G minor), all as in BWV 531. That the first eighteen bars of BWV 531 are almost entirely centred on a tonic pedal point is within character, though kept up longer than was customary; on the other hand, the overall harmonic shape of the prelude as tonic–subdominant–dominant–subdominant–dominant–tonic* is clearer and more systematic than the freer fantasy of the earlier composers would have produced. Other details will be found in other praeludia, such as the parallel sixths in b22 etc (see the Prelude BWV 568 or Lübeck's Praeludium in C); similarly, the material of b20 is wholly conventional. But the non-stop nature of the successive pedal points gives the movement a hectic quality unknown in such sectionalized toccatas as BUXWV 165 in the Möller MS. The harmonic repetition of bb23–7 or bb30–2 suggests a new version of the conventional reiteration of simple harmonies found in (e.g.) Buxtehude's Praeludium in C BUXWV 138 (bb10–14), where the repetition is simpler and achieves a winsomely obsessive charm. There is also unequal interest between (e.g.) b31 and b32 – a sign of immaturity – while the climax of the closing bars is out of proportion to the rest of the prelude even by the standards of Buxtehude and Bruhns. These composers are also unlikely to use both the top and bottom notes of the organ (C-c‴) in the final bars of a first movement.

The prelude therefore mingles the conventional and the unconventional, its chief contribution to the *oeuvre* being the array of various praeludium details expanded to a fully independent prelude of 40 bars. Similar points could be made of the Prelude BWV 568, where the phraseology is more regular and the melodic elements more numerous.

Fugue

Such a *perpetuum mobile* fugue subject is more characteristic either of the smaller keyboard canzonetta or of a variant fugue in the long praeludia of northern composers; it is less characteristic of a self-contained organ fugue which follows a toccata prelude, and which from Scheidemann onwards tended to be 'quieter' in style. The exposition of BWV 531 also has interesting features:

four entries distributed over three parts and resulting in a falling effect (g″ b1, c″ 3, g′ 6, c′ 9); the answers mostly subdominant, so that all dominant notes

---

* This point alone makes it unlikely that a missing pedal note in b36 (if there is one) is d, as suggested in *NBA* IV/5 p5; G is either implied or restated.

in the subject can be answered by tonics (cf. fugue subject of BWV 565), in the key in which the answer ends (4–5).

The 'falling effect' is said to be an early feature (Bullivant 1959 p344). Further development of the subject produces an individual shape to the fugue:

1   exposition
11   first episode, new material (in Italianate–Pachelbel manner)
14   stretto use of subject *caput* towards:
17   middle entry in dominant, followed by more 'Pachelbel' material
24   tonic middle entry, preceded *alla stretta* by simplified pedal version of subject *caput*; answer in tonic, followed by episode incorporating new *figurae* in relative minor
36   pedal tonic entry, followed by derived sequential episode
41   four-part harmonization of further tonic entry, followed by episode derived from different fragments of subject
49   dominant middle entry, followed by episode and:
53   tonic entry
55   merging into long final coda in which the subject is not heard again complete

Although the final bars are built on conventional flourish figures – scales, trills, pedal point, sudden tonic minor (cf. Böhm, end of prelude section of Praeludium in C major) – and thus draw attention to the separated and independent close, the form of the fugue could be better expressed as:

A   1–27   beginning and ending in C major; no full pedal entry
B   28–55   ending in C major; in the middle, a pedal entry
C   55–74   coda; pedal for *point d'orgue**

The free close is thus merely part of a longer coda. Moreover, section B is dependent on a passage not given in P 274 (see above) which includes somewhat unexpected changes of direction (bb30–1, 34, 52–3); this passage also contains conventional *figurae* found in section A but now used in more advanced style (compare bb19–21 with bb30–2). Similarly, while conventional figures can be heard in both section A (e.g., the subject's motif Ex. 62 is used in Lübeck's Praeludium in C

Ex. 62

major) and section C (e.g. the sequences from bb58 and 63), the harmonization of bb41–2 is both curiously original and surprisingly undeveloped. But the 'original' form of BWV 531 is uncertain. It could be that in the interests of 'improvement' most of section B was omitted from the fugue in P 274 (and/or its original source) rather than added to an otherwise short fugue by (or for) the scribes of such copies as

* The pedal G of b70 in BG 15 should be F♯ according both to sources (*NBA* IV/5 p9) and to convention in the seventeenth century, when dramatic use of a dominant $^{6}_{5}$ was common (e.g. Buxtehude's Praeludium in D major BUXWV 139 bb89–94).^{3} The following c″–b′ *trillo* is also characteristic of the seventeenth-century praeludium.

the Möller MS. That b25 ends with the same notes in the right hand as appear at the beginning of b55 is difficult to use as evidence of what the authentic or eventual form of the movement should be. It could be evidence both that P 274 omitted the already composed section bb26–54 (leaving an unconvincing join) and that in the Möller MS the section bb27–54 was the result of an addition by the composer (in order to avoid the unconvincing join and to develop the material farther). Similarly, although the pedal entry in b36 may seem out of character in view of the previous simplified pedal subject in b23, the manner in which it is paired off with the left-hand countersubject recalls the contemporary (?) Fugue in A minor BWV 551.ii b45.

The apparently *ad hoc* shape of the fugue BWV 531.ii anticipates a later C major organ fugue (BWV 547), where harmony and counterpoint are both richer, as the form is more closely reasoned. Both prelude and fugue BWV 531, unlike BWV 547, depend greatly on keyboard figures other than those found in the themes themselves; but as the last six bars show, these figures produce a sense of drive however varied the texture, suggesting to Spitta 'a spring storm at night in March' (I p401) and to Frotscher the 'dark harmony' of minor chords as used by Buxtehude and Bruhns (1935 p866).

---

532   Prelude and Fugue in D major

No Autograph MS; copies in Württemberg Landesbib. Cod. mus II.288 (owned by W. H. Pachelbel 1685–1764), P 204 (C. F. G. Schwenke 1781?), and P 291 (2nd half of 18th century); prelude only in P 287 (2nd half of 18th century) and Lpz MB MS 7, 11 (J. N. Mempell), fugue only in P 1095 (J. N. Mempell), P 567 (J. F. Doles? 1715–96; in C major), P 595 (J. Ringk 1717–78), Brussels Fétis 2960 (late 18th century), P 834 (c1800, in F major), P 924 (Grasnick), Lpz MB III.8.20 (Dröbs), III.8.22 (early 19th century), a Schubring MS (*BG* 15) and late copies ('Oxford MS', Scholz MS).

Two staves; title in Lpz MB MS 7, 11 'Praeludium', in P 287 'Preludio' and in P 204 and 291 'Piece d'Orgue'; in an 'old manuscript' owned by Griepenkerl (see Peters IV p. iv) headed 'Concertato'.

The occasional title 'Pièce d'Orgue' seems to justify the view that the prelude of BWV 532 has points in common with the Parisian organist's *Offertoire* (Klotz 1962), points which can be summed up as a festive character and a sectional plan. But the details neither of the musical idiom nor of the form itself are Parisian, since there are none of the characteristic French harmonies or textures, nor are there fugal expositions as found in the earlier *Offertoires*. In both prelude and fugue the composer seems rather to be working many conventional elements towards a massive composition in which those various elements are exploited more fully than before, less capriciously than in Buxtehude or Bruhns. Griepenkerl's idea (Peters IV 1845) that the title 'Concertato' suggests 'a non-church use' for the work cannot be substantiated, not least since 'concerto' was a common term for a church cantata itself (e.g. Cantata 65, autograph MS P 147). Other attempts to classify or describe this prelude – e.g. that each of its three sections has three further sub-sections (Schöneich 1947/8 p66ff) – are no more than suggestive; moreover, while clearly the fugue subject has a sequence in common with the *alla breve* passages of the second section (Dietrich 1931 p60), it would be an exaggeration to see the fugue as actually 'derived' from the *alla breve* section. It is not as close as (e.g.) the fourth section of a Buxtehude Praeludium which uses a subject from the second. Similarly, had the composer wished to underline any 'similar character' between the 'end of the fugue and the beginning of the prelude' (Keller 1948 p63) it could have been achieved much more explicitly, given the simple nature of the material. That the fugue theme has points in common with at least one subject of Pachelbel may indicate the work's ancestry; but the sequences in the *alla breve* section were also common Italian and south German property, while the overall plan must be seen as drawn from the northern praeludia, as should the patterns and figures of the fugue. Spitta's suggestion that Bach wrote the work 'for an occasion, such as one of his artistic travels' (Spitta 1 p404) has no documentary backing.

Prelude

First section

Although no clear parallels are to be found in any of his extant works, the style of the opening scales and broken chords – all on a tonic pedal point – is close to Bruhns. Many of the same elements can be seen at the opening of the D major Toccata BWV 912, of which two older sources (Möller MS and P 804) tie the notes of the broken chords, producing an organ-like effect. The subsequent dominant pedal, and its manual figures in simple stretto, conform with toccata tradition, both southern (Pachelbel, Fischer) and northern.

Second section

The dramatic rest followed by mediant pedal point is all ultimately within the Bruhns tradition, though surprise chords are usually – in true recitative fashion – first inversions, not root positions. Both tremolo chords and quick scales are to be found in the Toccata BWV 912, the tremolo chords being an equivalent to the trilled thirds in Buxtehude, Lübeck or Bruhns. Indeed, the whole first sixteen bars suggest an eighteenth-century composer's response to the caprice of the northern praeludia in which *ouverture* elements (dotted rhythms) are usually absent but deserve to be considered amongst the repertory of toccata effects. The rhetoric of these sixteen bars is new, particularly the stormy B minor passage into and from which the listener is plunged without warning.

Third section

The idea of a simple, sequential main theme interspersed with conforming episodes is also to be found in the Allegro of the Toccata BWV 912. The main theme of the present *alla breve* centres on a conventional chain of suspensions which, depending on the inversion, can be described as *7–6* (b21), *5–6* or *5–4* (b32), *2–3* (b65) or *9–8* (b34); in three parts, the sequence would be a conventional $\begin{smallmatrix}7 & 6\\3 & 3\end{smallmatrix}$, but in four parts it requires the fifth of the chord. The result of these patterns is to create a movement which appears almost a kind of well-improvised basso continuo: a series of solutions for the figured-bass player. In this respect, though not comparable in complexity, certain praeludia of Buxtehude offer parallels, e.g. the G minor BUXWV 149 and the F sharp minor BUXWV 146: Ex. 63. The episodes are distinct from the *alla breve*

Ex. 63

BUXWV 149

b55

BUXWV 146

suspensions, despite the overall continuity of the section. Thus the episode bb37–47 introduces triadic harmonies, repeated phrases, repeated notes, parallel harmonies without suspension – all elements calculated to contrast with the main material, which has none of them. The sequences and plain rhythms may at times remind the listener of the style of Cantata 4 (1708), and it is clearly right to see the main theme of b20ff as similar to passages in Corelli and Handel (Keller 1948 p63). But more than that: the movement is created from basso-continuo formulae, familiar in (e.g.) the late *Gründlicher Unterricht des General-basses* (1738) attributed to J. S. Bach (see *Dok* II pp333–4 and Schulze *BJ* 1978 p39).

The clear episode structure of the movement is usually taken as an indication that manuals can or even ought to be changed; the difference in content between the main theme and episodes suggests a second manual for the latter, as in the G minor Fantasia BWV 542 (Kloppers 1966 p77). But it is not quite clear at what points the 'episodes of different content' begin: b37 rather than b31, b62, b71 etc? Perhaps it is rather a question of taking off the quasi-echo bars on to a manual contrasting with the *plein jeu* of the opening theme, such as at b41 (end); but that is scarcely possible in b39 (end). Perhaps a tutti with and without pedal is sufficient contrast for such passages; but the notation of bb62–3 in the surviving sources certainly suggests change of manual.

Perhaps only the left hand (playing both inner parts?) in such bars as 37, 39, 41, 52 etc is taken off, indeed on to a manual whose *petit grand jeu* might contrast with the *plein jeu* of the rest (Klotz 1975 p390); but that would be an exceptional treatment, in theory suiting French *dialogue* style but matched nowhere else in Bach. As in the fugue, the manner of keyboard writing allows the player to change manuals without particular difficulty (e.g. over bb71–96), but this factor cannot be conclusive proof that he is required to do so.

Fourth section

Not for the only time in a sectional work of Bach (cf. end of the Gravement in BWV 572), an original interrupted cadence is produced by resolving the dominant on to a diminished seventh. While the *adagio* harmonies are certainly in the 'Buxtehude manner' (Spitta I p404), an instructive comparison can be made with the Grave of the C major Toccata BWV 564, with respect both to position (short interlude ending on the tonic of a following fugue) and idiom (scale line, diminished sevenths, augmented triad, ninths, angular pedals). The part-writing of BWV 532 is stricter, pedal appears to be *doppio*, and the suspended harmonies are broken by runs, two of which concern Neapolitan sixths (bb98, 104). Thus, though the two pieces are similar in *genre* – compare the last two bars of each – they are very different in the way they present that *genre*. Despite also such particular chords as the $^9_7$ it would be a mistake to see this sustained/chromatic idiom as French. J. S. Bach's use of the diminished seventh and Neapolitan sixth is more systematic than that of any French composer, and may even be more German in tradition, judging by the Neapolitan sixth above rests in a Bruhns Adagio (Praeludium in G minor b30, also copied by J. Ringk).

Fugue

The striking fugue subject and even more idiosyncratic countersubject have sent commentators to find parallels elsewhere: Ex. 64, next page. The style of such *Spielthemen* is even more general: for example, compare bb3, 4 of the subject with the closing pedal line of the G major Fugue BWV 550. These resemblances merely confirm that in BWV 532 the composer was working with yet a further distinct type of keyboard fugue subject and producing at the end of the fugue not a final toccata-postlude but a virtuoso coda, derived from but not wholly devoted to a long final tonic.

The form may be expressed:

A	1–26	exposition, four parts, two real answers
	26–9	derived then free episode
	30–53	middle entry or re-exposition (tonic–dominant–tonic) with four bars of episode 42–5; followed by two further bars of episode towards:

> B   53–64   middle entry in relative minor (first bar of subject repeated), leading to derived then free episode*
>
> 64–76   answer in dominant of relative, first manual then in part (without subject-*caput*) on pedal
>
> 76–84   subject-*caput* on pedal to pass to: further answer, broken up and shortened, in dominant of dominant of relative
>
> 84–96   episode (similar to first two episodes) leading to partial entry in supertonic, altered to modulate back to:
>
> C   96–124   final entries in dominant (followed by lengthy derived episode) and tonic, the last intact
>
> 124–37   coda, picking up second half of subject, running to material derived from first codetta (b12), last six bars using the opening motifs of both subject and countersubject

In particular, the episode structure could be differently expressed, but such a scheme draws attention to the essential ternary plan of the whole. It is the cut-up nature of the lines, rather than the overall form, that

Ex. 64

subject
Pachelbel, Fugue in D

BUXWV 172 (LM 4983)

countersubject
BUXWV 145   b40

Reincken, Fuga in G minor   b37

development
BWV 71   (1708)

---

* The apparent abruptness with which the stretto in bb58–9 is cut off in b60 is avoided by the shorter episode of BWV 532a at this point.

allows for changes of manual; even so, it is no more than interesting conjecture to think of the fugue as planned for no less than 'the four manuals of the great Hamburg organs' (Klotz 1975 p391).

The spacious exuberance of the fugue should not disguise either its strategic or its tactical ingenuity. Thus, after the first section it is never clear whether the opening phrase of the subject is going to herald a simple entry (b96), be used as an episode (b77, bb103ff), be taken over by another voice (bb90–1) or be merely delayed by it (bb53–4). In this longer version of the fugue (see also BWV 532a) the anchoring effect of the long dominant preparation for the final entry (bb103–16) is highly desirable but is nonetheless contrived in a manner quite distinct from strict fugal technique. At the close, Spitta heard similarities to the end of Buxtehude's F sharp minor Praeludium (repetitions of the tonic, etc), while others have heard there a reference to the opening of the prelude itself. But the timing and expansiveness of BWV 532.ii are unique, however logical a conclusion to the opening bars of the prelude the end of the fugue may seem. At the same time, despite the length of the final section no other fugue in the literature actually ends so succinctly, with such an exclamation.

532a   Fugue in D major

No Autograph MS; Peters IV, from 'a very good old MS'.

Two staves; heading, 'Fuga'.

This simplified, shortened version of BWV 532.ii differs from it as follows:

BWV 532a		BWV 532.ii	
1–27	A	1–27	similar
28–9		28–9	different content
30–52		30–52	similar
52–8	B	52–8	pedal entry distributed between hands and feet in 532a
59–61		59–64	different episode
62–71		65–76	similar, but entry shortened in 532a
71–3		—	episode in 532a
—		76–96	in 532, further episode and (shortened) entries in C$\sharp$ minor / E major
74–98	C	96–137	same entries but longer episode material in 532

The shorter version is usually taken to be the earlier, 'simpler' version (Frotscher 1935 p868), 'Pachelbel-like in form' (Schöneich 1947/8 p66ff), and showing with BWV 532 the ways in which the composer extended a fugue when for some reason the desire arose. Similar points are often made about the two Albinoni fugues BWV 951/951a and the extended Reincken fugue BWV 954, though with what justification will not be clear until their sources are assessed.

As the comparison above shows, BWV 532a may be a shorter but is hardly a simplified version of 532 technically, since the manual and pedal parts are equally difficult. Nor is it easy to see that the 'most brilliant parts' are missing in 532a (Keller 1948 p63), unless this includes the remoter keys. More plausible is Spitta's suggestion that 532a represents a later version, made by the composer himself to present the fugue in a 'more concentrated' form (Spitta I p405). Why he should do this can only be conjectured. There remains the possibility that a copyist shortened it – though the cadence at bb92–3 required a good composer – but there then remains also the question why he has a different version of bb27–8. Perhaps he did not care for the texturally plain sequences provided in bb27–8 and 86–9 of the BWV 532 version, changing the first and cutting the second. As the two fugues stand, the final passage in both –

	BWV 532a	BWV 532.ii
dominant preparation	80–6	103–16+2 bars
tonic entry (final entry)	87–93	119–24
coda	93–8	124–37

– is equally convincing, but it is easier to imagine the frenetic element of BWV 532 being cut out in order to make the fugue shorter than to envisage its being added to a short fugue in order to make it longer. But Griepenkerl's remark in 1845 that 'it is a pity one cannot be sure whether J. S. Bach was responsible for the differences [between BWV 532 and 532a] or not' (Peters IV preface) still holds.

---

533   Prelude and Fugue in E minor

No Autograph MS; that once thought to be autograph (Lpz Bach-Archiv Mus MS 2, fugue only) copied by 'Anon 18' (Kilian 1962; and cf. BWV 545); copies of later 18th century: P 287 (Michel), P 289, P 320 (Kittel), P 425 (J. Ringk), LM 4838, and of early 19th (often dependent on MSS of Kittel circle): P 282, P 923, P 319 (Westphal), P 557 (Grasnick), P 671 (Grasnick), Lpz Go.S.26, unnumbered Oxford Bodleian MS, BB 30289; BG 15 used a Schubring MS; 18th-century copies of prelude only (P 301) or fugue (P 804) by known copyists; BB autogr. Mendelssohn 2 (prelude), Scholz MS (fugue).

Two staves; heading in P 287, 'Praeludium et Fuga ped'.

For a version without pedals, see BWV 533a. That the work circulated widely is suggested by the extant sources; perhaps from one of them Mendelssohn made his copy of the prelude in 1822 (BB autogr. Mendelssohn 2). Spitta was full of admiration for the work, not only hearing many specific expressive qualities in both prelude and fugue ('gloomy pride...melancholy...magic...gentle strength') but seeing the movements as 'closely related, more so than usual with Bach preludes and fugues' (Spitta I p401); it is an 'inner connection' rather than any explicit inter-allusion, a point repeated often and more recently (e.g. Schöneich 1947/8 pp156ff). Disagreements arise, however, between commentators who hear in the work characteristics of the composer's maturest styles (Widor, quoted by Keller 1948 p60) and those who think it so early as to be perhaps the first extant example of a separate, independent prelude and fugue (Schöneich *op cit*), i.e. without interludes, toccata-postlude etc. Certainly it is striking that while the prelude contains three traditional toccata elements – a solo line (b1), a free passage (b6) and a regular passage with suspensions (bb12ff) – the fugue contains none of them, being even freer of suspensions. Such factors suggest that the two movements are carefully planned complements to each other, characteristic of a style-conscious composer.

Prelude*

That the opening solo line has points in common with the Prelude of the Lute Suite BWV 996 (copied by J. G. Walther in P 801) – such as the improvisatory figures running around an underlying chord of E minor, settling on a low E after four or five bars – suggests that such openings were traditional. However, BWV 996 is closer to the average solo run-in of a Buxtehude praeludium than is BWV 533, whose question–answer shape is more regular and hence alien to the opening lute line: Ex. 65.

Ex. 65

BWV 996
b1

BWV 533
b1

It is thus an exaggeration and possibly an anachronism to claim that the E minor Prelude 'owes its type to the E minor Lute Suite Prelude' (Frotscher 1935 p872). Either way, it should be noticed that the organ prelude begins much more obviously in its tonic key than in many openings by Buxtehude.

Since BWV 533 proceeds in b6 to a freer passage that introduces three rather vigorous ideas familiar from Buxtehude, Lübeck and others – Ex. 66 – it is possible that the 'gloomy weight' familiar in performances of this prelude is also an anachronism. All three ideas appear in a further E minor work – the Toccata BWV 914 (Adagio), which shows little sign of 'melancholy...' etc. Similarly, in the third section, which is given to firm rhythmic harmonies, it may be less relevant to hear 'atmospheres' than to note that such textures grow from ideas known in (e.g.) such chorale fantasias as in Ex. 67. Moreover, despite the undeniably organ-like textures and general idiom, such details as the final repeated cadence recall those cadential echoes or tonic re-affirmations found in vocal works, namely the early cantatas 131, 106 (1707?), 4 and 71 (1708?).

* Bar numbers as in *NBA* iv/5 (b18 is omitted in *BG* 15).

Ex. 66

Ex. 67
Bruhns, 'Nun komm' (P 802)

Throughout the prelude, whether in the opening solo, the subsequent free passage, the middle section of sequences or the final pedal phrases, the phraseology is highly discontinuous, relying on one-bar phrases or fractions of one bar. This is an unusual feature and one which heightens the significance of the prelude's most original section, i.e. the chords from b18, where the one-bar phrasing is itself a kind of *pesante* development of a half-bar figure found in the previous passage. As in other early works of Bach, the harmonic power of the section is derived from simple diminished sevenths, although in this case they have the function of dominant minor ninths.

Fugue

The first half of the fugue is taken up with five entries (subject or answer), i.e. one more than the number of parts, as is the case with other 'early fugues' (BWV 531, 549 etc):

1–15	subject, tonal answer, codetta, subject, tonal answer, real answer (in pedal – cf. the fugue BWV 550)
15–18	episode derived from codetta
19–23	tonic entry, accompanied by non-thematic pedal
24–9	answer and further tonic entry
29–33	episode (derived from the countersubject's dactyl figure)
33–6	final entry in pedal, no coda

This is one of the classic fugue shapes – brief, like the prelude, but like it incorporating many hallmarks of the *genre*. The subject leads to a texture not unlike that of the central part of the prelude (compare bb19 and 24 of the fugue with b15 of the prelude), although such a melodic resemblance as that between b18 (alto) in the fugue and b29 (pedal) in the prelude is presumably no more than coincidence. The entry in bb24-5 gives a texture found in chorale fantasias (see Ex. 67), while the harmonies produced by the entry *en taille* (bb19-24) are particularly happy and suit a piece obviously intended to present the form, texture and figuration of fugues in a very different guise from such works as BWV 531 and 532. Despite its unextravagant nature, such a passage as bb322-3 shows a natural sense of contrapuntal melody combined with an ability to spin out the lines – the pedal entry of b33 could have appeared 1½ bars earlier than it does – while the episodes themselves (e.g. bb15-18) are less 'neutral' or frankly preparatory than those of (e.g.) the C minor Fugue BWV 549. The final bars too, though apparently simple and undramatic, have a harmonic resonance typical of the succinct five-part writing in a cantata interlude of Buxtehude or in an early string prelude of J. S. Bach (Cantata 4.i).

533a

Prelude and Fugue in E minor

No Autograph MS; copy in Lpz MB MS 7, 19 (J. G. Preller).

Two staves; heading 'Praeludium et Fuga'.

BWV 533a differs from 533 in two main respects: pedals are neither specified nor required by the spacing; and two extra bars are contained in the prelude, so that bb6-13 of BWV 533a are equivalent to bb6-11 of 533. Though referred to amongst the 'early versions' of Bach organ works (*NBA* IV/6 p. vi), BWV 533a is not demonstrably earlier or later than BWV 533. The last five bars of each prelude suggest that the keyboard version is a reduction of the organ texture. Similarly, while extra bars found earlier on in a keyboard prelude might suggest in other cases that the organ piece is a reduced (shortened) version of it, in fact the passage in the organ prelude contains a recurrent or unifying motif absent from the keyboard prelude (tremolo chords). Perhaps the arranger of BWV 533a, whether composer or transcriber–copyist, began to add harpsichord figures, omitted the 'unifying motif' but extended the Buxtehude-like idea in the second half of b6, and went no farther than b13 in this manner. Why he should change the harmonies of the long sequence from b20 is even less clear; it can hardly have been carelessness (as the different harmonies two bars from the end of the fugue may have been) and almost suggests that the organ version is indeed a later 'improvement'.

The fugue as it stands in the organ version is also playable by hands alone, although this does mean that the real answer in b12 would not then be so conspicuous; this cannot be assumed to be a 'fault', however, but merely a characteristic of a harpsichord fugue.

---

534   Prelude and Fugue in F minor

No Autograph MS; only source: Lpz MB III.8.21 (Dröbs, early 19th century), also used for Peters II (*BG* 15 p. xxii).

Two staves; heading, 'Praeludium et Fuga ex F moll pedaliter'.

Whether or not it is a question of 'new paths' being opened up by BWV 534, 537, 540 and 546 – with all that would suggest about chronology – Spitta was obviously justified in thinking this group of pieces 'related in so many exterior and interior details that they [must have] originated during the same period, following Bach's practice of exhausting certain characteristics of form – once he had discovered them – in several works, one after the other' (Spitta I p581). These 'certain characteristics' include a tighter or more integrated form for the preludes, whose material is in any case melodious rather than merely motivic, and more finely worked and spacious counterpoint in the fugues, whose subjects leave in their melodic lines 'a quite different impression from the earlier' fugues (*ibid* p582). The poor source material for BWV 534 means both that such grammatical errors as the doubled leading-note in b128 of the fugue are of doubtful origin and that textural similarities felt between the prelude and the fugue – 'obviously conceived together as a whole' (*ibid* p581), 'closely related in their final passages' (Keller 1948 p80) – are not confirmed by any authenticated source, however plausible they may be. The same is true of the key itself, F minor.

Prelude

The form of the prelude may be expressed:

A	1–11	tonic pedal point; three parts, of which two in canonic imitation
	11–32	series of sequences (including pedal sequences), working towards hemiola close in C minor; four parts
B	32–43	dominant pedal point (material as bb1–11); three parts, of which two in canonic imitation
	43–67	series of different sequences (including pedal sequences), working towards final cadence; four parts, framing a section of three parts
	67–76	final cadence begun with dominant pedal point, interrupted by diminished seventh* from which cadenza springs

The movement is thus cast in an unusual binary form between whose 'second subjects' only a family likeness of motif can be claimed; episode material on any large scale does not return, nor does the first subject reappear constantly in the manner of a ritornello. The 'series of sequences' is made clear in particular by the pedal, which engages in some of the important sequences (bb11, 17, 43, 64) as well as a few

---

* The poor source material again leaves uncertain whether or not the composer wrote this chord in ten parts; compare the diminished-seventh interrupted cadences in BWV 532 b96 (four parts) and in BWV 572 b185 (six parts).

briefer sequences (bb15, 21, 28); the transitions in between produce a figure that returns throughout (bb21, 26, 50) until it creates a sequence of its own (bb64–6). Although these pedal phrases may be thought to reveal careful or planned inter-quotation, it would be truer to the nature of the movement to claim only that the composer was (still) working with small motif-patterns between which connections can often be heard, e.g. Ex. 68. These motifs are not yet built up towards original

Ex. 68

or free, melodious lines. Almost all begin off the beat – one reason for the ambiguity of metre when they first do not (e.g. b17).

The somewhat elusive character of the movement has sent commentators looking amongst books of the period which outline the *Affekten* of music (e.g. Mattheson's description of F minor as a key 'full of anxiety and despair' – Keller 1948 p80) or amongst such conceivable influences as contemporary dance-suites (e.g., BWV 534.i is a spacious sarabande – Klotz 1962). Neither the melodic phraseology nor the binary form necessarily suggests Italian models or influence, as is sometimes hinted, since the former is built on motifs familiar to German toccata-composers and found in such contexts as Ex. 69. Nor is the

Ex. 69
Toccata in E minor BWV 914

binary form like the binary movement found in Italian sonatas; rather, it recalls the German toccata of the Pachelbel type, i.e. planned as long tonic and dominant pedal points, interspersed with and followed by other material. This 'pedal-point toccata' conception is also found in the Toccata in F major BWV 540 and the ritornello Prelude in C minor BWV 546, though in a yet further developed manner. That the inventiveness of J. S. Bach often seems geared to creating variety of treatment from what is basically a single conception may be seen by comparing the details of the Toccata BWV 540 with the present prelude, whose differences of metre, key, form, texture and 'style' disguise their common roots as preludes shaped around tonic and dominant pedal points, with manual parts in canonic imitation for the main subject, and episodes based on tutti sequences.

It is not only the last 2½ bars that the prelude appears to share with the fugue: the final 8 bars of the prelude trace in a freer, more prelude-like way aspects of the melodic line of the final 6 bars of the fugue. An important difference, however, is that the prelude 'cadenza' changes harmony over its course, whilst the fugue 'cadenza' does not. On the contrary, the fugue close is highly derived from its own subject, and no facile inter-quotation between the movements is likely to have been intended. The bar-by-bar structure of the prelude is more homogeneous, with a musical control of sequence so that the basic interest of each is pointed up by the differences between one and the other – for example, in phrase-length (two-bar sequence bb9–10, three-bar 11–13, four-bar 17–20, etc). Since the texture is full and widely spaced – closing up for the halfway cadence bb30–2, opening out for the final close bb71–6 – the result is a concentrated movement of unusual character, at times almost bleak in its wide spacing, at others warmly congested (b64). The pedal lines are more 'powerful' than the merely agile lines typical of difficult pedal solos in the usual toccatas.

Fugue

The form of the fugue may be expressed:

1–27	exposition in five parts; no constant countersubject, but counterpoint created from the crotchets of the subject (b3); fifth entry followed by 'prolongation episode' typical of ricercar subjects (Bullivant 1959 p516)
27–46	episode-entries in tonic and dominant, in three, four, two parts
47–55	entry in relative major; episode to:
56–72	dominant and tonic entries, each followed by episodes
73–80	entry in relative major; episode to:
81–96	tonic and dominant entries, each followed by shorter episodes, with pedal
96–119	tonic, dominant and tonic entries, each followed by shorter episodes, without pedal
120–38	dominant final entries (bb120, 123); episode; followed by implied tonic final entry and cadence

The frequency of the tonic and dominant entries is highly original and leads to an unusual fugue in which the subject is constantly accompanied by new countersubjects. Spitta's judgment that the countersubjects soon peter out and that the subject therefore 'must always look around for help' (I p583) can be accepted only if the composer is not allowed to be creating a specific type of fugue whose subject and answer (real, since a fully subdominant answer would otherwise be necessary) sustain the drive by appearing always on the same three notes but in succession or alternation, in different voices, with different countersubject, in different textures, and spaced at different intervals of time. That the entries appear in succession or in alternation, in different voices and textures is clear from a glance; less clear is the ingenuity with which the many entries are spaced at different distances along the fugue: bb1, 4, 8, 12, 17, 27, 31, 37, 38, 42, 47, 56, 64 etc. Similarly, the countersubjects have a subtlety not immediately obvious, since not only do they vary in rhythm from (i) minims to (ii) crotchets and (iii) quavers – Ex. 70 – but they also vary in the number of parts.

(i) b12

(ii) b4

(iii) b120

Thus the 'countersubject' to the entry in b27 is rightly in two parts not one: Ex. 71. Within these areas of rhythm and number of parts, immense variety is achieved. The parts countering the subject vary from

Ex. 71
b27

one (b3) to four (b123), not in the normal way of fugal texture but as a conscious attempt to present the subject – which remains in as few keys as is compatible with a length of nearly 150 bars – in various guises. It is instructive, for instance, to compare two harmonizations – b17 and b81 – where both are in five parts, both are in the tonic, and the subject is in the top part in both: they have but one chord in common. Similarly, although the countersubjects at b38 and b90 both centre on quavers, or those of b17 and b96 both on crotchets, obviously there are essential differences between the two in each case, almost as if they were demonstrating the possibilities. Both crotchet countersubjects are in the tonic, both quaver countersubjects are in the dominant, the first in each case on the beat, the second off the beat.

The movement also shows how to derive and develop episodes. The first codetta (b7) inverts the previous bar taken from the subject; the short episodes of b11 and bb15–16 extend crotchet lines; so does the episode bb20–6, but now in a five-part counterpoint that produces easy suspensions and rich progressions. Important episodes bring forward a free sequence (bb50–5) or derive it from what has just gone before (bb61–3). Contrasted with the freer episodes of b69 and b93 is the close-wrought four-part counterpoint very characteristic of J. S. Bach's *alla breve* style (bb105–9); contrasted with the truncated sequence of one episode (e.g. b69) is the repetitious sequence of another (b113).

Ex. 72
b130

Finally, the fine, idiomatic organ writing of the last twelve bars should not hide what is perhaps the most imaginative element in the whole fugue, namely the paraphrased final entry or entries of the closing bars. Perhaps even further references can be found than this skeleton suggests: Ex. 72. And perhaps it was for the sake of such a coda that the tonic already reached in b119 suddenly turns to the dominant for the full entries of b120 and b123.

535   Prelude and Fugue in G minor

No Autograph MS (see BWV 535a); copies in P 1097 (Oley? 1738–89), P 1098 (J. G. Preller), Lpz MB III.8.7 (c1740–50, same copyist as BWV 768; but with 2 bars said to be copied by J. S. Bach), P 288 (2nd half of 18th century), P 320 (Kittel), P 804 (J. P. Kellner, prelude only), later sources in Kittel circle (P 557, Lpz Poel 19, Lpz Go.S.26), Am.B. 606 (2nd half of 18th century, fugue only); *BG* 15 used a 'Schubring MS'; Göttingen Bach-Institut, copy signed by 'J. C. Bach' (anon. scribe, 1st half of 18th century?).

Two staves; title in Lpz MB III.8.7 ('written in J. S. Bach's circle' – Krause 1964 p16), 'Preludio con Fuga per il Organo', in Schubring 'Preludio con Fuga pro Organo pleno', in P 804 'Praeludium'.

For a different prelude, see BWV 535a; that of P 804 has 39 bars, 4 shorter than P 1097 etc. In the two Leipzig sources, as in P 288, P 1097 and P 1098, BWV 535 was copied as an isolated work; only in P 320 and P 557 is it part of a collection. Both the sources and musical details suggest that BWV 535 is the 'later version' of the work, and the relative restraint of the 'earlier' fugue version BWV 535a makes the final toccata postlude more suitable and traditional for it than for BWV 535.

Prelude

The cello-like passage-work above an implied pedal point in the opening bars is a complement to that of (e.g.) BWV 536 and conforms with the opening *passaggio* lines of the E minor preludes for organ (BWV 533) and for *Lautenwerk* (BWV 996); the term 'passaggio' appears in the 'early version' (see BWV 535a). In comparison with BWV 535a, however, the present prelude picks up an idea in b3 and uses it for the whole tonic section before it passes to the expected dominant pedal point. Though simple, the effect is striking (like the chordal passage from b14 of BWV 533.i), leading to conventional *9–8* progressions (bb8–9), conventional Buxtehude-like repeated chords (b10), and – rather puzzlingly – an apparent reference in the pedal to the head of the fugue theme to follow. Insofar as bb10–11 can be seen to be based on Buxtehude-like repeated chords above a moving bass and on a passing from tonic to dominant pedal point (like the pedal-point toccatas of the whole period between Frescobaldi and Pachelbel), there does not seem much likelihood that the composer intended those bars to refer to the fugue subject, particularly since that reference is incomplete.

The following section (bb14–34)* appears as a kind of afterthought to the version BWV 535a; but it is significant that the opening and closing bars of the section are based on a dominant pedal point. This means that the series of scale figures and diminished sevenths, although descending even beyond the twelve degrees of the octave,

---

* Bar numbers as in *NBA* IV/5, where each figure of b31 of the *BG* 15 version is played twice to produce bb31–2.

returns to where it began, and the harmonies pick up where they left off. Such single-minded pursuit of a motif or harmony, not paralleled in any other organ prelude (hence its appearance here? – it is worth a place in any list of 'prelude effects'), is not allowed to divert the plan of the whole. In turn, the resumed dominant pedal point passes to a figured version of the closing bars of BWV 535a. Unlike the plain diminished-seventh sequence in the Gigue of the B flat Partita BWV 825 (which also returns to the harmonic point of departure), the descending chromatic sequence of BWV 535.i centres on the ease with which $^{\flat 7}_{\flat 5}$ is changed to $^6_{\flat 5}$ (so that each seventh is a suspension from the previous bar), while the plain sevenths are reserved for the final two bars.

Fugue

The fugue subject begins with crotchets and passes to quavers and then to semiquavers. Thus, although the first bar has the appearance of a conventional subject-*caput* and the following two bars have a broken phrase like the sectional subjects of BWV 549, 575 etc, the progress of this subject is like neither of those, passing to an answer before it is fully complete. Such 'uncompleted' subjects are rare in J. S. Bach, and subtle variety in the fugue is achieved in the different consequences of this 'incompleteness' each time the subject enters and runs its course. The form of the fugue is as clear as (e.g.) BWV 578:

1–25	exposition of four parts but realized in only three; 'uncompleted' subject passes without break to first episode (b21)
25–46	series of tonic–dominant–tonic entries in the three manual voices, each followed by episode
46–55	entry (without answer) in relative, with pedal, followed by episode
55–70	dominant and tonic entries, each followed by episode
70–7	coda, with pedal solo, scales, Neapolitan sixth, tonic pedal point, and with the highest and lowest notes of the fugue (C/c''')

Further subtleties in the figuration are referred to under BWV 535a; the present fugue provides a long list of conventional figures in the subject (b4), first countersubject (b6), episode (bb21–2, 37ff, 52ff, 60ff) and later countersubjects (bb33ff, 40ff, 55ff, 64ff). That of b62 looks like the closing passage of the prelude, that of bb69–70 like the pedal-point figure in b6 of the E minor Prelude BWV 533. The scale figures of the coda differ interestingly from those of the prelude, and it is possible that the composer consciously intended the B-A-C-H figure in the pedal solo (end of b71). The Neapolitan sixth of b72 is not fully integrated as it is in (e.g.) BWV 534.i b30, nor is it followed by a dramatic rest as in (e.g.) BWV 582 b285.

Despite all such details, the chief interest of the fugue centres on the sense of cumulation and climax, not only through well-conceived counterpoint (in particular, the four-part passage from b46 to b57) but through the 'new and increasing liveliness' of that counterpoint 'each time the theme enters' (Spitta I p405). The consistent countersubject of the exposition is soon dropped, and countersubjects become livelier: at b55 a canonic figure runs in contrary motion, at b64 the subject is countered by wide-ranging arpeggios. In one sense, the toccata postlude is 'unnecessary' to BWV 535.ii, since it has already had climactic moments. It is not certain that the dramatic and quickly modulating final ten bars belong to BWV 535a; but as in BWV 531, they supply a climax otherwise missing from it.

535a

Prelude and Fugue in G minor

Only source: Autograph MS in Möller MS.

Two staves; title and headings, 'Praeludium cum Fuga ex G♭ pedaliter', prelude 'Passaggio', fugue 'Allegro' (at least the last two inscriptions are not autograph).

BWV 535a differs from BWV 535 as follows:

prelude: from b3, a solo line above an implied pedal point; last 6½ bars similar to last 7½ bars of BWV 535, but simpler figuration; intervening passage has different material (total length of prelude 21 bars).

fugue is incomplete in the Möller MS (where writing breaks off at the foot of a page), lacking the last 12½ bars of the BWV 535 version and giving rests in the upper parts after the first chord of b65; bar by bar, the versions are similar (exposition, entries, episodes), but BWV 535 has a busier and more inventive figuration (manual, pedal) with a more continuous line. The right-hand tessitura of BWV 535 is also in general lower.

Since the Möller MS is still uncertain in date and provenance, the autograph excerpt can be put only tentatively at 'before 1707/8?' (Dadelsen 1958 p75), although its being a fair copy suggests that the work may well have originated before 1707 (Emery 1966). Musical details – such as that the pedal enters in the fugue only with the subject, unlike (it seems) BWV 533 – suggest that the work does not count amongst the earliest, despite the simplicity of the prelude.

Prelude

That the final 6½ bars, already the fullest-written passage of the prelude, appear in a decorated version in BWV 535 – the five parts there taking in more continuous motion, including demisemiquavers – may suggest that an inventive composer could always have understood them as a skeleton and treated them to improvised figuration. Certainly the *durezza* formulae of those 6½ bars are open to figural decoration by the player, and the figures found in BWV 535 are of the conventional kind known to such theorists as Printz and Walther.

A similar point may be made about the previous 6 bars of BWV 535a:

the slurs may indicate that some figuration could be applied, as may the term 'passaggio' added above the first bar of the movement. As with the Suite in E minor BWV 996 (see BWV 533.i), the first movement in P 801 is labelled by J. G. Walther 'Passagio', in the sense defined by Walther himself as

Variatio. Sonsten auch Passagio genannt ist, wenn an statt einer grossen und langen Note, allerhand geschwinde Läufflein gemacht werden (Walther 1708 p153)

Variation. Otherwise is named *Passaggio*, when instead of a large and long note, all kinds of quick little runs are made.

Walther's examples of such figures show them to be not unlike the opening bars of BWV 535a, 996 or 533. The question therefore remains whether the term in BWV 535a indicates that the passage-work has been added already or whether the player is free to add it to the simpler bars; perhaps both. Moreover, the diminished-seventh sequence of BWV 535.i is 'passage-work' of an obvious kind, providing a passage between the two dominant pedal points far more extensive than any between the tonic pedal points of BWV 535a; but 'passaggio' appears not to have suggested 'passage-work' in this more general sense. As it stands, BWV 535a provides four sections, only the first of which has lively figuration of a kind familiar from preludes for keyboard or lute.

Fugue

The different lines brought out by bar-by-bar comparison between the BWV 535 and 535a fugues presumably reflect (*a*) a change of mind by the composer, or (*b*) changes brought about by copyist(s), or (*c*) changes made traditional by players, or (*d*) some combination of these. Thus, insofar as it is easier to assume that the composer was responsible in the 'later version' for the greater sense of climax in bb23–4 or the smoother continuity of bb35–8, it is possible to trace the composer's maturity in such terms. But decorative figuration remains in the strict sense superficial, and such differences as exist between the two versions of bb17–19 suggest that the composer may have been preoccupied with the same *figurae* (Ex. 73) now re-shuffled for reasons of continuity and imitation – qualities which could have been attended to as well in *c*1705 as later.

Ex. 73

Whether therefore certain changes are due to (*b*), (*c*) or (*d*) above must remain open. Particularly significant differences occur between the versions of the passage bb46–65, and it does seem that BWV 535a was strikingly restrained at two points (bb50, 54), and possibly at a third – i.e. b65, where the incomplete bar in the Möller MS has tutti rests above the (unharmonized) pedal subject. Entries in BWV 535a are no more climactically treated than they are in the fugal section of a Buxtehude praeludium, where the true climax is reserved for the toccata postlude, as was presumably the case in BWV 535a. The common observation, therefore, that the 'later version' achieves a rise or gradation of intensity and thus follows 'the famous rule that the first part of a fugue must be good, the second better, but the third outstanding' (Keller 1948 p62) seems not to apply to BWV 535a and is anachronistic.

536

Prelude and Fugue in A major

No Autograph MS (see BWV 536a); copies in P 804 (prelude copied by J. P. Kellner, fugue by unknown copyist), P 837 (early 19th century); *BG* 15 used MS from Rust Collection, Peters II copies by Schelble, Hauser (P 837?) and Kellner (P 804?)

Two staves; title in Rust Collection MS, 'Praelud: con Fuga ped:'.

For a variant or 'early version', see BWV 536a. Some assumptions usually made are that its source was autograph (as claimed in Peters II), that it was composed in the Arnstadt years, and that it was later 're-worked' during the Weimar years when pedal e' was available (Keller 1948 p81) – none of which is demonstrable. That the 'later version' has a clearer motif-development in the prelude than BWV 536a was taken by Spitta not to mean that BWV 536a was a variant or simplification but that BWV 536 was formed with a 'more lively organism' (Spitta I p581). Presumably because of its fugue, the work has also been dated as late as 1715–17 (Besseler 1955); this would accord with Cantata 152 (1714), the fugue subject of whose opening 'Concerto' movement is often said to resemble that of BWV 536.ii (Spitta I p580): Ex. 74. In both fugues, the subject enters as a distinct melody in a

Ex. 74
BWV 152.i
b5

consistent and homogeneous texture, and there are naturally some similarities of figuration countering the subject; but the resemblances are not so striking as to suggest that the pieces 'originated perhaps directly one after the other' (*ibid*). Rather, the rhythm of such subjects is to be seen as alluding to that of triple-time dances like the forlana (Krey 1956 p191).

Prelude

Open broken chords may have been typical of improvised preludes in major keys, judging by Buxtehude's Prelude in D major BUXWV 139 and by the opening lines of the G major Prelude BWV 541. In fact, the opening ten bars of BWV 536 show the conventional harmonies of a pedal point spread over a large canvas – $\frac{5675}{3443}$ etc, and as convention required in a major key, the first chromatic tone in this bland spectrum is the dominant leading-note (b11). The result is a prelude in which tonic–dominant–tonic pedal points frame the movement (as in BWV 534, 535 etc) and between the limbs of which one or more motifs are developed. In the present prelude this development stretches across the whole section bb15–27.

While the pedal motif of b20 is clear in its development through manual and pedal, it should not be missed that the true seed of the movement is the opening arpeggio, informing the piece from first bar to last: Ex. 75. Characteristically, the similarity is clearest at the end,

Ex. 75

with obvious thematic reference (as in e.g. BWV 541). Deriving a movement from such a motif is the aim of many a prelude of that period, e.g. no. 5 in C major from J. K. F. Fischer's *Blumenstrauss* – Ex. 76

Ex. 76   J. K. F. Fischer, *Blumenstrauss* (pub. 1732?), Praeludium 5

– and such figures go on appearing in mature chorales, e.g. BWV 651/651a. But BWV 536 accepts the limitations of an arpeggio figure and changes it subtly as opportunity arises; the manual version of bb20–1 (see BWV 536a) retains the grouping clearly, while the same phrase divided between manual and pedal (BWV 536) is less obvious. The resulting *ton* of the prelude is brighter than that of the Buxtehude

Prelude BUXWV 139, chiefly because of the wide tessitura and the fact that the progressions underlying the section bb15–27 are familiar suspensions, usually expressed in sequences of a more 'serious' non-arpeggio kind, and thus very dance-like in such a context as this. Similarly bright and playful are the harmonies realized above the tonic pedal of bb5–10, where the line falls and rises in dancing figures.

Fugue

The form may be expressed:

1–41	exposition of four parts, first dominant answer tonal, second real; countersubject almost consistent
41–65	'false stretto' entries from b45, anticipating tonal answer of b49, which is answered *en taille* in b57; 'rocking' countersubject
65–85	'false stretto' entries, anticipating tonal answer of b69, which is answered in the bass in b77
85–110	entries in F♯ minor and B minor, each prefaced by episode from previous entry; F♯ minor entry with 'rocking' countersubject
110–36	entry and answer in D, the first prefaced and the second followed by episode
136–53	closer stretto entries, with full tonic entry in b145
153–82	episode, final entry (pedal), coda built on scale pattern

Although such divisions are conveniently shown in this form, in fact the entry in (e.g.) b69 is disguised by its context; only as it proceeds does it become clear that this is an entry, not an episode stretto. The overall shape could be shown as:

A	1–45
B	45–153
C	153–82

in which section B is characterized formally by pseudo-stretto, the last example of which (from b136) is stretto at the bar not at two bars, and which requires both subjects to be altered more or less. The original countersubject is stated or hinted at several times before its clear return above the final entry, and it is striking that the 'rocking' countersubject is highly suitable as a quasi-episode (from b115).

Particularly remarkable is the sustained three- and four-part counterpoint of the fugue (with a 'wonderful intensity' from b153 – Spitta I p581), in which the entries have a more singing quality than even those of BWV 535 or 578. The whole fugue has a smooth, effortless counterpoint that treats the subject almost as an ostinato, an effect or impression heightened by its rhythm and eight-bar phraseology, both of which are typical of ostinatos. An unusual overall effect is also given by constant series of thirds and sixths brought about by the strettos and the 'rocking' countersubject. Pretty dance-like cadences add to this effect (in bb76, 88, 114, 122, 181), although in the interests of continuity required for a long fugue of 182 bars, the cadences are not so marked as those of the fugue in Cantata 152. Some phrase endings avoid cadences (e.g. end of exposition, b41). The particular sweet flavour of such bars as 60–70 is unusual in an organ fugue, being perhaps more characteristic (at a slower tempo?) of an organ chorale between cantus-firmus phrases. In general, as the fugue progresses there seems a move towards non-stop quaver motion, in the context of which the relatively simple scale patterns in the coda – now above a pedal point and hence in five parts – are the more fluid. The thematic reference at the end of BWV 536a gives a touch of the musette, whereas the short final chord of BWV 536 suggests a strong final rallentando.

536a

Prelude and Fugue in A major

MS said to be Autograph once in the possession of Guhr (Griepenkerl in Peters II); five copies in Scholz MSS (four of fugue only, one of which in G major); also unnumbered Oxford Bodleian MS (fugue).

Called 'a variant' by Rust (*BG* 15 p. xxiii) and assumed to be the earlier version (*BG* 15; *NBA* IV/6), BWV 536a differs from BWV 536 as follows:

Prelude
bb5–9, 12–13: in the inner voice, a single line of quavers only
bb10, 15, 16, 20, 25–7: lowest voice played by left hand, not pedal

Fugue
notated in $^3/_8$
bb33–41, 159, 160: pedal an octave lower
bb42–3, 89, 90: lowest voice played by left hand, not pedal
bb182–4: three further bars beyond BWV 536, incorporating references to the subject-*caput*

If *NBA* IV/6 is correct to give bb177–8 of this fugue to the pedal, an e′ is required on the pedalboard, which makes it clear that those earlier entries written an octave higher in BWV 536 are so written not because the compass available was larger than it was for the copyists of BWV 536a. Indeed, the subject in b33 ought to be at a higher octave in order to keep the exposition answers without a gap between successive voices (entries at e′ a′ e″ b). Yet the differences between the two versions of the prelude at bb20–1 and 25–7 are such as to suggest that BWV 536a is a deliberate simplification: the pedal bass of BWV 536 produces a line of motifs much more clearly articulated than the so-called 'earlier version'. The difference in the notation of the inner voice from b5 of the prelude may be due to BWV 536 clarifying what BWV 536a merely implied (compare the version of a movement from F. Couperin's B flat Ordre in the *Klavierbüchlein für Anna Magdalena Bach*, BWV Anh. 183, where Couperin's sustained notes are not shown). But only if Guhr's lost MS was an autograph, or derived ultimately from an autograph, can the status of BWV 536a be upgraded from that of a simple variant; the relation between manual and pedal parts in the fugue at bb42–5 – i.e. pedal dropping out when manual agility is required, but re-entering before the fugue subject – suggests that BWV 536a is an inferior variant.

537

Fantasia and Fugue in C minor

No Autograph MS; source, P 803 (fantasia and 89 bars of fugue copied by J. T. Krebs, the rest by J. L. Krebs); unnumbered Oxford Bodleian MS (19th century).

Two staves; heading, 'Fantasia con Fuga', at end (J. L. Krebs) 'Soli deo gloria d[en] 10 January 1751'.

The copy made by J. T. and J. L. Krebs, evidently made in the period just before 1751 (Zietz 1969 pp68, 98), has added glamour through Griepenkerl's report that the MS was almost used as waste paper (Peters III). Many commentators have heard some close relationship between fantasia and fugue, not least since the two themes of the fantasia and the two themes of the fugue produce together an *overall* shape of *A B A B C D C* (Kloppers 1966 p22), i.e. one similar to developed ritornello movements. Certainly the half-close at the end of the prelude is unique in the organ works, and the very details of this half-close – the bass descending in hemiola, the wandering semiquaver lines – recall such half-closes as that of the middle slow movement of the E major Violin Sonata BWV 1016. Perhaps because it is highly organized and achieved throughout in four parts, the fantasia was renamed 'Praeludium' in *BG* 15. In playing time, fantasia and fugue are compatible (more so than is often the case), and their conception as complements is striking: both in four parts (though the fantasia is more consistent and dense); binary fantasia, ternary fugue; short themes treated in imitation and stretto (fantasia), long themes treated fugally (fugue). Despite some possible forebears, neither fantasia nor fugue can be matched by works of other composers, the fugue subject itself, for instance, still appearing to have that power 'that was Bach's own' (Spitta I p583).

Fantasia

Like the triple-time Prelude in F minor BWV 534, the fantasia takes a binary form followed by half-close or phrygian cadence (a toccata close in BWV 534) as follows:

A	1–11	tonic pedal point, imitative upper parts; subject of *B* anticipated in pedal of last bar of *A*
B	12–21	imitative upper parts; closes with hemiola bar (b20)
A	21–31	dominant pedal point, imitative upper parts; virtual repetition of first ten bars with the counterpoint inverted (top part avoiding d''' in b25)
B	31–47	denser development of *B* subject, including *inversus* (bb32, 35,

36) and pedal entries; bb41–6 = partial decorated repetition of bb15–20 in inverted counterpoint

47–8   final phrygian cadence already anticipated at the end of A_1 (bb9–10) and A_2 (bb29–30)

The details of the form and style, however, produce a fantasia very different from any Italian binary movement that may ultimately have influenced it. Indeed, its ancestry is as complex as its originality is obvious. The opening bars, with the resting pedal point and the expressively wandering voices of bb5–7, are perhaps *sui generis* with such cantata first movements as those of BWV 8 or 27, the manual lines looking rather like woodwind obbligato counterpoint. Equally, the opening seven bars have a texture very like those French *en taille* movements in which the eventual tenor solo is first anticipated by the upper parts, often in $^6/_4$ above a partial or complete pedal point (cf. *Récit de tierce en taille* from de Grigny's *Livre d'Orgue*, 1699). Equally, fugal/imitative lines above a pedal point (itself returning in the dominant later on) were known in German organ music, being found in (e.g.) Buxtehude's F major Toccata BUXWV 156 and G minor Praeludium BUXWV 150 (Pauly 1964 p119), as well as the F minor Prelude BWV 534. Other detailed similarities to the latter prelude can also be found, such as the hemiola bar leading to section A_2 (b20 of BWV 537.i, 30–1 of BWV 534.i). Similarly, the eventual passing of the opening tonic pedal point to one on the dominant halfway through is paralleled in BWV 534 and thus in many southern toccatas, whose form or figuration allow their skeletal shape to stand out more clearly than they do in BWV 537.i.

Of all these influences on the C minor Fantasia, the most instructive are the cantata first movements. All the main material, including the semiquaver lines that accumulate towards the end, is well within the melodic character of woodwind obbligatos: Ex. 77. Despite its *points d'orgue*, the pedal also shares the characteristics of a good basso-continuo line (e.g. bb12–21). That the texture of bb35–46 in particular is obviously organ-like does not diminish the instrumental qualities of the themes themselves. Subject B (b12) is almost an analogous theme, i.e. one by nature associated with certain texts or scriptural context and thus – without necessarily intending to convey a verbal or other image – used by an organ composer as a reference to other kinds of music.

To the player, as remarkable as the fantasia's mixed origins and tight form, from which 'all inorganic passage-work' has been excluded (Spitta 1 p582) and in which a well-worked texture is sustained, is the 'noble, elegiac' atmosphere (*ibid*) which it can be claimed to share to some extent with the C minor Prelude BWV 546. While none of the opening harmonies produced above the pedal point is itself original, the phraseology is masterly: by b6 or b7 the pedal-point harmonies require (because of their associations) the turn to the dominant in b10, but this is achieved by taking the opening motif itself into the 'necessary' progression of the bass-line. The result is an exceptionally well-conceived paragraph over bb1–11, natural and unforced despite the

Ex. 77

b1

b3

b6

b12

b42

etc

difficulty of producing four-part contrapuntal harmony with this degree of conviction. Technique gives the appearance of being geared to expressiveness. Thus the inversion of the secondary theme in b32 is surely introduced for reasons of expressive beauty, both of melody and harmony, and not in the interests of ingenuity or even for variety; similarly, although the section in bb31–41 (B_2) has the theme in every bar, it is no more obliged to do so than section B_1. A further remarkable feature of the movement, aiding the qualities Spitta heard in it, is the almost complete absence of passages or even cadences in major keys. Clearly, B_2 must be the section with most modulation; but even its respite in A♭ major (bb41–2) is very short-lived, as was the corresponding key of bb15–16.

Although Spitta regarded the fantasia as a 'twin sister' to the C minor Prelude BWV 546, a more striking complement is provided by the other C minor Fantasia BWV 562, the very openings of the two movements having enough in common as to suggest comparison and hence pointed differences:

BWV 537.i	BWV 562.i
four parts, $^6/_4$	five parts, $^4/_4$
two subjects, binary form	one subject, monothematic development
tonic/dominant pedal points	tonic, dominant, subdominant and relative major pedal points

85

The operative difference is that of form and the use to which the themes are put; they both suggest French elements and both derive in principle from the pedal-point toccata, but each solves the problem of extension and organization in its own way.

Fugue

The violin/organ fugue subjects of Bach referred to by Mattheson (see BWV 539.ii) seem to suggest that there was also a recognized fugue type behind the subject of BWV 537; at least, this may be suspected by comparing it with a theme quoted by Mattheson (1739 p209), who drew attention to the striking semitone: Ex. 78. This is not to lessen either

Ex. 78

Mattheson 1739   (transposed from G minor)

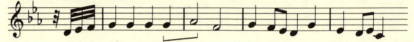

the 'demonic power' of Bach's subject or Spitta's admiration for it, but to suggest that it contains regular, even textbook-like, examples of fugal features: the repeated dominant, the broken chord (diminished seventh), the fall to the tonic at the end. Every performer will have his own way of trying to describe the exhilarating effect of such moments in the fugue as the sequences derived from the subject (b18), but he should note too that the subject contains the classic intervals discussed by Mattheson and other writers on fugue.

The form of the fugue, which tends towards the *da capo* shape perfected in the E minor Fugue BWV 548, can be expressed:

A	1–28	exposition, followed by sequential episode tutti, with a further tonic entry *en taille* during which the pedal drops out
—	28–57	manual episode, taking in entries in dominant, tonic and tonic (for the opening of the subject as it appears in b37 and b45, see Mattheson's example, above); after pedal tonic entry, sudden half-close
B	57–104	irregular fugal exposition of two new subjects
A	104–28	repetition of bb4–28, partial in that the final *en taille* entry is re-harmonized to allow dominant pedal point
—	128–30	coda

In general contrapuntal style, the fugue recalls the organ chorale 'Nun komm der Heiden Heiland' BWV 661, although its having no cantus firmus allows it to be less angular in line. As is customary in a Bach organ fugue, the pedal is not kept exclusively for passages with middle entries; there is no marked end to the exposition, since it passes to a sequence, and a further entry of the subject runs across the end of the pedal paragraph. The 'decorated-suspension' style of the first manual episode (bb29–37) is characteristic of the counterpoint of which the composer seems to have had an inexhaustible supply.

Apart from its subject and its drive, the most striking features of the fugue are the overall impression it gives of an *A B A* movement – not entirely justified by an analysis of its shape – and the contrasting nature of the middle section. Although, as is often pointed out, the two subjects of the middle section are not combined with the first subject – as might be expected by analogy with BWV 540 and other fugues – there is a precedent for both of the new subjects. The rising chromatic theme is common as one of the themes of a standard double-fugue subject; it is as close to tradition as the rising/falling scale of another double fugue in the middle section of a Bach movement, namely the Prelude in C minor BWV 546.i. The origin of the quaver countersubject is more specific: not only is it 'introduced in a masterly fashion seven bars before' the *B* section begins (Keller 1948 p83), but it has been gradually emerging throughout the first 57 bars. Its chief motif is in fact a countersubject to the original main theme: Ex. 79. Therefore,

Ex. 79
b24

although the composer does not combine his three themes, one of them is constructed of motifs that combine with the other two, thus producing a multi-subject fugue with an unusual element and one adding new variety to the corpus of such complex fugues in organ works (BWV 540, 546, 552, 574, 590 etc), suites (BWV 808, 830) and elsewhere. That the motif concerned has many uses can be seen by its appearance in some movements already referred to (the Fugue BWV 546.ii and the chorales BWV 661 and 677), as well as (e.g.) the Italian Concerto for Harpsichord BWV 971 (pub. 1735): Ex. 80. It also has a family resemblance to other motifs developed at length in quite different kinds of music, for instance Ex. 81 (next page).

Ex. 80

Ex. 81 Violin Sonata BWV 1016.ii

The *A B A* shape itself is not yet fully crystallized in BWV 537.ii, nor is the transition to or repeat of the opening section yet easy. The bass line and /or harmonic progressions leading to the bass entry of b110 and to the pedal point of b124 appear more 'forced' than do the corresponding bars of the first section. Both problems are dealt with neatly in the E minor Fugue BWV 548 by (*a*) dropping out the pedal after the beginning of A_2 until its own entry, and (*b*) already including a dominant pedal point in A_1, so that it is automatically there in A_2. As to the middle section *B*, the continuous quaver runs disguise the irregular entries of the chromatic subject, which is treated imitatively rather than fugally. The effect of section *B* with its two themes is that of a series of sequences, since the second bar of the subject is a rising sequence to the first, etc. The phrase structures of the *A* and *B* sections are therefore quite different. A further detail is that not only does section *B* close with manual trills reminiscent of a passage in another C minor work (the Passacaglia BWV 582 bb269–70), but its final half-close cadence in bb103–4 is very like that which came before its entry in b57.

---

538   Toccata and Fugue in D minor

No Autograph MS; copies in P 803 (J. G. Walther), P 1099 (J. G. Preller), later-18th-century sources (P 275, P 277, P 286, P 290, P 416, P 596), and 19th-century (P 282, P 837, unnumbered Oxford Bodleian MS); also in sources of Kittel circle (P 319 Westphal, LM 4842h J. C. H. Rinck, LM 4839e, Lpz MB III.8.16 Dröbs); toccata only in 'Schubring MS' (*BG* 15); fugue only in (late) sources: Salzburg Archiv des Domchores MN 104, Vienna Gesellschaft der Musikfreunde VII 14399 a/B, and BB 30377 (shortened).

Two staves; title in P 803 (by whom?) 'Toccata con Fuga'; in P 286 (copyist Anon 300) 'Toccata per l'Organo a due Clav. è Pedale col la Fuga'; in P 275 (Palschau *c*1742–*c*1780?) and a 1785 Catalogue (*Dok* III p273), 'Preludio in Organo Pleno con Fuga'; and in Forkel's list (1802), 'Prel.'.

The 'Dorian' Toccata and Fugue has little right to its name – already given it by Spitta (I p688) – since sources also transmit the other D minor Toccata (BWV 565) without the key-signature of one flat. Truer distinction is owed the work not only for its various masteries but because, with the exceptions of BWV 552.i and the concerto movements, it is the only work in which 'authentic' registration or manual changes are related to the structure. The so-called dialogue* technique of the toccata produces an exceptional movement without exact parallel as a conception within or outside organ music, although in theory the technique may be related to the *dialogues* of the classical French organ mass. Further distinction is owed the movement for what appears to be a unique clue about its early use, even its origin: it seems to have been played on the rebuilt organ of the Martinikirche in Kassel in September 1732 (*Dok* II pp226–7), according to a remark by Kittel's pupil M. G. Fischer in the copy LM 4839e: 'bey der Probe der grossen Orgel in Cassel von S. Bach gespielt' ('played by Sebastian Bach at the examination [inauguration?] of the large organ in Kassel').† Of itself, this provides no evidence against the view that the work originated during the Weimar period and was revised at Leipzig (*MGG* I col. 1013) – for which, however, there is also no documentary evidence despite the possibility that Walther made his copy at Weimar. Useful as a gauge of the composer's versatility in prelude forms is that the toccata is virtually monothematic, like the C minor Fantasia BWV 562 – however, this is not a five-part fantasia wrought closely around a pedal point and various French motifs, like BWV 562, but an apparently free development, in a concerto-like framework, of an elementary motif which is itself more 'north German' in style. The fugue counters the apparent freedom that results from this treatment with exceptionally well-reasoned counterpoint in which at least two almost independent countersubjects are joined by unusual harmonies produced by strettos. As elsewhere, therefore, prelude and fugue provide a reciprocal complement: they are similar enough in length to form a more obvious pair than (e.g.) BWV 540.i and ii, and their styles are similar enough for them to form a more obvious pair than (e.g.) BWV 542.i and ii.

Toccata

Resemblances between the basic material of this movement and that of works by other composers have been suggested by Pirro, Grace and Keller – Ex. 82 – and further examples could easily be found. But there is an undeniable individuality about the movement, in both form and melody. The squareness of motif – Ex. 83 – seems to bow to north German organ idioms, to the various keyboard figures taken up but never so thoroughly explored in the praeludia of Lübeck, Bruhns and others. At the same time, all dialogue movements, whether in an Italian concerto, a French organ dialogue, an English double voluntary, or a Spanish *medio registro* movement, can be shown to share common characteristics: two manuals are used in alternation with the same melody, alternately in bass and treble, alternately as brief accompaniment to each other, and the form of their music is often such that both hands close the movement on the same manual. Particular parallels may well be drawn, concerning any one feature, between BWV 538.i and one

---

* Strictly 'duologue', 'dramatic piece with two actors', rather than 'dialogue', 'conversation' in general, i.e. with more than two.
† Neither stop-list nor disposition of manuals in this organ is known.

Ex. 82

A. Raison, Messe du Premier
   Ton (1688), second Agnus

BWV 540.i
b229

etc

Pachelbel, Praeludium in D minor b85

8va bassa

Pachelbel, Toccata in D minor b33

8va bassa

Fischer, *Blumenstrauss*, Praeludium I

etc

Ex. 83

or other of the foreign categories listed above. Thus the antiphonal use of two manuals for the sequences in bb43–5 or 73–7 provides a more sophisticated working of a similar idea in the concerto transcription BWV 595.i from b3. To use the manuals in this way – i.e. in more or less simple alternation – is indeed the chief aim of the dialogue technique of the movement. Since there is no *récit* or *en taille* melody as such there can be no clear parallel to French dialogues, and since there is no fugal development there can be no clear parallel to the English double voluntary. Nor would it be true, despite the first change of manual in b13, to say that the two manuals are used only to mark the sections or structural limbs of the movement. Rather, both are used in both the main and the secondary sections irrespectively – an integration of tone matched by the sameness of themes.

   A thesis has been constructed to show BWV 538.i as a duologue movement arranged according to rhetorical principles of the kind implied in the writings of Mattheson, Scheibe and others (Kloppers 1966 pp80–93). The shape of the movement could then be expressed (*Ow* = *Oberwerk*, *Rp* = *Rückpositiv*):

Ow	1–13	*Exordium* by first speaker A, entry of main theme, becoming: *Narratio* or report showing how the theme develops; then *Propositio* from b5: further repetition, emphasis and development, but closing in tonic (closing cadence – cf. Contrapunctus III, *Art of Fugue*, engraved version)
Rp	13–20	*Confutatio* or controversy: subject taken up and developed by dialectic partner B, also closing in tonic
Ow	20–5	*Confirmatio*, confirming main theme, incorporating further repetition (i.e. sequential imitation)
Rp	25–9	*Confutatio*, taking up bb1–5 in dominant, parts inverted
Ow	29–37	*Confirmatio*: speaker A answers and develops, in the course of which speaker B interrupts with antitheses (31–2)
Rp	37–43	*Confutatio*: B takes variant theme from previous section (tenor b34), in the course of which A interrupts with antitheses
Ow	43–67	*Confirmatio*: new variant on original theme proposed by A, answered at once by B, further developed at length by A, who at b47 re-introduces material as originally discoursed upon in bb1–5
Rp	67–81	*Confutatio*, B interrupting when his material from b37 is referred to by A (66–7); after B closes the section in 73 (tonic), A re-introduces previous material from b43, whereupon B answers twice, eventually speaking at the same time (from bar 78); motifs repeated and accumulated (*congeries*) for reasons of dialectic climax (*gradatio*)
Ow	81–94	*Confirmatio*: A takes over before B has finished his line, referring back to main section from b53, confirming the dominant pedal point (b88) and producing his own high point (90–4, this time in contrary motion) towards D major
	94–9	*Peroratio*, exit, conclusion, coda

In no other work of J. S. Bach is there 'such a complete approximation to speech', suggesting amongst other things that the work originated 'during the maturer Leipzig period' (Kloppers 1966 p90). However, the analogy to the rules of rhetoric and dialectic is achieved purely musically, without extra-musical 'meanings'. Such words above as 'controversy', 'speaking' or 'answers' are analogous and not literal. Nor is there further evidence to support attempts to date BWV 538 on such grounds. Only in a general sense can J. A. Birnbaum's defence of J. S. Bach in 1739 against Scheibe's attack be taken as meaning that J. S. Bach was conversant with the rules and terms of rhetoric:

Die Theile und Vortheile, welche die Ausarbeitung eines musikalischen Stücks mit der Rednerkunst gemein hat, kennet er so vollkommen, dass man ihn nicht nur mit einem ersättigenden Vergnügen höret, wenn er seine gründlichen Unterredungen auf die Aehnlichkeit und Uebereinstimmung beyder lenket; sondern man bewundert auch die geschickte Anwendung derselben, in seinen Arbeiten (*Dok* II p352).

He understands so thoroughly the parts and benefits which the composing of a piece of music has in common with oratory that not only does one listen to him with a satisfying pleasure whenever he directs his profound conversation to the similarity and conformity between the two, but one also admires the clever application of the same in his music.

The context of Birnbaum's remarks, chiefly apropos the composer's 'profound conversation' known only to his intimates, is too uncertain to produce from it a theory on the origins and date of BWV 538.

The musical technique of the toccata is as remarkable as its oratorical. While the general plan is that of a ritornello movement –

1	A
13	episode
20	A
37	episode
47	A
53	episode
58	A
66	episode
81	A (but as b53)
94	coda

– homogeneity is produced by the episodes taking material from the main theme so that the ritornellos are rarely clear or striking; the plan above is only one of several possible readings. Some motifs seem to be related to the main theme, some merely similar: Ex. 84. Presumably

Ex. 84

the accompanimental motif x used throughout (including the coda) is related to an idea picked up in the first Rp section: Ex. 85. But that the movement has no ordinary ritornello form is clear from the close

Ex. 85

relationship between sections, however we label them; for example, compare the passages from bb7 (pedal), 15 (rh), 30 (lh), 53 and 81. Similarly, the main motif can be used to create a pedal point (b86) or can be put above a pedal point in imitation etc (b30). A similar use of uniform material in a partial ritornello movement can be seen in the F major Toccata BWV 540, but in BWV 538.i the episode material is more closely related.

The complex unity of the movement should not disguise the fact that the rhythms are unusually square, to some extent counteracted by phrase-lengths (e.g. six-bar phrase bb37–42) but throughout producing remarkably few tied notes. The result is a highly unusual movement characterized from first bar to last by groups of four semiquavers. Allied to this is a bland harmonic spectrum, bowing to (e.g.) 7–6 progressions as commonly found in lively organ music (compare bb8–9 with harmonizations of the fugue subject in the D major Fugue BWV 532), but otherwise producing 'interesting' chords only at carefully timed intervals (bb12, 35, 52, 65, 72, 93), three of which have similar contexts and are thus like a ritornello (51–2, 64–5, 93–4). When there has been some rich harmony, the following passage 'clears the air' with a simple figure or sequence (e.g. bb35–7, 52–3). It is difficult to see how these various formulae or ideas sustaining the movement could have been applied again to another composition; the toccata must remain an *unicum*.

Fugue

The fugue is an unusually complex movement based on a theme with *alla breve* elements ($^2/_2$ metre, suspensions, dactyl countersubject) which is curiously symmetrical (rising and falling an octave, the closing syncopations balancing the opening minims). The subject is aeolian rather than dorian and in some sources (P 177, P 290) is ornamented. From a formal point of view, the most unusual features are that the main basis for the episodes is canonic (more characteristic of entries than episodes in *The 48*) and that the subject has two countersubjects (b18), producing not so much a permutation fugue as an ideally matched invertible counterpoint often overlapping and thus confusing to the ear. Although the pedal has three conspicuous tonic entries, they do not mark what has been called (Bullivant 1959 p705) the canzona-like ternary construction of the fugue: part I in the tonic b1, part II relative b101, part III tonic b167.

The form of the movement may be expressed:

I	1–36	exposition; two consistent countersubjects (the first with a motif that seems to be an inversion of that in the toccata: Ex. 86); from the codettas (bb15–17, 25–8) an imitative sequence *x* is taken for later development (see Ex. 87 below)
	36–42	episode, brief canon at fifth in outer parts
	43–50	entry in dominant
	50–6	episode, three parts imitative–canonic *x*
	57–63	entry in tonic, its beginning decorated
	64–100	further entries in dominant (b71 as bb18ff) and tonic (b81), preceded and followed by episodes based on sequence *x*
II	101–66	series of entries in F (canonic, bb101–2), C (115), G minor (canonic, 130), B flat (146) interspersed with episodes based on *x*
III	167–74	tonic entry in canon
	174–202	episodes based largely on *x*, surrounding a dominant entry (188)

> 203–11 tonic entry in canon (soprano entry decorated)
> 211–22 coda based on four-part version of *x*; final homophony

Ex. 86 b12   (cf. Ex. 84)

The array of suspensions from exposition to coda (e.g. bb43–56) forms a stark contrast to the harmony of the toccata (see above). Already in 1777, Kirnberger was quoting excerpts from it to demonstrate the composer's use of sevenths and ninths (*Dok* III pp226–7). It is noticeable that neither of the countersubjects, first seen together in b18, contains suspensions or tied notes; rather, the mainspring of the movement comes from the canonic–imitative potential of bb2–3 of the subject itself, particularly in what seems to be a derived codetta (bb15–16) which yields '*x*', an exceptional series of imitative episodes recurring throughout the fugue: Ex. 87. From the canonic seed grow sequential

Ex. 87

b2   b9   b15   *x*

imitations at all intervals except the third and seventh above, either at the full or half bar, all naturally invertible. Yet despite the uniformity, variety is achieved in the fugue as in the toccata by avoiding simple repetition and by creating episodes differing from each other in the canonic intervals, in the number of parts in which the canon is pursued (four in the coda), and by the varying number of added free parts. The free parts themselves vary – e.g. becoming chromatic from b156 – while other passages of yet freer quaver lines grow out of the current and throw the canonic entries or imitative episodes into greater relief (bb64–7, 195–202). The canon to which the subject itself is susceptible produces parallel rhythms (as in the A minor Fugue, *The 48* Bk I after the first two bars); clearly it is the episode material that offers widest variety.

This variety may be shown by comparing treatments of the same phrase in soprano or bass: Ex. 88. Alternatively, two different settings of the same bass line may be compared, such as bb36–42 and 211–17. Such use of episode material results in a *tour de force*, so that one crucial passage (from b125) has been said to 'defy harmonic analysis' (Bullivant 1959 p539), a pardonable exaggeration in the circumstances.

Though it is (with BWV 547.ii) the most involved of Bach's organ fugues, BWV 538.ii shows a tendency towards rich harmonic effects by no means clear from any paper account of it. The sixths of b109 or b212

Ex. 88

are simpler examples of some of the most carefully argued four-part harmony in the organ repertoire. In any pair of similar passages, two of the four voices may well be identical; but the other two, without apparent contrivance or difficulty, display a totally different harmonic character (compare bb43–50 with 115–22, for example). Although such constantly varied harmonies are typical of J. S. Bach's subject entries, BWV 538 offers an unusually fruitful series of such harmonizations. For the completeness of the canonic imitation in thirds and sixths, an extra manual part is added at one point (b164, immediately after the loosest texture of the fugue), while the final chords of the fugue dispel any doctrinaire contrapuntalism. Indeed, the last four bars are the most surprising of the fugue, almost suggesting a return to the dialoguing of the toccata and offering an uplift to the spirit. But the contrapuntal complexity is also carefully gauged throughout; thus, it is the densest episode that just precedes the middle entries in the relative major, producing a splendid inner line in minims which may or may not be referring to the head of the subject but which stands out even in such a texture (alto b93, tenor bb95ff). A further effective detail is that each middle entry is preceded by a strong perfect cadence (e.g. bb114, 129), although in each case the key is prepared well beforehand. But the naturalness with which the subject is re-harmonized and the episodes varied in their imitation still distinguishes the fugue. For example, on each occasion that the countersubject motif – Ex. 89 – appears, it does

Ex. 89

so naturally and itself helps to produce homogeneity; but on most occasions it is approached in different ways, the rest of the phrase that originally preceded it (i.e. the original countersubject) being usually absent. Not the least surprising thing about the coda is that the quavers gradually drop out, leaving behind an impression of immense harmonic richness.

539

Prelude and Fugue in D minor

No Autograph MS; copies in P 517 (early 19th century), and fugue only in Am.B. 606 (2nd half of 18th century), P 213 (ditto; a copy?) and later sources (e.g. P 304 c1800, P 282 19th century). The fugue is a transcription of a violin-sonata movement (see below).

Two staves (no indication of pedals in the Prelude).

Although it is usually assumed that the differences between the violin fugue (BWV 1001.ii) and the organ 'transcription' are due to J. S. Bach's own revisions made in the course of transcribing the violin original (Spitta 1 pp688–9),* and although these differences are often seen as highly indicative of the composer's methods and skill (Geiringer 1966 pp237–8), in fact it is not certain who made the organ version or when.

* Spitta's claim that J. P. Kellner had already made a copy of the organ transcription by 1725 (Spitta 1 pp689, 825) appears to be based on a misunderstanding of a note in *BG* 15 p.xxv, where Rust is speaking of a copy of the violin sonatas. BWV 539.ii shows certain readings of the violin fugue as it appears in a copy of the sonatas made by Anna Magdalena Bach (P 286) dated between 1725 and 1733/4 (Kilian 1961 p327).

Nor is it known who wrote the prelude, whether it was composed for organ, or who coupled the two movements as they exist in P 517 and are listed together by Forkel in his thematic catalogue of 1802. It is therefore unfruitful to speculate on 'why Bach did not also transcribe the sublime and deeply passionate prelude' of the violin sonata instead of substituting 'a little, insignificant praeambulum' (Keller 1948 p99), whose authenticity, however, can 'scarcely be doubted', despite its having no pedal part (Kilian 1961). Presumably the transposition down from G minor to D minor was to lower the required compass from f''' to c''', but it also enables the violin texture to be widened by putting an entry up an octave in the organ version (b4), in addition to the new tenor or bass entries. The pedal does not rise above a, crosses the (written) left hand at three of its four entries, and is reserved largely for a bass line – three features untypical of Bach's organ fugues.

The fugue (without prelude) was also transcribed into French lute tablature, probably before c1730 (Schulze 1966a) and perhaps under the guidance of the lutenist J. C. Weyrauch (A. Burguéte *BJ* 1977 p45). Both lute and organ versions appear therefore to be later arrangements of the violin original, and as such are probably unconnected with each other (Kilian 1961). That all three fugues or fugue subjects in the violin sonatas (G minor, C major, A minor) appeared to some contemporaries to have archetypal properties – the A minor (BWV 1003) a short theme of great potential, the C major (BWV 1005) a model for chromatic counterpoint, etc – is suggested by Mattheson's quoting two of them, in 1737 and 1739 (see *Dok* II pp294–5).* BWV 539.ii is a complete organ transcription of the third of these: a fugue with a model canzona subject. It thus pinpoints the violin-sonata fugues as archetypes: each of them presents an example of a basic fugue type worked from a basic subject type. The Albinoni Fugue in B minor for Harpsichord BWV 951, found in some of the same sources (Am.B. 606, P 213, P 304), would supply an example of yet a further type of violin fugue: an expansive fugue written on a melodious subject of the kind found in earlier violin music such as Frescobaldi's.

Prelude

While it is perhaps an exaggeration to see this movement merely as a *durezza* type (Dietrich 1931), with traditional suspensions and slow-moving harmonies, it may well have been meant to allude to the latter-day appearances of this tradition, namely in the *plein jeu* or *petit plein jeu* pieces of classical French organ masses. Such suspended chords as the $\frac{9}{7}_{5}$ of b20 and such lines as the quaver figures (bb1, 2 etc) could be found elsewhere: Ex. 90. It is doubtful, however, whether a German organist would have interpreted the scale figures of bb4, 10, 41 etc as *notes inégales*. Although in length of phrase and types of sequence the possible French models for such a prelude are much less regular than

---

* It is not known whether Mattheson quoted them from memory or verified them from a written source.

Ex. 90

de Grigny, Plein jeu (Fin de la Messe) from *Livre d'Orgue* (1699)

b69

BWV 539.i, it is certainly an unusual piece in the repertory of German organ music of the mid-century; this is also clear from the part-writing, much of which (bb3, 9, 19, 34 etc) is closer to a frenchified harpsichord idiom. Of all the organ music in the BWV corpus, therefore, BWV 539.i is the piece most plausibly treated with *notes inégales*, irrespective of what a German organist of *c*1750 might have done with it.

One harpsichord piece with several sections and textures close to BWV 539.i is the A minor Fantasia BWV 904.i. (Both BWV 904.i and 539.ii occur in the early-nineteenth-century MS Lpz Go . S . 318a, though not together: see Schulze 1977 p79.)

In its 43 bars, the prelude makes some attempt at closed form:

        1–6
        7–12   = 1–6 in dominant, outer parts in inverted counterpoint
        13–24   sequences towards half-close
        24–33   sequences towards return to tonic
        34–9   = 1–6 in tonic
        40–3   coda (41–3 = 22–4 in tonic)

In a varying texture uncharacteristic of J. S. Bach, some simple, frenchified use is made of familiar figures (e.g. the three-part sequence from b24), one of which is used in an inventive, integrated way (the scale line of bb4, 5, 10, 13, 21, 22, 37, 38, 41). The suspensions lead to striking harmonies and colour the first beats of more than half the bars; in contrast, the cadences are unsyncopated and without suspension, a detail not particularly typical of French *durezza* styles. The result is a prelude of mixed *genre*, full of charm and interest.

Fugue

Like the other violin-sonata fugues, BWV 539.ii has a clear rondo structure in which both the entries and episodes have a curious weight and musical originality not suggested by the theoretical properties of either. That the subject has the repeated notes, and its countersubject the implied suspensions, of countless canzonas merely explains the neat, traditional invertibility of the three-part counterpoint (b3), or the ease with which an extra entry is fitted in (b5). But this canzona-like character (borne out by the irregular, almost Palestrinian exposition) hardly explains the fine sense of progression and tension that results from the first six or seven bars, even more strikingly in the organ version than in the violin original: Ex. 91. It is also in accord with the condensed nature of the organ version that not only does it have an extra entry in b5 and b29, but the implied violin harmonies of b6 (= b5 of the violin version) are realized in the form of a further subject entry – a detail of some ingenuity. In this respect the top part in b6 of the organ version is as remarkable as that in the pedal of b5 and b29. Similarly, it would be a mistake to view the accompaniment added to the episodes (bb8, 44, 66, 89) as elementary block chords necessarily filling out the organ texture; an intense, detached way of playing them, so 'placed' as to achieve the opposite of the fluency or fluidity aimed at in the violin version, aids the total effect of tension and condensed harmony that they give. Of all the organ fugues of J. S. Bach, BWV 539.ii can achieve the most remarkable intensity if played with a kind of halting exactness; only a theoretical comparison of its counterpoint with the subtle, understated style of the violin version can lead to the opinion that the arrangement 'nowhere goes beyond the scholastic' ('über das Schulmässige': Siegele, quoted in Kilian 1961).

The shape of the fugue may be expressed as:

1–7	irregular exposition, including two pairs of octave strettos (subject–answer–answer–subject–subject) and a sixth part on the mediant
7–15	episode, including reference to subject
15–30	entries, beginning as conventional exposition in tonic, but incorporating strettos or imitation at third and fourth; then 'stretto episode' at bb25ff
30–57	episode, first based on melodic extension of subject
57–60	stretto as at b25, now in subdominant, passing to relative
60–76	episode, first based on melodic extension of subject
76–81	partial entries in which subject is developed and followed by:
82–92	episodes and coda

Ex. 91

BWV 1001.ii

BWV 539.ii

Ped.

The entries thus become less and less marked, although the change in texture from episode (semiquavers, open texture) to entry (quavers, more closed) makes it clear enough to the listener. In this respect, the violin version is even less ambiguous, since chords for the entries are mostly contrasted with semiquaver lines for episodes.

Throughout the fugue the strettos compensate for the brevity of the subject. A curious result of this technique is that the subject could be introduced into the harmony as it stands far more often than it is (e.g. in bb11–12, 55), but presumably the harmony 'as it stands' is no mere background into which entries can be 'introduced'. The tendency for the fugue to go into five parts particularly either when stretto entries are involved or when the harmony is suspended in a manner reminiscent of certain string concertos (bb37–9, 85 – cf. the Vivaldi Concerto BWV 593.i b9) is itself an equivalent of the tendency for the violin version to use four strings when feasible. But the respective passages do not necessarily coincide. The musical strain produced by the four violin strings may inspire the arranger of BWV 539 to seek a different climactic effect – Ex. 92(i) – while at other points lower or upper entries are enriched – Ex. 92(ii). Even more so than is the case with

Ex. 92

(i)

BWV 1001.ii b58

BWV 539.ii b60

(ii)

BWV 1001.ii b80

BWV 539.ii b82

the Vivaldi and other organ arrangements, many subtleties of this 'transcription' can be seen only by careful bar-by-bar comparison of the violin and organ versions. Both the clarity of form and the content are altered – enriched, even – in the organ version in ways already outlined: 'harmonic and polyphonic texture is intensified...there are new entrances of the theme, a bass part is supplemented, and mock imitations of the original are replaced by real imitations' (Geiringer 1966 pp237–8); and some solo-episode lines are widened to appear as two parts. This last is achieved rather tentatively, however, though certainly not 'unklavieristisch' as has been claimed (Kilian 1961 p327).

It seems to be coincidence that organ and lute arrangements are both two bars longer than the violin original, since the additions occur at different points (organ at b5 and b28 of the violin version, lute in b2 and b5). But both change the nature of the fugue, in particular its opening exposition. As the following shows, the lute version has a fairly regular exposition of tonic subjects and dominant answers, the violin something less regular, the organ (through its additions) less regular still (t = tonic, s = subdominant, d = dominant, m = mediant):

violin: BWV 1001 bb1–5	d t t d
lute: BWV 1000 bb1–7	d t d t s d t
organ: BWV 539 bb1–6½	d t t d d m

The arrangers of BWV 1000 and 539, whoever they or he were, added entries for different purposes, making one more regular than the violin fugue, the other less regular.

In addition, the movement BWV 539.ii as a fugue in its own right has many points of interest. Obviously its violinistic rondo structure gives it a shape and progress very different from any mature organ fugue, but there would be no justification in regarding such a shape as inferior or unidiomatic. The episodes produce new organ textures and carry weight even when they at first appear undistinguished (e.g. b66). The sudden springing up of fiery episodes from static entries is (in both violin and organ versions) very much in the Italian manner already perfected by Corelli: Ex. 93. Conversely, the final violin cadenza in BWV 1001.ii conforms (on a smaller scale) to the codas of old organ praeludia and is directly transcribed for organ: the figure used in b95 recalls some

Ex. 93
b87

Corelli, Violin Sonata Op V no. 1, 2nd movement

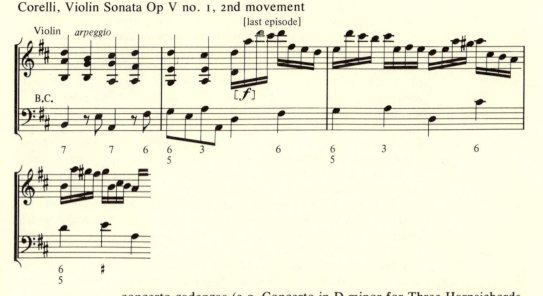

concerto cadenzas (e.g. Concerto in D minor for Three Harpsichords BWV 1063.ii). The harmonic detail of such passages as bb82–5 is so often enriched in BWV 539 that the tautness of the subject is amply countered: that is to say, the driving fluency of the other mature organ fugues is replaced in BWV 539 by constantly re-worked harmonies, rarely original but re-positioned and re-thought in every bar. Despite the Italian formulas of subject and countersubject each entry and each bar is thought out anew, often with a melodic inspiration in the right hand that is not found in the violin version (bb32–7, 77–9) and that is difficult to attribute to any composer but J. S. Bach, despite the unusual pedal part and the accompanimental style of the episodes.

540   Toccata and Fugue in F major

No Autograph MS; copies in P 803 (toccata copied by J. T. Krebs, fugue by J. L. Krebs), P 277, P 290, P 596 and P 287 (18th century), also 'Schubring MS' (*BG* 15); toccata only, in 18th-century (P 1009 Kittel?, P 289) and 19th-century copies (BB 30387 Dröbs, Lpz Poel 16); fugue only, in 18th-century (P 287, P 409, Lpz Poel 28, Lpz MB MS 3, 2 J. A. G. Wechmar?, a MS once owned by Rust) and 19th-century copies (P 282, Lpz MB III.8.29 Dröbs, BB 30377 shortened).

Two staves; heading in P 803, 'Toccata col pedale obligato'; first movement, 'toccata' in P 289, BB 30387 etc, 'preludio' in P 277, P 290, Forkel's list (1802) etc.

Several conjectures have been made about this work: that the toccata 'dates from a later, maturer stage of mastery' than the fugue (Rust *BG* 15 p.xxvi); that the toccata was written for a performance on, or a visit to, the Weissenfels organ with its pedal f', perhaps in 1713; and that the so-called 'Aria in F' BWV 587 may have been an interlude between prelude and fugue (see BWV 587). While many sources hand down the work in separate movements (Lpz Poel 16 has a different, anonymous fugue), and while it does not appear, complete or incomplete, as part of a regular collection of Bach works (in P 290 it is amongst miscellaneous works, in P 409 amongst chorales), there is no documentary evidence for any of these three conjectures. P 803 gives a variant of the toccata in which the pedal part rises only to c', perhaps for the sake of a particular organ and copied by c1717, the fugue later (Zietz 1969 p66); such dating, however, is most uncertain. Furthermore, to assume that the fugue is earlier can also lead to a conjecture that the toccata dates from the Leipzig period (Spitta II p687), a questionable conclusion in view of formal and other details. Nor, in view of the version copied in P 803, does the fact that in the fugue the pedal compass rises only to c' argue that the movements did not originate together (Keller 1948 p91).

While it is only conjectured that the toccata and the fugue were composed at the same period, and that they were intended to be played together, the very degree of contrast in length, fluency, shape and 'effect' between them would be no disqualification and could itself suggest a favourite Bach conception, that of 'complementary movements'. The drama of the toccata is contrasted in *Affekt* with the contrapuntal ingenuity of the fugue. That such ingenuity is often used elsewhere for more climactic purposes than in BWV 540.ii, or that a fugue elsewhere with two subjects may seem to dominate its prelude much more obviously (e.g. F sharp minor, *The 48* Bk II), does not have any bearing on BWV 540, where the different conceptions behind the two movements should not be misunderstood as mere discrepancy. The toccata is the longest extant prelude; but the fugue is the only thorough-going double fugue in the organ works of J. S. Bach. They therefore have complementary, exceptional qualities.

Toccata

Since this gigantic movement is a combination or rather pairing of pedal toccata and ritornello form, it is possible to see them as distinct units in the movement as a whole (Keller 1948 p92):

A   1–176   pedal toccata (tonic and dominant pedal points, two pedal solos)

B   176–438   ritornello movement in which the main theme is Ex. 94(i) and the episodes Ex. 94(ii), not vice versa

Ex. 94
(i) b177   **(ii)** b219

However, this idea of the movement suggests a demarcation and even discontinuity not otherwise felt. Rather, the shape may be seen thus (Voigt *BJ* 1912 p36):

A   introduction
B   ritornello movement, of a form related to the preludes BWV 544, 546, 548, 552
C   coda

In further detail, the movement is constructed as follows:

A_1 1–55   tonic pedal point below two-part near-canon
         55–82   pedal solo, its chief figure throughout derived from b1; cadence figure *x* in C major (see Ex. 95)
A_2 83–137   dominant pedal point; exactly as 1–55 except canon inverted and 114–21 altered because of crossing parts
         137–76   pedal solo, derived from same figure as before but towards cadence figure *x* in C minor
B_1 176–218   new but related figure treated imitatively in four-bar sequence (176–92), then extended, developing cadence figure *x*; interrupted cadence, Neapolitan sixth, final cadence in D minor
A_3 218–38   opening material in three-part octave imitation, D minor
B_2 238–70   as B_1 in D minor but without interrupted-cadence section
A_4 270–90   as A_3 in A minor, three parts inverted
B_3 290–332   as B_1 in A minor (including interrupted-cadence section) but sequence changed to pass to G minor
A_5 332–52   as A_3 in G minor, three parts inverted
B_4 352–438   begins as B_1 in G minor; during the last of the four-bar sequences (352–67) it changes direction, passing from B♭ to F to C, on which a dominant pedal point prepares final cadence as in B_1 (thus 352–63 = 176–83, and 417–38 = 197–218)

This plan, too, disguises the continuity of the movement, for 'main themes' and 'episode' are related, as both being keyboard figures – Ex. 95 – and as both being treated canonically or imitatively throughout.

Ex. 95

It is to be noted, however, that *b* differs from *a* more obviously than do any of the variants quoted below in Ex. 100. The toccata is by no means monothematic.

Very striking to the listener is the rhythmic figure ⁷𝄽♩♩, so much so that its punctuating effect against a background of continual semi-quavers has itself the function of a rondo episode. That this same little figure leads to one of the most startling interrupted cadences even in J. S. Bach's repertory of them – Ex. 96 – emphasizes its formal

Ex. 96   (b203)

importance yet further, particularly at the end (bb423–4), where such a cadence is even more startling in a major key.

As in other ritornello movements of Bach, material can be modified or its order changed without any perceptible break. At some points, one cannot foretell what the next section is to be. It does not seem unnatural that section B_2 passes to a return of A without the interrupted cadence heard in B_1, for example, or that the first B sequence (from b176) is a less complete circle of fifths than a later exemplar (from b352). Both these sequences and the main theme itself – octave canon on a subject used in various guises by various composers including J. S. Bach (e.g. the Two-part Invention in A minor BWV 784) – are somewhat simplistic, throwing yet further weight on the interrupted cadences and the novel ways of treating other progressions,

Ex. 97   (b432)

e.g. the Neapolitan sixth: Ex. 97. Similarly, while the rhythmic figure ^{7} 𝄐𝄐 can hardly be seen as original either in itself (e.g. the closing cadences of other $^3/_8$ or $^6/_8$ movements such as BWV 543.ii, or C sharp major Prelude, *The 48* Bk I) or in its first appearance in the toccata (b81), its extension and sudden minor turn in b169 are most striking. This figure was later taken up by J. L. Krebs in his Prelude in C major and Toccata in E major. The whole melodic idea of the opening theme – octave imitation above a pedal point in $^3/_8$ – can be heard at the beginning of the motet BWV 226, while the chief formal idea of the movement as a whole – ritornello motifs heard in episodes – can also be found in several of the English Suite preludes, which indeed have a family likeness to BWV 540.i. The stylistic context for this movement is that it seems to combine ideas current in other kinds of organ toccata: the tonic/dominant pedal points found in so many 'southern' toccatas (Pachelbel, Fischer, Kerll etc) and the pedal solo found in the 'northern' type (Buxtehude, Bruhns etc).

This F major Toccata can therefore be seen to be built on material not itself original but working towards originality of overall form, contrapuntal handling, some new harmonic progressions, and dramatic pedal points. Of these four, the counterpoint is apparently the least distinguished, by no means tortuous or even particularly ingenious, although the three-part invertibility of A_3, A_4 and A_5 is not found so clearly stated in any contemporary organ music. It could well be that these invertible passages, like the opening 'octave canon' itself, are an acknowledgement of some keyboard device familiar to other organists: a commonplace of counterpoint found in (e.g.) Ex. 98. Similarly, the

Ex. 98

Handel, 'Aylesford Pieces', Allegro (cf. BWV 540.i bb219–22)

Reincken, Sonata (BWV 966.ii)
b16

imitative sequence during the *B* sections has none of the originality of motif and treatment in (e.g.) the C minor Fantasia BWV 562; it is easily adapted to the patent series of modulations back to F major from b365 onwards and to the dominant pedal point that follows. More complex counterpoint is reserved for the double subject of the fugue.

To player and listener, the sustained energy of the toccata is virtually incomparable and relies on, as it springs from, simplistic elements. Although the key-structure hangs between tonic and dominant pedal points – i.e. simple, traditional elements – the tonality is varied and balanced. Even the final cadence is no platitude and almost serves as a surprise. Obviously the motifs themselves are open to development, i.e. alteration for the sake of or towards a modulation. The second pedal solo is an interesting case, for – if the sources* convey the composer's intentions – there may be an intentional change in the structuring of the phrases as the line approaches the celebrated high pedal f':

bb137–68, 32 bars built up from two- and one-bar phrases thus:
2, 2, 1, 1, 1, 1, 1, 2, 2, 1, 2, 2, 2, 2, 2, 2, 2, 2, 2

This itself may suggest that there is a textual crux, since the isolated one-bar phrase† just before halfway seems unlikely and indeed at variance with the structure of the *first* pedal solo a hundred bars earlier. This crux would not be solved by assuming either that bars 152–65 or 156–9 could have been omitted in performance, or even that they were added later by the composer (Williams 1972 p34), since this does not affect the isolated one-bar phrase. Moreover, quite apart from other objections to thinking these bars optional, the second solo would not then balance the first, as presumably it should.

* Other than P 803, which may be a special case or may imply a different history.
† 'Phrase' in this context indicates a structural and not necessarily a practical conception: a question of what was in the composer's mind rather than what might be in the performer's.

The fact that the key motif of the movement is open to a two-bar or one-bar interpretation – Ex. 99 – is itself remarkable (other examples of such motifs in single- or double-length versions can be found in

Ex. 99

b139

etc

Orgelbüchlein chorales, e.g. BWV 625). Such ambiguity again belies the motif's apparent simplicity. Also belying it is the sheer number of variations on the motif, as in Ex. 100. Therefore, in addition to the

Ex. 100

formal control of the movement, the planning of keys, and the contrapuntal detail, the movement is ingenious in its use of the two basic motifs (*a* and *x*, Ex. 95) and in the simple contrast between them: one is imitative, the other homophonic. This very contrast provides much of the tension, and it is very likely no coincidence that the final dominant pedal point seems halfway between the two, uniting the rhythm of one with the simple harmony of the other.

Fugue

While the rhythmic character of the fugue is not unlike that of the D minor Fugue BWV 538, or the idea of combining themes not unknown in the fugues in C minor BWV 546 and E flat BWV 552, the present movement is a unique example of the thorough-going ricercar or *alla breve* fugue in which two themes are separately exposed and then combined:

A	1–23	exposition, consistent countersubject
	23–70	series of tonic (30, 49, 56) and dominant (39) entries, interspersed with episodes based chiefly on the original countersubject
B	70–93	irregular four-part exposition of new subject (subject b70,

answer with subject-*caput* b75, further answer b81, further subject b88; 'subject' in tonic, 'answer' in dominant)

	93–128	further entries of new subject (without answers) in D minor, G minor and C minor, interspersed with episodes based chiefly on the countersubject of *B*
A	128–33	return of subject *A* in tonic
A + B	134–70	further entries of subject *A* in C, D minor, D minor, B♭, F and F, on each occasion accompanied by subject *B*, complete (134), almost complete (142–3, 153–4, 158–9, 163–4) or incomplete (147–50)

The cumulative nature of this fugue is therefore based on three levels: thematic (*A*, *B*, then *A + B*), rhythmic (increasing quaver activity), and tonal (most key changes occur towards the end). It is probably for the sake of the second of these that the composer 'disguised' most combinations of *A* and *B* by changing the first bar or so of *B*, since its original *caput* would have held up the rhythm and harmony and drawn too much attention to the combination. Throughout, the organ writing is characteristic of a style as practised by this composer elsewhere (e.g. Magnificat Fugue BWV 733). Even for J. S. Bach, however, the apparent ease with which convincing counterpoint has been achieved over, for example, the last twenty bars is striking: the two subjects, the derived quaver lines, the diatonic grasp (subdominant, tonic, tonic entries in near-stretto), the idiomatic organ texture (opening to its widest points at the final entry over bb162–4), all most expertly rounded off by a three-bar close even more succinct than others of the type (e.g. BWV 537) and producing a good example of the 'cantabile polyphony' (Besseler 1955) heard in BWV 534, 538, 540, 545 and 546.

Some of the important details in the style of the fugue are concerned with the way it adapts traditional *alla breve* counterpoint. Thus, the subject has the white notes, the incipient chromaticism, the suspension and the simple cadence of such *alla breve* themes (e.g. Pachelbel, J. C. Bach); even the absence of codettas between subjects and answers alludes to an antique style. Also, the countersubject incorporates the important crotchet phrase equally typical of the style (cf. E major Fugue, *The 48* Bk II), including the traditional elements of contrary motion and even a kind of *nota cambiata* (*x*): Ex. 101. The

Ex. 101

b6

dactyl *x* is important not least since it later flavours the second fugue subject *B*, though in a significantly different form, i.e. as a broken chord. The crotchet countersubject of theme *A* provides further hallmarks of stricter *alla breve* style – Ex. 102 – while the quaver lines accompanying

Ex. 102
b55

subject *B* obviously increase the drive of the movement as a whole. The crotchets produce passages familiar from elsewhere (e.g. compare bb61–2 with the A minor Fugue, *The 48* Bk I); they can be used *inversus* (first time in b37) or can be made to run across an entry, e.g. the second subject in bb69–70.

The second exposition has a 'character theme' of strong rhythm ('more characteristic of the Cöthen period', Krey 1956 p180ff) and produces a quaver line that is as true to its tradition – at least in the hands of J. S. Bach – as the crotchet line was to the first. This quaver line can assume various shapes – Ex. 103 – and in that way continues

Ex. 103
a b73   *b* b80   *c* b74   *d* b101   *e* b131

to appear through to the end of the Fugue, including the three-bar close. Such quaver lines usually produce fertile developments, and BWV 540 is no exception. They are both fluent and infinitely adaptable, as can be seen by the quaver lines accompanying both the reappearance of *A* with its countersubject (at bb128–33) and the combination of *A* and *B* at bb134–8. The familiarity of such lines in J. S. Bach should not disguise their virtues; though they are merely built up of the three- or four-note *figurae* outlined by Walther and others, no known composer worked them to happier result. Codettas or episodes derived from them (e.g. from bb79 or 115) appear to have a kind of neutral effect against which a subject is easily conspicuous (b119) and against which other kinds of quavers (e.g. the broken chords from bb122 or 164) introduce a new, exciting element. Furthermore, such quaver lines can produce figures which themselves turn out to be of melodic interest (e.g. the figure *e* in Ex. 103, in the final section of the fugue),* or they can be twisted to produce harmonic effects against which a subject entry stands out (bb125–8). Although it has been claimed that in bb125–8 Bach's 'diatonic sense failed him' (Dalton 1966), it should not be missed that the modulation from C/F minor to D minor has the effect of

* Also used to make a melody or a good bass line in (e.g.) the A flat Fugue, *The 48* Bk I (here semiquavers).

Ex. 104

BWV 540.ii   b96

Italian Concerto BWV 971.iii (pub. 1735)   b118

presenting the same quaver *figurae* in a new, disturbed light. At other
moments, the line is much like that in other works: Ex. 104.

The inventiveness of the F major Fugue is only hinted at in such
general remarks. A further understanding of the composer's methods
could be gained by studying and comparing the bars that follow each
complete subject entry, or by tracing such formal strategies as the way
in which the minor middle entries of subject *B* occur in successive
voices (bottom, middle, top). More so than the toccata, the fugue is
working on several different levels at once, combining a careful
adherence to style (*alla breve* elements), composition through *figurae*
(quaver lines), fugal counterpoint (combination and invertibility of

themes), key-structure (the first half exclusively tonic and dominant), and organ texture (close opening, wide final entry). To the composer, the toccata and the fugue must have represented perfect complements.

541   Prelude and Fugue in G major

Autograph MS listed as Lpz MB MS a 1 (removed to USA in 1945; Krause 1964 pp23, 54); copies in P 288 (owned by J. P. Kellner), Lpz MB MS 7 (J. G. Preller, 'Poss....1749'), Am.B. 543 (Kirnberger?), P 320 (Kittel); other sources of 2nd half of 18th century (P 290, P 595 J. Ringk, P 597, Brussels II.3914, LM 4839) and later (P 837 etc), including further sources perhaps dependent on Kittel (P 319 Westphal, P 557 Grasnick, Lpz Go.S.26 fugue only, Brussels Fétis 7327 fugue only); *BG* 15 also used a 'Schubring MS' and a further MS owned by Rust 'with many corrections in the hand of the composer'.

Two staves; autograph heading, 'Praeludium pro Organo con Pedal: obligat:' (source for heading in Am.B. 543?) and 'Vivace' (also given in Forkel's catalogue, 1802); in Lpz MB MS 7, 'Praeludium et Fuga'.

The chordal technique of the prelude, with its 'north German' opening on a solo line, could indicate an early origin for the work, while the tendency of those chords to dissolve into counterpoint could indicate a later. In theory, BWV 541 could be an early organ piece worked upon at a later period (Kloppers 1966 p222). Certainly the impression given by the prelude is one of very confident technique: a mature salute to older forms and styles, like BWV 538.i now promoted into an organized ritornello form. But the, or an, autograph MS (evidently a fair copy – *BG* 15 p. xxvii) has a watermark that is said to imply a date c1715 (Emery 1957 p104), which would then accord with the idea that the work originated at the time when the composer began to work in Italian concerto forms, even specifically on Cantata 21, the theme of whose first chorus is often said to resemble the fugue subject of BWV 541.ii. Spitta thought the autograph MS showed signs ('diplomatische Merkzeichen') that suggested a date of 1724 or 1725, which in turn would accord with a three-movement version found in later sources (see below); the piece would then have belonged originally to the pre-Leipzig years when Bach 'had the idea of composing a three-movement organ work on the analogy of the concerto' (Spitta II p688). However, the extant autograph has more recently been dated to the 1730s or even 1740s (Kilian 1969 pp16–17), though it is uncertain whether this indicates the date of composition, copying or revision; perhaps the last is most likely. There may be confusion in the accounts of these sources. There must have been at least two autographs, but neither can be the one referred to by May (1974 p275) when he says that Lpz MB MS a 1, P 288 and P 595 all 'apparently depend on the Weimar autograph (now lost)', for the 'lost Weimar autograph' is now thought to be identical with the lost MS owned by Rust (Kilian *NBA* IV/5 *KB*).

In two MSS there are signs that at one period or another, with or without the composer's authority, a middle movement was played or planned. Such a third movement was suggested presumably because, as with the C major Prelude and Fugue BWV 545, the external dimensions of the work can seem out of scale with its internal tensions – i.e., the preludes seem too short. The middle movement is a fragment (first thirteen bars) of the early version of the Un Poco Allegro from the Sonata in E minor BWV 528; both copies of the fragment (P 288, P 319) were written by Westphal, both were crossed out, and both follow the fugue with the direction 'Trio so nach dem 1sten Satze folgen muss' ('Trio to be played after the first movement'), all of which amounts to poor authority for playing three movements. Kellner's copy of the work in P 288 is marked after the prelude 'verte fuga' ('turn to the fugue'?), and after the fugue 'Il fine' (Kilian 1969 16–17). It is not known whether Westphal had any authority for adding the middle movement, whether it 'was at one time meant to be played between the prelude and fugue', or whether the composer 'gave up the idea of a middle movement after writing thirteen bars' of it (Emery 1957 pp103, 104), although all three seem unlikely. Certainly Spitta's parallel with the three-movement Italian concerto is over-bold.

Prelude

As the keyboard figures of the C major Prelude BWV 545 can be compared to those of other pieces in C major, so the scales, broken chords and homophony of BWV 541.i can be compared to those of other pieces in G major, in particular the Toccata BWV 916: Ex. 105. BWV

Ex. 105
BWV 916

916 is cast in elementary ritornello form, a form yet more contracted in the organ prelude BWV 541.i:

1–29   toccata opening in tonic; important keyboard figures to follow (a 12, b 16, c 18, d 24: see Ex. 106, next page)
29–46   toccata return (allusion) in dominant; figure a developed; figures b, c, d much modified
46–59   further development of a and b
59–82   tonic; further development of b and c; from 74 a return to the opening toccata material; from 79 a return (now in tonic) to the cadence phrase of 44–6

It may be a mistake to see such shapes as intentional ritornello forms,

Ex. 106

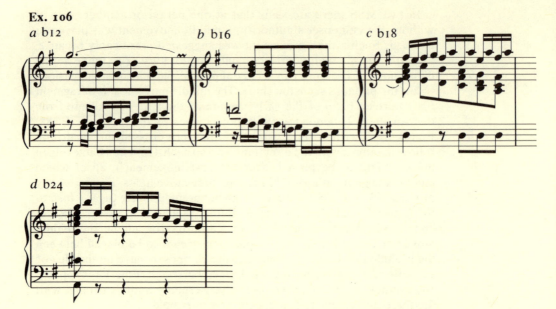

a b12   *b* b16   *c* b18

d b24

since the returns of the main theme have none of the clarity or emphasis usual in the concertos. Rather, BWV 541.i suggests a composer working the conventional toccata elements – opening tonic, dominant (b29) and final pedal point (b63) – into an organized movement for whose cohesion themes will obviously be re-quoted or re-used in the course of the movement as a whole, though in what order and manner is anything but stereotyped.

The figuration itself is an interesting blend of German organ toccata and what seem at times elements borrowed from the new concerto traditions: Ex. 106. Thus the pedal part of figure *a* will be found in (e.g.) Bruhns's fantasia 'Nun komm', der Heiden Heiland' bb102–3, while figure *b* (in both manual and pedal parts) will be found in the Vivaldi Concerto BWV 593.iii from b70 (a passage owed only in part to Vivaldi). Thus the repeated chords found in figure *b* and throughout the movement are not specifically 'north German' but are in a more general instrumental style. More north German is the semiquaver pattern of figure *c*, particularly as it occurs in bb43–4 or bb63–4; comparable passages, not so systematically worked, will be found in the first part of Buxtehude's Praeludium in D minor BUXWV 140. It is also the various elements of figure *c*, particularly the violinistic semiquavers, that seem to leave the biggest mark on the movement; many bars – the movement works very much in one-bar units – are developed from these component parts in highly varied ways (bb18, 19, 20, 59, 60, 63–8, 78–80 and possibly 39, 40, 50). Figure *a* is also used widely and in similar ways (bb12, 14, 32, 34, 36, 47, 51, 53–6), while figure *d* – a texture rather than a motif – is particularly open to development (bb13, 15, 24–6, 33, 35, 37, 41, 46, 48, 52, 57, 69, 74–6*).

* The last has the diminished seventh serving much the same purpose as the Neapolitan sixth – which might have been used in a less mature work – in BWV 532, 535, 565, 582 etc.

Indeed, the movement could be described as a series of single bars, restless in their drive (particularly around b70) and derived more or less in turn from one or other of the opening figures. Not only can it not be forseen at any one moment which figure is likely to be developed next, but the kind of development itself is unusual. There is no simple repetition; instead, a bar-by-bar composition process takes up the basic figures, extracts a shape or a texture or a rhythm from them and creates a kind of *ad hoc* form whose unity is ensured by the fact that both the opening and closing bars are heard elsewhere in the movement (b29 and b45 respectively).

In that the movement is not long-limbed enough to be called concerto ritornello form, the G major Prelude can be seen as a salute to the old praeludia, its elements cemented together to produce an *ad hoc* form not so far removed from the praeludium but here both more continuous and more given to composition by *figurae* than is usual with Buxtehude, Bruhns etc. The use that the passage from b12 to b16 is put to in bb32–38, for example, would not be found in Buxtehude on the one hand or in Vivaldi on the other.

Fugue

The fugue subject has been a happy hunting-ground for those who recognize in it some kind of formula well known during the period. Spitta not only heard in it the rhythm of the opening chorus of Cantata 21 (1714, 1723) but found that same rhythm 'serving the prelude as a motif working freely in it' (Spitta II p689), presumably a reference to what were called above figure *a* (rhythm) and figures *b* and *c* (repeated notes); or perhaps he was referring to such bars of the prelude as 61–2. Such observations have also been made to bolder effect, e.g. that the prelude and fugue 'have a close inner, even thematic, connection' (Keller 1948 p111), or that the fugue develops out of the prelude's own motifs (Emery 1966). However, such a conclusion would depend on the value given to functional analysis, since no overt inter-reference between prelude and fugue can be demonstrated. Nor do similar but shorter themes of G. F. Kaufmann ('Von Himmel hoch' in *Harmonische Seelenlust*, Leipzig 1733–6) or F. A. Maichelbeck ('Fuga Octavi Toni' [G major] in *Der auf dem Clavier lehrenden Caecelia* III, Augsburg 1738) suggest either influence on or influence from J. S. Bach,

Ex. 107
BWV 21.ii b2

BWV 596.iv

since the subject follows a harmonic and rhythmic norm – repeated notes on *4–3* and *7–6* suspensions. Such subjects form a study in themselves. For example, it is surely correct (Dürr 1951 pp167–8) to see a close resemblance between the chorus theme in Cantata 21 and the finale of the Vivaldi Concerto BWV 596, both of which were probably written in or by 1714 – Ex. 107. They are both in the minor and both exploit the stretto from the beginning – unlike BWV 541.i, where stretto is reserved for the close. But that the 'repeated notes on *4–3* and *7–6* suspensions' can be found in many contexts is also clear from the opening of Cantata 77, where the material is derived from a cantus firmus: Ex. 108.

Ex. 108

BWV 77.i

Strings

The shape of the fugue can be expressed:

1–17	exposition; first dominant answer tonal, second real (b14; see also BWV 550, 536); new countersubject for the second answer
17–26	episode, using in particular the quaver figure from the subject (b2) and semiquaver figures from countersubjects
26–35	tonic entry followed by derived episode in relative
35–52	relative entry (tenor) followed by free (?) episode towards:
52–63	dominant entry, codetta–episode, supertonic entry
63–71	derived episode, G minor entry (as if a dominant tonal answer to subject in C minor), dominant pedal point in minor
72–83	stretto at the ninth, followed by stretto at the fifth below; then final entry on a new fifth voice (b79, subdominant); inverted then doubled final tonic pedal point

Though modest, the variation of the subject as it appears in b66 or the second half of b72 looks ahead to the sophisticated treatment given the subject of the C major Fugue BWV 547, while the passing, flagging turn to the minor before the final entries resembles that of several movements, not least the prelude itself (compare prelude bb76–7 with fugue bb71–2). As a striking melody, the subject is open to patent development in its repeated notes and suspensions, leading to such clear-sounding quasi-entries as the soprano line of bb30–2. A particularly successful use of it is to be heard over the section bb20–5, where the question-and-answer sequences are song-like in their melody and lead to a trio-like dialogue (bb23–4).

Form and harmony in the fugue are conceived with respect to each other. Thus a tendency in the first and last thirty bars or so is for semiquaver figures to spin around themselves, as in Ex. 109. Of all

Ex. 109

composers, J. S. Bach was a master of such creative figuration; it also at times produces somewhat complex harmony (e.g. second half of b14), clearly more mature than that produced by other themes based on a repeated note, e.g. the Toccata BWV 566 bb34–8. These lines can also reach out towards wider, capricious effects achieved in the interests of good harmony (from b30) or of climax and cadence (b34). But real contrast is provided by the middle episode, the only passage without pedals, without clear reference to the subject, and without consistently shifting harmonies. The broken chords of this episode supply the relief given in different forms in other fugues, e.g. the scale passages before stretto entries in the D minor BWV 538.ii. But in BWV 541 the structure is shorter, simpler and in general not so dense as BWV 538. While for an *alla breve* subject like BWV 538 the few bars of contrary-motion scales produce great contrast, for BWV 541 the relief episode can be lighter still, more charming, dance-like, fitting the aria-like nature of the fugue subject itself. The whole episode bb38–52 suggests passages in the first movement of the Fifth Brandenburg Concerto, i.e. a light ritornello form, not a fugue. At its close, this central episode in BWV 541.ii also brings in figures beginning on the main beats, a detail of some importance in a fugue whose themes and lines usually begin on up-beats. But never are the motifs allowed to become either repetitious or dominant; the combination of fine harmony and fine melody achieved through rhythmic drive is the purpose of the movement. In the interests of those three aims, new figures can be produced up to the last two bars, figures which pick up the tail of the subject. Thus bars 60–2 use a motif – Ex. 110 – which is found in (e.g.) the *Orgelbüchlein*,

Ex. 110

but now taken up and used in the interests of the 'fine melody, harmony and rhythmic drive' of BWV 541.ii, producing amongst other things a fine bass line and powerful $\sharp\substack{7\\5\\2}$ harmony (b62) beyond the imagination of the many French composers who used it as a matter of course. The 'inverted' pedal point at the close is not common; that at the end of Cantata 77 is a conventional bass pedal point, in which the original subject and its figures are used in a less condensed manner than in the G major Organ Fugue.

---

542   Fantasia and Fugue in G minor

No Autograph MS; copies of fugue only, in P 803 (J. T. Krebs), P 1100 (J. C. Oley), P 598 (J. F. Agricola, between 1738 and 1741), P 288 (J. P. Kellner), other 18th-century (P 290, P 203 J. S. Borsch c1744–1804) and 19th-century sources (P 282, P 837, Lpz MB MS 4, Lpz Poel 21, BB 38276, 'Schubring MS', etc); fugue alone in F minor in P 320 (Kittel), P 287 (J. S. Borsch), P 204 (C. F. G. Schwenke 1767–1822), P 518 (c1800), P 557 (Grasnick c1820), LM 4838, Lpz Go . S . 26, probably all dependent on Kittel sources; fantasia alone in Lpz MB III . 8 . 20 (J. A. Dröbs, early 19th century); fantasia and fugue together in Am.B. 531 (18th century), P 288 (2nd half of 18th century or later), P 595 (ditto) and P 924 (Grasnick); together but in reversed order in P 1071 (c1800).

Two staves; heading in P 803, 'Fuga'; in P 288 (the earlier copy) 'Fuga . . . pro Organo pleno cum Pedale obligato'; in Am.B. 531 and Lpz MB III . 8 . 20, 'Fantasia'; in P 288 (the later copy), 'Fantasia e Fuga in G m: Per l'Organo pieno, col Pedale Obligato'.

Two problems concern BWV 542 as we know it: Do the movements belong together? and Were the movements composed at the same period? Although the latter is often assumed – suggesting that the contrast between the movements was deliberate – in fact the fugal counterpoint, texture and figuration point back to the period of or even before the Passacaglia BWV 582, while the enharmonic modulations of the fantasia suggest a later date, no doubt in the years after Weimar (last suggestion in Spitta I p635). Against such conclusions, however, it should be pointed out that the techniques of fantasia and fugue are so different as to make such comparisons doubtful. Other writers have not only heard 'a certain connection' between fantasia and fugue, but also think the fugue to belong to the Hamburg visit of 1720, the fantasia to a previous period (Keller 1948 p86); this seems to be based on the compass (d''' is required for the fantasia but could not be found on the organ of the Jakobikirche in Hamburg), while the style would suggest the opposite. Whether the movements belong at all together is uncertain (Emery 1957–8). While it is true that even the E flat Prelude and Fugue BWV 552 are found apart in their printed edition and were often copied separately in later MSS, and while the preludes and fugues of other major pairs were sometimes copied separately (e.g. BWV 540), the list of sources for the G minor Fantasia and Fugue is unusually suggestive in this respect. Moreover, in some MSS such as P 203 and P 204 this fugue is included alone with other fugues of various origins (*The 48*, etc), while in others such as P 1100 and P 288 (first copy) it was written out as a separate and single piece, i.e. not in an album. Also, although in some copies the fugue appears transposed into F minor (which requires that allowances be made for the original pedal Cs), the fantasia is not known in an F minor version. There was therefore at least a tradition of playing the fugue alone: one copy in F minor (P 518, *c*1800) even has a different prelude or so-called *intrada*. The fugue as given in *BG* 15 has been claimed as a variant form 'adapted' for a less proficient eighteenth-century player from its original version; both variants are contained in P 288 (Keller *BJ* 1913).

The conjecture that the movements, whether or not belonging to different periods, were coupled by the composer is thought to be backed by – and is then taken as evidence for – one particular incident in the composer's life: viz., it is claimed that BWV 542 'belongs without doubt to the Cöthen period' (*BG* 15 p. xxviii) and was composed 'for the visit to Hamburg' in 1720 (Spitta I p635). This was the occasion on which the composer applied for the organist's post at the Jakobikirche (*Dok* II p77) and, according to the Obituary, which seems to refer to this visit, the occasion on which he played to the ancient Adam Reincken, last representative of an old organ school (*Dok* III p84). Allusions to Hamburg music have been heard in BWV 542; for instance, in the fantasia Spitta hears Bach 'seeming to wish to surpass the Hamburg organists on their own ground'. But the link with Hamburg depends on a more objective circumstance, namely Mattheson's remark in his *General-Bass-Schule* (Hamburg 1731, pp34ff) that the competition for a new organist in Hamburg Cathedral on 24 October 1725 included an

Ex. 111

(i) Mattheson, *General-Bass-Schule*

(ii)

extemporized fugue on the subject of Ex. 111(i), which was complete with a countersubject (ii). Mattheson adds that

ich wuste wol, wo dieses Thema zu Hause gehörte, und wer es vormahls künstlich zu Papier gebracht hatte

I knew well where this theme originated and who worked it artfully on paper.

However, a simplified version of the subject was published in 1700 as the song *Ik ben gegroet* – Ex. 112 (*Oude en nieuwe Hollantse Boerenliedjes*, Amsterdam; see *Dok* II p219) – and it is possible that Mattheson's phrase 'zu Hause gehörte' refers to its Dutch origin, which may or may not have been known to J. S. Bach. The date of the Dutch publication makes it impossible for it to be a later, simplified version

Ex. 112

Ik ben gegroet

of the fugue subject rather than vice versa, as was suggested before the dates came to light (Emery 1957–8). Also, it is uncertain whether the little discrepancies between BWV 542.ii and Mattheson's version indicate that the 'fugue as we know it must have been touched up later' (Spitta 1 p635). Of even less certain significance is the question of compass: of the C♯, E♭, A♭ and d‴ required for the fantasia or the E♭ and A♭ required for the fugue, none were available at Reincken's church, the Katharinenkirche, nor (except the A♭ on *Rückpositiv* and pedal only) were they available at the Jakobikirche on the organ as Schnitger left it (Fock 1974 pp63–4). The question is further complicated by the (later?) history of the fugue as transposed to F minor, and by the need for any organ on which the fantasia is played to be well-tempered, though not necessarily equal-tempered as is sometimes said. Possible solutions to all these questions offer themselves – e.g. that the fantasia demonstrated enharmonic possibilities in some tunings, that the fantasia was not written for (or even by the time of) the Hamburg visit, or that the fugue may have been composed or copied for an 'ideal' compass which many organists must have been used to dealing with, however roughly by modern standards, when they played on short compass. But all such solutions are conjectural.

Fantasia

The shape of the G minor Fantasia is unusually clear; that it expresses musical–rhetorical form is highly likely, as then is its distribution on two manuals, *Hauptwerk* and *Positiv* (Kloppers 1966 pp76–7):

A	Hw	1–9	*Propositio*: main material; roulades, scales etc on tonic, then dominant; pedal point
B	Pos	9–14	*Confutatio*: opposing statement; imitative, more modulatory, with moving bass line; strict four parts
A	Hw	14–25	*Confirmatio*: partial return to the main material (in particular, roulades and multiple suspension); more chromatic idiom; enharmonic modulation
B	Pos	25–31	*Confutatio*: as before but a fifth lower, upper parts inverted, lengthened by one bar
A	Hw	31–49	*Confirmatio*: further development of chromatic idea (31–9) *Peroratio*: return to tonic (b40), roulades etc; chromatics finally resolved in final pedal solo and cadence

What cannot be clear from such rhetorical analyses, however, is the vital question whether the composer had them in mind and composed accordingly, or whether such natural contrasts are merely common to verbal and musical rhetoric in the wider sense. Are they form preceding or shape superimposed? That the *St John Passion* in its revised form begins with a chorus incorporating opening progressions similar to those in BWV 542.i for the *exclamatio* 'Lord, Lord' (Kloppers 1966 p114ff) is not conclusive, since that too is governed by musical laws and has its own logic as a series of pedal-point harmonies. Similarly, although the opening accented chord (*emphasis*), the crying-out of the opening bars (*exclamatio*), the repetition of demisemiquaver motifs (*anaphora*), the falling/rising lines (*anabasis/katabasis*), the contrapuntal discussion of motifs from b9 on (*declamatio*), even the manual rests in the penultimate bar (*aposiopese*) may have equivalents or analogies in verbal rhetoric, it cannot be claimed either that any element is there as a kind of demonstration of the theoretical figure of rhetoric or that every element has such equivalents or analogies. Thus, all that can be said about bb31–4 from the point of view of *ars rhetorica* (Kloppers 1966 p120) is that they follow the previous section 'without sharp contrast' and that they incorporate such rhetorical figures as *gradatio* ('rising' towards climax) and *congeries* ('accumulation' of part-writing). But even in this extraordinary movement, that passage is one of the most striking in its major–minor modulations, its chromatic lines (very different from their origin in the pedal of bb22–3), its contrary motion and its crescendo effect.

Even were it to be accepted that the fantasia is 'to be understood as a little instrumental oratory' of its own (Kloppers 1966 p111), its stylistic roots must not be forgotten. The opening pedal-point harmonies, considered as a spacious progression, can be paralleled in many

Ex. 113
Violin Sonata BWV 1001.i (Adagio)

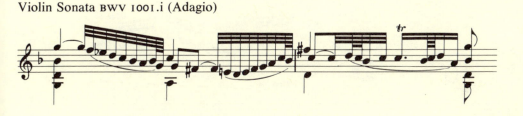

Violin Sonata BWV 1005.i (Adagio)
b39

other movements, including those of a less extempore cast (e.g. BWV 546.i), but rarely, if ever, will such a pair of consecutive diminished sevenths be found as in the second and third chords here. Another device, that of chords punctuating roulades, can be found in more refined contexts: Ex. 113. Such figures may themselves derive from the kind of roulade added by violinists to sonata movements, judging by one edition of Corelli's Sonatas Op V, though this is poor justification for seeing the G minor Fantasia as a 'secular' piece (Hammerschlag 1950). Either way, the violinist's added runs and decorations are unlikely ever to have been so systematic, so simple or so dramatic as in BWV 542.i. In that the opening eight bars consist of a tonic and then dominant pedal point, the fantasia also begins like a conventional *Orgelpunkttokkata* with later chromatic harmonies of a toccata–*durezza* kind. Indeed, although the line woven by bb6–7 can be shown to be a highly developed composition which repeats (*anaphora*) and extends its figure – Ex. 114 – there is at this point little indication that the

Ex. 114
b6

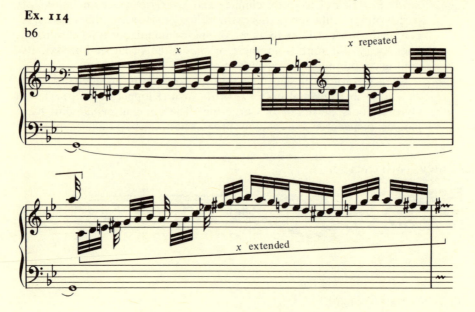

fantasia is going to develop beyond its toccata-like beginning (compare the pedal point at the beginning of BWV 543) into a chromatic, modulatory and sectional fantasia. Even the startling penultimate bar can be seen as a mature adaptation of an older idea: compare the penultimate bar of the E minor Prelude BWV 533.

Although the shorter pedal points in the rest of the movement often seem to encourage relatively conventional harmonies (bb13, 18–19, 30, 41), these moments are by no means simplistic, relaxed or uninventive. Nevertheless, it is the other harmonic effects that give the movement its original element. By b49 an impression of immense harmonic complexity has been gained, aided by the exceptional discontinuity of the movement and its equally exceptional contrasts from section to

Ex. 115

b1 (*a*)   b8 (*b*)   b14 (*c*)   b20   b38

b32 (*d*)   b35 (*e*)   b43 (*f*)   b44

section. The harmonies – Ex. 115 – can be seen in several categories: (*a*) pedal-point harmonies, including (*b*) the important multiple suspensions, (*c*) the diminished sevenths treated enharmonically (as in some older and contemporary Italian recitative), (*d*) chromatics, particularly those moving to unexpected minor chords, (*e*) consecutive diminished sevenths, and (*f*) 'interrupted' cadences or unexpected resolutions. More conventional harmonic effects also find a place, such as the Neapolitan sixth (middle b11, end b16, end b41, end b45), and one or two chords distinctive to this movement, such as the $\frac{\flat9}{\frac{\sharp7}{\flat6}}$ of bb19–20 (usually heard in 'opened-out' form, as in b8 or b11). The effects are given further power by the dramatic rests or *tmeses* (in particular bb15, 20, 35, 44), by the variety of texture from one to eight parts, by the extreme changes, and not least by the 'ordinary' passages that set the others into relief (e.g. bb39–41). The development of the six harmonic devices *a–f* replaces more conventional kinds of development. Thus it is a combination of *b*, *c* and *d* that lies behind bb21–3 and bb36–8, and only the two *B* sections develop a motif in familiar ways, i.e. stretto imitation in invertible counterpoint over the same motif augmented in the pedal part. As with the motif-development of *Orgelbüchlein* chorales, however, this intense development of harmonic ideas or devices does not preclude more or less straightforward inter-quotation (e.g. bb15–17 in bb44–6). Indeed, whatever the origin of BWV 542.i may have been, this element of inner repetition seems to be a speciality of middle-period Bach.

Despite the closely reasoned detail suggested by such descriptions of the chief events of BWV 542.i, it could still be thought that, as with Schubert, the most startling harmonies are those produced not by chromatic ideas or diminished sevenths as such but by changes of direction. Thus, while sevenths and chromatic ideas are certainly involved in bb23–4, the most startling event is in fact the conclusion of the phrase not in Eb minor (the key of the previous bar) but in F minor; then in turn, the change of direction towards the G of the next bar. It is as if the dominant chord at the beginning of b20 had merely been delayed by a few bars; but the effect is unique in music.

Fugue

In important respects, the fugue subject is also unique: it may have originated in an old Dutch song; it may have been known to, used by or regarded (by J. S. Bach) as a salute to Reincken who had lived for a time in Holland; and it may refer to specific subject types of north German origin (e.g. those in Reincken's *Hortus musicus* sonatas copied in P 803 and P 804). The subject contains two sequences, the first of half-bar and the second of one-bar units; this itself is a unique feature and must be one reason why the subject is so memorable.* The unmistakable jollity of the subject usually brings forward more 'earnest' countersubjects in the course of the fugue, but at least one episode (from b43) matches the subject in this respect. Both the copyist of P 287 (who thought it 'the best of all the pedal works of J. S. Bach') and Spitta (I p636) are unboundedly enthusiastic about the fugue, but its form is a good deal slacker than (e.g.) BWV 538 or 534. Perhaps in the 'slack' moments there is a reference to Reincken, either in general or specifically to his own G minor Fugue: Ex. 116.

Ex. 116

Reincken, Sonata in G minor (*Hortus musicus*)   b56

BWV 542.ii   b50

The form can be expressed:

G minor	1–17	exposition, two countersubjects
	17–21	episode derived from subject-motif *x* (semiquavers)
G minor	21–36	further tonic–dominant–tonic entries, inverting the counterpoint; followed (b32) by episode derived from same motif *x*
	36–65	entry in relative; extensive episode (including two entries in D minor); answer in relative dominant (b54) followed by return to G minor and a drawn-out thematic anticipation of:
G minor	65–72	tonic entry; episode derived from subject-motif *x*
	72–93	entries in subdominant and relative of subdominant (b79)

* In simplifying its sequence, the pedal of b78 seems closer to Mattheson's version of the subject. It is also a curious detail that, as bb51–3 show, each one-bar sequence can be accompanied by two half-bar sequences in a countersubject.

interspersed with episodes, the last (b86) with a change of direction to remoter keys before:

G minor   93–115   tonic entries in the course of the episode (94–103 = 44–53 down a fifth); then full three-part entry (103), followed by returns to a previous episode (106–10 = 32–6 now in tonic); final entry without countersubjects

Thus the fugue is a rondo in which the tonic key is the ritornello idea, as can be found on a smaller scale elsewhere (e.g. E minor Fugue, *The 48* Bk II). On each entry the subject stands out from its context. The episodes are derived from the subject-motif *x* and from episode-motifs *y*, *z* – Ex. 117 – which are presumably related; subject-motif and

Ex. 117

episode-motif combine naturally, since as cells they are easily adaptable and extendable. An unexpected result of the rondo key-structure is that the entries themselves are somewhat demoted in their importance to the form as form. The 'final entries' appear in the course of an episode, and that heard in the pedal at the end serves as coda. Yet on the whole the length is achieved without apparent effort, and balances the multi-limbed length of the subject itself.

While (as was noted above) Mattheson seems to have known the first countersubject of the fugue, he makes no reference to the second, Ex. 118. That this second countersubject seems related to the *B*

Ex. 118

material of the fantasia (bb9–10) has no doubt occurred to some commentators; but closer still to both is the same kind of imitative sequence found in other fugal episodes, such as from b17 of the B minor Fugue, *The 48* Bk I (see also a remark on BWV 544). If the original subject and first countersubject had also been given to the Jakobi competitors in 1720, the second (Ex. 118) might well have been contributed by J. S. Bach. But such biographical speculation is not productive, since the result of the three lines is to produce the elements of a conventional permutation fugue – like another G minor fugue,

BWV 578. Two countersubjects can be found occasionally elsewhere (e.g. Bruhns's E minor Fugue; Buxtehude's D minor Fugue BUXWV 155 b63); but in BWV 542.ii as a whole the chief inventiveness or ingenuity is concerned rather with the development of the little motif x (Ex. 117). While the three subjects may have their counterpoint inverted or even varied (e.g. soprano b56), the episodes contain material that is not inverted and depend more on the melodiousness of the subject and on the *perpetuum mobile* that can be built up from x. But again, x is not used for ingenious counterpoint; on the contrary, its most remarkable development is the passage bb61–3 when it produces a very unusual homophony. In no way is the harmony of the fugue obscure; if Mattheson was hinting at a criticism of BWV 542.ii when he remarked that in working such a fugue

lieber was bekanntes und fliessendes genommen...darauf kömt es an, und es gefällt dem Zuhörer besser, als ein chromatisches Gezerre (*Dok* II p219)

rather, something familiar and fluent [should be] taken...that is what matters, and the listener will like it better than some chromatic affectation

then he cannot have known what 'chromatisches Gezerre' was to be found in the Fantasia BWV 542.i. The little passage bb40–1 of the fugue does not justify such terms. But that is not to deny the fugue interesting and unusual subtleties. Of course, were Mattheson to have known both Fugue and Fantasia BWV 542, he might well have been showing here his approval of the 'fluent' fugue after the 'chromatisches Gezerre' of the fantasia. The hidden repetitions have been referred to; these are required to give the fugue a rounded shape. Otherwise it derives fresh sequences up till b91, keeps up semiquaver motion, and in the second long series of episodes from b68 turns the motif x into an ascending phrase (Ex. 119) when it has previously been descending.

Ex. 119

b83

On the whole, the repeated episodes produce a fugue somewhat different from that implied by the first thirty bars or so, making change of manual neither more difficult nor indeed any more disruptive than is usually the case. The movement is also held together by the passages of reiterated perfect cadence (bb68–71, 89–93, 113–14).

543

Prelude and Fugue in A minor

No Autograph MS; copies in Am.B. 60 (a Berlin copyist, after 1754) and other sources of mid or later 18th century (Am.B. 54, P 276, P 290), and early 19th (P 819 prelude only, P 505 Grasnick, P 837, Lpz MB III.8.14 Dröbs, P 925 and arrangement for four hands dated 1832).

Two staves; title in Am.B. 60 'Preludio e Fuga per l'Organo pieno', in Dröbs's MS '...für die volle Orgel'.

It seems that the prelude had an earlier version (see BWV 543a); but the fugue is still often claimed as a revision or a re-written, shortened version of the keyboard fugue in A minor BWV 944 copied into the Andreas-Bach-Buch (*MGG* I col.1013), so revised because 'only in the organ fugue' did the composer 'seek and find adequate expression' (Oppel 1906 pp74ff). But this view can only be based on certain resemblances between the subject and shape of the two fugues BWV 543 and 944, since they have little else in common. The subjects and countersubjects of the two fugues follow similar melodic lines and tessituras, both fugues have something of the nature of a *perpetuum mobile* (BWV 543 less so), and both have a rather free close (BWV 543 more so). These 'resemblances' may well be only the result of A minor associations for the composer, even if the organ fugue does contain playful figures (e.g. b83) in the style of the harpsichord fugue (Hering 1974 p49).

Other inter-resemblances have been found: the outline of the subject BWV 543.ii is like that of the A minor Fugue BWV 559, as is a (pedal) figure in the closing stages of both preludes (Beechey *MT* 1973 p832), while the same subject BWV 543.ii can also be traced somehow in the opening right-hand figure of the prelude (Oppel *op cit*) – a resemblance that unfortunately requires b2 of the fugue subject to be ignored. What is more, the subject can be paralleled by a (non-fugal) Corrente in Vivaldi's Op II no. I (Venice, 1709) and a Fugue in E minor by Pachelbel (Keller 1948 p84). It is doubtful whether any such similarity proves that J. S. Bach was influenced by others. The conclusion ought rather to be that a minor subject with a *caput* or head motif tracing the triad, which is then followed by a sequential, figurative tail of some length (as BWV 543, 944, Corelli etc), will produce only a certain degree of variety. In the instance of BWV 543, the result is a *perpetuum-mobile*-like subject – unusual for an organ fugue of J. S. Bach – and one which, like BWV 564, requires some kind of broken-up postlude towards the close, since a final entry on classical lines (as in BWV 538 or 540) would not convey the correct sense of finality. Either way, it is difficult to justify Spitta's much-repeated conjecture that prelude and fugue did not originate in the same period (Spitta I p405), for both show signs of immaturity, and the common assumption that the 'early version' of the prelude (BWV 543a) long preceded the 'later version' is supported by neither contents nor sources.

Prelude

It is true, as Spitta also pointed out, that the so-called early version of the prelude shows 'certain characteristics reminiscent of the Buxtehude School' (Spitta II p689), but his instances of Buxtehude-like figures – Ex. 120 – are also found in the 'later version' and would therefore suggest that it is unreliable to date a Bach work (in any of

Ex. 120

b22

8va bassa

b33

etc

its versions) on the degree to which this or that figure may be reminiscent of Buxtehude.* Other characteristics of the northern praeludium are: the idea of an opening right-hand solo based on an extended figure; the pedal version of it twenty-five bars later ('replacing' the Pachelbel-style dominant pedal point that might be expected); and the kinds of figures in bb1, 23, 30, 33, 36 (and pedal quavers), 50–3. Of more general origin in keyboard toccatas, including those of Pachelbel, Kerll and others, are: the idea of tonic pedal point (from b10) followed by dominant (only briefly, in b25†) and closing with further tonic; and running figures isolated above other pedal points (b33 etc). What may be regarded as characteristic of J. S. Bach are: the regular phraseology of the nine bars of the opening manual solo; the dramatic use of the tonic pedal point of b10 (low beginning, gradual rise in tension); the very careful planning of distinct note-values (semiquavers, triplets, demisemiquavers) to aid the tension, as a climax to which the trilled chord in b23 is used before the tonic pedal point moves away; and the clear division in the piece between the opening pedal points (implied or stated) and the systematic use of an antiphonal figure in the second half. From tradition, therefore, an original piece is moulded. Thus, the trilled figure in b23 may be heard in Buxtehude and elsewhere, but its appearance as the climax of a well-paced tonic

Ex. 121

b28

* Spitta does not make it clear whether the bb22ff and bb33ff he refers to are those of the prelude now numbered 543 or to 543a; whichever it is, however, does not affect the argument.
† From the point of view of structure and logical 'answer', the pedal solo of b25 would best begin in the minor (i.e. with g♮), a detail missed by the various copyists. A performer should also draw attention to the change of direction here by observing the break.

paragraph may not. Other conventions are also used, but pushed farther than would normally be the case. For example, the little broken-chord or *brisé* effect in b29 is unusually complete (Ex. 121) and is not likely to be found so clearcut in any French organ piece. Similarly, the pleasing keyboard idiom of the motif over bb36–46 (a figure obviously derived from the opening bar, now exuberant and in the major: Ex. 122(i)) almost disguises the simple, even commonplace progression of harmonies that underlies it, Ex. 122(ii). These harmonies

Ex. 122

(i)   b36

(ii)

are exactly the kind of thing that countless organists all over Europe improvised on or composed, on any registration from a single Open Diapason to the *plein jeu*, depending on local tradition. In comparison, the closing bars are distinctly more static harmonically, including the last four bars which amount to a tonic pedal point elaborated with a motif typical of the northern composers.

Despite the differences in figuration and harmonic activity between one section and another, the piece is by no means subject to illogical caprice and may rather reflect the composer's interest in integrating different traditional approaches to preludes. A dangerous moment is the return to the tonic halfway through (b31), but a simple 'countersubject' in the left hand – the only such figure in the movement – sustains motion and disappears as a new figure strikes up in the next bar. Such a bar-by-bar technique must be accounted 'northern', as perhaps should such details of the writing as the little obsessive g♯ (bb10–14) and c♯ (16–20) slipped into the broken figures of the tonic pedal point. These dissonances have the effect of chromatic acciaccaturas and help towards what must be the most striking originality of the prelude as a whole, i.e. using a tonic pedal point for gradual and dramatic build-up, then answering it by the dominant.

Fugue

The subject comprises a head motif (b1) and a lengthy sequential tail (bb2–5); the general impression is of a series of broken chords producing a figure convenient for organ pedals but usually so played as to confuse the ear about the beat:* Ex. 123(i). Inventive use of this

* It may be some such confusion that led to the garbled extract in Schumann's *NZfM* xx (1844), p121 – Ex. 123(ii) – although the point of the brief article was to survey disagreements, already current in 1844, about tempos in J. S. Bach.

Ex. 123
(i) b2   **(ii)**

figure is in fact not typical of the fugue. The codetta (bb11–14) already allows a drop in tension, and the episodes (bb56, 66 etc) rarely rise above a certain level of melodiousness against which the fugue subject itself is bound to be conspicuous.

The form of the movement can be expressed as:

1–30	exposition, in regular four parts, of a subject 4½ bars long; consistent countersubject; two codettas
31–50	episode 'extending' the exposition without a break; pedal in sequence, otherwise new material; tonic entry (after hemiola cadence), head motif in stretto
51–61	after further hemiola cadence, entry in dominant (subject head hidden); episode based on a further circle-of-fifths sequence to:
61–95	relative major entry *en taille*; episode; answer in its dominant; episode (all episodes based on circle of fifths)
95–125	four-part entries (tonic stretto 95/96, dominant stretto 113/115 after hemiola cadence, tonic 131), each followed by circle-of-fifths sequential episode on derived material and incipient pedal points (101, 126)
135–51	pedal point finally picked up and developed with pedal solo and quasi-cadenza manual figures

In general, the fugue is long-phrased, 'tight' neither in its counterpoint nor in its succession of entries, which in each case appear after a somewhat drawn-out episode. The technique of 'quasi-delayed entries' is as effective as it is unusual, since at each of its entries the subject heightens the sense of melody.

Like the opening solo of the prelude, the final manual solo of the fugue is not at all free in the manner traditional in northern toccatas but is so phrased (two sets of five half-bar phrases, the second set in sequence to the first) as to lead without a break into the final perfect cadence, itself a figure associated with finality (e.g. Toccata BWV 540.i). This momentum also characterizes the pedal solo (again as in BWV 540). 'Antique' features of the fugue centre on the sheer profusion of circle-of-fifths sequences, sometimes rising (e.g. b65) but usually falling, like that in the fugue subject itself. Other details may also be considered characteristic of an early period in the composer's development, such as the array of Neapolitan sixths (bb85, 111, 134) which, like the *brisé* figures of b51 and elsewhere, may suggest a close relationship with the prelude (Neapolitan sixth in the prelude b43). Such harmonic turns as the diminished sevenths in sequence (bb146–50) were not only highly inventive at the period, like the penultimate acciaccatura chord* Ex. 124(i), but have particular point in view of the predictable

* Richer than the harpsichord figure Ex. 124(ii) in the D minor Concerto BWV 1052.i b166.

Ex. 124

(i)

b150

(ii)

BWV 1052.i b166

sequences earlier in the fugue. As in the C major Fugue BWV 564, there is a contrast between the simplistic figures and the brief moments of complexity for the player (bb 26–7 etc).

In contrast to such condensed fugues as BWV 539 and 547, the chief characteristic of this A minor Fugue is its fluency, springing from a sequential subject whose lively figures still produce only two different harmonies per bar – hence the significance of the hemiolas early on in the fugue and of the 'cadenzas' towards the end. The $^6/_8$ metre itself gives a foil to the careful repertory of note-values in the prelude (see above):

> *prelude*: semiquavers, triplets, demisemiquavers
> *fugue*: $^6/_8$ quavers, semiquavers, demisemiquavers and sextolets*

Most of the semiquaver groups of the fugue can be traced to its subject; and considering the first codetta, the fugue remains surprisingly empty of scale figures until the last episode. The singable nature of the subject sustains the fugue as a whole, inspiring countersubjects to the last moment (bb132–4) and justifying the cumulative episodes (e.g. bb83–95). Perhaps the ultimate inspiration had been the 'motoric' subjects and their working at the hands of Reincken, Buttstedt, Heidorn and others, in which case such sequences as bb28–33 were highly original in their complexity. At times the fugue almost looks like an essay in the art of writing sequences and, just as important, in how to close them and lead off into a new entry. What they finally lead off into is a pair of pedal and manual solos, themselves sequential like other solos (e.g. in the C major Toccata BWV 564) but obviously breaking the pattern of the previous sequences and forming a climax to both prelude and fugue.

543a

Prelude and Fugue in A minor

No Autograph MS; copies in P 803 (1st half of 18th century, autograph 'corrections' in e.g. bb110–12 of fugue), P 288 (probably J. P. Kellner) and LM 4839g.

Two staves; title, 'Praeludium cum Fuga ex A♭ pedaliter'.

---

* It is difficult to justify the view that the demisemiquaver sextolets at the end of the fugue should or could be played half as fast as they are written and therefore represent a 'written-out rallentando' (Emery *MT* 1967 pp32–4, reiterated in *Bach-Studien*, ed. R. Eller and H.-J. Schulze, Leipzig 1975, pp109–11). Would this not result in a wrench to the motion, and weaken the natural rallentando of the penultimate bar?

The fugue being the same in BWV 543 and 543a, the differences between the two preludes in *NBA* IV/5 and IV/6 are as follows;

BWV 543.i		BWV 543a.i	
1–9		1–6	similar idea of broken chords descending chromatically first in rh and then lh, but the chromatic descent in 543a more contracted; in 543, lh version inverts the rh figure
10–21	=	7–12	identical, but 543a appears to be notated twice too fast (demisemiquavers)
22–5	=	13–16	identical, except that 543a distributes the runs between the two hands
26–8	=	17–18	pedal of 543a again uses a shorter form of broken-chord figure
29–53	=	19–43	almost identical

The semiquaver/demisemiquaver question has led to such bizarre conjectures as that the composer intended a distinction between the two versions, thinking 'in the later version...on a larger scale' and preserving 'a calmer mood', and that the demisemiquavers 'make sense' as they stand and could be a means of inviting the player to 'feel free to improvise and elaborate the score' (Beechey *MT* 1973 p832). The crucial differences between the versions – bb1–9, 26–8 (first and fourth sections above) – are generally assumed to suggest that BWV 543a is the 'earlier version' (*NBA* IV/6), but in fact the opening figure as it appears in BWV 543 is more conventional in harmonic implication, i.e. a series of prepared and resolved sevenths – Ex. 125 – despite the

Ex. 125

fact that the lower of the two parts is delayed each time. Nevertheless, the extended and more developed triplets that follow in b4 of BWV 543 look like the result of revision, as does the altered first figure when it passes to the left hand. That no further revision seems to be in question perhaps indicates how classical is the logic behind the harmonic progressions of the second half of the prelude.

544

Prelude and Fugue in B minor

Autograph MS (now in private possession); copies in P 891 (owned by J. P. Kellner), Am.B. 60 (Berlin copyist, after 1754), LM 4720 (J. P. Kellner's hand in the fugue; dated '1740'), other 18th-century sources (Am.B. 54 copy of Am.B. 60, P 276, P 290), and later-18th- and early-19th-century sources (LM 4839i, P 560, Lpz MB MS 1, 17 Wechmar?, Lpz Poel 24 Weigand c1817, BB 30380, P 922 Grasnick, Lpz

MB III.8.21 Dröbs, P 925 arrangement for four hands dated 1832, P 837), some presumably from Kittel sources.

Two staves, pedal in red ink (Autograph MS); title in Autograph MS 'Praeludium pro Organo cum pedal obligato', in Lpz Poel 24 'Praeludium et Fuga...pro Organo pleno cum Pedale oblig.'.

The fair copy Autograph MS has a watermark dated to 1727, and its handwriting must be before 1740; however, it is doubtful whether it is correct to assume that the copy was made from a late Weimar 'sketch', as has been suggested (Emery 1966). The similarity between the structures of the preludes in B minor, C minor and E minor (BWV 544, 546, 548) suggests that they should be roughly contemporary, while the mature pedal-point harmonies (e.g. final bars) might also be thought to belong to the Leipzig years. In general, the prelude is of a highly original and individual melodic type, perhaps ultimately aria-like but in texture and counterpoint unique to the variety of newer organ styles typical of those years. The 'chromatic sequences' have elsewhere been compared with the first Kyrie of the B minor Mass, and the 'melismatic nature' with 'Erbarme dich' in the *St Matthew Passion* (Keller 1948 p121); however, whether such views can be used as more than an expression of admiration for the work or as attempts to put its unique character into context is as doubtful as other attempts to date it. That it does have a unique character is suggested by the key alone.* Yet Mattheson's description of the *Affekt* of B minor as 'unlustig und melancholisch' ('listless and melancholy') is little more than suggestive (Mattheson 1713 pp250–1), while Schubart's label 'the key of Patience' (1806, quoted by Frotscher 1935 p899) betrays an aesthetic yet more removed from BWV 544. Spitta hears the fugue as 'quiet and melancholy', the prelude as striking a 'deeply elegaic note not heard so intensively anywhere else in Bach's organ works' (Spitta II pp689–90). But whatever terms are used in the discussion of the work, its stylistic confidence should not be forgotten. The very opening bar is startlingly unlike other organ preludes (even BWV 546 and 548 have a family likeness between them), and the bold effects dependent on appoggiatura harmonies are created with immense skill and inventiveness. Since the tone of BWV 544 conforms closely to what musical aesthetics since J. S. Bach have considered to be *affecting*, it would generally be considered a more powerful work than the D minor Toccata BWV 538. Yet the two works are equally skilful – and even perhaps contemporary – in the creative use of their respective forms, themes, motifs, harmonies and texture. Each could be considered a fully realized *exemplum* of a certain musical form and a certain keyboard style.

* Keller's attempt to relate it to the 'Affettuoso' B minor slow movement of the Fifth Brandenburg Concerto is understandable.

Prelude

The concerto or ritornello shape of the prelude can be expressed as:

A 1–17 two-part imitation settling on to a tonic pedal point (answered eight bars later by dominant pedal point)

B 17–23 fugal exposition of a new theme

A 23–43 scale idea from *A* picked up, linked to a return of *A* in dominant (27–33 = 1–7); further sequences before settling on to second pedal point (40–2 = 14–16)

B 43–9 fugal exposition of *B* theme (43–8 = 17–22)

A 50–73 complex section, with old and new material: 50–6 sequential motifs from A_1 (50–2 = 11–13) now in relative major
56–60 new theme (appoggiaturas) against earlier scales
61–4 *A* theme (63–4 = 6–7)
65–8 beginning as b54
69–73 simple sequence from new appoggiatura theme of b56; scales to:

B 73–8 imitative exposition of *B* theme *rectus* and *inversus* (77–8 = 49–50)

A 78–85 return to figures from *A*, extended (79–80 = 38–9; 82–5 = 40–3 = 14–17; 81 = new)

However, the limbs of the movement are not so clearly defined as they are in BWV 542 or 552. It is possible to see the return of *A* not at b23 but at b27 (rh first quaver, lh second quaver), in which case there is no clear return from the *Positiv* manual to the *Hauptwerk*; but that remains true either way, for any return to the *Hauptwerk* in b50 is also somewhat abrupt. The question must remain, therefore, whether the limbs of the movement are to be distinguished by change of manual or stops (the latter of which is highly unlikely at the period) or whether – since the *BG* heading 'pro organo pleno' may be inauthentic – a modest *Hauptwerk* chorus be registered and played throughout. The prevailing two- and three-part texture of the episodes would suffice to produce the required contrast with the prevailing four and five parts of the ritornellos, aided by the change in keyboard touch (detached quavers in the episodes). Moreover, the section bb50–73 could itself be interpreted as *A B A B*, in which case the subsidiary *B* sections (i.e. the new themes at b56 and b69) would, in a two-manual interpretation, be played on the *Positiv*. This is not out of the question, since the pedal at these points is strikingly discreet and continuo-like, and such manual-changing would require the same kind of approach as at the other junctures, i.e. a tactful break in continuity. But all such manual-changing today is based on at least two assumptions – that structure should or can be expressed in this way, and that the *pleno* of the organs concerned was so coarse or loud as to require change – neither of which can be established by documentary evidence.

The elusive style of the B minor Prelude depends on several factors. First, the opening bars, though based on the unoriginal idea of invertible counterpoint imitated at the octave/unison (cf. the Two-part Invention in E major BWV 777), explore a somewhat unusual tessitura, more characteristic of Buxtehude openings yet, unlike Buxtehude, involving appoggiatura harmonies on every main beat of the first three bars. Secondly, the harmonic language heralded by such appoggiaturas, suspensions or accented passing-notes is continued further, with the curious result that apart from minor exceptions (the first note of all, or the first beat of b6) every main beat of the whole opening ritornello of seventeen bars has a harmony which depends on one or other of these discord effects. Thus while in theory the pedal-point harmonies of bb14–15 reflect the tradition of pedal-point toccatas (*Orgelpunkttok-katen*), in practice the five parts create a rich, lush harmonic spectrum characteristic of this piece and of little else, including even 'Erbarme dich'. The dotted rhythms are anything but siciliano-like; however springingly played, what they supply is heaviness or emphasis. Similarly, though the lines of such bars as 23ff or 49–50 may look as if they are related to various passages in the Corrente of the E minor Partita for Harpsichord BWV 830, there is nothing courante-like or corrente-like in the tempo, the texture, or even – though this is more difficult to show – the harmonic rhythm of BWV 544.i. The combination of slow compound time, harmonies based on appoggiaturas etc, and exchanges between bleak and warm textures helps to produce the individual effect of the main sections. In comparison, the episodes are mostly without the dotted rhythms, without harmonies based on appoggiaturas etc, and more consistent in texture; on the other hand, their phrase-structure is more cut up, being based largely on units of one bar's length rather than the two or more bars of the ritornello sections. Thus ritornellos and episodes are in all details reciprocal complements, in which the new themes at b56 and b69 are a paper compromise, having the appoggiaturas from one and the phraseology from the other.

The figuration itself is to some extent derived from a set of patterns which appear in the earlier bars of each main theme: Ex. 126. All of

Ex. 126

them, except *a*, which produces lines based on it, are re-worked on most occasions. From the idea *b*, for instance, all the scale lines of the movement could be claimed to grow (both ascending and latterly descending), but the point of the bar at which they begin or at which they curl back on themselves varies. The figure *a* is probably the subtlest from the composer's viewpoint, but to the listener *b*, *c* and *d* are the most striking.

Stylistic details have their own points of interest. Thus the fugal theme *B* can produce both a pretty sequence (bb46–7) and the kind of *inversus* idea (bb74, 76) that smacks more of the didactic: the deliberate solving of a compositional problem, in this case perhaps contemporary with the *inversus* working of the fugue subject BWV 547. The cadence which prepares the new theme of b56 (which appears twice in that bar, the second time decorated) is similar to others elsewhere (e.g. the Loure from the G major French Suite) and is most fitting to introduce the new woodwind-like theme, which itself one can imagine as having occurred to the composer on the spur of the moment and which he is careful to rein in over the following bars. Both the scale figures that come so easily to hand in bb58–9 or 69–70 anticipate or are reminiscent of the keyboard style of the E minor Prelude BWV 548, whose opening bars are most curiously hinted at in b61 – a detail that would be more often observed if that bar were not so well integrated within the chromatic web. 'Integrating within a chromatic web' is well managed in this movement, so that bb59–61 seem to be approached and quitted more smoothly than are the two bars preparing the final imitative episode (bb71–2) which have the effect of breaking the sequence of the previous bars and holding up the overall move back to B minor, in a relatively commonplace texture that is too patently setting the scene for the *inversus* imitation that follows. In comparison, the extra bar slipped in between b80 and b82 is masterly, extending the falling chromatic harmonies up to a minor ninth and forming the harmonic climax of the movement. It could be thought that the section bb71–8 has to be there to satisfy the requirements of superimposed form, whereas the five-part harmonies of b81 (particularly the D major chord) are inspired.

Fugue

In its restrained line and simplistic harmony, the fugue contrasts strongly with the prelude, as too the Fugue in G minor BWV 542.ii contrasts with its prelude, the G minor Fantasia. But the scale-like patterns of this B minor Fugue – lines move predominantly by step throughout – seem to give it a maturer harmonic spectrum than the G minor Fugue; perhaps the plain quavers themselves suggest a driving subject of the kind known to such later-seventeenth-century composers as Heidorn, or remind players of another B minor movement (cf. bass line of Prelude 24, *The 48* Bk I). On the other hand, its overall form as a tripartite fugue (i.e. with relaxed episode in the middle) is closer to that of the G major Fugue BWV 541. The shape of BWV 544.ii can be expressed as follows:

1–11   exposition (pedal third, not last, to enter – cf. BWV 541); consistent countersubject

12–17   episode derived from countersubject; further entries in tonic and subdominant, followed by further short episode derived from subject

18–23   entry in relative, answered in its dominant, followed by short episode derived from subject and countersubject

24–37 modulatory entries in dominant, dominant (b28 with new countersubject), tonic and subdominant, interspersed with short episodes (bb32ff from subject and second countersubject)

37–49 episode derived from second countersubject (b29), followed by
further modulatory entries in supertonic and dominant; episode
from subject

49–59 quasi-entry in relative, followed by episode derived from subject

59–67 tonic entry with two countersubjects (top one new), answered in
dominant; followed by episode derived from subject and
countersubjects

68–78 modulatory entry in supertonic, with the 'new' (third) countersubject; episode to subdominant entry, followed by episode (cf.
b32)

79–84 chain of three modulatory entries in pedal, accompanied by lines
derived from countersubjects

85–8 final entry with two countersubjects

A good deal of art has gone to the make-up of this fugue, an art
springing from two particular conceptions: the creating of successive
countersubjects, and the working of the contrapuntal lines in terms of
a very few basic figures. It is the latter conception in particular that
produces the striking smoothness of the counterpoint.

That the subject itself contains classical four-note *figurae* is clear
from its essential similarity to (e.g.) the countersubject of the fugue on
'Jesus Christus, unser Heiland' BWV 689 (from b3); these four-note
figures naturally work well in diminution and go towards the making
of the semiquaver lines that run through the fugue as a whole: Ex. 127.

Ex. 127

These in turn are very much within the same family of motifs as *a* and
b of the prelude (see above, Ex. 126). The *ambitus* of this apparently
neutral fugue subject accords with phrases in the prelude (compare the
soprano part in the penultimate bar of the prelude with the opening bars
of the fugue) not because of conscious quotation but because each is
founded on scale-like or in-turning *figurae*. But the composer seems to
have taken trouble to produce countersubjects which indeed are not
founded on these *figurae*: the countersubjects heard for the first time
in b3, b28 and b59 respectively counter this figuration quite deliberately,
producing angular lines (first countersubject), non-stop semiquaver
scales (second) or up-beat motifs (third). The second of these is most

like the prevailing scale-like line, and it is significant that for the
ensuing episode the composer uses not the semiquaver scale figure but
the broken-chord tail (second half b29). Similarly, the final episode at
bb73–7 concentrates on broken figures before the final entries, with their
smooth lines, are heard.

The movement thus becomes an extremely ingenious working of, and
at times reaction to, a basic figure. Why did the composer reject (as
he must surely have rejected) the idea of stretto, either of the quaver
subject or of its diminution? At times, he approaches stretto closely
– Ex. 128 – which is not surprising in view of the 'basic' quality of the

Ex. 128

figures concerned. Perhaps for the final stretch from b79 onwards
stretto would have been too commonplace; perhaps it was reserved for
other contexts (e.g. the chorale BWV 689, already referred to), or for
fugues specializing in contrapuntal techniques (e.g. BWV 547). In BWV
544 the interest seems rather to have been in the *figurae*: the subtle
contrast that can be achieved between a broken and an unbroken
semiquaver figure, the variety that can be achieved within a keen
economy of means (e.g. different results from·the same broken motif
in bb24, 41, 50, 72), and the many fleeting countersubjects that can arise
with such a subject. Despite such theorizing, however, it would be a
mistake to see the exploring of *figurae* as doctrinaire or all-absorbing
in BWV 544.ii; it is far less so than in the chorales of *Clavierübung III*.
Subject and two countersubjects can be heard in b59 and b83, but there
is no attempt to use the second countersubject in such a *summa
contrapuncti*, any more than there are 'statutory' strettos before the
coda. Constant re-harmonization of the fugue subject leads to happy
results (e.g. the sixths of bb71–2), while on the contrary detailed
combination of countersubject motifs (e.g. from the first and third
countersubjects in b63) leads to relatively colourless moments, as do
such obvious traditional elements as the invertible sequences in bb32–4
or 44–7. It is easy for a performer to miss the special flavour of the
fugue even at the potentially intense moment around b50, since there
is nothing extravagant about the melody or lines – e.g., b51 has a brief,

simple sequence heard elsewhere (BWV 542.ii). A not dissimilar figure is used in the B minor Fugue, *The 48* Bk I, apparently for periodic relaxation: 'quiet' episodes, curiously similar to passages in Domenico Scarlatti's D minor Fugue (Sonata K417) and even hinted at in BWV 542.ii. It could be that BWV 544.ii becomes more obsessed with its figures or motifs as it proceeds, dropping some of those heard early on (e.g. pedal b14) and relying on others, so that (e.g.) b65 or b86 is a mass of allusion to the motifs *x*, *y* or *z*, often in diminution. Hence, perhaps, the caprice that keeps back the dominant entry in b28 from appearing in b27 where it has been prepared: the tenor delays the entry with a fragment of inversion. At the same time, that half-bar delay could suggest that the entry appears on a different manual, returning to the original manual in b59 (lh only; rh two bars later?); but on the analogy of the tripartite BWV 541.ii, where if there is any such return it is less simple, such manual-changing was probably not expected. More to the point is the density of four parts in the final stages of the fugue, giving its own sense of balanced climax.

545

Prelude and Fugue in C major

Two-movement version

Clauss MS once thought to be Autograph fair copy (*BG* 15 p. xxx), now lost; copies known to Kittel circle (P 658 Kittel, Lpz MB III . 8 . 21 Dröbs, LM 4839 Ringk); copies of variant text in sources of mid or later 18th century (P 276, P 290, Am.B. 60 and Am.B. 54, P 602) and still later (P 916, P 816 and P 521 fugue only, P 559, P 837).

Three-movement version

Moscheles MS once thought to be Autograph (*BG* 15 p. xxx) but copied c 1727/31 by 'Anon 18' (i.e. J. C. Vogler: see Schulze *BJ* 1978 p31), now in Stockholm, Stiftelsen Musikkulturens Främjande; other copies LM 4718 (J. G. Walther), P 286 (J. P. Kellner) also P 282 (c1800).

Two staves (prelude and fugues; pedal part in red ink in Am.B. 60); title in Clauss MS 'Praeludium pro Organo cum Pedale obligato' (as in a 1785 catalogue, *Dok* III p273), in Moscheles MS 'Praeludium in Organo pleno, pedaliter', and in Am.B. 60 'Preludio e Fuga per L'Organo pieno'.

It is not known whether the complex history and variant texts of the C major Prelude and Fugue are as exceptional as they now seem, or whether accidents of extant source material make them appear so. Four clear conceptions of the work exist: a shortened prelude form with fugue (BWV 545a); a 'later' and longer version of the prelude with fugue (BWV 545 two-movement version); the same separated by a trio movement (BWV 529.ii, placed before the fugue by Vogler but after the fugue by Walther); and the B flat version of the 'early' prelude, followed by an arrangement of a gamba-sonata movement (BWV 1029.iii) and then the fugue, the three movements separated by two short sections (BWV 545b). The four conceptions may be shown as follows:

(i)	(ii)	(iii)	(iv)
BWV 545a.i	BWV 545.i	BWV 545.i	BWV 545.i
545.ii	545.ii	529.ii	1029.iii
		545.ii	545.ii

The B flat version may have been made in order to avoid d''' in the prelude and trio movements, though this made impossible the final low pedal entry; any 'crude' detail arising from the transposition would not disprove its authenticity (Emery 1959 p. vi note). The inclusion, in extant sources made by copyists, of two different slow middle movements in trio form (BWV 545 three-movement version, and BWV 545b) may or may not reflect the composer's own wish or wishes, but each was made probably because the particular prelude is so brief.* The trio movement BWV 529.ii appears in an 'early' form (Emery 1957 p104), which may suggest that Walther or Vogler had authority for adding it, though the contrary could also be proposed. There would seem less reason to doubt the authorship of the 'extra' bars of the prelude in its 'later' form BWV 545.i, since their musical sense is clear: they give a three-bar framework to the movement, which is *perhaps* a sign that the composer revised it in c1730 when he can be assumed to have preferred the closed form that such a little prologue and epilogue would provide (Kloppers 1966 p222). The date would agree with the watermark noted by Spitta in one or other of the so-called 'Autograph MSS' (1723–35: Spitta II p689 and Emery 1959 p. vi note).

A possible order of composition for the work is as follows (Emery 1959):† (A) BWV 545a, as published in *NBA* IV/6; (B) BWV 545b (this has three further bars at the close of the prelude referring back to the opening bars of BWV 545a, which may suggest that BWV 545a was itself an abridgement); (C) BWV 545 three-movement version, as published in *NBA* IV/5 (involving the replacement of the final bars of BWV 545b.i by a new coda, also used as a preface, and the replacement of BWV 1029.iii by BWV 529.ii); (D) BWV 545 two-movement version, 'variant text' (slight variant readings in both prelude and fugue); (E) BWV 545 two-movement version, as in *BG* 15. Three questions still open to speculation are: What is the original form of the prelude (is it with the coda as known in BWV 545b.i?); is BWV 545b authentic; and what is the date of its source if it had one? For example, the term 'replacement' under C above may give BWV 545b an authority that it cannot be shown to deserve. See also BWV 545a and 545b.

* This may also have been the case with the G major Prelude and Fugue BWV 541, where the added movement was a fast trio.

† Not all of Emery's hypotheses are included in this summary, nor do all of those here concur with his.

Prelude

The movement retains the general framework of a pedal-point prelude:

tonic	1–3	suspensions, broken chords above pedal point
	4–7	main motif *a* (see Ex. 129)
interlude	7–11	four-part counterpoint using *a*
dominant	12–16	motif *a* above pedal point
interlude	16–22	as before (16–19 = 7–9 in dominant)
dominant	22–6	motif *a* above dominant pedal point, then below tonic pedal point; followed by cadence bar
tonic	28–31	similar to 1–3

The miniature quasi-*da-capo* form is unique and could well be regarded as a sign of mature revision, though in practice it merely makes clearer the most traditional element of the movement, i.e. its tonic–dominant–tonic pedal-point structure. The idea of a framework is created by more than the prologue–epilogue bars. For example, the number of parts in the composition is five or more at the beginning and close, while at b7 and b23 there are four, at b13 and b20 three, and at b16 (the centre) four. A pattern is thus created – 5–4–3–4–3–4–5 – though it is not exploited to any doctrinaire degree. Particularly instructive is that the framework also has no doctrinaire symmetry (e.g., it does not end as it began on top c′′′). The effect and even the cause of the three added prefatory bars of BWV 545.i is to show the top and bottom notes of the organ – while manual begins on top c′′′, pedal falls to bottom C, and the whole compass is thus exposed from the first moment. Indeed, beginning an organ work on the top note of the keyboard may well be unique, although the means themselves are traditional (alternate-foot pedalling for the bass line, sustained manual parts, etc).

Motif *a*, with which BWV 545a and 545b begin, may well have been for J. S. Bach a kind of standard C major prelude motif, judging by a further instance shown in Ex. 129. In both cases the prime motif is

Ex. 129

BWV 545.i b4

Das Wohltemperirte Clavier, II
C major Prelude BWV 870.i b32

15ma bassa⌐ _ _ _ _ _ _ _ _ _ _ ⌐   8va bassa⌐ _ _ _ _ _ _ _ _ _ _ ⌐

extracted and worked into a contrapuntal texture, in the course of which it often changes shape but does not lose its identity: Ex. 130. The Prelude BWV 870.i (*The 48* Bk II) itself exists in several versions and, like BWV 545.i, soon introduces a B♭ over the opening pedal point and an A♭ diminished seventh at the closing cadence. Indeed, BWV 870 has a more extensive development of motif than BWV 545, which in keeping with its *Orgelpunkttokkata* conception has a somewhat simpler

Ex. 130

BWV 545.i
b10

b24

BWV 870.i
b30

8va bassa_ _ _

technique. Perhaps, too, the splendidly expansive manual writing of both prelude and fugue BWV 545 can be understood as having some kind of association with C major – Ex. 131. Such 'C major angularity' may well be found elsewhere and should not be overstressed; but, equally, the resemblance of *x* in Ex. 131 to the opening pedal line of the prelude should not be missed.

Ex. 131

BWV 545.i   b5   Fischer, *Blumenstrauss*, Praeludium 5

BWV 545.ii   b35

The highly idiomatic organ writing of BWV 545.i contrasts particularly well with highly idiomatic harpsichord writing of BWV 870.i. Comparison shows in BWV 545.i a much more open texture, a somewhat simpler use of motif, and a natural tendency to throw out fine pedal lines, whether strong sequential ideas (bb7, 17), pedal points, or simple basso-continuo roles (bb10, 20). Much of the prelude is based on the unit of the single bar, but at least two passages break from this and form longer phrases (bb14–16, 24–6). Such a bar as 21 is highly susceptible to sequential treatment, and perhaps it was only a wish for structural variety that prevented it: from the second half of b18 to the 'epilogue' there is a touch of caprice, a neglect of the obvious. The harmony of the main motif is also worked with great variety and conviction. It is probably no accident that when the first syncopated, suspended pedal phrase, which will colour later harmonizations of the main motif, makes its first appearance against *a* (b7), *a* is at the same pitch as it was in b4 (i.e. beginning on g'); but the change from f' to f#' in b7 pushes it most inventively in other directions and beyond the point reached by any other composer working in the 'standard C major prelude' idiom.

Fugue

The shape may be expressed:

1–19   exposition (pedal third, not last, voice to enter); no consistent countersubject

19–51   series of dominant (28, 35, 45) and tonic (41) entries prefaced, interspersed and followed by episodes derived in part from the subject; countersubject, b45

52–72   entries in relative and dominant of relative, spaced out with episodes; sudden turn in b72 to:

73–99   entries in dominant, tonic, subdominant and supertonic spaced out with shorter derived episodes; longer episode before:

100–11   final tonic entries, b100 in bass, b106 above pedal point; cadence previously anticipated (b108, see bb81, 18)

The composer of the *Orgelbüchlein* and *Clavierübung III* will have been aware of the motivic unity offered by the opening of the subject (*caput*), whose rising tetrachord proves so useful in different guises later on in the fugue – Ex. 132. Despite the vigour of the movement, therefore,

Ex. 132

and in addition to an inventive opportunism that creates new idiomatic sequences on all possible occasions (e.g. bars from 19, 31, 49, 65, 77, 96 – that before the final entry is the most regular), and even despite the fertile broken chords colouring the manual writing, the fugue is also engaged in a certain amount of playing with motifs. Passages built on the tetrachord will be found more or less in alternation with passages built on the broken chords or arpeggios. It can be assumed that Ex. 133 is therefore no coincidence; nor is it by accident that the entry

Ex. 133

at b35 is anticipated in the alto of the previous bar, as if in another key. Some not dissimilar points could be made about the B minor Fugue BWV 544, which however is obviously less robust in style than BWV 545.

But despite even the similarity that exists in theory between the subjects of BWV 544.ii and 545.ii – narrow compass, scale-like line –

the entries in the latter have a quite different character. The simplistic final episode certainly prepares the final tonic entries; but otherwise entries have tended to slip in during the working-out of a sequence or episode, as if they were part of the background (see bb28, 35, 52, 79, 84) – which is not so in BWV 544. Similarly, the ends of entries pass each time into an extended discussion of what the other voices were already concerned with, which is only sometimes true in BWV 544. Often the subject is altered at its close in order to enable the other voices to develop in their own way (e.g. bb31, 103). A further distinction is that while BWV 544 has three returning countersubjects, BWV 545 has at most only one, being more concerned with changing harmonies and counterpoints. Thus any of the lines that continue to accompany the subject – e.g. the alto in b73, the bass in b79, the soprano in b62 and b100 – could have been regular countersubjects. In this respect it is important that although the initial countersubject of b5 re-appears only once in the whole fugue (b45), it chief distinguishing features – contrary motion, suspensions/syncopations – colour the counterpoint throughout. Thus, while in the texture of the first episode the quaver patterns can be seen to derive from the subject – Ex. 134 – the minim

Ex. 134
b21

syncopations give equal if not greater drive to the passage. By way of contrast, the sequences without syncopation add strong rhythmic punctuation (bb56, 65), and the figures produced give continuity and unity – compare the tenor of b58 of the fugue with the pedal of b1 of the prelude. As so often with the mature Bach, it is difficult to say whether the harmony produces good contrapuntal lines or vice versa (e.g. the augmented chord in the relative-minor entry of b53); even the unusual block harmonies of the final entry are cantabile in each part. Apparently independent lines are naturally created against subject entries (e.g. the tenor line against the final soprano entry – compare a similar situation in the G minor Fugue BWV 542 bb43–4), and the quaver patterns work ceaselessly to create the counterpoint.

545a   Prelude and Fugue in C major

No Autograph MS; copies in sources of 2nd half of 18th century (P 290, Lpz Poel 12, the latter once owned by Forkel – hence 545a not 545 quoted in his thematic index of 1802?).

Two staves; title in Lpz Poel 12 'Praeludium et Fuga'.

The chief differences between BWV 545a and 545 (according to the editions in *NBA* IV/6 and IV/5) are as follows:

BWV 545.i	BWV 545a.i	
1–3	—	
4	1	(two further manual parts in 545)
5–26	2–23	
27	24	(different in detail; dominant pedal point in 545a)
—	25	
28–31	—	

The fugue differs only in minor variant readings, e.g. no semiquavers in bb96–8.

Whether BWV 545a.i is an abridgement of an earlier or original version in which there was a coda requiring d''' and referring back to the opening bars (i.e. as now known in the transposed version BWV 545b) is a question that has been asked before (Emery 1959 pp. v, vii) but still not answered. It is a curious coincidence that in addition to BWV 545a the prelude is known in versions with two different codas, one of which is also found as a preface to the same prelude in most extant copies. In comparison with the others, BWV 545a.i closes somewhat abruptly, thus suggesting either that the composer later felt the need for a coda (both examples of which restore a tonic pedal point, thus giving a tonic–dominant–tonic shape to the whole) or that the composer, or one copyist or more, took out the 'first' coda to avoid d'''. There may be other reasons why BWV 545a is shorter: the sources were poor, the revision was not completed, etc. As it stands, however, BWV 545a opens with allusive C major prelude material to which attention was drawn above (see BWV 545.i) and with which Bk II of *The 48* begins.

545b

Prelude, Trio and Fugue in B flat major

No Autograph MS; source, London RCM MS 814 (copied by B. Cooke Sen. 1734–93 and B. Cooke Jun. 1761–72).

Three staves; headings 'Prelud[i]um pro: Organo Pedaliter', 'Adagio', 'Trio a 2 Clav: e Pedal', 'tutti', 'Fuga pro Organo. Pedaliter'.

The chief differences between BWV 545b and BWV 545 (as in *NBA* IV/5) are as follows:

key, with the many octave displacements this entails
five movements

prelude:	BWV 545.i		BWV 545b.i	
	1–3		—	
	4	=	1	with two further manual parts in 545
	5–27	=	2–24	
	—		25–8	coda referring to opening bars
	28–31		—	

Chronological inferences based on the compass – e.g., that the transposed version avoiding d''' was necessary for the Weimar organ, that BWV 545a dated from the Mühlhausen years, etc – are too speculative to show the history or chronology of the work. For the Trio used as the middle movement, see BWV 1029.iii; it is a further curious coincidence that the trios associated with BWV 541 and 545b are both fast movements and not, as might be expected, slow. The Adagio and Tutti movements, though brief, are evidence of their composer's knowledge of styles (Adagio built on dotted figure, Tutti on recitative line); both are the work of J. F. Kleinknecht, the first from a Prelude, Toccata and Fugue in B flat (Ansbach Schlossbibliothek MS), the second 'simply a rather primitive transcription' of bb34–8 from the second movement of a Violin Sonata in G major (J. S. Schwarzschild *MR* 1959 p184). On the grounds that BWV 545b contains such 'improvements' to the bass line of BWV 545a as Ex. 135, it is possible to claim

Ex. 135

BWV 545a.i
b4

BWV 545b.i (transposed from B♭ major)

that 'the transposed text contains corrections that are not likely to have been made by anyone else', and that it can therefore be 'best ascribed to Bach' (Emery 1959 p. v). But this does not mean that J. S. Bach either transposed it or authorized its transposition by a copyist, since BWV 545b could have been made by a copyist from some (amended?) version of BWV 545a. Either way, BWV 545b provides an unusual glimpse of the ways in which copyists, or the copyists of copyists, dealt with music from several ultimate sources very likely not known to themselves. In this instance, it is a question of an organ prelude and fugue and an instrumental trio sonata by one composer, an organ work and a violin sonata by another. Perhaps it is 'obvious that the Kleinknecht MS of the Bach...was Cooke's principal source; or at least Cooke must have copied from a MS based, in turn, on Kleinknecht's' (Schwarzschild *op cit*). Did Cooke's master Pepusch (1667–1752) possess works by Bach and/or Kleinknecht and give them to Cooke's predecessor Robinson (to whom Cooke attributed the work)? Did Kleinknecht's brother Johann Wolfgang (1715–86), who worked in Eisenach, serve as some kind of link? Both J. W. and J. F. Kleinknecht published chamber music in London (1774 and c1760 respectively). Did Cooke give his young son copying experience by using a completed source already made by Robinson from miscellaneous German MSS? These and similar explanations are all plausible; some direct German link is certainly implied by the headings of the first, third and fifth movements, which could be the wording of Bach himself.

---

546   Prelude and Fugue in C minor

No Autograph MS; copies in P 286 (J. P. Kellner), P 320 (Kittel), Am.B. 60 (Berlin copyist after 1754) and other good 18th-century sources (P 276, P 290, Am.B. 54, P 1104 fugue only plus Fantasia BWV 562.i) and later sources (Brussels II.3915, LM 4839e, P 596, P 557 Grasnick, P 837, P 519 fugue plus BWV 562.i, Lpz MB III.8.22, Lpz Go.S.26, P 925 an arrangement for four hands dated 1832), some of which sources dependent on Kittel.

Two staves; title in P 286 'Praeludium con Fuga ex C mol. pro Organo cum Pedale obligato'.

Two problems concerning BWV 546 as it is now known are: Do the movements belong together? and Were the movements composed at the same period? The discrepancy commonly felt between the gigantic, powerful prelude and the plainer fugue has suggested to some that the fugue was written earlier, perhaps with another prelude, such as the Fantasia BWV 562.i (Griepenkerl in Peters IV 1845). The present prelude, 'completed in Leipzig', is in 'the form of the first movement of a concerto', and 'is so powerful that it almost overwhelms the Fugue' ('fast zu Boden drückt', Spitta II pp687–8). Or, to put it another way, of the four fugues BWV 534.ii, 537.ii, 540.ii and 546.ii – which 'have so much in common, both intrinsically and externally', as to suggest that they 'originated at the same time' – two (BWV 540.ii and 546.ii) later received other preludes (the present BWV 540.i and 546.i), whose 'gigantic construction stands in all too great a contrast to the fugues' (Spitta I p581). Though this argument has been adopted in various guises and degrees by many commentators ever since, it is weakened by two factors: there is no evidence that BWV 562.i was composed earlier than 546.i or that it was the original prelude to 546.ii;* and it was not uncommon for the composer to couple a prelude and fugue whose form and technique are totally different and therefore complementary. On the first point, the appearance of the fugue alone in a nineteenth-century copy is hardly conclusive; on the second point, it is clear that the concerto-like prelude – a ritornello movement whose tutti is massive and whose solo episodes are fugal – is countered by a fugue with varied elements: a few *alla breve* details, a long middle section developing *figurae*, use of homophony. Similar points may be made about BWV 537 and 540; while the complementary pairing of this C minor prelude and its fugue may be less well matched than the E minor BWV 548, in concept the two cases are similar. It is an anachronism to assume that the fugue must be similar in tension to the prelude and outstrip it by

---

* Rather, BWV 546.ii replaced the unfinished fugue BWV 562.ii in some of the sources for BWV 562.

its close; rather, they couple and contrast two varied forms and techniques. Though this is not conclusive evidence, the close of the fugue BWV 546.ii is similar enough to the close of the prelude – richly scored, climactic, static harmonies on a pedal point unusually long for a fugue – to suggest that the composer consciously paired them, whether before, during or after the composition of the fugue.

Prelude

The ritornello shape of the prelude is of particular interest, since only fragments of the main material A return in the course of the movement before the final reprise. In principle, such highly sophisticated 'sporadic recapitulation' was probably learnt from examples in Vivaldi, in particular the first movement of the A minor Concerto transcribed as BWV 593. But it is possible that such shapes would have evolved without Vivaldi's model, since the idea is not far removed from the composer's treatment of quasi-ritornello form in organ chorales and cantata first movements, i.e. movements in which the chorale lines act as episodes of a sort.

24 bars	A A_1	1–5	homophonic dialogue between hands; tonic pedal point
	A_2	5–13	distinct quaver motifs; then dominant pedal point
	A_3	13–25	several ideas (pedal motif from A_2, subdominant pedal point, Neapolitan sixth, triplets over moving bass, perfect cadence)
24 bars	B	25–49	irregular fugal exposition of new (but derived) figures; followed by episode
48 bars	A A_1	49–53	dominant
	B	53–70	more regular fugal exposition (answer intact, shorter codetta); followed by episode
	A A_2	70–81	original pedal point of b10 now (b75) providing a triplet *figura* for following four-bar episode
	B	82–5	short statement
	A A_3	85–97	as 13–25 in subdominant, upper voices inverted
24 bars	B	97–120	two entries (97, 117) separated by long episode built on sequential developments (including chromatic) of motifs from first codetta (b31)
24 bars	A A_1	120–4	as before, final *tierce de picardie*
	A_2	124–32	
	A_3	132–44	

The prelude thus becomes a particularly clear example of a basic rhetorical form (Kloppers 1966 pp74–5), its *overall A B A* character clearer than that of BWV 538.i or 542.i:

A	*Propositio*	no introduction; main and most striking theme; contains essential features of the movement (dialogue chords, triplets, pedal points, scale-like bass)
B	*Confutatio* and *Confirmatio*	repetition or spinning-out of triplet figures causes the 'high points'; A material restated ('confirmed') in three extracts
A	*Peroratio*	conclusion or exit

Yet a strict interpretation of the movement either according to Vivaldian ritornello form (with its implications for change of manual) or according to conventions of rhetoric does not seem quite to fit the shape. Thus *Peroratio*, defined as a counterpart to the *exordium* or introduction (Kloppers 1966 p64), is not what would normally be understood as the *da capo* section of a piece of music, however complex the middle section had been. Also, it seems open to doubt where the sections begin: Kloppers (*op cit* p220) understands the third *B* section to begin in b78, while Keller (1948 p115) regards the whole passage bb70–96 as one section on the *Hauptwerk*, an idea which confirms the bar-plan of the movement (24–24–48–24–24). In any case, manual-changing over the middle section is too awkward if the player is to preserve continuity.

The material and motifs of the prelude are unusually colourful. The dialogue chords Ex. 136 may be likened to those in the coda of the D

Ex. 136

minor Fugue BWV 538 but are more in a frank concerto style, like the close of the C major Concerto for Two Harpsichords BWV 1061. Although section *A* has contrapuntal elements and section *B* homophonic elements, the prevailing character of each is in fact the opposite of this. The startling contrast between the beginnings of the two themes (*A* in b1, *B* in b25) suggests the opposite effect from such preludes as those of the English Suites (BWV 807, 809) where the opening material is contrapuntal, the episode material more homophonic. Moreover, the opening tonic pedal point followed by 'interlude' and soon answered by dominant pedal point (in addition to that of bb49ff) is reminiscent of the old 'pedal-point toccata', already much altered by BWV 534 and here changed almost beyond recognition. Thus the traditional pedal-point element gives the movement the impression of already being or containing its own prelude and fugue (prelude b1, fugue b25), as is the case with (e.g.) the E flat Prelude, *The 48* Bk I, where the two themes go on to combine. It is striking that the pedal points of BWV 546 are not there for climax or excitement, as they might be in the sonata form of a later composer. At b97, the episode themes take over the pedal point of the ritornello section, thus uniting material from sections *A* and *B* and 'conforming to the concerto element' of the movement as a whole (Frotscher 1935 p895).

As in many highly organized Bach movements, there seems at times no particular reason why one theme or section appears rather than another, e.g. A_3 at b85. Similar episodes at bb68–9 and 115–16 (inverted) lead to different sections, the first to A_2, the second to *B*. To be sure, there are formal reasons: the middle section includes the whole of the *A* section (first two in dominant, third in subdominant) split up by episodic/fugal material, in which case A_3 is required. Yet it may not necessarily be required at that point (b85), and indeed both there and on other occasions (in particular b120) there is a degree of abruptness unexpected from the composer of the best seamless Brandenburg movements. Perhaps this is itself a sign that no manual-changing is required, since that abruptness scarcely needs emphasizing by any additional change of timbre; perhaps it is also a sign that the composer was governed by the twenty-four-bar structure.

The figures or motifs used have their own points of interest. The opening chord is like an exclamation, the rhetorical character of which is best conveyed by a *non legato* approach (Kloppers 1966 p105). The contrasting figure that follows – Ex. 137 – has a conversational effect;

Ex. 137   b6

it springs naturally to mind when the composer requires contrast (see B minor Prelude BWV 544.i b56) and only hesitantly is the player to associate it with the pathos (Keller 1948 p115) implied by the same figure in vocal music. The triplets that follow continue the acceleration (minims, crotchets, quavers, triplets); the pedal point ensures a simple harmonic idea which is countered in the strict invertible four-part counterpoint of the following bars (from b13) which in turn passes to semiquavers decorating and thus emphasizing a Neapolitan sixth, whose dramatic contribution to C minor works was nothing new. The repeated rhythm of the closing triplet section (b21) corresponds to the repetition associated with the term *anaphora* in rhetoric (Kloppers 1966 p107), coming just before the cadence. Both this device and the triplet sequences in section *B* (*polyptoton*) are so natural to music that such rhetorical parallels need scarcely be stressed. Just as clear is the connection between material* shown in Ex. 138, which is not so much direct quotation as a result of a compositional technique whereby crotchets in the movement tend to move by step, triplets by leap. Those

Ex. 138   b20

* The Neapolitan sixth in b26 suggests that the second and third a″ of b29 should be flat (cf. the answer in b57).

triplet leaps themselves lead to unusual harmonic effects when inverted and thus 'unresolved' (bb109–11); they are the easiest figure of the movement to develop (bb3–34, 41–4, 58–9, 62–5, 99–101, 105–11) and obviously relate to the other triplets (from b10, 25, 35 etc), whether or not they have the crotchets against them. The ease with which they can be developed leads to the little episode bb78–81, for example, where the figure Ex. 139 from the pedal point three bars earlier can be heard

139

b78

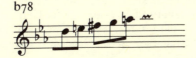

at least six if not eight times. Even so, it is hardly to be expected that the triplets can be doubled in thirds against the subject also doubled in thirds (= *canon sine pausa*), which is what happens in b82. This tonic prepares the subdominant entry in b97, which combines subject and countersubject of *B* over the pedal point from *A*, in turn passing to the only chromatic episode of the movement. Despite, or in addition to, such formal considerations, the triplets are treated very inventively from a melodic point of view, bursting out into pretty sequences time and again (bb44, 102, 109) in a manner that transcends mere musical rhetoric.

Fugue

The fugue is a further example of construction with two subjects, different from BWV 537 and 540 though in its formal aspects close to the former: from the first part of *A* a quaver motif emerges, on which a new section *B* is based, followed by extensive working of *A* combined with a line derived from *B*. It is not correct to call this a 'double fugue' in any sense, since *B* is itself not exposed fugally, nor does it accompany the second *A* without much re-writing, i.e. lengthening. Nevertheless, the collaboration of initial five-part exposition, motivic or figural composition, and thematic combination produces a movement of great technical interest – in this sense a complement to the prelude. It can only be conjectured how far the first forty bars or so suggest that BWV 546.ii began as a quite different fugue, from which the composer was led away by the potential of the quaver figures.

The form may be expressed as:

A	1–45	exposition in five parts (pedal last), second/third and fourth/fifth entries separated by spacious episodes developing *alla breve* counterpoint
	45–59	episode using quaver figures, followed by final tonic entry whose perfect cadence is consolidated in two further bars
B	59–86	invention-like development in three-part imitation of a quaver figure (*d* in Ex. 140) which is found in every bar of section *B*

A₂   86–121   combination of the quaver figure *d* (which persists in almost every bar of the A₂ section) with original subject; exposed in the style of a double fugue to b98, then episode, followed by double entry in relative (b104), further episode, double entry in subdominant (b116)

(C)   121–39   free episode, quaver figures (perhaps derived from *d*) embellishing crotchet figures of a kind heard earlier (e.g. pedal from b99)

(A₃)   140–59   final double entry (pedal + tenor/soprano); coda from b145, incorporating figures from *A* (pedal 'theme' 151–2), *B* (e.g. b153) and *C* (crotchets b147 etc?); cadence like that to A₁ (thus 140–159 = 50–9 extended by coda and pedal point)

The most puzzling section within this ingenious plan is the 'free episode' from b121. Spitta must be right to see that 'the most it has

Ex. 140
section A
b37

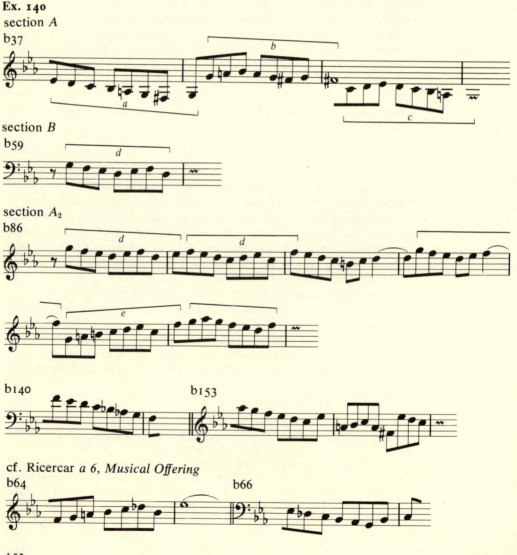

section B
b59

section A₂
b86

b140   b153

cf. Ricercar *a 6, Musical Offering*
b64   b66

in common with the rest is the on-flowing quavers' (I p583), but this says more than it appears to say, since the 'on-flowing quavers' are what has characterized the fugue since the end of the exposition, and all the quaver lines can be interpreted as derived from the basic *figurae*: Ex. 140. These little groups of notes take over the fugue from b37 onwards; *a*, *b* and *c* are aspects of the *figurae* adopted for section *B* (often misleadingly described as a fugue or fugato by the commentators), as the countersubject for A_2 is in turn developed from *B* – hence the long, almost *galant* final episode at b121, which produces a passage unlike any other in the whole corpus of Bach's organ music, though in the same family as the second subject of the E flat Prelude BWV 552. Its quasi-homophonic figure develops from the previous quavers: Ex. 141. From a structural point of view, at least some of the

Ex. 141
b119

bars 121–37 are unnecessary: the final tonic entry is more effortlessly prepared in BWV 545.ii, where indeed the penultimate entry is a step further removed from the tonic than is the case in BWV 546. It is as likely that this episode of BWV 546 originated as a free expansion of the quaver figures which change constantly in the final stages and produce such lines as Ex. 142.

Ex. 142
b107   b41

b147

Moreover, although as many objections against manual-changing could be raised in this fugue as in most others, the way the quaver motif winds in and out of the texture could lead to unusually feasible changes of manual: *Positiv* with the left hand of b59, *Hauptwerk* with the right hand of b86, *Positiv* with the left hand of b115, *Hauptwerk* with the left-hand f′ of b140 (and with the right-hand g′). However, there still remain such problems as the unresolved b♭ of b115. The quaver lines themselves and the counterpoint they produce are often like those elsewhere. Such bars as 59–86 belong to the same family as passages in BWV 540, 537, 661, 733 etc, while the counterpoint of b73 or b98 will be found note for note in BWV 694 (b1) and 646 (b2 – note inverted form in b1). Yet it will be seen that the motifs *a*, *b*, *c* and *d* do not dominate the movement beyond what the composer's invention will accept as proper. The episode at b121 seems to be an attempt to reach out beyond doctrinaire motivicism; and an interesting detail of the closing bars is that two separate phrases are each used twice (alto b151 modified in 152, soprano 153–4 = tenor 155–6), like a very subtle reference to the opening dialogue chords of the prelude. That the composer remained absorbed in the exploitation of *figurae* is clear in works ranging from the *Orgelbüchlein* to the *Canonic Variations* BWV 769; in particular, BWV 546 is an important if formally unusual example of a work concerned with figures familiar from elsewhere. Thus, the first phrase in Ex. 142 above is virtually identical with the countersubject of the A flat Fugue, *The 48* Bk 1.

---

547   Prelude and Fugue in C major

No Autograph MS; copies in P 274 (J. P. Kellner), Am.B. 60 (Berlin copyist, after 1754), P 320 (Kittel), Lpz Poel 32 (C. F. Penzel?), LM 5056 (J. Becker c1779), and other good 18th-century sources (P 276, P 290, P 286 Forkel); also sources based on Agricola (Am.B. 54) and Kittel (P 557 Grasnick, Lpz Go.S.26, Lpz MB MS 1, 8 Wechmar) and later (P 837, Brussels II.3914, P 925).

Two staves; title in P 274 'Praeludium pro Organo pedal.', in Lpz MB MS 1, 8 'Praeludium con Fuga ex C♯ pro organo pleno'.

Both the prelude and the fugue of this work, obviously very mature in many details, have very dramatic harmonies near their closing tonic pedal points, harmonies not only exceptional in themselves but suggesting as close a relationship between the movements as can ever be demonstrated in a Bach organ work. Irrespective of any fancied similarity between the main motifs of each movement, the prelude and fugue 'refer' to each other in the way they apply different chords at the key moments: modulatory dominant sevenths in the prelude (picked up from the previous bar), unrelated diminished sevenths in the fugue (also picked up from the previous bar). Thus it is probable not only that the movements were composed with regard to each other and were always coupled, but that they are to be seen as complements characteristic of the 'ideal' Bach prelude and fugue. Both are built from short subjects which, in each first bar, look hardly likely to lead to expansive, original treatment; in this way they are more regular 'complements' than (e.g.) BWV 540 or 544. Unlike other pairs they begin on the same note. In melodic detail (prelude) and thematic treatment (fugue) the pair of movements is also highly original. The first exemplifies a type of prelude in which the nature of the material dictates form or leads to an unusual shape; in the second can be seen a fugal technique in which both the particles of the subject (*figurae*) and the subject itself are open to wide development, spontaneous and *ad hoc*. The result is a work of a unique character both melodically and contrapuntally – with, moreover, a carefully planned climax and sense of finality. The grand pedal point of the fugue 'answers' the succinct close of the prelude, and the final stages of both movements are derived from the basic theme. Overall and in detail, BWV 547 is a particularly good example of originality resulting from an inventive composer's personal interpretation of numerous traditions affecting him.

Prelude

The tradition of octave imitation at the beginning of a prelude or set of pieces is not difficult to demonstrate (e.g. Two-part Inventions nos. 1–4; first *Canonic Variation* BWV 769.i; J. K. F. Fischer's *Ariadne musica*; etc), but the combination with a pedal quasi-ostinato is more arresting. Even then, triple-time octave imitation above a pedal ostinato can also be found elsewhere ('In dir ist Freude' BWV 615). But the working-out of the theme is more complex than in any of these pieces.

Although the movement may at first seem a free development of the two subjects heard in manual and pedal, the form is intricate, based throughout on three subjects or ideas, the second of which is a kind of decorated or 'coloured' version of the first: Ex. 143. These three

Ex. 143

ideas are themselves heavy with implication: each presents a key rhythmic unit of compound time, a fourth unit ♩ ♪ appearing at the end of *c*. They also contain within themselves the principle of *inversus* (see the motifs within *b*), and they supply all the rhythms of the movement except continuous semiquavers, which are first heard as the second countersubject (right hand b6). Thus the countersubject (right hand b2) mostly drops from view, having little part in this scheme,* while the single detached pedal crotchet *d* becomes homophonic *a 5* at the dramatic moment before the coda.

The general pattern of the movement may be expressed:

---

* That the countersubject rhythm is not the same as motif *c* but its opposite (trochaic not iambic) is clear not so much from any conjectural phrasing but from the ornaments on the longs. Whatever functional analysis might suggest, the different beat distinguishes the countersubject from the pedal ostinato, which cannot be said to 'originate' from it, despite claims to that effect (Keller 1948 p117); nor, to the organist, are they phrased in the same way. Motifs are not purely paper ciphers, and they require particularly careful phrasing in BWV 547.i, not least since their tempo and style should presumably avoid *too* light and gigue-like a manner.

I	1–8	four rhythmic–melodic subjects in turn (*a b c d*), all in tonic
	8–13	modulatory derived episodes (mostly *a* and *d*, some *b* and *c*)
II	13–20	as 1–8, in dominant, parts inverted, often with new extra part
	20–31	modulatory derived episode (*a* and *d* at first, then *b* and *c*)
III	31–48	octave imitations in A minor (*a c b d*), then D minor (*a c b d*), followed by episode (*b c*; from b44, *d*), so that 39–43 = 25–9 a step higher (tonal not real, counterpoint inverted); last bar developed sequentially (*b d*) towards:
IV	48–54	octave imitation in F (*a c b*) followed by episode (*b d*) to:
	54–60	octave imitation in C, so that 54–7 = 48–51 (upper parts inverted); followed by episode (*a b d*) 58–9 (cf. 22–3)
	60–79	octave imitation in G with chromatic colouring, then in C (60–7 = 31–8 down a tone, some parts inverted); the chromatic hint is latterly extended in episode material (68–72 = 25–9 in minor); dominant pedal point (*d b*) and modulatory chords (*d*)
V	80–8	tonic pedal point, above which *a* and *c* used; final reference to opening subjects (83 = 5, 84–5 = 4–5) including *c* in octaves

However, this is not so much a form or shape as merely a plan of how the basic material is developed, combined or extended. The common-chord nature of the material, including themes not listed above as basic (e.g. right hand b4), allows easy combination of motifs, so that (e.g.) *c* can either follow *a* (bb56–7 etc) or be combined with it (b60 etc), *a* can combine with *b inversus* and *d* (b58) or *d* with *b rectus* (b63), and so on. In view of the later metamorphoses of the fugue subject, a particularly interesting quality of such themes is the ease with which they slip into other keys (b9 etc) – not remarkably, at first, but eventually leading to a harmonic crescendo (b32, b37, b62, then bb66ff) resolved by Neapolitan sixth (b72 – the comparable point in b29 had been a phrygian cadence) and so to the detached chords before the final tonic pedal point.

Thus the chief 'formal' elements of the movement are the pair of expositions in tonic (b1) and dominant (b13) – which could be seen as influenced by Vivaldi ritornellos (Klein 1970 p77) or by traditional pedal-point toccatas – and the close on a derived pedal point at the end. Otherwise the movement is a motivic fantasia in which (as in *Orgelbüchlein* preludes on a smaller scale) there is a degree of internal repetition, but in which a constant re-working or re-exposing of the basic themes is the true nature and purpose of the movement. The four-part harmony is most skilfully planned so that passages of static harmonies alternate with others less static. A further subtlety is that the harmonic rhythm is varied, so that chords change as shown in Ex. 144. One curious result of this is that on the first beat of each bar the harmonies are almost always either $\frac{5}{3}$ or $\frac{7}{3}$, which only such a scheme of modulation – with important sections in minor keys – could save from monotony. The most didactic textbook example is hardly likely to lead to a greater harmonic homogeneity. Another curious factor is that the movement is based mainly on one-bar phrases which result from the basic motifs and between which there are very few tied notes of any kind – only a few outside the main sequential episodes beginning at bb25, 39 and 68. The pedal alone has a complementary function in

Ex. 144

b19

harmonies:

the two movements: without either the main theme or any tied notes (suspensions) in the prelude, but with both* in the fugue. It is partly this predominant repetitiousness of the $^9/_8$ metre on strong beats that gives the prelude its particular rhythmic character. Clearly there is some kind of similarity to the horn motif and triadic counterpoint in the first movement of Cantata 65 (1724) – Ex. 145(i) – not least since another

Ex. 145

(i) **(ii)**

BWV 65.i

b1 b51 Und___ des Her - ren Lob ver-kün - - - - di - gen

coll'8va bassa _ _ _ _ _ _ _ _ _ _ _ _ _ _ _ _

motif (*b*) appears with it in 'praise of the Lord' (ii). Both motif *b* and the element of bare octaves in these, the closing bars of the cantata movement, occur in the organ prelude. But the $^9/_8$ metre of the prelude BWV 547.i itself becomes a motif – an element contributing to, not merely an aspect of, the movement's unity. The performer who cannot easily accept a light, springing style and tempo for this piece would agree with Kirnberger's remark (in the 1770s) that $^9/_8$ as distinct from $^9/_4$ can 'easily have the appearance of the light and trifling' ('kann . . . leicht den Schein des Tändelnden gewinnen' – Kloppers 1966 p159), which he then illustrates with Ex. 146.

Ex. 146
Kirnberger, *Die Kunst des reinen Satzes* (1774–9), II.i, p128

* See the very first pedal note in b49 of the fugue.

Fugue

The fugue is one of the most interesting of all the organ fugues, combining new solutions to formal problems with ingenious counterpoint and far-reaching treatment of the subject itself.

The formal intention of the movement is to present a series of expositions, as follows:

I   1–15   tonic exposition, episode, dominant answers (tonal b9, real b10, tonal b13); perfect cadence

II   15–27   tonic exposition with new semiquaver countersubject and motif (*x*: Ex. 147), which is further developed against entries in other keys; imperfect cadence

III   27–34   irregular exposition of subject *inversus*, against which motif *x* is further developed *rectus* and *inversus*; followed by episode

IV   34–48   exposition of subject *rectus+inversus* on E (34–5), A (36), D (37–8); then three entries *inversus* (on A D G); three *rectus*, either tonal (C minor, G minor) or real (C minor); link (*brisé* chords) to:

V   48–72   mass-exposition of subject *rectus*, *inversus* and augmented (pedal); from b56, subject transformed, as far as the two pedal entries *inversus in augmentatione*; tonic pedal-point coda, above which foreshortened subject is stated in stretto and dismembered

Ex. 147   b17

The movement is thus a distinctive fugal type, in which the first opening statement of fifteen bars – itself very like a complete fughetta of traditional type – is followed by a series of increasingly intricate expositions, unlike BWV 548 where a similar statement becomes the *A* of an *A B A* fugue, or BWV 546 where it is followed by a new subject *B*, or BWV 544 in which the subject is given a series of successive counterpoints. Whereas most of the organ fugues are sectional in one manner or another, BWV 546, 547 and 548 offer particularly important solutions to the formal plan of a fugue whose first opening statement closes in the tonic with a clear perfect cadence. That this 'statement' can vary in length reflects only the different lengths of the subjects, and other fugues such as BWV 541 or 545 have no such clearcut section of this type. It is the new conception of fugal form in BWV 547 that makes the delayed pedal entry of b49 even more significant; while delays of the pedal are of little significance in Buxtehude (see Pauly 1964 p186) and produce a simple, climactic coda in BWV 549, the delayed pedal in BWV 547 draws attention both to its augmentation and to the piling-up of subject-motifs above it. In the C minor Fugue, *The 48* Bk II, an extra voice enters with a bass augmentation, also in the tonic, towards the close of the fugue; perhaps the composer associated such devices with the tonality of C major, for both the pedal entry and the final pedal point of BWV 547.ii anticipate the piled-up climax of the *Canonic Variations* (in C) BWV 769.

Probably in no other fugue of Bach does the subject appear so many times (over fifty, according to Keller 1948 p118), and its type is familiar from elsewhere. The opening motif incorporates the common *figura suspirans* (*y*), while the angular line *z* can also be heard in such subjects as the B major Fugue, *The 48* Bk II: Ex. 148. But the most striking

Ex. 148

BWV 547.ii

Das Wohltemperirte Clavier, II
B major Fugue b10

Ex. 149

BWV 547.ii

BWV 677

resemblance is to be seen in the exposition of the fughetta on 'Allein Gott' BWV 677: Ex. 149. It would be difficult to find two other keyboard works of J. S. Bach with quite such a correspondence; it is equally curious that the motif in the subject of BWV 547.ii which is not found in the first subject of BWV 677 (i.e. the opening figure y) can actually be found in the second line or subject of the same chorale – Ex. 150

Ex. 150

BWV 677

b7

– which, as can be seen, also continues in similar vein. Yet it would be a mistake to see the resemblance between BWV 547.ii and the several fughettas of *Clavierübung III* as confined to the examples above: in addition to these, the piling-up of motifs and thematic derivations from b48 and b66 is within the same style of counterpoint. So is the use of a motif in its *rectus* and *inversus* forms with impunity: Ex. 151.

Ex. 151

b27   b30

The somewhat strange harmony produced in (e.g.) b29 accords with *Clavierübung III* insofar as it arises from a subject which for the moment is in an ambiguous key (the entries of the previous two bars have been less ambiguous, merely changing direction). The short, intensive composition with motifs is itself within *Clavierübung III* style.* More remarkable still is the astonishing metamorphosis of the subject in its entry (and answer at the tritone) in bb56–7: Ex. 152. Nor is this

Ex. 152

b56

transformation merely an aspect of the diminished-seventh harmonies which the composer often marshals in other works, and which he goes on to use in this fugue before the final pedal point – the most

* Moreover, it has not escaped the attention of commentators (Siedentopf *BJ* 1974 p73) that the prelude of BWV 547 'represents the Trinity' in its 3×3 quaver motif (*a* in Ex. 143).

remarkable progressions of bb56–8 are not a diminished seventh at all, but the augmented sixth resolved in b57 and the melodic diminished third (tenor) in bb57–8. The fugue has other examples of entries altered for the sake of modulation – Ex. 153 – and it is noticeable that of the

Ex. 153

b9

b39

two augmented entries in the pedal at b59 and b62 it is the latter, with its altered (diminished) interval in the second half, that produces the more convincing harmony.* Bach subjects are often transformed for harmonic effect – e.g. D major Fugue, *The 48* Bk II: Ex. 154 – but in this and similar cases the transformation produces interesting harmonies rather than far-reaching modulation. In such respects too, BWV 547.ii is unique.

Ex. 154

Das Wohltemperirte Clavier, II, D major Fugue

b43

In addition to the form of the fugue and its treatment of the subject, its bar-by-bar composition shows equal skill and originality. In theory, the episodes of bb6, 12, 23, 31, 46 and 53 are unimportant; but each is characterized by a most striking sequence, with the exception of b47 which, like other preparatory bars in J. S. Bach (e.g. the D minor Toccata BWV 538.i bb12–13), contains a broken chord or two. The

Ex. 155

b6

b22

---

* This is a subjective point: while the harmonization of the pedal b at the beginning of b61 is ingenious and imaginative, it cannot be said to satisfy all ears.

Ex. 156

sequences, in particular bb6, 23 and 53 (the last two of which refer to b6) have a melodious counterpoint that in the context is rather conspicuous, and only familiarity with the mature motif techniques of J. S. Bach enables the listener to see that they derive from the same motif x: Ex. 155. In fact, this motif – which itself picks up the head motif (y) or *caput* of the fugue subject – colours the fugue as a whole, so that every bar (with the important exception of the lead-in to the final pedal entry) contains it in one form or another. Like motifs in certain *Orgelbüchlein* chorales, it exists in two forms – y single (four semiquavers) and x double (eight): Ex. 156. Motif x, though it has distinctive shapes, is clearly of a family with those listed under BWV 537.

From the y motif spring the subject, the prevailing motif, the sequential episodes, the *rectus/inversus* contrast, the running semi-quaver lines, the counterpoint above the pedal augmentation and the final pedal point. As the examples above show, the variety with which the *figura* is wielded is immense, and it should not be forgotten that it is one of the most basic or 'elementary' of all: the *figura suspirans* (see e.g. BWV 628). But just as this *figura* is used to produce many varied lines, so the final stretches of the fugue include many varied fugal techniques, obviously looking towards the ingenuity of the *Canonic Variations*. The techniques are: *rectus/inversus* forms, stretto, aug-mentation, transformation of the subject, homophony, rhetorical rests, pedal point, final turns towards the subdominant, intense development of *figurae*, and valedictory reference to the subject (cf. tenor, penultimate bar). Some of these are already unusual in organ fugues (e.g. augmentation and rhetorical rests), while others achieve here a new concentration: 'preparatory chromaticism' before a final perfect cadence can never have been more richly employed that it is over bb56–65 of this fugue. The accumulation of all these effects from the modest start of the fugue on middle c' to the five-part close is not only a preview on a bigger scale of one of the *Canonic Variations* (whose basic motifs are in the same family as x or y) but is itself a fugal device quite different from BWV 548, where the *A B A* form, though masterly and spacious, is not cumulative in the same way.

548   Prelude and Fugue in E minor

Autograph MS P 274 (prelude and first twenty bars of fugue; the rest copied by J. P. Kellner?); other good 18th-century sources (Viennese MS in private possession, copied by Anon 5; Lpz MB MS 7, 18 J. N. Mempell; Am.B. 60 Berlin copyist after 1754, further copied in Am.B. 54; P 276, P 290, LM 5056 J. Becker c1779, LM 4839, P 287 Forkel) and later sources, some of which also probably derive from Kittel (Lpz MB MS 1, 9 Wechmar?, P 228 fugue only, P 553, P 837, P 925, Lpz MB III.8.21 Dröbs; BB autogr. A. W. Bach 2, fugue only, much shortened; Lpz Poel 14, fugue only, Lpz Poel 15 J. L. Weigand 1815/20, the last two without bb54–172 of fugue).

Two staves; title in P 274 (Autograph) 'Praeludium pedaliter pro Organo', in Lpz MB III.8.21 'Praeludium pedaliter pro Organo pleno'.

That the composer and his friend J. P. Kellner* each wrote out about half of the total length of BWV 548 may suggest collaboration between them, but different reasons could be argued as to why Kellner took over; whatever the explanation for the change of hand, the composer's writing and the watermark are the same as for the autograph MS of BWV 544. The two fair copies, like that for BWV 541, were presumably made from older autograph(s), perhaps from the Weimar period (Kilian 1978 p62). It seems hardly open to doubt that prelude and fugue were intended to be, and always were, coupled. This is borne out by the complementary techniques in form and figuration employed: the intricate concerto–ritornello form of the prelude is matched by the clearcut *A B A* of the fugue. Thus, because the overall shape of the fugue is close to that of the C minor Prelude BWV 546.i (*A B A* in which *B* refers to *A*), it is better paired with a different kind of prelude, one containing thematic sections, such as BWV 552.i or indeed BWV 548.i; conversely, the C minor Prelude is paired with an open, sectionalized fugue that contains several expositions. It would be contrary to Bach's practice to couple such a fugue as BWV 548.ii with such a prelude as BWV 546.i. In BWV 548, 'inner relationships' are also often felt between the two movements, very likely depending on such factors as the use of scales and scale motifs in the harmony. At least since Spitta commented on the work's 'life energy' and the 'extreme daring' of the fugue subject, christening the whole a 'two-movement symphony' and pointing out that it is 'the longest amongst Bach's organ fugues' (Spitta II p690), the work has held a rather special position which can hardly be gainsaid. But it could well be that the riveting power of the work is due not only to its material and the use of it but also to the length of the movements in relation to each other: given their vigour, their scope accords with views which have grown up since its time on what constitutes balance and climax. While it may be possible to show that to the composer the movements of BWV 540 or 546 were balanced conceptually, no listener needs persuasion to hear for himself the balance, tension and climax of BWV 548. But whether that was the intention behind the *A B A* form can only be conjectured. Rather, the movements of BWV 548 represent a further experiment in, or demonstration of, musical form: coupling a ritornello prelude with a fugue whose shape gives yet a different solution from BWV 547, 546 or 538 to the question of how to organize an extensive but homogeneous fugue.

* 'Either a later phase of Kellner's own hand' as authenticated in other MSS 'or the hand of one of his students' (May 1974 p270).

Prelude

The sectional ritornello shape of the 'Wedge Prelude' is the most involved amongst the organ works:

A_1	1–5	homophonic, pedal continuo; an 'instrumental' rhetoric
A_2	5–7	contrapuntal possibilities open to development
A_3	7–19	various sequential phrases before perfect cadence (following Neapolitan sixth) in tonic
B_1	19–24	new but continuous material, to dominant
B_2	24–33	inner supertonic pedal point broken in 27–31 as material from A_2 is newly developed
A_1	33–7	now in dominant, upper parts inverted
A_2	37–9	ditto
A_3	39–51	ditto except 46–8 not inverted; sequence so transposed that 40–3 = 7–10
C	51–5	no pedal
B_1	55–61	inverted form, now in major; closing with reference to A_1, now with new bass
C	61–5	as before, down a fifth (rh top line re-phrased to avoid d''')
B_1	65–9	as 55–61, down a fifth, followed as before by:
A_1	69–81	not a return but a longer development of A_1 material over a new bass, followed by freer episode (75–81) which refers to same bass; b80 reaches same cadence as b69 before its interruption in b70
A_1	81–5	not a return but more direct development of opening theme towards
A_1	86–90	subdominant return, upper parts further inverted (see also 33–7)
C	90–4	an *inversus* form
B_2	94–111	94–103 similar to 24–33 a tone lower, upper parts inverted; followed by freer episode (103–11, manual line derived from A_1) above a running bass
B_1	111–15	as 55, 65 but now in C major
C	115–21	C motifs *rectus* and *inversus* developed in sequence, in order to approach key of:
B_1	121–5	as 55, 65, 111 (i.e. B_1 used as pedal-point material) but parts inverted above dominant pedal point for:
A_3	125–37	125–36 = 7–18 except lh re-written to allow full descending scales from b'' down to C; close on *tierce de picardie*

Where this differs from a concerto movement is in its more succinct length and in a kind of hectic continuity that avoids (e.g.) the 'false final recapitulation'* heard in some concertos. Although the writing in general is highly conducive to manual changes, they could not be said to be as inevitable as those of the E flat Prelude BWV 552, a factor which further distinguishes the movement from any concerto model it may have had.

That the first subject of the prelude is basically homophonic while other subjects are polyphonic is a sign of how finely and totally

* I.e. the return of the main subject in the tonic near the end, only to break off into a further episode. Kloppers (1966 p220) hears a return to A_1 in b103, but both the running bass and imitative upper parts are more like the episodes of the movement.

complementary prelude and fugue are, since this antithesis is exactly reversed in the fugue. Most of the prelude seems to be focused on the sensitive soprano range around e″, which also contributes to the intensity of the writing. Also, 'the movement avoids strict imitation' (Frotscher 1935 p894). As has been seen before (Keller 1948 p119), sequences are particularly significant in the movement as a whole; spontaneous and inventive, they seem to rise and fall constantly. But sequences are only one aspect of the continuity. There are strikingly few cadences in the movement, and what cadences there are usually rush into another section of the involved ritornello form. Most of the sections are in the minor, and it is striking that the new episodes at b75 and b103 both work towards a melodious appearance of subjects in the major. The ritornello plan has the effect of constantly juxtaposing material in non-stop sequence, so that sections follow each other in almost random order (e.g., B_1 is followed on successive occasions by B_2, C, A_1, C, A_3). The finality of the last A_3 gains both from its unexpected if logical appearance and from the fact that it alone in the movement quotes substantially from the original exposition. Although any fancied thematic similarity between sections A, B and C does not quite follow J. S. Bach's usual methods of melodic/motivic derivation – i.e., the motifs cannot be shown to develop from each other – there are certain resemblances between phrases (Ex. 157), which must

Ex. 157

add something to the continuity of the movement. In particular, the writing at any one moment seems engaged either in a question-and-answer phraseology (e.g. bb1–2) or in a harmonic sequence (e.g. beginning in bb7 or 12), which cannot be said of such preludes as the C major BWV 547. In addition, although the keyboard writing is obviously idiomatic, it is not traditional in the manner of (e.g.) the C major Prelude BWV 545; like the partly imitative, partly melodic writing of the preludes in B minor BWV 544, C minor BWV 546 and C major BWV 547, the movement achieves an original and scarcely imitable organ style, new to the corpus of organ music as a whole. That the keyboard writing is characteristic of a certain point in the composer's development is clear from (e.g.) the curious resemblance of the main subject to a bar in the B minor Prelude (BWV 544.i b61, cf. BWV 548.i b2), from the important appoggiatura chords (compare BWV 548.i b2 with BWV 546.i b2), and from the scale lines familiar also from the B minor Prelude. In BWV 544, scales are used by way of decoration to other themes, or as countersubject; in BWV 548, they are used rather to enrich sequences and aid continuity. No other composer before Beethoven made such well-reasoned use of scales. But despite these and other devices, the texture is surprisingly consistent, from three to five parts, with something of a planned alternation between the two.

Subjects are both re-introduced and developed, the two processes being kept in balance. Thus, in b86 the first subject returns in exact form, while five bars earlier its shape and motifs have passed between the voices and created modulating appoggiatura chords; similarly, the second subject B_1 returns each time developed as a pedal point, while the third subject C both repeats and develops. Such use of material recalls the ritornello plan of Vivaldi (e.g. BWV 593.i), in which the main theme returns partially throughout the movement in a pattern that looks intricate but probably arose from the bar-by-bar caprice of the composer.

Fugue

In both subject and form, the E minor Fugue has a clear historical context heightening the originality of both. That the subject* may have influenced some of the Bach pupils is suggested by the similar though less graphically drawn wedge shape in J. L. Krebs's Fugue BWV Anh.181. Perhaps there was a tradition of E minor subjects incorporating chromatic broken chords, like the two shown in Ex. 158, both of which are more than the merely decorated *passus duriusculus* or descending chromatic fourth associated with *tonus primus* or D minor (e.g. BWV 614). The rocking figure of the first main episode subject (b60)

Ex. 158

Muffat, *72 Versetl* (1726), 11.ii

BWV 855

* 'A wonderful theme', according to Schumann (*NZfM* XV (1841) p150), who was pointing out that b4 ('a single note') was missing in the Haslinger edition, vol. VI.

Ex. 159

(i) Bruhns, Praeludium in G major   b93   (ii)

has been compared to that of Bruhns's G major Praeludium – Ex. 159(i) – (Keller 1948 p120) but is obviously more complex; although merely a group of semiquavers, it leaves the ear with an impression of a broken chord plus an acciaccatura – Ex. 159(ii) – like the opening chord of the Sarabande of the E minor Partita BWV 830. Its underlying harmonic movement (Ex. 160) is not unlike fugal material elsewhere, such as that

Ex. 160
b60

etc

in the last movement of Vivaldi's D minor Concerto, arranged as BWV 596.iv (b4). Although, like the scales in the prelude, this figure demands manual dexterity, it is not quite correct to see it as 'toccata-like', since toccatas at that period were not built upon such figures.

Nevertheless, it is tempting to see the E minor Fugue as a combination or bringing together of fugue (with a regular exposition, etc), concerto (with 'solo' episodes), toccata (with running scale figures), and aria or *da capo* form. Against a concerto or tutti/solo interpretation of the movement is the fact that manual-changing, if at times perfectly feasible, is no more straightforward than usual, particularly the return to the tutti manual at the reprise in b172.* On behalf of a toccata interpretation of the work is the fact that much of the figuration in the central episode – scales, broken-chord figures, the patterns from b120 – accords with the praeludia of northern composers, and may even be an allusion to them (see below). Against a toccata interpretation, however, is that this allusion remains purely conceptual, and all the figures, of whatever origin, are incorporated into a massive structure of non-stop drive and impetus; certainly there are no liberties of the kind associated with the term 'toccata' before and after Bach.

The *da capo* fugal form may be expressed as follows:

> *A*   1–23   regular four-part exposition (pedal last) with consistent countersubject, from which springs motif *a* (Ex. 161), used in the codetta
>
> 23–38   episode derived from motif *a*, whence a sequence develops above a striding bass; tonic entry in b34 (with pedal countersubject)

---

* In the final tutti return in the fugue of the B minor Ouverture BWV 831, the composer directs that subject and countersubject should immediately appear on the *forte* manual.

	38–59	episode derived from a figure related to *a* (with suspensions etc); subdominant entry and tonic answer (the latter on dominant pedal point), with further development of *a*
B	59–71	episode, manual only, new figure; truncated tonic entry in pedal
	72–83	same as 59–71, up a fifth (modified ending); truncated dominant answer in pedal (upper parts inverted)
	84–93	episode, scales; full pedal-point entry in D minor/major *en taille*, with countersubject
	93–112	episode in three sections, the second on manual only and based on motif *a* from countersubject; the third, like the second, includes a pedal-point entry with countersubject (i.e. 106–12 = 87–93)
	112–41	episode in several sections: b112 scales now extended to two octaves; 116 episode as 25; 120 new figure (much in the Buxtehude tradition – Ex. 162) interspersed with references to first episode (124 and 130 as 60 etc) followed by pedal entry in supertonic, with countersubject
	141–60	episode, *alla breve* counterpoint (sequence, 141–4 = 145–8 inverted counterpoint); non-modulating sequence from b151 towards pedal-point entry in C major, with countersubject
	160–77	episode, scales similar to those from b93 but developing into further sequence; followed by pedal-point entry *en taille*, with countersubject
A	172–231	*da capo* return, so that the entry following the previous episode is itself the opening subject of A_2. From b178 = exactly as from b6, except for the *tierce de picardie* (as with the return of A_3 in the Prelude)

Ex. 161   b9

Ex. 162
b135

BUXWV 146 b77

The hidden nature of the *da capo* return is very striking. The entry at the end of b172 has a double function, perhaps the only instance in the organ works of J. S. Bach:* its pedal point is itself a kind of quasi-coda

---

* At least, it is the only instance of overlapping bar numbers in the outline 'analyses' presented in this book. The 'extra' bars of B make an even more accurate equation in number of bars: $B = A + A$.

and indeed corresponds to the two *da capo* codas from b51 and b223. But the true logic of its position is that it is providing an entry corresponding to the entries provided at the close of each previous episode section. At b172, it is not at all clear that a full *da capo* is about to take place.

The position of this *da capo* conception in the fugal work of J. S. Bach has already led to some comparisons (see notes to BWV 547.ii), and it is scarcely still necessary to find the shape as 'inadmissible in fugal composition' as it once was (Schreyer 1911). A_1 is itself a formally complete fugue in that it contains exposition, episodes, entries and coda. What an early full close in the tonic (b59) can next lead to is a question given different answers in the three fugues BWV 546, 547 and 548. Obviously as a whole the alternation of contrapuntal main sections with semi-homophonic episodes mirrors or reverses the formal pattern of the E minor Prelude BWV 548, which is not in *A B A* form; but the C minor Prelude BWV 546 is, demonstrating another movement type in which the main material is quasi-homophonic and the episodes are fugal. *Da capo* fugues as such are by no means unknown. Like the theme itself, the form may have influenced a band of admirers or pupils, as is suggested by the *A B A* fugal movement of the spurious Lute (or Flute and Harpsichord) Partita BWV 997 known to C. P. E. Bach (P 690), Agricola, and Kirnberger (P 218), or the Lute Fugue BWV 998. The E minor Fughetta no. 10 of Telemann's *XX Kleine Fugen* (Hamburg c1731) is cast in a simple *A B A* shape in which *B* is derived from *A*, and it is possible that the C minor Fugue BWV 906 was intended to be *da capo*,* as was already the case with the finale to the Fifth Brandenburg Concerto, which has fugal elements. Amongst the organ works, the C minor fugues BWV 537.ii and 526.iii had approached an *A B A* form in which A_2 is modified in some way – shortened, with a coda added (BWV 537), or with its counterpoint inverted (BWV 526.iii). One clarified *A B A* structure can be seen in the F major Duet BWV 803 (*Clavierübung III*), the significance of which lies in the composer's evident desire to present in the four Duets four specific fugal techniques or shapes (see notes to BWV 802–805). In one important respect, the C minor Fugue BWV 537.ii is less clearcut than BWV 548.ii: its middle section is more noticeably divided into two large paragraphs, and there is not quite the same *A B A* simplicity.

Closest to the E minor Fugue is the type of fugue contained within a suite prelude or French Overture, such as the D major Suite for Orchestra BWV 1068, the English Suites in D minor and E minor BWV 808 and 810, and the B minor Ouverture BWV 831 from *Clavierübung II*. In all of them, section *B* contains simpler episodic material, often quasi-homophonic, in which the subject from A_1 appears shortened or in the form of isolated entries, and in which A_2 enters unobtrusively or in any case without a halting break. In this respect, the E minor Organ Fugue is a version of a form realized in the E minor Harpsichord Suite BWV 810, now perfected in the originality of its material, in the inherent drama of an organ fugue (tutti counterpoint contrasted with

* For other spurious works, see *BJ* 1921 p46.

manual episodes, etc) and in such details as the rhetorical effect of well-spaced pedal points.

In addition to the formal perfection of the E minor Fugue, which is realized by means of a striking rhythmic–contrapuntal drive, there are many details of importance in the bar-by-bar composition. Thus, although neither subject nor countersubject otherwise yields any motif patently used later on, the motif *a* does have sections to itself: bb9–12, 22–31, 37ff, 55–8 etc. Once or twice, the motif and its leap are inverted – Ex. 163 – and, as often in the composer's treatment of such motifs

Ex. 163   b57

(compare that of the C minor Fugue BWV 546), the same motif can be observed working over a stretch of several bars (e.g. bb22–31), incorporating or leading to sequences and easy imitation (e.g. the invertible counterpoint of bb29–31). The chromatic subject leads to a strained harmony of which good use is made (e.g. augmented sixth followed by augmented triad, bb20–1) and which therefore contrasts with the easier imitation of the motif *a*.

Remarks on episode material have already been made above. The tendency of the pedal to use striding figures – typical of episodes (bb25, 38, 84, 93, 116, 163) – is hardly to be seen as a development of the de-embellished pedal form of the subject at b21; rather, it contrasts on the one hand with the quaver chromatics of the subject (bb19, 81 etc) and on the other with the carefully spaced pedal points. The episodes use scale figures in such a way as to suggest that the composer was intent on presenting a whole series of them, a repertory of scale motifs either half-bar or whole-bar, either ascending or descending, either straight (e.g. b160) or convoluted (e.g. b164). The scale lines also produce at times bleak textures reminiscent of other works: compare bb86ff of this 'Wedge Fugue' with bb71ff of the B minor Prelude BWV 544. At other times they weave in and out of harmonic sequences that occur quite as often here as in the prelude itself – another element in which prelude and fugue are like reciprocal complements. The final pair of episodes presents an interesting repertory of organ effects, placed in juxtaposition:

132–5   Buxtehude-like figure
141–9   four-part *alla breve* style
150–5   organ-sonata style (invertible upper parts over a bass)
160–4   scales decorating a 'French' progression of the kind found in four-bar *rondeau* ostinatos (Ex. 164, next page)

In a composer of Bach's stylistic alertness, such a 'repertory' is unlikely to have come about by accident. One result is that the homophonic episode of bb120–35 is better integrated within the fugue as a whole than is the final episode of the C minor Fugue BWV 546, where

Ex. 164

b160

a not dissimilar but simpler and more modish effect is sustained longer and, in comparison with this repertory of styles in BWV 548.ii, is out of proportion with the fugue. The episodes of BWV 548.ii give the impression of a limitless invention, sequence succeeding sequence (e.g. bb168–70 following bb164–7), and the return of A_2 is the more striking for there being no obvious flagging of invention during the episodes. Not the least remarkable feature of the fugue is that the truncated entries in the *B* section merely quote the fugue subject, in no way developing it or transforming it in the manner made familiar by *The 48*. As in other long fugues (such as the three-part Ricercar in the *Musical Offering* or the Fuga of the C major Violin Sonata BWV 1005), the composer seems to be deliberately walking a tightrope by interpolating new material, sharply differentiating episode from entry, controlling his material with great tension, yet at the same time giving it a feeling of unplanned caprice and 'inspiration'. He achieves all this in the E minor and *Musical Offering* fugues not least by the melodic power of the themes themselves.

549

Prelude and Fugue in C minor

No Autograph MS; copies from later-18th-century (P 320 Kittel, P 287 Michel, P 289, P 301 prelude only, LM 4838) or 19th-century sources (P 282, P 319, Lpz MB III.8.22, Stift Göttweig MS J. S. Bach 35, Lpz Go.S.318a, Lpz Go.S.26, Warsaw Bib. Univ. Rps Mus 98), perhaps from sources circulating in the Kittel circle (*BG* 38 used a further Kittel MS owned by Hauser); for copies in D minor see BWV 549a.

Two staves; title in Hauser MS 'Praeludium', in P 287 'Praeludium pedaliter', and in P 289 'Praeludium et fuga pedaliter'.

Sources containing BWV 549 frequently also contain the Prelude and Fugue in E minor BWV 533, which may imply that they originated at the same time. But a more basic question concerns the original key: Is it C minor or D minor? That the oldest extant source is in D minor supports the claim that C minor was the later version; moreover, 'there was no reason for transposing it up, but a very good reason for transposing it down' (Emery 1959 p. iv), namely to avoid pedal d′ in the opening solo (b2–3 etc). A similar point could be made about the two-key versions of BWV 566 and 542.ii. It is not known whether the composer himself made this, or any, downward transposition of BWV 549a, though the usual assumption is that he did.

That the only two preludes and fugues for organ copied in the Möller MS* were the C major BWV 531 and D minor BWV 549a draws attention to a particular similarity between them, even perhaps confirming the suggestion that 'they were conceived as complements to each other' (see notes to BWV 531). Some particular aspects of the prelude–fugue–postlude shape – derived perhaps from Böhm, and familiar from such other works as BWV 565 – are common to the two works:

BWV 531, BWV 549
A   pedal solo
     manual develops pedal motif
B   fugue (four subjects or answers, but in two or three parts), in which
     the pedal entry is delayed
C   coda, beginning as an integral part of fugue, but later developing
     demisemiquavers

Within these general guide-lines for or by the composer, the differences between the two works are striking and consistent:

	BWV 531	BWV 549
	major	minor
A	pedal detached, and thematic textures broken	pedal points only, and consistently in four or five parts
B	descending exposition	ascending exposition
	tonal pedal entry integrated	pedal entry accompanied homophonically
C	coda without pedal until pedal point and final perfect cadence	coda with pedal, which is thematic at first; no pedal point; plagal cadence

It is also possible that (e.g.) the sudden turn to the minor towards the end of BWV 531.ii is to be seen as a kind of reversed *tierce de picardie* – a gesture perhaps meant to be as conventional as the final chords of BWV 549.i and BWV 549.ii. Further detailed differences will be seen in the way other conventions are exploited. Thus, the alternate-foot technique of the opening pedal solo leads in BWV 531 to figures that are repeated, in BWV 549 to sequences; while in BWV 531 the final detached octave leap of the pedal solo is followed by pedal rests, in BWV 549 it is followed by a pedal point, etc. A catalogue of such differences within similarities would be possible between many' pairs of preludes and fugues, but they are striking in the case of BWV 531 and 549.

Prelude

The opening motif-gesture and careful phrase-structure of the pedal introduction are as much like the extant praeludia of Böhm as those of any other composer; but the following four-part development for manuals and pedal is rather a more consistent and sustained version of the kind of counterpoint familiar in a Buxtehude praeludium once the opening pedal or manual solo has subsided. Bars 9 to 18 – familiar in style from *The 48* Bk 1 (E flat Prelude) and elsewhere – can be related to the traditional toccata style based on suspensions of the

---

* Except the autograph insertion BWV 535a.

durezza type, but here, in b15 or so, given a heightened colour not usually found in comparable examples by such composers as J. K. F. Fischer.* Also not out of character with Fischer – although his published volumes offer no exact parallel – are the homophonic passages in b20 and b24, regarded by Spitta as early elements thrown off later by the composer (Spitta I p246) and found in less contrapuntal movements (e.g. Buxtehude Toccata in F BUXWV 157). The dissolving of the counterpoint for the sake of these chords – both bars are occupied with dominant sevenths – anticipates the dissolving of the fugal texture in the second movement for the sake of manual chords (bb41ff); this seems to be in the Bruhns manner, though again no exact parallel can now be found. Similarly, the motif-repetition of bb25–6 is in the Buxtehude style. Since, given the harmonic progressions of the movement, the composer could have unified the motifs without trouble, it can only be assumed that he had as yet little interest in developing a single motif over twenty-nine bars; a kind of unity is provided by the pedal points of varying length, covering the diatonic steps between C and A♭.

Fugue

The fugue consists chiefly of a series of entries, the first five of which rise in tonic and dominant steps (bb1, 5, 9, 13, 17) and are spaced, as the bar numbers show, at regular four-bar intervals. This regularity is itself out of the question with genuine five-part expositions such as the C sharp minor Fugue, *The 48* Bk I, but the effect of three voices yielding more than three subject answers is familiar elsewhere (e.g. BWV 531). Though this is not a permutation fugue, the first counter-subjects share a common rhythm (an undeveloped dactyl figure); also striking in its simplicity is the implied harmony of the subject, i.e. a series of tonics and dominants which can be enlivened only by good contrapuntal texture in such bars as 17–22.

The two- and three-part counterpoint is gradually overtaken by semiquavers which, in b33, anticipate the broken chords above the eventual pedal entry of b40. The episodes (bb21, 31, 36) show the spinning-out technique useful in later fugues. The final or pedal entry of b40 is anticipated in elementary stretto,† and the same motif is then picked up and spun out by pedal below toccata-like chords. The coda is reached with the tonic of b46. Like that of BWV 531, the coda is first concerned with a spacious if simple development of derived material, before quicker scale passages succeed it. The final plagal cadence recalls that of the prelude, whereas both cadences of BWV 531 are perfect; a further, if subjectively based, difference between the two

---

* The motif given to pedal in b14 of *BG* 38 is rightly returned to the left hand in *NBA* IV/5; perhaps the pedal d or D should run through bb13 and 14 (as in BWV 549a). It is probably also correct to hold the final pedal C through to the last bar of the prelude (as suggested by Bruggaier 1959 p177), whether or not the tenor c is added to the last chord (again, as in BWV 549a).
† Hence the undesirability of cutting out the last four beats before the pedal entry, as suggested in *BG* 38 p. xvii; the passage also appears in BWV 549a.

closes is that the demisemiquavers of BWV 549 suggest a more gradual rallentando than the less continuous figuration of BWV 531.

The fugue is original in form insofar as it relies totally on tonic and dominant entries. The late pedal entry consolidates this feature, emphasizing the tonic (under a kind of chordal countersubject in the manuals) and with its final cadence signalling the end of the fugue proper. At least one commentator, Schöneich (1947/8 p89), sees the pedal entry itself as marking the beginning of the third section. Both prelude and fugue are preoccupied with tonic and dominant to an extent seen in few, if any, other organ works of Bach, although the same element may be found on a smaller scale in e.g. Buxtehude's C major Fugue BUXWV 137, which does indeed become an ostinato movement on those harmonies. A further kind of originality lies in the subject itself and hence – since in this fugue the subject is so often prominent – the total impression of the piece. The subject's length and three-bar structure (cf. BWV 575) are not as unusual as its rhythm and the prosaic squareness of the melody, neither of which in practice detracts from the idiomatic keyboard style and rhythmic panache of the whole but which at first seem to be removed from any elevated style.

549a   Prelude and Fugue in D minor

No Autograph MS; copies in BB 40644 (Möller MS), later-18th-century (P 218, shortened) and 19th-century sources (P 308); also a 'Schubring MS'.

Two staves: title in Möller MS 'Praeludium ô Fantasia pedaliter', in P 218 'Praeludium pedaliter'.

Since the Möller MS is by far the oldest extant source for either BWV 549 or BWV 549a, the D minor version has been claimed by some as the original and elsewhere as an 'early version' (*NBA* IV/6); see also BWV 549.* The pedal note which had to be avoided (d') occurs only in the opening introduction, the pedal otherwise not rising above b♭. Unlike other works in D minor (BWV 538, 539, 565), BWV 549a does not go below D, nor does it seem to have been altered in that respect – a detail which no doubt made the transposition easier. As it stands, the coda of BWV 549a.ii offers interesting parallels with the closing section of the D minor Toccata BWV 538.i: in both cases, manual and pedal exploit square semiquaver patterns, BWV 549a naturally in a more conventional style but with equal vigour.

Sources of BWV 549a.ii make the closing plagal cadence in the pedal more direct than do those of BWV 549.ii; similarly, it is possible to believe that b8 of the prelude is authentic in BWV 549a but was altered in BWV 549 by copyists who did not understand that an opening pedal solo could have its own perfect cadence distinct from the following

---

* J. G. Möller, owner not copyist of the MS, was a Kittel pupil, a circumstance perhaps confirming the association of this work with J. C. Kittel.

passage for manuals (cf. Böhm's C major Praeludium). The result is that the pedal solo in BWV 549a (as in *NBA* IV/6) requires a more distinctly drawn close than that of BWV 549 (as in *NBA* IV/5), which runs straight into b9.

550

Prelude and Fugue in G major

No Autograph MS; copies in Lpz MB MS 7, 20 (J. N. Mempell?), P 287 (Michel), P 1090 (Homilius) and later copies (LM 4839a, Brussels Fétis 2960, Scholz MS prelude only, Salzburg Archiv des Domchores MN 104) including those of 19th century (P 642 etc, P 512 Grasnick, P 924 Grasnick, Lpz Go.S.318a (1819)); *BG* 38 also used 'old MS in Hauser's Collection' (P 1210, 1st half of 18th century, 'corrections' by J. S. Bach) and Dresden Sächs. Landesbib. Mus. 1 T 12 (destroyed).

Two staves; headed variously 'Praeludio in G dur con Pedal' (Lpz MB MS 7), 'Toccata, Praeludium pedaliter' (Dresden MS), 'Preludio con fuga' (Fétis 2960), 'Praeludium pedaliter' (Hauser MS); fugue headed in P 287 'alla breve e staccato'.

According to Griepenkerl (Peters IV p. iii), a copy by J. P. Kellner 'lacked several bars of the prelude before the fugue', as is also the case in P 642; if the missing bars are those marked 'Grave' in Peters IV and some subsequent editions, it is perhaps more likely that Kellner omitted them because he thought them cursory and stunted than that he made his copy from a supposed early stage of the work which did not include that passage. Considering the Bruhns–Buxtehude elements in the work (see below), its formal originality lies chiefly in the length of the fugue. Despite the Grave section, the polarization of a praeludium into a prelude and fugue is clear enough, and there is no question of a postlude. More than either BWV 549.i or 551.i, the prelude too is a consistently worked version of an idea that sprang from the northern praeludia – i.e. introductory passage for manual, then for pedal (or vice versa), followed by much the same material for both together. The conception of unified prelude followed by spaciously developed fugue is not found in BWV 531–533, 535, 549 or 551; on the other hand, such unified preludes as BWV 534 do not refer so clearly to the praeludium tradition as do the opening manual and pedal solos of BWV 550 or 541. The closest parallel in this respect is BWV 536.

Prelude

As Spitta pointed out, Buxtehude had already created a prelude from 'an imitative and developed motif', though less extensively than BWV 550 (Spitta I p403). Such a prelude as the A minor BUXWV 153 has points in common with BWV 550.i: open motif treated in imitation between the hands and taken up in a pedal solo; related motif developed in four parts tutti; final tonic pedal point. But BUXWV 153 is only one-third as long as BWV 550.i, and the expansion-within-unity of the latter appears to be highly original. Were it not that Bruhns's extant praeludia constantly change direction, it could be thought that the expansiveness of BWV 550.i is more in the Bruhns than the Buxtehude style.

Given the form of the prelude – manual/pedal introductions followed by prelude proper – certain details recall tradition as others anticipate future developments. The motif appears in two forms – Ex. 165 – of

Ex. 165

which the first produces a striking gesture, the second a continuity. So striking is this gesture that the metre of the piece is not clear for some time ($^3/_2$? $^4/_2$?), despite the fact that the work begins with three distinct four-bar phrases. This counteracting of square phrases (which are characteristic of other composers of the period) by a metrical ambiguity is no doubt calculated. The pedal solo produces the required continuity, although there is still no modulation away from the tonic until after (or momentarily during) the *point d'orgue* that follows. The motif itself resembles others found in the early period (e.g. *Versus* III of Cantata 4, 1708?) and naturally leads to brief harmonic ostinatos familiar from Buxtehude (e.g. bb9–10, 38–9). In the course of the pedal solo, the motif produces a line through 'the whole compass of the pedalboard from top to bottom' (Spitta I p403), rising to e′ in b34;* the following bass line is characterized by a clarity of metre and harmony not unlike passages in Buxtehude or Bruhns (including motet move-ments), but here more regular. Indeed, the very logic of the bass line leads to a tonic cadence in bb45–6 and so produces a 'false close' avoided in such maturer pieces as the G major Prelude BWV 541.

The $^3/_2$ metre is manipulated with some dexterity, producing hemiolas at unexpected points (bb28–9, 43–4) and sequences of either two-bar (bb31–4) or one-bar phrases (bb35, 36). Despite the develop-ment between b31 and b46, the beginning and end of the prelude are based on the tonic–dominant–tonic strategy traditional in the genre. The result in BWV 550 is a movement whose unity of motif has not yet produced a complex form comparable to (e.g.) the Toccata BWV 538, but one sufficiently more extended than (e.g.) BWV 531 or 549 to seem to require that complex form.

* The e′ has led some commentators to seek an organ on which it could have been played, e.g. Weissenfels (like BWV 653b; Klotz *NBA* IV/2 *KB* p68). Certainly, both C (b22) and e′/d♯′ (b34) are integral to the musical logic of the piece as transmitted by the source. It would be a groundless conjecture to suppose that the subtleties of the whole passage from b31 to b46 indicate something added later to what was already there; but compass of itself is a poor guide to when or for what organ BWV 550 was written.

'Grave'

Although in theory related to those sustained passages, enlivened with little *durezza* motifs, that introduce or (equally often) follow fugal sections in Buxtehude praeludia, these three bars are less traditional in two respects: the two diminished sevenths are more characteristic of the eighteenth century (see also BWV 532, 565 etc), and the overall design is a simple imperfect cadence. In this respect the three bars look ahead to such links as the phrygian cadence between movements of the Third Brandenburg Concerto and have a less intrinsic (and interesting) character than the usual *grave* sections in organ praeludia. But as Keller pointed out (1948 p79), there is a comparable link between sections in Buxtehude's 'Wie schön leuchtet der Morgenstern' BUXWV 223 (bb74–6).

Fugue

The direction 'staccato' might reflect a later copyist's ideas on how to play such figures and (eventually) chords as the fugue subject produces – effects of keyboard style standing midway between the preludes BWV 532.i and 541.i, and most like the style of the Jig Fugue BWV 577, particularly at the close. The subject itself contains the two figures primarily associated with this keyboard style, namely repeated notes and broken triads – Ex. 166 – both of which are used with a degree

Ex. 166   b62

of independence in the course of the fugue, and both of which are played detached.

The fugal working produces an unusual form:

62–95	exposition with five entries in three and four parts (compare BWV 531, 549); first answer (b68) tonal, second real (b83); fifth entry follows on directly (b89); countersubjects vary but are based on subject
95–117	episode accompanied at first by pedal, which drops out for the two entries (bb99, 107), with related and to some extent repeated countersubjects
117–44	two entries in relative minor, without answer; followed by derived episode to:
144–55	quasi-stretto entry in dominant of relative minor, followed by derived episode to:
155–65	quasi-stretto entry in dominant, followed by derived episode to:
165–76	quasi-stretto entry in supertonic minor, followed by derived episode to:
176–92	quasi-stretto entry in subdominant, followed by derived episode to:
192–202	two quasi-stretto entries in tonic
202–20	derived coda

The details show some command of structure – e.g., the pedal entries are timed asymmetrically – and the derivation of material is achieved with some variety, despite an apparent sameness in the series of entries. More to the point than the frequent criticism levelled at the piece (Spitta, Keller) is that the fugue develops triadic figures as exhaustively as the prelude uses *its* motif; in this sense prelude and fugue are complements, not using similar figures as such (as claimed by Schöneich 1947/8 pp149ff) but each developing its own, in prelude form and fugue form respectively. The episodes, though simple, do in fact use the triads to varying effect (compare bb139ff with bb171ff), and the subject itself is so easily transformed that there is curiously little exact repetition. The countersubjects share this characteristic, even if it is true that 'one cannot speak here of counterpointing' (Frotscher 1935 p866) in any strict sense. Similarly, though the sequences frequently threaten too much spinning-out they are held in check, each passing quickly to another (as in the prelude) and producing such well-timed preparation for entry as bb182–92. The concentration of four-part chords at the close is produced by extending in sequence both the subject and its various countersubjects, which join in naturally since they use the same motifs. The pedal line, for example, clearly belongs to the same idiom as much of the D major Prelude and Fugue BWV 532, but the sense of climax is more dramatic, ending in a close far more succinct than was usual in the new long unified organ fugues of the early eighteenth century, such as J. G. Walther's Prelude and Fugue in C (BB 22541/4).

---

551   Prelude and Fugue in A minor

No Autograph MS; copies in Lpz MB MS 7, 11 without first 11 bars (J. N. Mempell?), P 595 (J. Ringk), and 19th-century sources including Lpz MB III.8.20 (J. A. Dröbs), P 642 and P 924 (Grasnick).

Two staves; title in Lpz MB MS 7 'Fuga in A mol', in P 595 'Praeludium con Fuga...pedaliter'.

Commentators have usually agreed with Spitta in hearing no connection between the two fugal subjects of this five-section composition, which is said to have been written before the young Bach visited Buxtehude (Keller 1948 p48) and which shows signs of being 'only an imitation ...written before Buxtehude's manner had been fully understood and enlivened by the composer' (Spitta I p316). That the two fugal sections are 'independent' has been ascribed to the influence of the north German organ toccata (Frotscher 1935 p855). But it is not difficult to see connections between the two fugues; rather, the work can be shown to have a symmetrical plan of some ingenuity, even perhaps in a common tempo from section to section:*

* The bar-numbering is in one sequence through the whole of BWV 551.

1 prelude based partly on scale fragments . bb1–12
2 fugue with chromatic subject and key semiquaver figure *x* bb12–28
3 short sustained five-part section bb29–38
4 fugue with chromatic subject and semiquaver figure *x* bb39–74
5 postlude based partly on scale fragments bb75–89

The symmetrical elements grouped around a conspicuous if short central passage distinguish the work from such praeludia as Buxtehude's E minor BUXWV 143, where there is little resemblance between the prelude and postlude and no clearcut middle section. On the other hand, there is no such clearcut postlude in other multiform works such as the E major Toccata BWV 566. Like the three-section works BWV 531, 565 etc, this A minor Prelude and Fugue is a simple, logical presentation of a conventional shape now made clearer with its sections more obviously balanced. Only general parallels can be drawn between it and the 'Buxtehudian five-section toccata' in the harpsichord toccatas BWV 910–915.

First section

It is not known why Mempell's version does not contain the present first eleven bars of BWV 551; nor what the significance is of the further chromatic fugue subject in A minor that follows it in that MS copy. As it is, the tail-chasing figuration of these eleven bars is not unlike that occasionally found elsewhere (e.g. Buxtehude G minor Praeludium BUXWV 149, Lübeck Praeambulum in C minor), as are the clear, deliberate tonic in preparation for the fugue (bb11–12), such details as the pedal point after the semiquaver pedal entry (cf. Lübeck *op cit*), and the three-part texture widening only for the cadence.

Second section

The fugue subject has a chromaticism clearly reminiscent of many a seventeenth-century subject, not least in its elementary imitation, characteristic of south German fugues: Ex. 167. The fugue consists of

Ex. 167 b14

two similar expositions, the second moving towards C major, and both are based on the entries of descending voices – more entries than there are parts:

entries on e″ a′ e′ a e in the first exposition (12–19)
entries on e′ a e A in the second exposition (21–7)

The second is more 'correct' in its correspondence to the number of parts; both recall or anticipate the exposition of BWV 531. Such bars as b20 also suggest south German style. Spitta found the subject 'mechanically motivated and melodically expressionless' and heard in it an imitation of northern models (Spitta I pp316–17), but northern touches can be heard only in such motifs as Ex. 168.

b12

Third section

More strikingly northern are the three bars 29–31 and the seven bars 32–8, since both passages use devices familiar from the corpus of praeludia. The first passage clearly conforms to those moments in Buxtehude when a sharpened fourth obsesses the harmony until it is resolved (an idea from Frescobaldi); the rests or breaks are also part of the language. The sustained chords are as simple as, and no more chromatic than, similar passages in Buxtehude or Bruhns. Although the $^{6\ 6}_{4\ 3}$ harmonies resemble those of (e.g.) Buxtehude's A major Prae-ludium BUXWV 151 (passage from b64), the increase from four to five parts is less typical and may already suggest the interests of a composer who was to write the Grave of the C major Toccata BWV 564.

Fourth section

The passage in Ex. 169 from Sweelinck's Fantasia in G, preserved in a Lübbenau tablature, has been adduced by Seiffert and others (Keller 1948 p49) as an influence on the double fugue subject of BWV 551. But

Ex. 169

Sweelinck, Fantasia in G major

b35

it is more likely that BWV 551 reflects merely a tradition of double subjects (of which one is chromatic) and not specific influences. The 'countersubject' *b* in the Sweelinck example is one of several employed, in various note-lengths and species, throughout a 262-bar fantasia, from which bb35–9 are chosen somewhat arbitrarily. Being major and not minor, the chromaticism of the theme *a* is less pronounced than that of its counterpart in BWV 551. Nevertheless, the coincidence is striking and underlines the conventional nature of Bach's double subject.* More probable than any Sweelinck influence is that there are family likenesses between any such chromatically rising subjects or between any such semiquaver countersubjects. Whether it is correct to see the counterpoint to the second fugue subject as more than 'thematically related' to the first fugue subject (Schöneich 1947/8 p43) is uncertain; resemblances may be heard, but some common quality is also heard between the motifs of all three subjects: Ex. 170.

Ex. 170

If BWV 551 is seen as an exploration in fugal terms of such semi-quaver patterns – heightened by the sustained middle passage – the work can be seen to have a more important position in the composer's development than is suggested by the commentators' usual criticism of its fugal technique. It is true that neither fugal section goes much beyond two or three parts; but great variety of texture and tessitura can be heard, and such a passage as Ex. 171 contains both thematic

Ex. 171
b65

* It is unlikely that the countersubject ought to be given to the pedal (bb44, 51) as assumed in BG 38 and elsewhere; BWV 579 offers no parallel, since both subjects there are more plausibly pedal-like. Both BWV 551 and 561 are given more pedal phrases in the sources than their composer(s) probably intended.

cross-reference and the developed sense of semiquaver line useful in maturer works. That the top line looks like a phrase from (e.g.) Vincent Lübeck again confirms the traditionalism of the melodic technique; the two-part chromatic counterpoint (bb45–7, 51–9) is generally very like that produced in similar circumstances by such composers as J. C. Kerll. It should be noticed, however, that the lines are as close to the first fugal section as to the second, looking like a derivation from both. In each fugal section of BWV 551, the composer is preoccupied with invertible counterpoint against which a third part is rarely important; there is no attempt at a full permutation fugue, although stretto is found both in regular expositions (g″ c″ g′ c′ in bb62–4) and in irregular (d g d″ d′ a e a″ in bb67–72). So far as it goes, there is a sense of increasing complexity and shape at the close of the fourth section; its cadence is old-fashioned, clear, requiring no rallentando.

Fifth section

That the second fugue ends with a perfect cadence (b74) further isolates the final coda. Like the prelude, the postlude is built on semiquaver figures of various kinds, further enlarging the repertory of such figures presented in the course of the work as a whole. A typical comparison – Ex. 172 – shows how familiar are the ideas from other

Ex. 172

Praeludium in A minor BUXWV 153
b16

praeludia. Both manual and pedal figures sometimes resemble those of the first section of the work, but there is no intricate cross-reference or simple repetition. The postlude can be seen as one long drawn-out plagal cadence in A, finally incorporating the broken-up phrasing characteristic of many northern praeludia. Even the final bar with its d♯″ (see *NBA* IV/6 p67) recalls the Buxtehude cadence in which a sharpened fourth prepares acceptance of a tonic when the ear has become accustomed to its subdominant.* Points similar to those made about the manual sixths or pedal figures in BWV 531 can also be made here.

---

* As in (e.g.) Buxtehude's A minor Praeludium BUXWV 153. This 'explanation' of the sharpened fourth above tonic harmonies is conjectural; the effect seems to have been largely reserved to such organ music.

552   Prelude and Fugue in E flat major (*Clavierübung III*)

Published 1739 (for title, see BWV 669); no Autograph MS. Several subsequent copies, e.g. Am.B. 45, P 247 (fugue only), P 506 (prelude only), BB 30444 (three-part arrangement for manuals), Lpz Poel 355 (early 19th century).

Two staves; heading 'Praeludium pro Organo pleno', 'Fuga à 5 con pedale pro Organo pleno'. Inauthentic title in Lpz Poel 355, 'Concerto in Es-dur'.

Although united by key, number of parts (five) and number of themes (three), and understood by Forkel, Griepenkerl etc. as belonging together, the Prelude and Fugue in E flat were printed apart in *Clavierübung III*, were sometimes copied singly during the later eighteenth century (Tessmer *NBA* IV/4 *KB*) and were not always played together in the nineteenth.*

Prelude

The prelude – which with BWV 540 is the longest of the organ preludes – has a general shape as follows:

A_1	1–32	32 bars
B_1	32–50	
A_2	51–71	first part of A
C_1	71–98	
A_3	98–111	second part of A
B_2	111–29	
C_2	130–74	
A_4	174–205	32 bars

but each of the sections could be subdivided, and constant development takes place during the returns, particularly of the fugal C sections. The dotted figures that predominate in A are open to melodic extension, and in A_2 and A_3 the lines they produce are inverted or interchanged (compare bb17–18 with 1–2, and 104–11 with 25–32) and perhaps decorated (compare the scales of bb54–7 with the middle section of the E minor Fugue BWV 548). A_4 is the same as A_1 except that its return is disguised at first by its quite different opening at bb174–5 – a more drastic disguise even than the return of the *da capo* section in BWV 548.ii. The second C section not only is more extended than the other episodes but begins and ends in an unexpected manner: in b129–30 a return to A_2 or A_1 is more expected (compare bb50–1), and at b174 the music is firmly in C minor, not E♭. Other preludes also include fugal sections – e.g. BWV 544 and 546 – but there the fugal episode is the only full secondary material and not the third of three sections as in BWV

---

* E.g. Schumann's review of a concert by Mendelssohn (David & Mendel 1945 p372); in a letter to his mother on 13 July 1837, Mendelssohn defended the performance of the prelude and fugue together as a pair.

552.i, and in each instance it begins in the tonic after the previous section has come to a full close.

Despite elements taken both from the French Overture (dotted rhythms and short runs in A_1; the emphatic appoggiatura chords*) and from the Italian concerto (contrasting episode material within a developed ritornello form), the prelude is unique. The tempo, for instance, is too fast for a true French Overture, unless two bars equal one bar of an overture $^4/_4$, in which case more semiquaver runs would be expected; clearly, the overture idiom has been modified for organ. The contrast between the three ideas A, B and C is very striking:

> A five-part contrapuntal harmonies based on two-bar phrases open to extension and motivic development
> B staccato three-part chords of a distinctly quasi-*galant* nature ('pointing to C. P. E. Bach's and Haydn's keyboard style', Spitta II p690), with one-bar phrases open to echoes, repetition and simple sequence but not further developed
> C double fugue (or three-part invention with modified countersubject), built from running or broken-chord semiquavers

All three themes are uncharacteristic of organ music of the 1730s (e.g., the 'French Overture' was not a part of the French organ repertory) although the movement as a whole has been seen as a 'symbiosis of orchestral and keyboard style' (Trumpff 1963 p470). It has also been seen as a depiction of the Trinity (Chailley 1974 p262):

> A majestic, severe (Father)
> B the 'kind Lord' or 'freundlicher Herr' (Son)
> C fluid, incorporeal (Holy Ghost)

The three sections share the same written pulse but their styles are different, just as in the fugue the three themes share the same style but the written pulses are different. To the player, the stylistic differences make it difficult to find a common tempo suitable to both A and B; clearly, too, the pedal version of the fugue theme in C_2 is difficult to play, although fugue themes were often altered to give the pedals a line more suitable for alternating feet (cf. BWV 566.ii, manual and pedal versions) and the pedal part resulting from such alternate-foot pedalling is well within the convention (Bruggaier 1959 pp159–67).

The transformation of the theme for pedal in C_2 emphasizes the fact that the pedal does not take part in C_1 and that it is chiefly on its behalf that C_2 is so much longer. In general, the pedal fulfils a different function in each of the three sections:

> A a 'modern' bass, an instrumental basso continuo removed from the stated or implied *points d'orgue* of toccata basses (as still found in e.g. BWV 542.i)
> B a pedal quasi-staccato bass
> C_2 old-style pedal line (semiquavers for alternate-foot pedalling)

In none does it have its old role of providing pedal points, whether actual (e.g. BWV 546) or implied (e.g. BWV 548).

* Compare the opening chord of b2 with the same point in the Ouvertures of the D major Partita BWV 828 and the B minor 'Partita' BWV 831.

The two-part fugal theme C_1 resembles that of BWV 546.i (b25) both in the syncopations of the upper voice and in the steadier rising scale of the lower, which again does not at first appear in the pedal despite its conventional nature as a fugue subject (compare it with BWV 545.ii). The passage beginning at b161 is puzzling because of its sudden change to the minor until it is seen as (i) a contraction of the whole of C_1 (beginning in the minor, ending in busy figuration and a run down to *A*), (ii) a change of mode introduced for variety of key and a sense of impending close (cf. the subdominant and tonic minors at the end of the Prelude and Fugue in C BWV 547, or in A flat, *The 48* Bk II), and (iii) a reference to the previous change to the minor (b144) in keeping with other music of *Clavierübung III* (see also the E minor Duet BWV 802 bb35-7).

In the prelude the composer seems to have attempted to work an Italian form from elements varied in style and texture, through a key-plan centring on E♭ at crucial moments (notably the beginning of *B* at b32 and *C* at b130), and countering E♭ or its dominant by some unexpected modulations at bb91, 161 and 168. The contrast between one theme and another does not result in a Vivaldian concerto form as such but is worked towards an organ movement of alternation, one agreeing with the principle of rhetoric whereby the *dispositio* of the movement contains varied sections gathered together in, and framed and controlled by, the reprises or *confirmationes* (Kloppers 1966 p221). Thus while sections *A* and *B* differ from each other in style, they unite in contrasting with *C*. But the principle of contrast united by returns of key and theme has caused much misunderstanding about the movement, which is sometimes thought 'obviously inferior in inspiration...lacking in resource', with a 'monotonous result' in one section or another (Grace *c*1922 p226). It is often not seen that the conventional two-part figurations in bb86 or 147 and the three-part in bb93 or 170 (reminiscent of the Passacaglia BWV 582) are planned to contrast strongly with the descant-like harmonization of the theme *A* in b100, which is a newer kind of organ music. The conventional and the new are being joined. At least one kind of unity between sections is achieved by their each having a derivative of the opening French Overture motif: Ex. 173. Such

Ex. 173

a motif 'justifies' the unexpectedness of the *C* sections which is felt at several of its entries (bb71, 130, 161). Thus the scale in b98 and b174 is a useful link between *C* and *A*. However, it is, as Frotscher has already observed (1935 p896), too contrived to see the third theme as a 'variant' on the second.

Two further examples of the movement's allusion to specific styles are easy to overlook. First, the old-fashioned square-phrase sequence of bb138–40 is suddenly lifted up into a climactic return of the fugue theme *C* (without its *caput*) at bb140–1. Secondly, although the French element is much modified throughout the movement by a continuity of texture and rhythm unknown in the true French Overture, it is noticeable that the minor-key extension of theme *A* produces progressions of a more obviously French kind: Ex. 174. Both of these

Ex. 174
b65

examples – the fugal entry in b141, the harmony in b66 – could serve almost as textbook models of how to close sequences and continue after them, and of how to harmonize in the minor.

Perhaps more than any other prelude in the organ works of J. S. Bach, BWV 552.i repays close attention and an imaginative sympathy with the composer's intentions. Its frequent reliance on four-bar phrases, for example, is uncommon – perhaps unique – in Bach's organ music and is as striking in its strategy (e.g. the opening 32 or 4×4×2 bars) as in its tactics. It is further in the nature of the movement that its intricacies of style and form are not immediately communicable in performance. It would almost certainly be a mistake, for example, for the player to assume that the contrasts propounded in the movement's musical rhetoric require contrasts in registration. The composer's intentions seem to have been conceptual rather than perceptual, and no evidence suggests that the organist was expected to underline the sectionality of the work by changing stops for each of those sections.

Fugue

The fugue presents a more antique front than the prelude and continues the array of styles exploited throughout the pair of movements as a whole. Its three sections may 'represent' the Persons of the Trinity, as has often been suggested; the changing time-signatures seem to support the associations, as does the Eb tonality, long thought to express 'unity with Christ' in Bach works (Wustmann 1911). But from Frescobaldi onwards, the cumulative fugue with sections based either on different versions of the same subject or on secondary subjects that combine with the first had yielded good results, and Bach makes no attempt to clinch the Trinity association by combining all three – which would not have required unimaginable ingenuity. The tripartite structure of the fugue has naturally led many commentators to find parallels elsewhere, and it is true that the canzona and other fugal types by Frescobaldi, Froberger,* Böhm, Buxtehude, Weckmann and others often use themes in two or three forms (one for each section). However, the seventeenth-century convention of using different versions of a subject was one found mostly in canzona or capriccio fugues, i.e. those of a lighter nature, as in Frescobaldi's *Fiori musicali* (see BWV 588). Ricercar subjects more closely resembling the style of BWV 522.ii do not usually change metre, although they may be combined with different countersubjects. Such sectional fugues as Froberger's Canzonas I and II serve as a halfway point between the ricercare type of Frescobaldi and that of BWV 552.ii. Certain *stile antico* elements found in the work of Fux, Gottlieb Muffat and other composers are discussed elsewhere (see introduction to BWV 669), and clearly fugue subjects of the kind shown in Ex. 175 share with BWV 552.ii such details as the 'quiet' $^4/_2$ character, rising fourths, suspensions, narrow compass (a minor sixth) and Italianate invertibility.

Ex. 175

Muffat, *72 Versetl* (1726), 12th Mode, no. 1

The tripartite form of BWV 552.ii has little in common with the 'fugue of varied subject' by Buxtehude and others of the north German school, since Bach is both varying the subject and combining it with successive fugue themes:

A $^4/_2$ subject A, twelve entries, 36 bars
B $^6/_4$ subject B, then B (modified) + A, fifteen entries, 45 bars
C $^{12}/_8$ subject C, then C + A, 36 bars

Such fugues as the F sharp minor, *The 48* Bk II, or no. 11 in the *Art of Fugue* (BWV 1080.xi) demonstrate further the composer's interest in combining fugue subjects (although to different ends): this, rather than varying the themes themselves, is the intention of BWV 552.ii. The time-signatures are obviously significant (see below);† even the intervals of the subjects may be seen as complementary, with the prominent fourths of A, thirds of B and fifths of C: Ex. 176. But contrapuntal ingenuity is not given free rein. Strettos, for example, are modest, and those such as bb21–3 or 26–8 are made easy by the resulting parallel thirds and sixths. The natural ease of the *stile antico* subject pervades the counterpoint, even when the subject is not actually there (e.g. over bb43–7) and only gradually emerges each time from lines accompanying the secondary themes; for example, compare

* E.g. 'Canzona II' of *DTÖ* iv/i (Vienna 1897, ed. G. Adler) pp56–9 has three sections: regular fugue on traditional slow subject; regular fugue on derived subject, now in $^3/_4$; $^6/_4$ version of subject, now with quicker countertheme. The source of the work in question is listed as a Leipzig MS (Stadtbibliothek MS 51).

† The original time-signature 𝄴 (see *NBA* iv/4 p105) is probably a misprint for ₵ (Wolff 1968 p43).

Ex. 176

the accompanying parts in bb91–2 (which include subject *A*) with bb97–9 (which do not). Importantly, no indisputable attempt is made to combine all three subjects (cf. F sharp minor, *The 48* Bk II), not even in the final bars; that the subjects are in some degree related to each other* need not have precluded a clear, unambiguous combination of them (cf. BWV 1080.vi and vii).

The first subject itself would naturally offer its intervals for separate development (e.g. the rising fourths of bb21–3) and quasi-entries (e.g. b54); but what is less to be expected, if the fugue were simply a series of contrapuntal demonstrations, is the way that the second subject *B* has to be altered to fit the first (bb59–60). Moreover, the third subject *C* is extended until it passes to the main subject *A* (b88) before the two are combined; then it fits twice to *A*'s once. While the practical composer will soon have appreciated that such a subject as the first leads naturally to simple suspensions (increasingly so in the final section) and hence to ease of harmony, the Fuxian scholar will also have appreciated that such a subject could occasion 'proportional' countersubjects of various 'species': the first (b3) of $^4/_2$ crotchets, the second of $^6/_4$ quavers (the subject diminished and syncopated), the third of $^{12}/_8$ quavers and semiquavers (the subject augmented and syncopated). The proportional countersubjects may also imply that the tempos of the three sections are to be directly related to each other: $^4/_2 \, \rho = \, ^6/_4 \, \rho$, and $^6/_4 \, \rho = \, ^{12}/_8 \, \rho$. It should be noted that a 'proportional' interpretation of tempo accords with the didactic elements in the collection as a whole, and that the player is helped at each juncture towards understanding the tempos in this way. Irrespective of any rallentando at the cadence, the left hand in b36 continues naturally into the new fugue subject, while in b81 the hemiola directs the attention towards a minim beat and thus guides the tempo of the following bar. In general, it can be said that the 'rhythmic variations of the main subject' in the second and third sections are unique, producing 'a degree of rhythmic complexity probably unparalleled in fugue of any period' (Bullivant 1959 p652).

---

* Keller felt that the second fugue subject was 'contained' ('einbezogen') in the semiquavers of the third (Keller 1948 p125), but neither the truth nor the significance of this is clear, despite similar views more recently expressed (Trumpff 1963 p469; Chailley 1974 pp266, 268).

Each of the three sections of the Fugue in E flat has further points of interest:

A. The subject is of such familiar outline that many similarities have been found, in chorales (close of Cantata 144), vocal/choral movements (Handel, Krieger), older *canzone a la francese* (de Macque) and contemporary fugues (J. G. Walther).* Such melodic resemblances are to be expected in a work intended by the composer to have *genre*-associations; in this respect, the subject of the E major Fugue, *The 48* Bk II (BWV 878.ii) is more closely related to BWV 552.ii than is the C major Ricercare from Bertoldo's *Tocate ricercari* (1591) or the E major Fugue of Buxtehude (BUXWV 141), which have some or all of the same notes.

There is more in common between the E major Fugue BWV 878.ii and BWV 552.ii than the type of subject. The countersubject of moving or *transitus* crotchets is a common factor (that of the Credo in the B minor Mass is closer still to BWV 552.ii) and is of great importance to both fugues. The bass lines of both BWV 552.ii and BWV 878.ii are of stricter thematic character than those of (e.g.) the first two *stile antico* chorales of *Clavierübung III* (BWV 669, 670). While the E major is no doubt the 'strictest and most compressed of Bach's instrumental fugues' (Wolff 1968 p99), both demonstrate the *fuga grave* (J. G. Walther's term: *Lexicon*, 1732), belonging as they must do to the same period of the composer's development. An example of their similarity of approach is the stretto in both fugues beginning after the end of the first full exposition (BWV 552.ii b21, BWV 878.ii b9), or the parallel thirds and sixths that such contrapuntal lines encourage. Traditional in northern European organ music in general is (e.g.) the imitation (figural canon) between parts in bb11–12; familiar in J. S. Bach is the inner melody of the writing, so that (e.g.) an entry of *A* may be heard over bb35–6 though it cannot be found on paper.

B. It is not known whether the subject *B* was altered in b59 for the entry of subject *A*, or whether the composer, having found a running-quaver countersubject to *A*, decided it was unsatisfactory to stand as a subject itself and so altered it for the exposition that began in b37. In both bb44–6 (alto, then bass) and bb54–5 (soprano) subject *A* is hinted at, showing its essential blending quality. The *inversus* form of *B*, beginning in b47, is also both altered to fit subject *A* (bb73–4) and extended to run into it (b67, bass). Just as the hemiola in b81 heralds the new section, so that in b58 leads to the combination of themes, cutting the $^6/_4$ fugue into almost exactly equal halves. Important, too, is that the top note of the whole fugue (c''') occurs in each section shortly before the transition to the next (bb32, 57, 77, 105); its other appearance in p96 is more *en passant*. Much detail in the theoretical interpretation of the fugue as a whole – e.g. whether each theme pictures a Person of the

---

* Some thirty examples of variously similar themes are given by H. Lohmann in B & H edn 6588 (1971); he also sees the theme as adding up to 41 (a = 1, b♭ = 2, g = 7, c = 3 etc), the same total as J. + S. + B + A + C + H (A = 1, B = 2 etc).

Trinity, and if so in what order – depends on whether or not *B* can be heard as containing within itself both *A* and *C*, which some writers, by ingenious juggling, have persuaded themselves is so (Chailley 1974 p264 etc).

C. Subject *C*, which begins on the second beat of b82, seems to refer to subject *B* (compare notes 5–8 of subject *C* with notes 8–11 of subject *B*), as in its falling fifths and rising fourths it also does to subject *A*. When subject *A* appears it is both syncopated and accompanied by running semiquavers; *A* and *C* are first combined only in bb91–3 and then somewhat obscurely, *A* being merely part of the accompanying chords. Bars 87–91 (top part) and 92–6 (pedal) suggest that there is a new composite theme, *C*-followed-by-*A*. But this pairing is not continued, and the fugue is characterized by other elements: semiquaver groups suitable for climax and flow at the end of a long fugue, sequential treatment of *C*, pervasive reference to subject *A*, combination of subjects in the tonic at bb114–15. The semiquaver groups are perhaps related to subject *B*; see for example the right hand at bb105–6. The references to *A* are more various: hidden and circumstantial (e.g. inner parts in bb103–4), quasi-stretto (bb108–11), extended (pedal b110), even quasi–ostinato (four entries of *A* in the pedal against two of *C*). It is this quasi-ostinato effect that gives the pedal a power and finality even exceeding those of such fugues as the D minor BWV 538 and C major BWV 545.

Even so, the fugue by no means overstates or even fully exploits its potential for thematic combination. The semiquaver sequence in the alto of bb93–4, for example, could have yielded further results. Although a $^{12}/_8$ organ fugue is by tradition the final section of a composite movement, the material of section *C* would have been sufficient for a full-length working of its own. The composer's interests were more invested in the formal shape of the fugue, its position at the end of a major collection of pieces, its springing from a *stile antico* subject, and the distinctly *stile moderno* sense of cumulative tension leading to the drama of the final pedal entry. It is scarcely an exaggeration to see the prelude and fugue as together summing up many, even most, of the resources of organ praeludia which were superseded, current or anticipated during the lifetime of J. S. Bach, assembling styles and techniques known from the period of Palestrina to that of Haydn and beyond.

553–560   'Eight Short Preludes and Fugues'

No Autograph MS; complete source P 281; a lost complete source used for Peters VIII (1852), not known in *BG 38* (1891).

Two staves; P 281 headed 'VIII Praeludia èd VIII Fugen di. J. S. Bach. (?)'.

The main question concerning BWV 553–560 is: Who composed them? That sources – or at least, known sources ascribing them to J. S. Bach – are so meagre obviously bears on that question. P 281 may have been copied by J. C. G. Bach (1747–1814) and seems to have belonged at one point to J. C. Kittel (Kast 1958 p18); and P 508, which contains a copy of BWV 554, was made in *c*1820 by F. A. Grasnick, who often copied works known to the Kittel circle. The lost source for Peters VIII belonged at one point to Forkel but seems to have resembled P 281: i.e., one was copied from the other, or both were copied from a common source (Emery 1952 p5).

There have been many conjectures about who wrote the Eight and when. Spitta felt that they bore the 'stamp of commanding mastery' as well as signs that their composer was not free of north German influences. On the other hand, they must have been written after J. S. Bach had become acquainted with Vivaldi's violin concertos – i.e. later than might be imagined from the 'early' non-thematic pedal entry in the fugue of BWV 588 (Spitta I p399). Perhaps J. S. Bach wrote them for his pupils (Frotscher 1935 p878); but their 'standard of counterpoint and general musicianship' would not be expected of the period in which Bach must then have written them (i.e. from 1707/10 onwards), nor does the scarcity of sources suggest that they were much used by pupils (Emery 1952 p31), even if they were part of a set intended to be larger and more wide-ranging (Beechey *MT* 1973 p831). Details of their technique have led to other observations, such as that in the fugues the differences between subject and answer (or the incomplete second answer of BWV 555) are unknown elsewhere in J. S. Bach (Souchay 1927 p4), as is the high proportion of descending SATB expositions (Emery 1952 p27), or that in general the fugal style and subject types are more characteristic of south German composers, in particular Pachelbel (Frotscher 1935 p878) and J. K. F. Fischer (Oppel 1910 p65). The south German resemblances, in particular the figuration and fugal details from Pachelbel, have been pointed out by Emery (1952 p24ff) and are clearer and more likely than the direct influences from Corelli imagined by other writers (Dietrich 1931). Comparisons between the Eight and their fancied models in Lübeck, Nuremberg and elsewhere have led others to date some of them to the 1690s (!) or at least before 1705, while BWV 560 in particular is said to show eccentricities not unlike W. F. Bach (Beechey *MT* 1973 p831). The most plausible conclusion is that 'there seems no reason why they should not have been written about 1730–50 by some minor composer in *central* Germany, whether or no he was a pupil of [J. S.] Bach's' (Emery 1952 p42), since proto-*galant* elements in the various movements (see below) make an earlier date unlikely. But these 'late' elements have led yet others to see resemblances to known works of J. L. Krebs (Keller *BJ* 1937) and J. T. Krebs (Löffler 1940–8 p143), or to see 'the stamp of the epoch of Telemann' upon them (Keller 1948 p58) clearly enough to call for a further refutation: 'as J. T. and J. L. Krebs are eliminated on the stylistic grounds shown, one should for the moment allow Bach's authorship to stand, until other criteria are found' (Tittel 1966 p123). But since Keller and Löffler each believed he had already found such 'other criteria', it is not useful to claim yet again, without further evidence, that J. S. Bach was the composer. Rather, the combination of stylistic elements – little *A B A* preludes, a *durezza* prelude, concerto elements, short fugues with clearly varied subject types, square sequences, *galant* turns of phrase, preponderance of root-position chords etc – suggests a widely read but only mildly talented composer of the 1730–50 period, even perhaps later. Such a dating would allow the Eight to belong together as the work of a single composer: any earlier dating might suggest that diverse hands were the source of such a variety of stylistic elements. Certain minor parallels with the work of F. A. Maichelbeck (Augsburg 1738) and J. C. Simon (Augsburg c1750) have already been pointed out (Emery 1952 pp41–2). That P 281 also contains authentic and presumably much older works (BWV 913, 718, 916, 735a) carries little weight in the argument, since those other works were written by several other copyists.

---

553   Prelude and Fugue in C major ('Eight Short Preludes and Fugues')

P 281.

Heading 'Prelude', 'Fuga'.

Prelude

Dietrich's idea (1931) that the binary prelude resembles a Corelli allemande has been adequately discounted (Emery 1952 p24), but it is likely that its composer knew Italian concertos or at least keyboard works aping violin episodes in such passages as bb5–8, 17–18, 20–1, 23–5. Except for one bar, the pedal looks like a basso-continuo part in string music; the exception is b1, where a *point d'orgue* combines with the figure above to resemble the small-scale toccatas of south German composers. That manual figure (Ex. 177) contains two motifs: *a* is typical of northern praeludia (cf. alternate-foot pedalling in bb12, 28),

Ex. 177

(cf. BWV 550)

b runs through the prelude. In fact, given the 'southern' allusions (a Pachelbel idea in b26 etc), the movement is unexpectedly tight in its organization around this motif *b*. The sequences centring on root-position harmonies in half-bar phrases are uncharacteristic of J. S. Bach; so are details of the binary structure (tonic return b13, abrupt close b28) despite the 'abbreviated recapitulation' of b21.

Fugue

Very close to J. K. F. Fischer or Pachelbel is the subject's coupling of two basic motifs – Ex. 178 – each of which has a distinct role: the first as *caput* or head leading to the strettos (bb41–2, 49–51),* the second

Ex. 178

b29

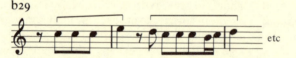

etc

giving continuity especially in sequence (bb52–3). Either detail can be traced in the organ works of other composers. Use is made of the countersubject, and again the movement is tightly organized around motifs – compact, but more than a mere fughetta.

554

Prelude and Fugue in D minor ('Eight Short Preludes and Fugues')

P 281, P 508.

Heading 'Prael[udium]', 'Fuga'.

Prelude

Such an *A B A* shape in which *A* is merely a framework for a *concertante* middle section would be unique in the organ works of J. S. Bach, irrespective of harmony or melody. The sources do not write out the *da capo*. The 'solo' section begins in b7 with a reference to the opening 'tutti' scale, then develops in a manner typical of string trio sonatas; the ensuing sequences resemble those of BWV 553. The return to the opening is both abrupt and too long in its F–Bb–D minor progressions – perhaps representing a minor composer's conception of miniature *A B A* form?

---

* In the discussion of BWV 553–560, the bar-numbering is continuous through both prelude and fugue in each case.

Fugue

There is no returning countersubject (except at bb45–6), although the alto of b36 or tenor of b39 would have been suitable. Bars 42–4 recall a familiar contrapuntal idiom, bb51–5 more one or another north German style. Whether the pedal enters in b54 (P 281, P 508) or in b52 (Peters VIII), it is still non-thematic, proceeding to a real entry only in b57; cf. BWV 533.ii b19. The closing bars not only resemble those of the prelude (themselves appearing twice in the *da capo* form), but both resemble the first and last lines of the melody *Jesu, meine Freude*: Ex. 179. The supposed reference is more conspicuous in the prelude.

Ex. 179

Although such references are unknown in J. S. Bach's free organ works, J. L. Krebs published a praeambulum to two settings of the same chorale in his *Clavierübung* (c1750/6; Löffler 1940–8 p143), beginning as in Ex. 180. Moreover, the chorale melody itself is an

Ex. 180

J. L. Krebs, Praeambulum to *Jesu, meine Freude*

etc

A B A framework like the Prelude BWV 554.i, i.e. with a last strain like the first, between which are longer, modulating strains. But whatever the significance of such observations, they further weaken the case for J. S. Bach's authorship of BWV 554.

555

Prelude and Fugue in E minor ('Eight Short Preludes and Fugues')

P 281.

Heading 'Prael[udium]', 'Fuga'.

Prelude

The *durezza* style of the movement, though unmistakable, is not pronounced and derives rather from *plein jeu* movements or organ versets of southern composers than from string trio sonatas. The picking up of melodic ideas (b1 in bb3 and 7, b12 in bb15, 18, 21) is less typical of the upper *durezza* style of the seventeenth century. Sometimes the idiom resembles passages in J. S. Bach, e.g. bb12ff in the D major Prelude BWV 532, while the Neapolitan sixth of b23 served such dramatic contexts as BWV 535.ii b72. Also, the metre is more squarely shaped around one-, two- and four-bar phrases than in older *durezza* styles.

Fugue

The fugue is stricter: the four-part fabric leads to progressions close to *durezza* idioms except for the metre (e.g. bb79–90), and the rising chromatic subject is an antique feature. It is probably this 'old' element that makes this the best-wrought fugue of the Eight, despite the truncated answer of b41 (tenor). Indeed, this shortened version becomes the true subject of the fugue, and the full subject does not appear again after the pedal entry bb45–50. But fugal devices are there: stretto (bb41–4), *inversus* (bb62–5) and stretto *inversus* (bb62–75),* and extension (b79) also in stretto. Further ingenuity would have been possible (e.g. a closer stretto in bb62/64); but the quaver motif from b32 is worked well throughout the fugue. The antique cadences are quite striking: the hemiolas of b96 (so notated in P 281) and bb68–9, and indeed the whole phrase bb66–70. Inverting the subject-head and the quaver motif produces counterpoint typical of earlier treatments of the descending chromatic tetrachord (bb64–5 in Sweelinck, etc).

556

Prelude and Fugue in F major ('Eight Short Preludes and Fugues')

P 281.

Heading 'Prael[udium]', 'Fuga'.

Prelude

Despite the hemiolas of bb12–13 and 42–3, and the rising sequence of bb15ff reminiscent of older concertos (e.g. finale of Third Brandenburg), it is difficult to believe that such mildly *galant* sequences as bb5ff are older than c1740, or that they were composed, even as a didactic example of a charming 'pattern-prelude', by the same hand that composed the faintly similar BWV 590.iii. The movement looks like an exercise in rising sequences, with a basso-continuo pedal part; despite the opening bars, the piece does not have a true minuet character; nor is it easy to see the influence of Italian toccatas of the period which Frotscher has suggested (1935 p878), although Soler's generation probably produced similar movements. As in BWV 554, the *da capo* (not written out in P 281) acts as a brief framework.

* The missing b71 surely centres on a soprano d' rather than the d♯' of *BG* 38, as has been well demonstrated (Emery 1952 p15).

Fugue

As in (e.g.) BWV 553, the subject contains at least two motifs: *a*, *b* and
c (Ex. 181) will be found in fugues of many a composer, northern or
southern. Perhaps such subjects were particularly characteristic of

Ex. 181
b59

Magnificat versets (Pachelbel). The doubled bass line of the closing bars
is not itself typical of any one *genre* more than another, and such bars
as b64 could be traced throughout the eighteenth century, particularly
in vocal fugues – which other bars also resemble (bb68, 69, 72, 73–7,
81, 86–7). As in (e.g.) BWV 555, an abbreviated form of the subject
appears in the working-out.

557

Prelude and Fugue in G major ('Eight Short Preludes and fugues')

P 281.

Heading 'Prael[udium]', 'Fuga'.

Prelude

Although beginning as a G major *plein jeu* verset in *durezza* style (cf.
BWV 902), the movement passes to simple figures of a kind justifying
Frotscher's phrase 'miniature toccata' (1935 p878). The pedal compass
may well exceed that of many southern toccatas, but it is written in
the long notes associated with such pieces – either a *point d'orgue* or
a phrase working towards a half-close. It is not certain from P 281 that
the pedal plays in bb13–17 (which would be exceptional in the longer
southern toccatas), although its solo is more in southern style (cf.
Pachelbel Praeludium in D minor). The succinct use of traditional
figures is combined with a melodiousness of cadence more in the
Fischer–Muffat tradition.

Fugue

Such syncopated subjects with potential for stretto seem more in style
with *The 48* Bk II than with any other fugal tradition; but the
foreshortened tonal answer (2½ bars instead of 3) is unlikely for J. S.
Bach (Bullivant 1959 p397). Each entry of the subject leads to and
follows a neat modulation* which the four parts join in to prepare.

* The G–C cadence in bb50–1 (cf. the B–E of b41) makes it the more likely that the C♯–D
in b51 (marked 'man.' in P 281) is indeed for manual, and not pedal as in *BG* 38.

Though also shortened, the strettos are varied (bb41–2, 46–8, 57–8), and the consistent countersubjects disguise the fact that one passage is repeated exactly (bb36–8 = 55–7).

558

Prelude and Fugue in G minor ('Eight Short Preludes and Fugues')

P 281

Heading 'Prael[udium]', 'Fuga'

Prelude

Only on paper could evidence be found for regarding this movement as an 'Italian courante' (Dietrich 1931); neither the form (*A B A B*) nor the figuration (one harmony per bar, decorated) is typical of any courante. Clearly the conventional cadence formulae have been well learnt (bb16, 22, 36), and the last might easily have been a phrygian half-close had it been conventional for preludes to end in this way. As elsewhere in the Eight, simple one-bar sequences above a basso continuo are so prominent as almost to suggest that their composer was consciously creating a series of samples.

Fugue

The subject again supplies three distinct ideas – Ex. 182 – any one of which can be found in other contexts, particularly canzona and ricercar subjects (e.g. *b* in a Pachelbel fugue, suggested by Emery 1952

Ex. 182
b38

p29). Motif *c* with its countersubject can obviously be extended in sequence, producing passages of a kind familiar in conventional fugues written under Italian influence, from at least 1675 to 1750. Although the counterpoint produced by *a* is invertible, there is no strict permutation-fugue technique, e.g. bb57–9 are not another version of bb54–5 or 86–7. Modulation is neatly managed (Spitta admired bb68ff in particular), and even the so-called non-thematic entry of the pedal at b75 (Spitta I p399) is in fact intrinsic: it is the countersubject from b43, showing the pairing of subject and countersubject throughout the fugue. That the composer had studied his south and central German models usefully is clear from the imaginative penultimate bar, very likely inspired by J. S. Bach.

559   Prelude and Fugue in A minor ('Eight Short Preludes and Fugues')

P 281.

Heading 'Prael[udium]', 'Fuga'.

Prelude

The demisemiquaver figures suggest the sample manual-play of the southern toccata rather than the caprice of the northern type, even though particular figures (e.g. b2) will be found in Buxtehude. For a note on sequences, see BWV 558.ii. It is not clear whether it was the figuration, sequences, tessitura or shape of the prelude that led Dietrich to see here the influence of Corelli's Op VI concertos (Dietrich 1931), though only the figuration is faintly reminiscent of these. The duet passage of bb11–13 must belong to 1730 at the earliest. Other features again show that the composer was close to certain organ traditions – compare the pedal of bb12–15 with the close of the first section of the A minor Praeludium BWV 543 (b24).

Fugue

That the second half of the subject follows the outline of the ornate A minor fugue subjects BWV 543 and 944 does not make either BWV 559 or 944 'in any sense a sketch for' BWV 543 (Emery 1952 p30), despite the suggestions made by earlier commentators (Oppel 1906). The subject of BWV 559.ii again resembles subjects of other $^6/_8$ verset–fughettas by central/southern German composers (e.g. F major II in J. K. F. Fischer's *Ariadne*), as does the sequential three- or four-part harmonies it easily produces (bb32ff, 37ff, 55ff, 63ff). As in other fugues of the Eight, the subject is shortened at times (bb46f, 48f, 59), the last occasion (bb66–8) resulting in an abrupt final cadence. The *point d'orgue* supports the least conventional harmonization of the subject throughout the fugue (see bb63ff).

---

560   Prelude and Fugue in B flat major ('Eight Short Preludes and Fugues')

P 281.

Heading 'Prael[udium]', 'Fuga'.

Prelude

No more than certain characteristics of the style – two-part writing, the melody-above-chords of bb14ff, the rising sequences – can be called 'orchestral' (Dietrich 1931). Rather, these details suggest a general keyboard style perhaps influenced by the newer oboe concertos of the 1730s but showing elements familiar in the Eight: the rising sequences themselves, the simple textures of bb18ff, the pedal solos, the general dependence on one extendable motif (as in the Prelude BWV 553). Specific elements are identical with those elsewhere: compare bb21–2 with bb16–17 of BWV 555.i. Presumably the varying texture of one to four parts is meant to provide the player with a complement to (e.g.) the three parts of BWV 556.

Fugue

The subject is not one likely to have been written before c1740: the motif of the first two bars and the broken-chord effect of bb29–30 would be traditional in $^4/_4$ but not $^3/_4$. The tonal answer of bb32ff is also uncharacteristic of J. S. Bach, having E♭s not E♮ until the close (i.e., it is not in the dominant). Such bars as 49–50 and 69–70 show the composer's familiarity with fugal imitation, but he surrenders the broken-chord figure to homophony from b35 onwards, despite some stretto (bb51–5 etc). The parallel octaves at the end are worse than those in BWV 556, since they reduce the number of real parts rather than duplicate one of them.

561   Fantasia and Fugue in A minor

No Autograph MS; 19th-century copies only (P 318, P 1066) and Peters IX (from a Schelble–Gleichauf copy).

Two staves; headed in P 318 'Fantasia in A moll (Preludio e Fuga per il Cembalo) compost: da Giovanne Sebast. Bach'.

Three questions are: Is the work for organ, and does it include a pedal part? Who wrote it? One common view is that it 'comes from Bach's earlier years and may have been originally composed for pedal harpsichord' ('Pedalflügel': Naumann *BG* 38 p. xxii), in which case the A major fugues BWV 949 and 950 should also be included amongst possible organ works. Another view is that whoever the composer was, he seems to have known the Prelude and Fugue in A minor BWV 543 (Keller 1937); perhaps it was J. C. Kittel, of whom the changes of movement from semiquavers to demisemiquavers may be typical (Keller 1948 p57). Why the work should also have been accredited to W. F. Bach (according to Frotscher 1935 p856) is also uncertain. Spitta assumed it to be a keyboard piece (Spitta I p432); despite *BG* 38 and subsequent editions, it seems that pedals are required only for the pedal points, i.e. not in the fugue and only with uncertainty elsewhere (see also BWV 551).

The formal intention of BWV 561 is clear: prelude, fugue, postlude. The sections are of a length comparable to the D minor Toccata BWV 565 and in certain details are not unlike BWV 543. The 'certain details' include such figures as the broken chords above an A pedal point, the harmonies of bb82–3* and the fugue subject itself, which not only includes similar notes and tessitura to BWV 543 but in both cases consists of an opening phrase (*caput*) followed by a figurative sequence – a fugue-subject type known elsewhere, amongst the work of contemporaries (e.g. Böhm's C major Praeludium) or pupils (J. P. Kellner's Fugue BWV Anh.180) and amongst doubtful Bach works (e.g. BWV 948). The prelude and postlude show the composer to have been directly or indirectly familiar with north German figures: e.g., bb1 and 29 can be found (in the same key) in Buxtehude's D minor Toccata BUXWV 155. Also, the sostenuto passages from b131 suggest a simplified and updated version of *durezza* harmonies, as those of bb73–4 suggest familiarity with Pachelbel. Other elements are those of a composer working traditional keyboard ideas in a modern idiom – the arpeggios of bb12ff have the flavour of c1750, and the expectancy aroused in the bar before the fugue (b48) is not typical of the Buxtehude period. The fugue, despite a fine theme, relies heavily on figures of an older type (e.g. from b63). To a Bach pupil, the example of the fugue section in the D minor Toccata BWV 565 would have justified (at least in theory) the poor, plain harmonies above the bass entry at b117, although such details as the supertonic pedal point so near the end of the work (b149)

* Numbering the bars in one sequence through the whole of BWV 561.

are not likely to have been known any earlier. Closing the fugue in the 'wrong' key (b121) is an extension of the idea of merging the end of a fugue with the following toccata passage, as in (e.g.) Buxtehude's D minor Praeludium BUXWV 140.

Despite the elementary nature of much of BWV 561, therefore, the work holds a certain interest – comparable to the Eight, BWV 553–560 – in its apparent cataloguing of effects or devices known in the north German Praeambulum and re-examined in a more modern light. It is difficult to believe that the thwarting of sequences (the weakness of A major in b20, the sudden A minor of b100) is the work of J. S. Bach.

562

Fantasia and Fugue in C minor

Autograph MS P 490 (fantasia plus fugue fragment); copies of fantasia in P 288 (J. P. Kellner), P 320 (Kittel), P 1104 (18th century, owned by Oley, later copied in P 519: both with the fugue BWV 546.ii), P 533 (J. F. Agricola 1720–74), P 277 and P 290 (2nd half of 18th century), Lpz MB MS 1, 3 (J. A. G. Wechmar 1727–99), P 557 (Grasnick, incomplete), and later sources (e.g. Stift Göttweig MS J. S. Bach 34, Lpz Go . S . 28, Warsaw Bib. Univ. Rps Mus 98, unnumbered Oxford Bodleian MS).

Two staves; headed in P 490 'Fantasia pro Organo a 5 Vocam [?] cum pedali obligato' (last phrase added later?).

All sources but P 1104 and Göttweig are based directly or indirectly on P 490 (the first page of which seems to be a fair copy), and a possible history of the work is as follows (Kilian 1962): (A) 'older' version of the fantasia (P 1104 and Göttweig), with simpler close and without penultimate bar of the (B) 'newer' version made before c1738 (P 288, P 533, P 277, P 290) and copied out in P 490; (C) a further stage at which the first page of a fugue was added in P 490, perhaps as late as 1747 (Kilian 1962) or at least in the period 1735–44/6 (Dadelsen 1958 p113). In P 1104 (perhaps copying an older autograph of BWV 562), the fantasia is followed by the C minor Fugue BWV 546.ii, which must, according to the scheme above, be dated before stages B and C; but there is nothing in their own sources to show that the Prelude and Fugue BWV 546 did not originally belong together (Kilian 1962).* In P 490 the fugue takes the last of the four sides of the MS, the final bar followed by directs to the next page, showing that the fugue was either continued/completed and lost, or planned but not executed. Other incomplete works of Bach do not have a full texture up to the point at which work stopped (e.g. the fragment 'O Traurigkeit, o Herzeleid' or the incomplete movement of the *Art of Fugue*), which suggests that BWV 562.ii was once longer; moreover, at least one other organ work

---

* Griepenkerl's supposition that BWV 562.i and 546.ii belonged together 'could not be maintained once the autograph had come to light' (Spitta II p691). In 1867 G. R. Wagener quoted the opening of the incomplete fugue BWV 562.ii in a letter to W. Rust (Schulze 1977 p69).

in an autograph score (BWV 548) breaks off during the fugue, which was then written out to the end by a copyist.

The differences in the final bars of BWV 562.i as they exist in P 1104 and in P 490 do suggest conscious amendment by the composer: compare Ex. 183 with *NBA* IV/5 p56. One might conjecture that the

Ex. 183
b76

simplicity of this texture results from a copyist's alteration – like the total omission of the 3½ bars 76–9 in P 320* – were it not that such 'simplification' would be unusual, that there is no particular playing difficulty or harmonic strain in the 'later' version, that the motif-content is more sophisticated in the 'later' version (eight-note figure instead of four-note; A♮/A♭ false relation), and that the rests in the 'later' version prepare the striking effect of the 'new' penultimate bar, with its doubled reference to the main theme of the fantasia. Such thematic reference certainly appears to be a sign of maturity – e.g., it is absent from the close of the F minor Prelude BWV 534, in which otherwise similar passage-work moves through a diminished seventh on a pedal point. As it happens, the coda in P 1104 also alludes to a previous motif (b52), now in diminished form.

Fantasia

While the open, even bleak C minor tonic and dominant pedal-point structure gives the fantasia some resemblance to the C minor Prelude BWV 537, its preoccupation with a single theme or motif is unusual – more so than the D minor Toccata BWV 538.i, whose motif is less melodious, more traditional to keyboard music. The six pedal points are separated by thematic pedal lines (cf. BWV 537) which are themselves new to the toccata traditions of southern Germany, and the

---

* It hardly makes sense for b80 to follow almost immediately on b75, and the version in P 320 cannot be given as much credit as that of P 1104.

contrapuntal treatment of the main motif is varied and inventive. It is not quite true that 'the whole work is developed from a single theme' (Keller 1948 p98), since the first twelve bars alone develop two motifs: Ex. 184. The chief melodic idea *a* is constantly treated to different

Ex. 184

countersubjects as well as being set in stretto (bb1/2 etc) and finally in sixths. A sign of the overall control of the fantasia is that it moves gradually towards smaller notes. New themes accompany the main melody at bb23, 40, 43–7, 51, 53, 54, 56, 57 etc, and the motif *a* is heard in more and more contexts as the piece proceeds. There is an abundance of countersubjects; one, particularly striking, is the crotchet pedal line of bb57ff, contrasting well with the pedal-point sections, while at other moments the intention is rather to incorporate the key figure as if unnoticed within an independent progression such as a cadence (e.g. b37), a sequence (e.g. b60), or an episode (e.g. b68).

The motifs themselves, not least in their ornamented notation, have often been claimed as French; it is no argument against the claim that the Frenchness lies more in appearance than in essence. Perhaps commentators are right to see here an allusion to melodies known from de Grigny's *Livre d'Orgue*, copied by J. S. Bach (*Dok* III p634) – melodies of which the Gloria fugue for the *petit plein jeu* (Ex. 185) is

Ex. 185

de Grigny, *Livre d'Orgue*, Gloria fugue

typical (Schrammek 1975 p102). In that connection, it is perhaps surprising that BWV 562 includes no *inversus* form of the subject. In general, it shares two particular elements with certain works of de Grigny: the decorative line that includes rising appoggiaturas (bb2, 3 in Ex. 185), and the five-part texture (not found in the Gloria fugue of Ex. 185) that is spaced thus: two parts right hand, two parts left, one part pedal: Ex. 186. Whether the five parts in BWV 562 are to be registered or divided up as de Grigny specified in his pieces – right hand on one registration (e.g. Cornet), left hand on another (e.g. Cromorne) – is very uncertain, not least because only a few organs (those of Silbermann) approached true French classical colours, which J. S. Bach would otherwise not have known. The use of paired manuals in the chorales BWV 619 and 633/634 is less ambiguous, since the texture is woven around a canonic cantus firmus.

Such appoggiaturas are not mere melodic ornaments but radical

Ex. 186

de Grigny, *Livre d'Orgue*, fugue *a 5*

b37

harmonic effects. Similarly, while the harmonic centres of BWV 562 are more in the pattern of the south German toccata (pedal points with quasi-fugal expositions above, etc), its shortness of phrase – different in principle from the phraseology of other mature preludes – brings it within the French mode as much as the appoggiatura harmonies themselves. That is, both the short phrases and some of the down-beat chords are certainly French in intention. It may have been these appoggiatura harmonies that attracted a later Leipziger, himself much versed in such techniques, to publish this fantasia in 1841 (Schumann *NZfM* Supplement 13, 3).

Fugue

The miscellaneous contrapuntal techniques of the fantasia are matched by the strict fugal texture of the 'Fuga', also in five parts and therefore complementary. The subject itself, incorporating a hemiola, would not be out of place in a *Livre d'Orgue* and does not conform to standard German fugue subjects; any resemblance between it and the Passacaglia theme (BWV 582) *inversus* is superficial. The texture promises to be full, and it is not difficult to believe such bars as 13–18 to be contemporary with the chorale BWV 678. That the stretto is already worked in b22 (i.e. after the first sectional cadence of the fugue) has suggested to some that the composer had intended to proceed to a double fugue, with a new subject (Keller 1948 p98; Kilian 1962); it is also possible that the theme would have been inverted later (as in BWV 547). However, it is not the subject that is of great interest in these twenty-seven bars but the motif [image: musical motif], which in various guises dominates the first section; its sequence in bb10–11, for example, produces a free upper part of little conviction. Both theme and motif are short for a fully developed five-part fugue, as are the subsidiary motifs that develop, whether crotchet (b13 pedal) or quaver (new motif in last six bars); there is as yet no broad sweep of line in the fugue, and it is possible that it was never continued.

563   Fantasia in B minor ('Fantasia con Imitazione')

No Autograph MS; copies in Lpz MB III.8.4 (Andreas-Bach-Buch), P 804 (Fantasia copied by J. P. Kellner, Imitatio by W. N. Mey, 1st half of 18th century), P 1091 (2nd half of 18th century) and later sources (P 279, P 308, BB 30069).

Two staves; headed 'Fantasia' (the second section 'Imitatio') in Andreas-Bach-Buch and elsewhere; 'Fantasia con Imitatione' in P 279; in P 804 no title for first section, second 'Fantasia' (*sic*).

That in P 804 the two movements are separated by nearly three hundred pages of music may be explained in several ways, all conjectural. Further questions are: Who composed the work? and Is it for organ? Peters edn 216 included it amongst the keyboard works, and Spitta regarded at least the 'light and minute ['leichte und minutiöse'] character of the first movement as not suiting the organ' (Spitta I p432). *BG* 38 and *NBA* IV/6 included it amongst the organ works, the former on the grounds of the 'organ-like nature' of the Fantasia, the pedal bass required for b15 and b20, and the crossed parts in the Imitatio at b129* (Naumann *BG* 38 p. xiv). There are several points against this: the sources do not indicate pedals; written-out sustained pedal points do not necessarily seem to indicate organ (cf. the A minor Fugue, *The 48* Bk I); the Fantasia is no more 'organ-like' than the Fantasia in A minor BWV 904 (also in P 804); and the Imitatio is neutral in keyboard style. More likely the work has a part to play in the pattern of 'stylistic experiments' operating in the Andreas-Bach-Buch (see notes to BWV 582), where with other works too the allegiance to any one instrument is doubtful.

   Although in principle a prelude and fugue, BWV 563 is unusual in its title and in its clear, even total, exploitation of two kinds of motif: the *figurae cortae* of the Fantasia and the $^3/_4$ figures of the Imitatio: Ex. 187. The former produces a clear four-part texture modified towards the end† with a slight cadenza and simple pedal-point harmonies; the

Ex. 187

* Numbering the bars in one sequence through the whole of BWV 563.
† In view of the strictness of motif treatment, the *NBA* IV/6 reading of b16 is certainly more in style than that of *BG* 38; but bb13–14 are still hardly convincing (should all the As be sharpened until the last three quavers of b14?).

latter produces a sectional fugue with a series of similar subjects. While the upper theme proper of a fugue may often not be heard complete after the first middle entry (e.g. Three-part Invention in C minor BWV 788), the several thematic groups of the Imitatio (bb25, 43, 71, 93) are more typical of the ricercar form of the seventeenth century.

Although neither movement pursues its use of motif to any doctrinaire extent, the pair do present an exercise not out of style with pieces exploiting some other set device, such as the canonic chorales 'Ach Gott und Herr' BWV 714 and 'Auf meinem lieben Gott' (anon.) in P 802 (copied by J. L. Krebs). The Fantasia also contrasts with the next fantasia found in the Andreas-Bach-Buch, BWV 944 in A minor 'pour le Clavessin'; on the other hand, the previous fantasia in that MS, BWV 570, is strikingly close to BWV 563 in its use of similar (but not identical) *figurae cortae*. That these three fantasias were copied by three different scribes at different dates does not invalidate such a comparison. The Imitatio too deals with a figure familiar from elsewhere in various contexts, e.g. the *Offertoire sur les grands jeux* from de Grigny's *Livre d'Orgue* copied by J. S. Bach (see BWV 562), the fugue theme of which is shown in Ex. 188. While therefore some

Ex. 188

de Grigny, *Livre d'Orgue*
Offertoire sur les grands jeux b90

commentators doubt the authenticity of BWV 563 (Blume 1968) and others date it to the early Arnstadt years (Dadelsen, notes to Telefunken record *BC* 635076), its origin is probably owed to an interest in *figurae* shown by J. S. Bach and J. G. Walther in c1707/8.

564   Toccata in C major

No Autograph MS; copies in P 803 (2nd half of 18th century), P 286 (mostly J. P. Kellner), P 1101 (18th century), P 1102 (fugue only, 18th century), P 1103 (without middle movement, 18th century), and later copies (Brussels Fétis 2960 or II.4093, unnumbered Oxford Bodleian MS, P 308) including incomplete copies (P 1071, up to b47; Stift Göttweig MS J. S. Bach 34, fugue only).

Two staves, headed 'Toccata ped: ex C' in P 803 and 'Toccata ex C♮ pedaliter' in P 286 (both also headed 'Adagio', 'Grave', 'Fuga' for the movements), 'Toccata' in a catalogue of 1785 (*Dok* III p273) and Fétis 2960.

The three-movement form of this work belongs at least to the period of the copyists, as can be seen in P 286 where all movements are on two staves and the Adagio begins on a verso page (after turnover). There is no known evidence in the sources that the Fugue was the earliest movement to be composed, as is sometimes suggested (Keller 1948 p77), or that the Adagio was a subsequent addition; but that the toccata includes manual d''' while the fugue seems to avoid it (bb4–5) may suggest that the fugue is later (Emery 1966). No sources suggest registrations or manual changes, but the opportunities for them are characteristic, perhaps intentionally so: quasi-echoes for both manual and pedal with rests allowing stop changes (first movement), manual dialogue within the ritornello structure (first movement), a solo line (second movement), a solo line merging into block harmonies (end of second movement), clear-cut fugal episodes (third movement). Such a repertory of organ effects may well seem to justify the idea that BWV 564 was composed for testing an organ (Gwinner 1968 115–17) – an impression also left by many a north German praeludium.

It is the clarity of form in three independent movements that caused Spitta to question the title 'Toccata' and to see behind it rather the 'model of Italian concertos' (Spitta 1 p415), a remark constantly resuscitated ever since. However, it is clear from (e.g.) BWV 545 that at least some preludes and fugues acquired slow movements at some stage in their history. Considered along with the Toccata in D minor BWV 565 and the Fantasia in G BWV 572, this C major Toccata can be seen rather as one of a series of essays in three-movement form, either so planned or so revised – the distinction between these two operations evidently being not crucial to an organist of the early eighteenth century. Like BWV 565 and 572, the C major Toccata remains a highly original example of organ form developed from elements current in and after 1700, with sections not only independent but each given a length, a form and a style not very like anything else. Each movement is highly original. The evolution of such a plan is clearly analogous to that of the chamber sonata of the period, with the crystallization of its sections into fully fledged movements. But the peculiarity of BWV 564, 565 and 572 is that they offer their three sections/movements in three very different forms. J. L. Krebs, who imitated details of BWV 564 in his Prelude and Fugue in C, did not develop or even keep the three-movement plan as a whole. This whole has been seen as close to the shape of the Buxtehude cantata, in which a solo is followed by a duologue (duet–dialogue), then an aria, then a fugue (Dietrich 1931); but the analogy can apply to BWV 564 only in outline. Equally highly organized are the details: the short phrases, the rests, the gaps and the occasional repeated notes – all of which are found in all three movements – contrast with the sustained, chromatic flow of the ten-bar Grave.

First Movement

A unique joining of toccata and ritornello form, the first movement comprises two distinct sections: (A) manual and pedal solo introduction, (B) a concerto-like dialogue. The join in bb31–2 is achieved so logically that B seems a natural consequence of A.

That section *A* is within the north German praeludium tradition is clear from the nature of the material, both manual and pedal, many phrases being of one-bar length. Ex. 189 shows some typical examples from elsewhere. The first is from a Reincken sonata arranged as BWV 965.ii (compare with BWV 564.i b33), the second from another Reincken sonata arranged as BWV 966.iv (compare with BWV 564.i b32). While the

Ex. 189
Reincken

Reincken

opening motif of BWV 564 is rather more arresting than is usual in north German praeludia (at least when they begin on the manual), the clear returns to the tonic followed by a rhetorical rest in bb2, 8, 10 and 12 are more typical – e.g. Lübeck's C minor Praeambulum. The three pedal Cs of bb8, 10 and 12 recall the familiar 'pedal-point toccata' and provide another example of how a convention has been applied to original ends. The opening motifs of the pedal solo are typical of such pieces (e.g. Buxtehude's C major Praeludium BUXWV 137, in the Andreas-Bach-Buch), and the systematic phrase-structure of this solo recalls Böhm (C major Praeludium). Less usual are the echo repeats of partial phrases and the bringing together of other important motifs (triplets, dactyls, trills). In fact, there is a careful control of figures in the opening thirty-one bars: the manual figures are demisemiquavers, scale-like, in-turning, smooth; the pedal figures are semiquavers, broken chords, varied, disjunct. Both seem to incorporate echo effects, the first in b5 (and b9?), the second in bb14, 16, 17(?), 18, 21–3, 28, and 30–1(?). Sequential patterns in the pedal solo are typical of (e.g.) Böhm, but the echo motifs themselves are of different length and type, again something carefully worked out – Ex. 190. Such variety suggests that the echoes should be brought out by the player – perhaps by taking off stops?

The section beginning at bb31–2 is marked less by its ritornello structure (episodes in bb55, 67) than by its dialoguing between two chief

Ex. 190

b21

b30

Ex. 191

ideas, each of which could have its own manual: Ex. 191. As Spitta observed, both ideas are anticipated in the pedal solo introduction (Spitta I p416), although Keller hears in the first of them the 'energetic bowing' of two violins (1948 p77). In some respects, the first

b32   b36

movement of the G major Harpsichord Toccata BWV 916 is similar: a ritornello movement based on short phrases constantly moving to cadences, with longer episodes as the movement proceeds, and returns of the main material in various keys. Also, the pair of short themes in BWV 916 has a theoretical resemblance to BWV 564 in that the first is scale-like, the second broken chords: Ex. 192. That such a form was

Ex. 192

BWV 916.i

b3   b5

not merely an early experiment is shown by its later appearance in less rigid, more sophisticated style in the G major Partita BWV 829. It should be noted that neither BWV 916 (Andreas-Bach-Buch) nor BWV 829 (published in 1730) distinguishes the two themes by changes of manual.

The 'general cheerfulness' and 'less church-like' mood of BWV 564 are not necessarily to be taken as showing the influence of Italian concertos (as suggested by Hoffmann-Erbrecht 1972), since Böhm's C major Praeludium is equally cheerful. Nor need the ritornello elements of this first movement, as of the fugue itself, be seen as originating in concertos; as has been pointed out (Klein 1970 p26), the returns of the ritornello material complete are not characteristic of Vivaldi concertos, nor does the movement follow a Vivaldian plan of exposition–middle part–reprise. Rather, the first movement is creating its own form based on short phrases each of which has an important contribution from the pedal; i.e., the texture is surprisingly consistent, more than in a concerto. It is possible that Spitta's phrase 'ganz concertmässig' ('entirely concerto-like') has misled later writers, who have seen the work as an attempt to transfer concerto form to the organ via 'German' toccata elements (Keller 1948 p77). A passage such as bb67–70 belongs ultimately to the north German style of praeludia (short phrases, pedal octaves etc), although its originality and charm should not be denied. Even the turn to the subdominant minor before the final cadence of the movement belongs to the toccata convention (e.g. tonic minor at the end of the first section of Böhm's C major Praeludium). Both the supposed tutti/solo contrast and the ritornello form of BWV 564.i are too ambiguous for the concerto analogy to be pressed too hard.

Second Movement

Obviously more concerto-like is the Adagio, which has 'no analogy in Bach's works' and whose melody, though 'conceived for organ', has an accompaniment 'reminiscent of a solo Adagio with harpsichord continuo' (Spitta 1 p416). The accompaniment has even been taken as one example of how a figured-bass part might appear when written out (Schneider 1914), not full-voiced but clearly rhythmic (Frotscher 1935 p870). Despite the structure of the melody – short phrases, in keeping with both outer movements – Italianate elements can be heard in the quasi-pizzicato pedal, the consistency of texture, the solo line itself, certain details of harmony (Neapolitan sixths etc) and perhaps the repeated or echo phrase at the close.* It is very uncertain how far any of these elements depended on specific acquaintance with Italian concertos or other orchestral music. Short melodic phrases, for example, can be heard in the Wedding Cantata BWV 196 (1708?). There is a simple, doctrinaire quality about the style of the movement that may reflect more than its early date when compared with the Air from the orchestral Suite BWV 1068. There neither the bass line nor the middle parts keeps entirely to a single motif as in BWV 564, and the melody is more clearly violin-like in its sustained notes and feer line. Indeed, is the concerto-like style of the Adagio in fact particularly string-like? It is possibly a newly devised organ idea independent of Italian concerto models and created within the spirit of invention shown so often in BWV 564. Quite apart from the reiterated rhythms associated with each of the three lines, there is a further didactic element in the very use of the Neapolitan sixths, of which there are five in a mere twenty bars (A minor bb2, 18, 20; E minor b7; D minor b14). Short dotted phrases are themselves consistent in style with earlier cantatas, and comparable decorative elements may be seen in the figures 'added' to the Reincken sonata arranged as BWV 965 (ascribed to J. S. Bach by J. G. Walther in P 803). The fact remains that the Adagio is amongst the most original of the new organ sounds attempted by J. S. Bach and has no clear parallels even amongst the chorale preludes. It is possible

* The repeated phrase is not found in P 286 and has been (later?) bracketed in P 803.

that the short stretches of melody-with-accompaniment attempted by Bruhns and others in praeludia (e.g. the longer E minor Praeludium of Bruhns in the Möller MS, bb90–4) suggested the kernel of the Adagio.

The Grave shows further clearcut musical intentions, being based not only on the harmonies produced by suspensions above a chromatic bass but in particular on the effect of a diminished seventh partly suspended over the next chord: Ex. 193. The same effect can be heard,

Ex. 193

not surprisingly, in the D minor Toccata BWV 565 b130 and the D major Prelude BWV 532.i b103; but in the Grave of BWV 564 it appears at least four times. It is this systematic use of a chord which distinguishes the passage from the chromatic *durezza* bars often found in north German toccatas, bars in any case based on simpler progressions (e.g. Buxtehude E minor Praeludium BUXWV 142, from b104). Such a use of suspensions may be associated in origin with Buxtehude (Spitta I p416) or with Frescobaldi and Bruhns (Keller 1948 p77), and the passage in BWV 564 may also be conventional in context, i.e. prefacing a lively fugue. But in general effect it belongs to the eighteenth century (as does that in the D major Prelude BWV 532), with its reliance on one particular and very striking harmonic device, its number of parts, the 'forbidden' intervals of its bass line and the clear recitative link between it and the previous Adagio.

Suspension harmonies can produce chords unusual in any period, as Frescobaldi, François Couperin and many others learnt; but the particular results of the technique employed in this Grave seem to have puzzled even the copyists. Thus in P 286 the pedal enters on a note consistent with the progressions in the next three bars, i.e. F♯ – Ex. 194(i). Although by association a pedal B♭ all through may seem preferable, the rising pedal diminished fourth is logical and consistent. So it is if the pedal rises a further diminished fourth two bars from the

Ex. 194

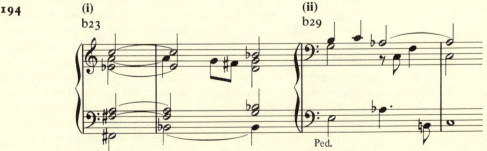

end, and the usual distribution between left hand and pedal (*BG* 15, *NBA* IV/6) is exchanged: Ex. 194(ii). This is the arrangement in one source, P 803.

Much speculation is required in order to solve the registration problem of the movement as a whole: How is the solo of the *Adagio* registered? Is the link played with the same stops? How is the Grave registered? In the absence both of information from the sources and of comparable movements elsewhere, it can only be pointed out that a single Principal 8′ for the Grave would accord with earlier Italian *durezza* practice and, on a suitable organ, would also have given suitable prominence to the right-hand solo of the Adagio.

Third Movement

The striking features of the fugue are the unique lightness of theme (and the mood it produces), the length of the working-out (middle entries answered at length), the modesty of the episodes, and the apparently low-key close. The form may be expressed as:

1–37	four-part exposition, with countersubject typical of the permutation fugue
37–43	episode, pedal and manual motifs derived
43–72	middle entry or exposition, in three voices
72–8	episode, motifs as before (invertible counterpoint)
78–96	middle entry, in two voices (answer imitated in stretto)
96–9	episode
100–9	entry, pedal only
109–23	episode, motifs partly as before
123–32	final entry, followed by:
132–41	coda, founded on various *brisé* figures

Much of the detail is highly unusual, including the moments in which conventional figures produce great technical difficulty. The rests within the subject, and its ending with a dotted-note cadence, are both features which can be found in fugue subjects of Buxtehude or Böhm; but nothing in their known work approaches BWV 564, even if long subjects incorporating broken-chord figures were known to the Reinckens and Buttstedts of the previous generation. A comparable motoric drive may be heard in the subject of BWV 532, and subjects whose rests divide the total theme into three phrases are not uncommon (e.g. BWV 533, 575); but again, nothing approaches BWV 564. The block chords produced by the simple counterpoint (bb25–6 etc) are also typical of such early fugues as BWV 533; less usual is the variety with which the main countersubject motif Ex. 195 is treated, such as the obsessive soprano part* to the E minor entry at b78. The episodes are too brief for the fugue to be considered a fully worked-out ritornello fugue, whether Italianate or not, but they often include a keyboard pattern that looks like a reference to the broken figures of a north German toccata: Ex. 196. Here the composer seems to be

---

* Which also in bb84–5 appears to avoid the c♯‴ and d‴ of the countersubject proper, i.e. notes outside the CD–c‴ compass.

Ex. 195　　　b11

Ex. 196　　　b118

integrating a familiar keyboard device within the fugal flow, instead of using it to break the flow as with Bruhns or Buxtehude. Like the subject, the broken figure returns rondo-like throughout; so does a characteristic cadence phrase.

The closing ten bars are interesting on several counts. The pedal cadence that might be expected at the close of a praeludium is again included 'within the fugal flow' (as it is in BWV 566), and the fugue closes with a held tonic pedal point, unlike the first movement where it is detached – a deliberate contrast. P 286 sustains the pedal C through to the final chord, which itself is given the length of a whole bar; the short detached final chord of P 803 suggests a strong closing rallentando, as do all such short final chords (e.g. BWV 547). From these two sources it is not clear what the original reading of the last bar was. Although the final bars of the chorale BWV 735 bear some resemblance to BWV 564, the held pedal note in the chorale invalidates the comparison; also, in BWV 735 but not in 564, the hands move up the keyboard. Whether the pedal is held or not, the close appears very unassuming. The allusion here may be to one of the north German conventions: Buxtehude's G minor Praeludium BUXWV 163 ends equally brusquely, and the north German allusion in BWV 564 is strengthened by the sharpened fourth (F♯) slipped into the closing three bars.

565　　　Toccata and Fugue in D minor

No Autograph MS; copies in P 595 (J. Ringk 1717–78) and 19th-century sources, some or all from Kittel circle (P 924 Grasnick, P 642, Lpz MB III.8.20 Dröbs); *BG* 15 used MS in possession of Schubring. All extant sources also contain BWV 551 and 532.

Two staves; heading, 'Toccata con Fuga' in sources (*NBA* IV/6), by Dröbs only 'Adagio', 'Fuga'. For tempo and movement indications, see below.

The lateness of the sources may well be reflected by the frequency and the 'modernity' of tempo and section indications (ten in *NBA* iv/6), as by the staccato dots of bb12ff and 34ff – neither of which could be expected in a toccata copied before *c*1740. The purpose of the pause marks (fermatas) in the first seven bars is not certain: it is more plausible to have them at least in part over the rests (as in *BG* 15) than over the final notes of each motif or phrase (as in *NBA* iv/6), since a free length for the rests seems more in line with the drama intended. However, it ought not to be assumed that a fermata does indeed indicate a pause or has any purpose other than guiding the eye to the phraseology, like some kind of *signum congruentiae*. At any rate, the notation of the first two bars is itself as unconventional as the musical gesture is original, quite apart from the potential phrasing of the opening figure: Ex. 197. More traditional are the variety with which

Ex. 197

the arpeggio of b2 is notated in the sources, the absence of manual indications for clear echo passages in north German style, and the 'superfluous' marking 'Fuga' (Rust *BG* 15 p. xxxiv) to distinguish the middle section.

Without doubt BWV 565 is one of the most original works attributed to Bach, its fugal movement in particular so 'simple' as to cause its authenticity to be questioned (e.g. Bullivant 1959). The overall form of prelude–fugue–postlude is within the north German tradition (BWV 561, 549, 551, 535a) and is itself a more codified or systematic development of the sectional toccata current in many areas by *c*1650. But three sections are less common than four or five, and where three do occur they are less cadenza-like than much of BWV 565, as in (e.g.) Buxtehude's Praeludium in D major BUXWV 139. No doubt Spitta is correct to see 'traces of the northern schools . . . in the detail' (I p402), but the figures and other motifs used for the 'stretches of recitative' or for the 'fleeting, rolling passage-work' are as original as they are often simple. Only analogously and not literally can the opening be seen as 'recitative formulae', as is often claimed (Frotscher 1935 p865). The simplicity with which the diminished seventh is treated, moreover, is such as to give it a dramatic prominence – a patent rhetoric – scarcely typical of *c*1705 when, on grounds of form and contrapuntal style, the work might otherwise be thought to have been composed. The chief influence on the work is probably not the 'north German or Buxtehude praeludium' in general but the prelude–fugue–postlude of Georg Böhm, perhaps familiar in Lüneburg at the turn of the century and represented by two examples in a later MS made by J. Ringk (BB 30381). Böhm's praeludia in C and in A minor each begin with a prelude involving various keyboard devices and end with a short section of freer cadential or even cadenza-like flourishes. The simple figures of the first part of BWV 565 are also somewhat within the Böhm style, while the figures towards the end of the work can be more easily imagined to fit Bruhns's idiom. But in extant works of neither Böhm nor Bruhns are there figures at all close to those of BWV 565, and even if there were, the treatment of such figures could hardly be as simple and as repetitive as in BWV 565. Its opening bar, for example, has 'extracted' a figure similar to those decorating held chords in a Bruhns prelude, taken it out of context and doubled it in octaves: the thinking behind this process, however achieved, is certainly more typical of the eighteenth century than of the seventeenth. The overall result in BWV 565 is to demote the fugue to an interlude between tutti toccatas, something characteristic neither of any composer who could have influenced the work nor of other Bach works in 'Böhm's form', e.g. the C minor Prelude and Fugue BWV 549.

First Section

Despite the apparently formless array of keyboard effects in the opening toccata, there are four sections divided by clear diminished sevenths:

1–3	short figures in octaves, then dim. seventh with resolution
4–12	triplet figures in octaves, then dim. seventh with resolution
12–22	two chief figures, then unresolved dim. seventh
22–30	triplet figure in sixths, resolved dim. seventh

The first, second and fourth of these sections end in D minor, which therefore dominates the pedal. The emphasis on diminished sevenths may recall or anticipate such works as the G minor Prelude BWV 535, as does the pedal's picking up its note after manual flourishes, i.e. reverting to the note it last had before those flourishes (BWV 565 bb22/27, BWV 535.i bb14/32).

The keyboard effects themselves provide a repertory of original details, none of which have obvious parallels elsewhere: the opening octaves of the first ten bars, the built-up diminished seventh,* the characteristic rhythm of bb3ff (which is uncertain in the absence of any analogy – are the pairs of semiquavers equal or unequal?), the violinistic passage from b12 exploiting the open A string, the fourfold phrase in bb16–20 interrupted by a scale, the long broken diminished seventh of bb22–7. Some of these effects recall other works, but only in general. Thus, the highly unusual octaves at the opening anticipate other works in D minor (Harpsichord Concerto BWV 1052 and its cantata version BWV 146.i, Triple Concerto BWV 1063) and have even been suspected of alluding to the fugue subject of the next section (Keller 1948, Krey 1956 etc): Ex. 198. What is more, the prevailing line and notes of these

---

* In view of the formal shape suggested by the four sub-sections, it is possible – even probable – that the diminished seventh of b10 should be spread in exactly the same way as that of b2. Since in Griepenkerl's edition (Peters IV) the arpeggio of b2 is signified only by a wavy line, it is possible that the sources also omitted it in b10.

Ex. 198

(b30)

(b1)

etc

two phrases supply motif-material 'related to the first line of Luther's *Glaubenslied*' or Credo (Gwinner 1968), for which melody see BWV 680. The chorale melody can indeed be traced in the figuration of the first three bars of BWV 565 (e.g. line 2 of the chorale in the very first phrase of the toccata), but a definite allusion to it is difficult to follow since beat and emphasis are quite different – apart from the unlikelihood of chorale-lines appearing in a praeludium. It is difficult too to see how the varied phraseology of the work can be shown to be 'determined by the numbers 3 (symbol of the Trinity) and 4 (symbol of the world)', tempting though such interpretations may be (Gwinner 1968).

The triplet figures of bb4ff (mobile) and bb22ff (static) are complementary, suggesting that the composer is engaged in a favourite occupation: inventing a motif which is then developed, in this case first in octaves and then in sixths. The treatment of diminished sevenths is very direct, as if putting a premium on simplicity has produced an unexpectedly modern approach to the chord. Despite the diminished sevenths, however, the prevailing pedal line of the toccata is in fact not so different from the traditional progression familiar in toccatas of Pachelbel and others, i.e. tonic–dominant–tonic. The violin-like figure from b12 – in which further reference to the fugue subject (*inversus*) may be suspected – is not a group of slurred semiquavers (Scheidt's *violistica* style) but a more patent reference to Italian violin figures, those belonging to the repertory of variations or 'divisions' developed more integrally in the Six Solos for Violin: Ex. 199. The dialogue figure

Ex. 199

BWV 1005.iv

b56

from b16 onwards – a manual figure answered by chords with pedal – is also somewhat removed from its ancestors, again because of its repetitive simplicity, though the falling line DCB♭A is clearly more traditional (e.g. Buxtehude BUXWV 155 bb6–10). It could be that the patently simple effects in the toccata – such as the chords in bb27–8 – could also be found in lost or obscure toccatas of north German composers; but such chords seem more typical of a Kerll than a Bruhns, who in such contexts would have broken his chords in the Frescobaldi manner. More characteristic of the north German schools are the triplet sixths (cf. Buxtehude G minor Praeludium BUXWV 149) and the pedal solo at the cadence; but even then, the simplicity of the harmony is striking, both for the triplet sixths (decorated diminished seventh) and for the pedal solo (decorated dominant seventh).

Second Section*

The subject itself sustains the simplicity of motif by being centred entirely on a pedal-point note (the same violin a' as in bb12ff) – (e.g.) the C major fugue BWV 953, whose subject moves off the reiterated note at the end. That the basic figure is both violin-like and organ-like is clear from many typical instances elsewhere, as in Ex. 200. The first of these

Ex. 200

Violin Sonata BWV 1001.ii
b64

Praeludium BUXWV 140
b4

Kerll (?), Fugue in D major (*DTB* II.ii p. lxi)

is actually lowered to the same pitch as BWV 565 in its arrangement for organ (Fugue in D minor BWV 539.ii b66). The associations of subject or motif therefore mean that the unique pedal solo fugal entry at b109 is itself a kind of reference to those pedal solos in the freer sections of north German praeludia (e.g. Bruhns in G major b27).

Although the exposition is the only strict section of the fugue, its countersubject, codetta and episode before the late pedal entry† in the subdominant scarcely scale the heights of ingenuity. The first answer is the subdominant: unusual, though known also in BWV 539 and 531, where too the subject centres on the dominant note of the scale. The first codetta (from b34) presents a simplified version of a texture also found in episodes of the Passacaglia fugue BWV 582, while the second (bb41ff) has the appearance of Italian violin style, as in a different way does the basso-continuo-like passage of bb50–1. On the pedal entry, the four-part 'counterpoint' uses the same countersubjects as the previous entry (b39) and thus hints at the permutation-fugue technique known in other early works. Most of the entries appear quite isolated, at a remove from each other; and there is no thematic imitation.

The episodes at b62 and b74 include repeated phrases that have suggested to some editors and players two kinds of echo: simple echo (bb66–70) and double echo (bb62–3 = 64–5, 73–4 = 75–6, each two-beat figure played twice). The evidence for either during the fugal section of a north German praeludium is poor, but certainly the simple echo

---

* The bar-numbering is in one sequence through the whole of BWV 565.
† For another late pedal entry see BWV 543.ii.

was common in chorale fantasias during the episodes. In Bruhns's 'Nun komm' (P 802, J. G. Walther's hand) a simple echo is registered so that the echo is played on the *Oberwerk*; but a potential double echo is ignored by Walther, and the second complete phrase is merely a repeat of the first. In general, the tradition in written sources was to register chorale fantasias but not free toccatas, presumably since in the former the references to the chorale melody had to be made unambiguous; or perhaps the discrepancy is an accident of sources.* In any event, the very freedom and length of the fugal section of BWV 565 – curiously rare features – put the work amongst the praeludia of north German composers from the point of view of manual-changing, so that the simple echo, if not the double echo, is within character.

While further episodes also contain such simple devices as echoes (b115) and sequences based on elemental keyboard figures (b98, b122 etc), the continuity of the fugue is not endangered since the composer has been careful to follow each subject entry by striking material (bb41, 54, 62, 74, 90, 95, 111, 122) and thus to produce a sense of drive. Only at times is this material founded on the subject (b42), and the other figures are rather newly worked versions of familiar devices (such as scales bb60, 85, 123) or broken chords. Conscious or not, the hundred bars of the fugue include a catalogue of conventional keyboard figures of this kind, one result of which is an occasional but marked similarity to other pieces: compare the texture and motifs of bb87–90 with b77 of the G minor fugue BWV 542.ii. The key-plan also suggests conscious structuring (tonic – F – tonic – C minor – tonic) in which the C minor entry at b86 (highly unusual in a D minor fugue) is important not only in itself but also to the pedal. The pedal has three entries, all of them unusual: G minor (a late point for the pedal to enter), then C minor (an unusual key) and finally D minor (an unusual fugal solo). This last is after a dominant pedal point which, not least in its quasi-*inversus* subject of b103, prepares the listener to assume that the close is near. However, the close is not in b112 as might be expected: a further episode leads to an impassioned final entry in b124. This pair of tonic entries (bb109, 124) anticipates those ritornello movements of J. S. Bach in which the main theme has a 'false' final tonic appearance, to be broken off and eventually followed by the true close (e.g. the D minor Harpsichord Concerto BWV 1052.i).

Bruhns, Praeludium in E minor
b95

etc

[Rp   Ow   Bw   Rp   Ow   Bw   ?]

---

* Bruhns's E minor Praeludium in the Möller MS includes, at the end of the fugue, the same cadential statement three times, in a manner reminiscent of string music by such composers as Biber, where echo effects are specified in the source. Three manuals could be used to give two degrees of echo, which might also be the intention behind the simple figure Ex. 201 in the same work. The absence of registration marks was conventional – to allow various interpretations, depending on the organ to hand?

Third Section

The interrupted cadence of b127 is not found in the Böhmian prelude–fugue–postlude works; final free sections usually consolidate a perfect cadence previously reached or approached in the final stages of the fugue itself. To break off dramatically appears to be more typical of J. S. Bach (e.g. C minor Harpsichord toccata BWV 911). In BWV 565, the tonic major of the episode in b115 has already confirmed the tonality, and a dramatic, simple interrupted cadence was logical. In fewer than twenty bars, this postlude also includes a large catalogue of effects: the *figura suspirans* (Ex. 202) for alternating hands,

Ex. 202

sustained chords hinting at the involved harmonies of *grave* passages in praeludia (b130), alternate-foot pedalling solo, change of tonal direction (b133) followed by new manual figure, a further passage scoring simple chords in a new manner (b137), a severely plain close. Each of these has points of interest: the pedal solo is in principle close to those of Buxtehude etc but in its plain diminished seventh is new; the second manual cadenza imperceptibly changes harmony as the figure descends (b135); the new-scored chords of bb137–40 seem both original and simple (see close of BWV 569), and add one more effect to the repertory of the north German praeludium. The simple close exaggerates the restrained final cadences (often marked by suspensions) found in Buxtehude etc; but the final minor plagal cadence (if the sources are correct) is rare, even unique.

*

*   *

In view of the originalities of BWV 565 – all achieved with means so simple as to be uncharacteristic of J. S. Bach – and in view of its poor sources, it may be useful to consider one possibility that may account for at least some of the puzzling details, namely that the work is an organ transcription of a piece for solo violin. The violin 'original' may not necessarily have been by J. S. Bach; it would certainly have been in another key (A minor, up a fifth).

Arguments against such a hypothesis would include the following: (i) there is no known violin piece by J. S. Bach or any other composer that had such a shape; (ii) certain chords are too full to be played on the violin, even up a fifth or a twelfth (e.g. b2); (iii) certain figurations such as octaves (b1) and sixths or tenths (bb22, 54, 99, 122) are not feasible on the violin; (iv) certain textures are totally out of the question for violin (e.g. bb86ff); (v) if it were a transcription, some passages must have been altered to a degree unusual in early-eighteenth-century transcriptions. Arguments in favour of such a hypothesis would include the following: (i) the absence of a suitable model does not amount to an absence of precedents; (ii) the simplicity of BWV 565 argues for its being written by a composer more of W. F. Bach's generation than of J. S. Bach's, or for its being transcribed by a composer no longer transcribing so straightforwardly as J. G. Walther or J. S. Bach; (iii) most chords, figurations and textures can be seen in other terms (see below); (iv) the violinistic details in BWV 565 (e.g. the 'open a' string' passages from b12, or the fugue subject itself) could have arisen from its being a violin piece, the open a' being originally open e' (with e.g. the fugue answer in b32 below, not above, the countersubject?); (v) so many unusual details would be less puzzling if they had not been written for organ (e.g. the opening octaves of bb1–10, the two-handed effect at bb12–15, the diminished-seventh cadenza from b22, the simplistic fugal 'counterpoint' in general, the fugal episodes in particular, the frequent harmonization in parallel thirds as at bb87ff, 103ff, 124ff, the solo pedal entry). Some textures in BWV 565 can already be seen as idiomatic violin music requiring very little change – the passage from b14, the chords punctuating the bass line in bb27–29, the echo episodes in the fugue (cf. the finale of the A minor Violin Sonata BWV 1003), the litle runs of bb85–6, and the cadenzas (particularly from b133). Those that cannot be easily seen as violinistic merely require more speculation as to what the original could have been: for example, the octaves of bb1–10 would not have been there (the opening top e″ mordent would then have offered a curious parallel to the opening notes of the E major Violin Partita BWV 1006.i), the spread diminished-seventh chords would have been spread in a different way, the sixths from b22 or b54 may have been there only as isolated double stops (e.g. the first note of each group) while other moments of harmonization by thirds or sixths may have been simpler (compare the sixths and thirds of bb13–14 in the Fugue BWV 539.ii with the same passage in its original violin version, BWV 1001.ii bb12–13), and in general the fugal counterpoint of BWV 565 would have been to its 'original' as the fugal counterpoint of the violin fugue BWV 1001.ii was to its transcription in BWV 539.ii (e.g., even bb86ff could be 'transcribed' back for violin on the analogy of bb40ff of BWV 539.ii, indeed so as to avoid the curious and perhaps significant third-less chord of b89 – a minor detail in the ill-conceived invertible counterpoint of those bars). And the final chord might have been an open fifth.

It is true that many organ works of J. S. Bach are unlike anything else: unique *genre*-creations to which his other music, and that of other organ composers, provides no more than a general context. But BWV 565 is particularly unusual in so many features that it can scarcely be useless to question whether J. S. Bach was the composer, whether it began as an organ piece and, if it did not, whether he was even the transcriber.*

---

* Had the solo violin sonatas not survived, the D minor Harpsichord Sonata BWV 964 (which also provides some parallel passages for the arts of keyboard transcription when compared to its original, the Violin Sonata BWV 1003) would no doubt have seemed a perfectly self-contained, idiomatic work: another lone masterpiece. One assumption is already commonly made about it, namely that J. S. Bach transcribed it himself.

566

'Toccata and Fugue in E major'
'Toccata and Fugue in C major'

No Autograph MS; copies in E major in Am.B. 544 (Kirnberger circle), P 320 (Kittel), later sources in Kittel circle (P 504, P 577) and unnumbered Oxford Bodleian MS; copies in C major in P 803 (J. T. Krebs), P 286 (J. P. Kellner), P 203 (C. F. G. Schwenke, dated 1783), P 658 (Kittel), P 277 (1st two movements) and P 416 (2nd half of 18th century), unnumbered Oxford Bodleian MS and P 837 (19th century). Of the E major version, P 320, P 557 and Oxford MS have first two movements only; of the C major version, Oxford MS has last two movements only.

Two staves in P 803 etc; headed in P 803 'Praeludium con Fuga'; in P 286 'Praeludium con Fuga e Fantasia con Pedal'; in Am.B. 544 'Preludio ou Fantasia con Pedal', in P 203 'Praeludium Concertato'.

Particular questions concern title and key. Although 'Toccata' was used in *BG* 15 on the analogy of BWV 564 and of the harpsichord toccata in four sections, the titles in various copies show the copyists to be less and less familiar with multi-sectioned organ works of the kind called 'Praeambulum' or 'Praeludium' by north German composers between *c*1650 and 1700. It is now assumed that the original key was E major (*NBA* IV/6) and that the C major version was made in order to avoid pedal notes higher than c' (Emery 1958 p. iv) or to simplify the playing problems of the first pedal solo (Keller 1948 p59). Evidence has also been heard in the ensemble of bb5–8, 'too thick' in C major and 'sounding badly on any organ' (Rust *BG* 15 p. xxxv). Whatever credit is given this last reason – and Spitta rejected it on the grounds that 'high organ pitch' during this period meant that it sounded higher (Spitta 1 p794) – the problem is still unclear in two respects: Which (if either) was the original key? Who authorized the transposition? The consistency of pedal motif in the upper stave of Ex. 203 suggests that C major

Ex. 203
b18

was the original, but there would have been no need for the transposer (whoever he was) to alter the line in the E major version. The absence of the first tie in the C major version has been seen as evidence that it was transposed from E (Rust *BG* 15 p. xxxv). However, the pedal line shown in Ex. 204* casts doubts on whether E major, C major or

* The bar-numbering is in one sequence through the whole of BWV 566.

Ex. 204

b127

E avoiding d♯′, e′

C avoiding AA, BB

D avoiding BB, C♯

even D major* was the original. Although the first two figures are satisfactory in the C and D versions, the higher position of the third figure seems, subjectively, to close up the toccata texture to its detriment. Further areas in which conjecture is also possible are the reason for a transposition up from C to E (didactic? for variety? for playing-practice?), and the reason for a transposition from E to C and not (as in the violin/harpsichord concerto BWV 1042/1054) from E to D? In a D major version, pedal C♯ would have to be avoided in Ex. 204, as has been pointed out (Emery 1958 p. iv); but some alteration is in any case necessary. That Vincent Lübeck (1656–1740) has left a four-section praeambulum in E major, to which BWV 566 might have been composed as some sort of acknowledgment, can hardly be taken as evidence that BWV 566 was originally in E major (suggested in *MGG* I col.1013), since it is unknown which was written first and whether J. S. Bach knew the Lübeck Praeambulum. It is just as possible that either the composer or the copyist of BWV 566 transposed it up from C to E in (later) acknowledgment of Lübeck. A serious objection to the E major version being either the original or even a transposition made or authorized by the composer is the passage at bb16–17, which in the E major version uses harmonies impossible in unequal temperament and unusual in J. S. Bach, particularly during the early Weimar or Arnstadt periods to which the work has been assigned (Geck 1968 p19). But the 'remote' harmonies, though approached in other organ works (e.g. Buxtehude's Praeludium in F sharp minor BUXWV 146 bb84–90), have also been seen by some commentators as evidence that the composer needed to transpose an 'original' E major into C major (Keller 1948 p59). The temperament problems, therefore, can be used to suggest both that E major was a later transposition and that it was the original key.

Despite unanswered questions on the origin and history of BWV 566, its formal type has long been recognized as 'the only essay of Bach

* Suggested because transposition by one tone – up or down – is more usual.

in the motivically extended fugue form...of Buxtehude' (Spitta I p322). Two fugues, the subject of the second a 'variation' on that of the first, are introduced and separated by a freer prelude/interlude. Unlike (e.g.) Bruhns's G major Praeludium, BWV 566 is not completed by a fifth section (postlude), which in other works is often reduced to a few bars, as in the harpsichord toccatas BWV 911, 912 and 915. In important respects BWV 566 resembles the D minor Harpsichord Toccata BWV 913, which contains four major sections: there too the second fugue subject is a 'variation' on the first, and the opening section includes such organ-like effects as a solo bass line typical of pedal parts. However, this and other harpsichord toccatas develop the third section more lyrically and melodiously than is common in organ toccatas – amongst which the fully independent Adagio of BWV 564 is very unusual. The four sections of BWV 566 are more distinct than is often the case with Buxtehude, but within his various forms of prelude–fugue–interlude–fugue as left by the sources (Pauly 1964 pp88–9) the G minor Praeludium BUXWV 150 in the Andreas-Bach-Buch offers certain parallels to BWV 566 both in the use of four sections and in certain details (e.g. opening with left hand, followed by pedal point, etc). Buxtehude's fugues with variant subjects are themselves part of a larger tradition (a fact not obvious from Spitta's generalization); but within this tradition, the several sections are open to many kinds of treatment. Thus, the third section of BUXWV 150 keeps vestiges of the *durezza* toccata (beginning with slow sustained and suspended chords), whereas that of BWV 566 is built entirely on keyboard motifs (scales for the hands, broken chords for the feet), and that of Lübeck's E major Praeambulum is entirely a fugato.

First Section

The free form of the section progresses from a single-line opening to a harmonic 'pedal point' in its closing bars (shifting harmonies below treble tonic, bb29–32); both features are familiar in the northern toccata, as are the details of the figures (triads for the hands, alternate-foot figures for the pedal, the unexpected note of b13, etc). Less characteristic of traditional opening toccata sections are the full chords suspended in *organo pleno* style (bb5, 13), though where these do occur in (e.g.) Bruhns's praeludia it is customary for motifs to be picked out and developed in a manner not unlike that of b15 or b22. The tendency to extract motifs and then to extend them in the manner of bb24–32, however, is more pronounced in BWV 566 than was usual. In this respect the passage bb28–31 is particularly interesting, since the motif is a simple *suspirans* and is saved from an ordinariness of sequence familiar to northern toccata composers by being lifted out in b29 and transformed to a miniature ostinato. There has already been an ordinary sequence (from b24) which, in the hands of a Bruhns, may well have had a charm absent from the more careful Bach.

In the richly harmonic passages certain infelicities suggest a composer less mature than he was to be in the middle section of the G major

Fantasia BWV 572: examples are the inconsistent part-writing and the details of the suspensions (last beat of b7, the ♯9–♮9 of b21). Possibly the sources are corrupt: the a♯ in b10 is unnecessary, the d♮ in b28 pedantic; and it is surprising that the pedal figure in the second half of b9 is not developed in sequence. In any case, the ability to spin out harmonies, with or without Neapolitan sixths (b14), is already clear from b20 onwards.

Second Section

The repeated-note head of the subject preserves the stylistic allusion running through BWV 566, since it is typical of the organ toccata with varied fugue subjects: Ex. 205. Although such subjects arouse little

Ex. 205
Bruhns, Praeludium in G major

Buxtehude, Canzonetta BUXWV 171

enthusiasm amongst modern commentators, their origin is probably not 'from violin music c1700' (Keller 1948 p60), nor are they merely 'characteristic repercussion themes' (Apel 1967 p598); rather, they developed from the varied fugue-subject types, long traditional, which sprang from the canzona: Ex. 206. The latter part of the fugue subject of BWV 566 is based on a sequence characteristic of a somewhat different tradition, e.g. the subject of the D major Fugue BWV 532. While the sequence figure in the subject is a half-bar long, the contrapuntal

Ex. 206
Scheidemann, Canzon in F

Frescobaldi, *Canzon post il comune*
 (*Fiori musicali*)

accompaniment is usually a whole bar (see bb45–6, 50–1, 62–3 etc): i.e., the sequence is not automatically treated in any uniform manner. As in other long but early fugues (e.g. BWV 532), sequences are typical of the total treatment, whether or not they are based on the subject itself (e.g. bb58–9, 84ff, 104ff); it is probably this factor, rather than thematic allusion as such, that provokes the similarity between (e.g.) bb84ff and the close of the prelude. Nevertheless, the four parts are worked and shaped carefully, without the harmonic maturity of the repeated-note theme of BWV 541.ii, but at times anticipating it in the harmony (compare BWV 566 b81 with BWV 541.ii b14). The countersubjects so consistently accompanying the subject recall at times those of a permutation fugue – especially when the complex of four parts incorporates them, e.g. bb73–6 and 101–4.

Third Section

Though short, this section includes the most obvious allusions to north German toccata traditions of the late seventeenth century: scales beginning off the beat, runs pitted against pedal motifs, simple overall harmonic progression (open to many kinds of figurative treatment), pedal *trillo*. However, the passage is more regular and less capricious than the interludes of Buxtehude, founded as they are more directly on the quasi-extempore toccata style of Froberger and others. Nor – as comparison with the corresponding moment in Buxtehude's E major Praeludium BUXWV 141 shows – do the north Germans prepare a linking imperfect cadence so dramatically, and so clearly in the manner of a curtain-raiser, as the linking bb131–3 of BWV 566.

Fourth Section

Widor's remark that the final section 'begins as a fugue, becomes a chorale and ends as a concerto' (Keller 1948 p60) is less apt than that this second fugue, now in triple time, reflects the tradition of final toccata sections. Its final flourishes are incorporated within the fugue itself.

As the example of BUXWV 171 above shows (Ex. 205), conversions of the opening fugue-*caput* into triplet time are often marked by dotted rhythms; repeated notes are also reminiscent of the Frescobaldi canzona tradition. The dependence of the final fugue subject of BWV 566 on that of the second section is slight (though unmistakable), and that too was traditional; any commentator who suggests that the triple-time fugue of such a work is a 'variation' on the previous fugue is exaggerating, since only the head of the subject is concerned. What is more a matter of variation in BWV 566 is the fugal treatment of its final section as a whole: the last true entry is less than halfway through (from b172), after which the subject is varied in witty stretto (b181) or modulates (b206), or its outlines are faintly suggested (bb218, 225).

While the textures may at times resemble those of other works (e.g., compare b209 with Variation 10 of the Passacaglia BWV 582 b80), there is a looseness of part-writing and fugal development which can presumably be traced not to faulty source material but to the composer's desire to include freer quasi-toccata elements in the movement and thus to contrast it with the more 'correct' treatment of fugue in the second section. The whole second half of this second fugue is anything but regular, since neither the subject entries nor the episodes are closely related to the opening exposition. Nor can the passage from b188 to the end be regarded as a quasi-chaconne. Yet its frequent returns to the tonic, its textures and figures, and its variety of style from bar to bar might suggest some distant relation to the ostinato technique found at the close of a few north German praeludia.

---

567 Prelude in G major

No Autograph MS; copy in Brussels Fétis 7327 (J. L. Krebs); later copies, c1800 (P 1071) or 19th century (P 637, P 837).

Headed in P 1071 and P 837 'Praeludium pro Organo pleno'.

Doubts about the authenticity of the movement must arise from the nature of the sources, as they have also arisen from such details as the augmented sixth in b26, which may point to a Bach pupil, perhaps Kittel (Keller 1948 p57). Spitta, in suggesting that certain elements in the piece were 'late' (consistency of three- and four-part legato harmonies – Spitta I p398), did not attempt to show that such elements led in the later eighteenth century to such textures as the break in legato at b20. While at least one passage shows that the composer was familiar with Bach keyboard idioms (bb10–15), and while the final five bars incorporate elements of finality well known in J. S. Bach (flat seventh, flat sixth), the 'tone' of the penultimate bar is alien to J. S. Bach, as are the harmonies in b8 and bb17–18. That $^3/_4$ preludes based on scales descending and ascending above pedal points may have been a distinct *genre* for improvisation is suggested by a similar but monothematic movement by J. K. F. Fischer (*Ariadne Musica* (1702?), Praeludium XIII). One commentator, having assumed that the lowest part is indeed for pedal, has seen BWV 567 as applying 'south German figuration' to the form of 'a brief toccata influenced by the north German' style (Frotscher 1935 p861). The source in Krebs's hand suggests him as the composer (Kobayashi *BJ* 1978 p46).

---

568 Prelude in G major

No Autograph MS; copy in P 1107 (18th century), Brussels II . 3917, Stift Göttweig MS J. S. Bach 34, unnumbered Oxford Bodleian MS, Salzburg Archiv des Domchores MN 104 and other late sources associated with Vienna (P 310, P 303, P 515).

Headed 'Praeludium con Pedale' in P 1107 etc.

That in P 1107, P 515 and P 303 the movement follows the 'Harmonic Labyrinth' BWV 591 (the only works comprising the first two of these MSS) does nothing to establish the authenticity of either. Further questions concern the pedal: the MS sources keep the pedal G for two bars only (*BG* 38 p. xxix); the pedal D is not sustained at all at the corresponding point at bb8–10; the crotchet motifs of bb26, 32, 35 and 56 do not have the consistent pedal line that might be expected of such bars.

Details of the inconsistent part-writing, the sequences and the pedal points suggest that the work, if it is in fact by J. S. Bach, belongs to his earliest period; the absence of thematic interest confirms this, particularly in view of the conventional nature of the figures (scales, alternate-foot pedalling, sixths above pedal point) characteristic of a Reincken or a Böhm. However, the work contains textures useful to a practising organist, e.g. held chords above uncoupled pedal lines in bb16–17 (minims), 18–21 (crotchets), 22 (dotted quavers). As in BWV 569, elements of 'written-out improvisation' are to be discerned: for example, the tonic pedal point of b1 is followed by the dominant pedal point of b8, as in toccatas of Pachelbel etc. Despite similarities of pedal motif, key, manual scale and chord figures, it is probably an exaggeration to suggest Bruhns's Toccata in G as a model for BWV 568 (Geck 1968 p21), a work much less static in key. At b26 of this prelude the semiquaver flow is broken for a move to the relative minor – exactly as in a little-known fantasia which accompanies the Fugue BWV 951a in one source. Although it is also an overstatement to see BWV 568 as 'chiefly in three sections' (Keller 1948 p52), there is evidence that the uses of returning material (bb1, 8, 23, 44) produce a formal organization unknown in north German praeludia. Rather, BWV 568 is best seen as a 'further working of the south German pedal-point toccata' in which the pedal now takes a more active part (Frotscher 1935 p861). Other material also returns (e.g. b36 and 51), but it is not difficult to agree with Spitta that the chief aim of the piece is to release streams of sound (Spitta I p397) already flavoured with verve and a sense of continuity.

569

Praeludium in A minor

No Autograph MS; copies in P 801 (J. G. Walther), Lpz MB MS 7, 22 (J. G. Preller), P 288 (J. P. Kellner), P 837 (c1829), Brussels II.3913 (2nd half of 18th century) and later sources including Kittel circle (LM 4842, P 1105, Lpz MB III.8.16).

Two staves; title-page in P 801 (written by J. L. Krebs) 'Praeludium pro Organo pleno con Pedal'; title by Walther in P 801 'Praeludium' only.

Walther's attribution to J. S. Bach seems to establish the authenticity

Ex. 207

b9

of BWV 569, in which case it may belong to the earliest period
(Dadelsen, notes to Telefunken record 6.35076). Several have heard in
it 'something monotonous' (Spitta I p398), though Spitta also admired
the inventive use of motif and harmony. The main motif takes various
melodic forms – of which Ex. 207 emerges only gradually as the
simplest and the most important – and the only invariable feature is the
rhythm $\frac{3}{4}$ ♪ ♪♪♪ | ♪, sometimes described as a feature of 'the south
German praeludium' (Frotscher 1935 p861): in fact, it is this rhythm
itself that is the true 'motif' and central concern of the movement. The
apparently diverse but in practice unifying use of motif over some
hundred and fifty bars is less characteristic of 'Bach's earliest years'
than of the period in which he and J. G. Walther seem to have been
particularly interested in *figurae*, from c1707/8 (see also BWV 571).

Several details suggest that the movement belongs to the chaconne
tradition, even perhaps the *chaconne en rondeau* (e.g. Muffat's
Apparatus musico-organisticus, 1690): its $^3/_4$ pulse in units of four or
six bars; the regular appearance of particularly simple sequential
episodes (bb9, 27, 54 etc); a preponderantly descending harmonic line
for each phrase; continuity combined with varied figures, many of
which are typical of the keyboard passacaglias of Muffat, Pachelbel etc
(e.g. from b73 or from b133). The last 24 bars, for example, suggest
an episode followed by three (or four?) chaconne variations, then a
coda. Other moments, particularly the opening, suggest a written-out
improvisation: a work that declares its triple metre only in b4 or even
b5. Some figures or harmonies suggest the organ music of Buxtehude
and other north Germans, particularly the 'harmonic pedal points' from
b36 or b80; and some suggest ideas developed by a maturer Bach (e.g.
the imitation of b49 and the Gigue of Partita no. 5 in G major BWV
829).

---

570   Fantasia in C major

No Autograph MS; copies in Lpz MB III.8.4 (Andreas-Bach-Buch),
P 804 (J. P. Kellner), P 279 (c1800) and later sources (P 308, BB 30069).

Two staves (no pedal cues); headed 'Fantasia' in Andreas-Bach-Buch,
P 804 and P 279.

Questions concerning the movement are: Is it for organ with pedals?
Is it authentic? Peters VIII published it on two staves, and Spitta not
only took it to be a manual piece but suggested that the keyboard Fugue
in C BWV 946 was 'perhaps originally connected with it' (Spitta I p398),

though sources do not confirm this. If BWV 570 is authentic, it must belong to the composer's earliest period: its non-thematic handling of the four parts does indeed give the impression of a didactic piece encouraging 'a very careful legato and facility in changing finger on the same note' (Spitta I p398). It is not known whether the heading in the Andreas-Bach-Buch 'Fantasia S J S B' (*Signor* JSB? *scripsit* JSB?) establishes its authenticity.

The stylistic origins of the movement have been seen in Pachelbel (Dietrich 1931), as has the idea of calling it 'Fantasia' (Keller 1948 p53). However, as the opening of the equally doubtful Prelude in G major BWV 902 shows, sustained four-part styles were common in several contexts; they could be found from *plein jeu* movements in a *Livre d'Orgue* to the Magnificat settings and other praeambula of the south German composers. Such styles are characterized by only a limited number of devices, and many parallels with BWV 570 can be found, such as Ex. 208. The motivic bass line of BWV 570 may distinguish it from

Ex. 208

BWV 570
b32

J. Speth, Toccata in C major (*Ars magna consoni*, 1693)
b3

etc

south German pedal parts (which are often optional) and at the same time may make it less likely that it was intended for pedal in the first place. The fantasia is also longer than most southern toccatas, and its motifs (quaver lines, then dactyls, then fuller semiquavers) are more cumulatively organized – not unlike BWV 571 in this respect.

571   Fantasia in G major

No Autograph MS; copies in P 287 (J. P. Kellner), Lpz Poel 28 and Brussels Fétis 2960 (both end of 18th century).

Two staves; headed 'Fantasia' in P 287, 'Concerto' in Poel 28, 'Partita' in Fétis 2960.

Although there are three pedal cues in P 287, Peters ix gives the work on only two staves; but the repeated notes and several of the textures suggest that the work is for organ. More basic doubts remain about its authenticity. To some extent, the three movements, the first of which leads directly into the second, bear signs of concerto shape: (i) ritornello-like theme of repeated notes, with semiquaver interludes; (ii) slow movement based not on a melody but on a theme treated in imitation (*rectus* and *inversus*); (iii) Allegro comprising a set of variations on, or different treatments of, the descending hexachord/ octave scale in minims. The working-out rarely rises above the invention of (e.g.) J. G. Walther, whose interest in specific semiquaver patterns and *figurae* in general may have led directly or indirectly to this work, although the commonplace subject of the first movement has been found in Kuhnau's *Clavier-Übung* (Frotscher 1935 p858). The several sections suggest a composer working with particular patterns and attempting to create a sustained movement with them; those of the third movement look like Waltherian *figurae* (Ex. 209).* Spitta heard

Ex. 209

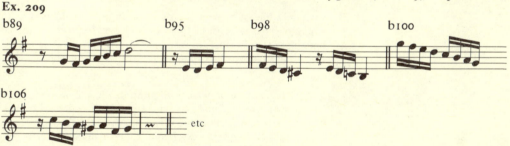

a thematic unity joining the three movements (the descending theme of the third is a simplified version of the second, which is an *inversus* of the first) and hence the influence of Buxtehude, so that 'it cannot be doubled when the work originated': it was the period when Bach's 'universal talent had the power to assimilate completely the various tendencies of his time' (Spitta 1 pp318–19). That the middle movement also recalls a theme of Kuhnau (Keller 1948 p54), and the third the opening of the fugal finale of the C major Concerto for Three Harpsichords BWV 1064 (of which the bass line itself had long been familiar as an ostinato phrase), is perhaps less a key to the work than its overt if simple development of *figurae*.

---

* The bar-numbering is in one sequence through the whole of BWV 571.

572   'Fantasia in G major'

No Autograph MS; copies in P 801 (J. G. Walther c1717–20?), P 1092 (owned by Oley), Am.B. 54 and Am.B. 541 (Kirnberger circle), P 320 (Kittel), P 288 (J. P. Kellner), Scholz MS, BB 30386 (owned by Goldberg; 1st section only), Bonn Musikwiss. Sem. der Univ. Ec. 252.2, and other sources of 2nd half of 18th century (P 837, two further copies in P 288) and later (P 414 1st section only, LM 4838), including those derived from Kittel (P 510, LM 4842h 1st section only) or arranged (St 626, c1800, and Stift Göttweig MS J. S. Bach 4: both 2nd section only, for five string instruments).

Two staves; heading common to most copies (including 1781 catalogue in *Dok* III p269) as given in P 801, 'Piece d'Orgue di Giov: Sebast: Bach', often expanded to (e.g.) 'Piece d'Orgue à 5 avec la Pedalle continu composé par J. S. Bach' (P 1092); but in Am.B. 54 and Am.B. 541 'Preludio per l'Organo col Pedale obligato...'. Heading above b1 'très vitement' in several sources (*BG* 38 p. xxvii); b29 'gayement' in P 801 but 'gravement' in most sources and 'Allegro' in Am.B. 541 and BB 30386; b186 'lentement' (P 801 etc) or 'lento', but not in all sources.

Walther's 'gayement' for the middle section – cf. 'gai' for the fugue of the French Overture in Cantata 61 (1714) – may well be a misreading for 'gravement', since a majestic centre to the movement seems without question to suit the simple and unique plan of the work:*

1–28	rh/lh solo line of broken chords incorporating 'pedal points' in soprano (bb1–2) or bass (bb3–4), and back-references to the opening, exact (b5 and, in P 801 and Am.B. 541, b15) or altered (b17 – 'partial recapitulation'); final broken tonic pedal point $\left(\substack{5\,7\,5\\3\,4\,3}\right)$
29–185	five-part *alla breve* or *plein jeu* harmonies based on scale lines (rising semibreves, falling crotchets); periodic cadences to new keys in which the semibreve theme is heard (bb29 G, 40 D, 59 B minor, 68 G, 76 A minor, 95 E minor, 118 A minor, 131 G minor, 142 D minor, 158 G) before its final appearance in thirds, rising above a dominant pedal point to produce six parts (b177)
186–202	rh/lh solo line of broken chords now enriched with acciaccaturas and placed above a pedal line which descends chromatically (in contrasts to the rising diatonic scales of the second section) to settle on to a dominant *point d'orgue*

Despite their distinct techniques, the three sections have in common a reliance not on melody or thematic counterpoint but on shifting harmonies linked by common notes between the chords, whether sustained and suspended (middle section) or broken and restated (outer sections). The 'linking notes' in the third section are often the non-harmony notes of the acciaccatura kind (see below). Quite apart from the charm of the first section or the majesty of the second, the

---

* The bar-numbering is in one sequence through the whole of BWV 572.

work is unique as a *tour de force* in harmonic manipulation. Its three sections are distinctly marked off; but otherwise either they have no disruptive cadence at all (outer sections) or else their cadences are prevented by suspensions from holding up the motion (middle section).

As a whole, the fantasia has no close parallel elsewhere, despite the tradition (conveyed by Buxtehude and others) of sectional toccatas. The simple tripartite structure of such toccatas as those of J. Speth (*Kunst-, Zier- und Lust-Garten*, Augsburg 1693) should not be credited with too close an influence (as in Dietrich 1931 pp62–4), since their three sections do not correspond to those of BWV 572 in formal techniques, except perhaps the (heavily disguised) pedal point of the opening and close. Nor, more importantly, is any of the three sections of such toccatas concerned with what seems to be the chief aim of BWV 572, i.e. the working of non-thematic harmonies towards varied ends, each section very sharply separated from the others. The maximum variety-within-unity of BWV 572 is indeed highly characteristic of its composer, despite its uniqueness. Only a few separate elements in each of the sections suggest obvious parallels elsewhere, some of which are discussed below. Particularly important to the player is the tempo relationship that may have been intended: a unifying common pulse between sections, so that $\emptyset = \emptyset = \emptyset$ (see also BWV 552.ii).

The French title may well be significant. In P 801 it contrasts conspicuously with the mongrel Latin title of the Albinoni Fugue BWV 951 (concerning such titles, see the Legrenzi Fugue BWV 574). But what is French about BWV 572? The key of G major itself may well be allusive (the key of Couperin's *Messe des Couvents* and of *plein jeu* music elsewhere) but can hardly be more than that. It is possible, as has been suggested (e.g. Klotz 1969a), that the first and third sections are to be played with a simulated *plein jeu* registration (*Oberwerk* or *Brustwerk* flue chorus) and the middle with a simulated *grand jeu* (*Hauptwerk* reeds, Cornet, Principal 4′); but the distinction between *plein jeu* and *grand jeu* music is not as clearly defined in any French *Livre* as BWV 572, if treated thus, would make it appear. Nevertheless, the *alla breve* harmony of the middle section does have French characteristics (described below), however foreign to the *Livre* tradition would have been the toccata-like framework around it or even the *plein jeu/grand jeu* contrast within one work.*

First Section

Despite the tendency of some north German composers to develop a figure within their free toccata flourishes, the opening of BWV 572 is highly original. Reincken's Toccata in G major from the Andreas-

---

* It is tempting to see the BB in b94 as an allusion to the long compass *en ravalement* found for the reed stops in some French organ pedals of the late seventeenth and eighteenth centuries. Its harmonic purpose in b94 is clear, but it is not known whether the note is authentic, whether the d′ of b138 and b171 proves that the piece cannot have been transposed down from A major, why BB is used only once and AA never (despite several entries of the subject on A), etc.

Ex. 210

Reincken, Toccata in G major (Andreas-Bach-Buch)
b73

Bach-Buch may play with such a figure as Ex. 210, but it does not begin with it, nor develop it so far, nor develop it in such regular patterns. No extant toccata by any other composer approaches the long-breathed solo line of BWV 572, although it has already been noted (Frotscher 1935 p604) that the idea of running semiquavers for hands followed by a sustained *durezza* passage with pedals is also found in (e.g.) a prelude by C. F. Witt (d.1716). Similarly, while such repetitions as in bb3–4, 11–12 etc might suggest the echo treatment required in a Bruhns praeludium, the repetition in BWV 572 is more sustained and the progressions less purely decorative. Were echo effects intended b24 could also have been repeated, but it is not.

Second Section

The middle section has more obvious resemblances to other works comparable in kind, though not in achievement. Spitta heard the rising bass scale as a device known to Bruhns and Buxtehude (Spitta I p319), but there are no obvious parallels there beyond simple four-part *durezza* harmonies. Such harmonies often led to rising semibreve scales (*a* in Ex. 211), falling crotchet lines (*b*) and pedal points (*c*), as well

Ex. 211

Fischer, *Blumenstrauss*, Praeludium 7
b30   b44

Ex. 212

Ricercar *a 6, Musical Offering*

b57

as to the suspensions that give the style its name. In his maturity Bach not infrequently adopted this idiom – as in Ex. 212, where the contrapuntal parts have been described as more independent than those in BWV 572 (Wolff 1968 p127). The contrary motion produced in such a *durezza* style helps – apparently without effort – to sustain long passages of fluent harmony. This fluency can work either towards quick, dramatic ends, as in the *Christmas Oratorio* – Ex. 213 – where the bass

Ex. 213

Christmas Oratorio, no. 21

Ex. 214

BWV 572

b158

is 'coloured' by quavers, or towards a kind of ideal species-counterpoint, where the bass is plain, i.e. written in First Species: Ex. 214. However, while the contrapuntal harmony may seem effortlessly continuous, the section is not without shape, being organized both *in toto* (into and out of planned keys) and in details (sequences such as bb105–13, rising/ falling lines such as bb114–24). That in the process the harmony proceeds with a rich series of various seventh and ninth chords is part

Ex. 215

de Grigny, *Livre d'Orgue*, Dialogue sur les grands jeux
b75

of the style, one found in simpler form in French organ music known to the composer – Ex. 215. Such harmonies establish a French background for the section better than the mere low BB *en ravalement* of b94, which of itself hardly indicates 'that the Fantasia in G was written completely in the French spirit for a French organ' (Schrammek 1975 p104).

But while the background for the middle section of BWV 572 is clear, its length (over 150 bars), its independence of fugal textures (contrasted with Ex. 212), its independence of word-painting (contrast the clamorous angels of the *Christmas Oratorio*), and its manner of organizing themes into an improvisatory style are found only here. Perhaps the last feature is the most remarkable. The many thirds, sixths and tenths produced by the five parts are often abandoned at the cadence points, which are in turn characterized by a falling bass octave (bb48, 58, 75 etc); in addition to parallel thirds, a device necessary in any five-part piece is the contrary motion already referred to (bb113–15 etc). Further unity is provided by the crotchet lines (usually moving by step), the periodic climaxes usually independent of sequences, consistent harmony (suspensions, Neapolitan sixths at bb57, 139 etc) and a steady rhythmic flow using few quavers. That the pedal semibreves and their lines in contrary motion appear at regular points in different keys gives the section its greatest single unifying element. No idle repetition results from this technique, as can be seen by comparing sections which begin with the same progression (e.g. b76 and b118); and the scale is always capable of new, dynamic treatment, as can be seen from the two-octave ascent of the final bass entry (bb157–71). The whole is achieved without conventional imitation or fugal counterpoint.

Third Section

The broken chords enriched with acciaccaturas are kept up until the last cadence bars – Ex. 216(i). It is very uncertain which of the various acciaccatura traditions – French, Italian or German (Williams 1968) – could have led to the conception behind the final section of the G major Fantasia. One influence may have been d'Anglebert's *Pièces de Clavecin* (Paris 1689), of which at least the table of ornaments was known to J. S. Bach (*Dok* III p634) and in which volume the basso-

Ex. 216
(i)
(b186)

(ii)
d'Anglebert, *Pièces de Clavecin*,
preface

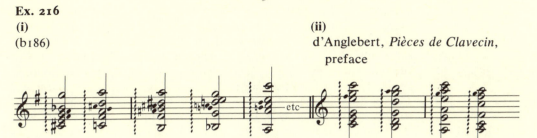

continuo player is recommended to play acciaccatura chords – shown in Ex. 216(ii) in the same form as in Ex. 216(i). More extravagant acciaccaturas were suggested by F. Gasparini in *L'armonico pratico* (Venice 1708) and by those German writers whom he influenced (e.g. Heinichen 1711, 1728). It was not an effect normally recommended for the organ, although the tradition may suggest that the notes in BWV 572.iii are momentarily held over to produce a harmonic effect. The chromatic notes apparently 'slipped in' conform to acciaccatura tradition and do produce strange combinations which are only gradually, though undeniably, softened or resolved towards the end.

Thus, as in the first and second sections of the fantasia, none of the putative influences on the third section is enough to suggest a movement so single-mindedly bent on exploitation of its technique or device as BWV 572 is throughout. Each section of BWV 572 pushes its 'idea' beyond the bounds of its supposed tradition. Moreover, in its solo line and inner repetitions the third section is like the first, but in its harmonic continuity more like the second; thus there is a unity binding the three sections, borne out by their proportional tempos but irrespective of their registration.

573

Fantasia in C major (fragment)

Autograph MS in P 224 (*Klavierbüchlein für Anna Magdalena Bach*, 1722).

Two staves; headed 'Fantasia pro Organo', pedal line 'Ped'.

The fantasia follows immediately after the last page of the French Suite no. 5 (BWV 816) and is written not in fair copy but as it was composed ('Konzeptschrift', Dadelsen *NBA* v/4 *KB*). The movement breaks off before the end of the page, after which an empty side follows before the next piece (*ibid* p15). The order in P 224 is as follows: BWV 812, 813 (incomplete), 814 (incomplete), 815, 816, 573, 991, 728, 813 (further movements), 814 (further movements), 841.

A movement in four and five parts is exceptional in the Anna Magdalena books, and Spitta may be correct to ask whether Anna Magdalena intended to learn the organ (Spitta 1 p756). However, the presence of BWV 991 (fragmentary set of variations), of BWV 728 (decorated chorale) and of the suites suggests rather that a wide repertory of keyboard music was desired for the purposes of an album. Musically, the fantasia is very promising. The pedal line, which is hardly suitable for a beginner, develops its own motifs and antiphonal character; the five-part writing allows both a massive statement (bb1–4) and several sequences in thinner textures (bb5, 8, 10); the idiom is close to that of the maturest organ music (compare the last two bars with the Fugue in C BWV 547). Melodious phrases such as the cadence at the end of b4 seem to arise naturally from the quasi-improvisation of an inventive composer working in a style that is basically derived from a (French?) *plein jeu* idiom. The decorated suspensions of bb2–4 and 6–7 are related to the more simply decorated suspensions of the middle section of the Fantasia in G major BWV 572.

---

574   Fugue in C minor ('on a Theme of Legrenzi')

No Autograph MS (MS owned by Guhr, said to be autograph in Peters IV); copies in P 1093 (J. G. Preller), Scholz MS and sources in or after c1800 (P 247, Brussels Fétis 2960; Lpz Poel 355 (J. G. Weigand) and Lpz MB MS 1, 18, without final section; Lpz MB Pölitz Mus. MS 13), some of which are from the Kittel circle.

Two staves; while the 'Autograph MS' did not name Legrenzi (Griepenkerl, Peters IV), the heading shared in most copies was already found in the Andreas-Bach-Buch (see BWV 574b): 'Thema Legrenzi-anum. Elaboratum per Joan Seb. Bach. cum subjecto. Pedaliter'.

Two unanswered questions concerning the work are: What is the theme? and What is the history of the Fugue? For the second point see also BWV 575a and 575b; it is unlikely that extant sources will ever yield clear indications of what the composer first wrote, particularly as the authenticity of the shortened versions is suspect. It is possible that the two versions of the B minor Harpsichord Fugue on a Theme of Albinoni (BWV 951, 951a) may serve as a useful parallel; but its shorter version is relatively less expert than that of BWV 574. However, the titles given the Albinoni piece are usually similar: e.g. 'Fuga. ò vero Thema Albinoninum. elaboratum et ad Clavicimbalum applicatum per Joa. Bast. Bachium' in P 801 (J. G. Walther).* But while the subject of BWV 951 is well within the north Italian tradition of melodious violin fugue subjects with both wide-spaced intervals and a chromatic phrase, that of BWV 574 does not look like a violin theme. Rather, it resembles keyboard subjects incorporating a well-known cadence, like the subject from the E minor Toccata BWV 914: Ex. 217. Such Legrenzi pupils as Lotti (Dresden, from 1717) and Caldara (Vienna, from 1716) travelled and no doubt helped to disperse works not known in

---

* Compare the title of Heidorn's fugue in the Möller MS: 'Fuga, Thema Reinckianum a Domino Heydornio elaboratum'. Titles establish a *genre*.

Ex. 217   BWV 914
b14

published editions; but no close connection has yet been established between BWV 574 and any known Legrenzi work. Internal evidence for Legrenzi is much weaker than that for Corelli in BWV 579 or Albinoni in BWV 951. Nor is it clear why Spitta thought that the phrase 'cum subjecto pedaliter' in the title referred to the 'countersubject' or second fugue subject (Spitta I p421).

The fugue is an interesting, presumably early attempt to work two fugue subjects towards a spacious movement, perhaps exceeding Legrenzi's fugue (if there was one) in length and pretensions as much as BWV 579 and BWV 951 exceed Corelli's and Albinoni's fugues. The shape is:

1–37	four-part exposition, episode, dominant entry, relative and tonic entries of fugue subject; first exposition with consistent countersubject; other entries with mostly changing countersubject
37–70	second theme with three- and four-part exposition; pedal subject simplified; subsequent entries with new countersubjects (bb53, 57) before:
70–104	two main themes combined in fugal exposition (double fugue) so that invertibility is possible (first subject lower from b70, higher from b76); two main episodes and further entries; coda pedal point implied
105–18	toccata section thematically unrelated (including pedal thirds of bIII etc)

Spitta thought the firm cadences prefacing each subject entry gave a 'disjointed and short-breathed' effect (Spitta I p421), but the nature of the various subjects (all of which begin off the beat) counteracts this. Moreover, the beginning of the subject implies no divisive perfect cadence like the beginning of the subject of BWV 579. Nevertheless, the frequent perfect cadences are no doubt a sign of an early date, as too they may be for the 'first version' of the slow movement of the E minor Organ Sonata BWV 528 (Emery 1957 p101); they also tend to have a melodiousness (e.g. bb18, 23) known in other early works such as the Capriccio BWV 992. Frotscher had no evidence for suggesting that the many cadence points were taken over direct from Legrenzi (1935 p860). Spitta also interprets the first 33 bars as 'going back to Legrenzi's original', with 'Bach's real manner' taking over in b34, but it is difficult to see the four-part counterpoint of this section as different in kind from that of the first. On the contrary, the fugue shows a gradual change of texture within a specific, barely Italianate keyboard style. The quavers and the dactyls of the first section flow quite easily into the semiquavers of the second, just as these in turn spin towards the end of the third and become less intricate there; then follows the toccata figuration as a logical next step. This gradual progression towards the toccata is absent from the Albinoni Fugue BWV 951, where the semiquaver movement is more continuous and sustained. The counterpoint may be Italianate in inspiration, but the use of the keyboard is more central German in style, resulting in a careful texture and producing some quasi-cross-references (see b67 and b21), the whole very comfortable and assured in idiom. The fluency of the decorated suspensions in b33 etc is as Italianate as any other element in the Fugue and could have led – as it did elsewhere – to long drawn-out passages; but here it does not, and throughout the fugue there is little of the *alla breve* facility of counterpoint familiar in Corelli or in BWV 589. But whether the counterpoint is facile or not, the toccata close is in comparison less fluent, working with broken chords and scales often similar in detail to (e.g.) Buxtehude's: Ex. 218.

Ex. 218

BUXWV 156
b65

Ped.

But the toccata close* is no mere pastiche: the particular broken chords from b107 onwards may be known by Buxtehude, Bruhns, Lübeck and others but are not treated by them in such an organized manner over so great a span as five bars. Also more highly organized than usual are the arpeggios of bb111–12 (though not in the Andreas-Bach-Buch copy – see BWV 574b) and the sequential runs of bb113, 116–17. In the process of organizing or developing such toccata motifs, the composer runs the risk of losing that capriciousness typical of both the seventeenth century in general and the Hanseatic organists in particular.

574a

Fugue in C minor ('on a theme of Legrenzi')

No Autograph MS; copy in P 207 (2nd half of 18th century).

Title: see BWV 574.

Called a 'variant' in *NBA* IV/6, as distinct from the 'early version' (BWV 574b), BWV 574a has 'often a more continuous and better-written

---

* The sources make it clear neither whether manual or pedal plays the last two notes, nor whether the pedal C is to be taken off or held through from the previous bar (cf. the close of BWV 564).

part-writing' than BWV 574 (Naumann *BG* 38 p. xlix); also, its 'leaving aside' the last fourteen bars 'points to a later, simplified re-working' (*ibid*). However, the shortened version is puzzling. The absence of a toccata section that included the traditional keyboard ideas (broken chords, scales, pedal points, rhetorical rests etc) might easily suggest that BWV 574a is a version closer to any original Legrenzi string fugue than the longer BWV 574. Alternatively, the shorter version can be seen to present, without the distraction of a toccata flourish, a fugue closely fitting its context in P 207, where it follows an incomplete copy of *The 48*, in which there are also fugues using more than one successive subject before combining them (F sharp minor and G sharp minor, Bk II). Perhaps the copyist of P 207 was responsible for the shortened form.

For a note on the 'more continuous part-writing' see also BWV 574b. Both BWV 574 and 574a are each 'more continuous' than the other, at different points; but the differences are not systematic enough to support any hypothesis about the order of events. Thus the 'omission' of a part in bb50–1 of BWV 574 may be an early copyist's error, while the extra fifth part in bb66ff of BWV 574a may have been added by a copyist. Internal evidence suggests that both treatments of the approach to the final cadence (b103/b104) are equally plausible: with held pedal point but no final toccata section (BWV 574a), or with final toccata section but no pedal point (BWV 574).

574b   Fugue in C minor ('on a Theme of Legrenzi')

No Autograph MS; copies in Lpz MB III.8.4 (Andreas-Bach-Buch), P 805 (J. G. Walther), Lpz MB III.8.29 (Dröbs, shortened), P 279 (*c*1800), Brussels Fétis 2960 or II.4093.

Title: see BWV 574.

Called an 'early version' in *NBA* IV/6, as distinct from the 'variant' BWV 574a, BWV 574b differs from BWV 574 chiefly in having more ornaments and fewer continuous semiquavers in certain bars (21, 34, 67, 77, 86), and a less clear fall and rise of arpeggios in bb111–13.

The main question about BWV 574/574a/574b is whether the differences between the sources are sufficiently frequent or significant to justify the term 'versions', in the sense either that the composer made or intended revisions, or that the sources reflect those several intentions. For example, the ornamentation of BWV 574b is so inconsistent as to suggest (if it is authenticated at all) either that the composer wished many more ornaments to be added in similar phrases later or that it was not fully thought out in the putative source from which copies were made. Suggestions about the shortened version of the fugue were made in connection with BWV 574a. Increased semiquaver continuity in BWV 574 would also not be difficult for a musical copyist to incorporate, since no radical use of motif is involved. The arpeggio of bb111–13 in both versions is more suggestive: the clear falling-and-rising shape in BWV 574 is less like older German toccatas than the passage in BWV 574b and has a sense of climax more typical of the eighteenth century.

---

575   Fugue in C minor

No Autograph MS; copies in Lpz Go.S.310 (1740/50), P 247 (probably *c*1730), P 213 (2nd half of 18th century), Scholz MS, MS in Göttingen Bach-Institut (*c*1800), P 536 (*c*1800), P 820 (Grasnick, dated 1819, without last three bars), LM 4839c, Stift Göttweig MS J. S. Bach 35.

Two staves; headed in P 247 'Fuga di Bach'; 'Adagio' at b65 only in P 213; 'Adagio' at b76 in P 536 and Peters IV (neither 'Adagio' in P 247).

Doubts about the work concern its authorship (C. P. E. Bach, according to Grace *c*1922 p19 and Keller 1937 p63) and the instrument ('Flügel mit Pedalbass' in *BG* 38), although Griepenkerl (Peters IV 1845) thought it was 'written for organ', and Schumann (*NZfM* Supplement 5, part 3) published it as a work of J. S. Bach. The sources specify pedal for the last twelve bars. In ornamentation and even in countersubject, the sources as reported by *BG* 38 offer only uncertainties about the original form and/or later evolution of the fugue.

Admiration has often been expressed for BWV 575. Spitta became lyrical over the 'swelling and stretching' of the fugue, as well as over the tonal ambiguities he heard in the subject itself (I pp248–50); Keller recognized that it required a good player, not least to give the correct sense of pulse to the subject (1948 p52); Dadelsen hears in it 'probably the best example of the young Bach's treatment of the fugue style of the north Germans, particularly Buxtehude' (notes to Telefunken record 6.35076); and very likely it was its 'freedom' of form that

Ex. 219
BWV 914
b71

prompted Schumann to publish it as the first of his Bach supplements (Plantinga 1967 p89). Spitta already recognized a relationship between BWV 575 and the E minor Toccata BWV 914, although he did not say in what way; presumably it centres on the fugue subject of the final section of the toccata, which supplies similar figures and continuity:

Ex. 219. The entries are also similar, being provided with a simple accompaniment in each fugue. The final toccata section of BWV 575 has also characteristics of *genre* in common with BWV 914:

BWV 575 bb67–8   see   BWV 914 bb63ff
　　　　bb75–6　　　　　　　　 b67

and no doubt others could be found. The subject of BWV 575, however, recalls figuration found in other C minor works (see BWV 549.ii bb52–3).

The canzonetta-like subject produces a rondo-fugue in which the subject is mostly accompanied by its countersubject and the episodes are brief interludes between entries. As such, the *genre* is both that of the Buxtehude canzonetta, now extended and given character by a fugue subject built up of three phrases, and that of the final section of a longer toccata for keyboard, in which the sections are virtually separate movements. In fact, the question must remain whether BWV 575 is not perhaps the final section of a complete toccata now lost. The uniqueness of the opening phrase – beginning on the submediant – may well support this possibility. Various stylistic details can be seen to operate in the work: the suspensions in sequence (from b34) known not only in Italian string music but in early organ works (see e.g. BWV 532.ii b32); other string-like motifs during episodes (e.g. bb41–2), the characteristic surprise effect of the concluding toccata section (F♯ of b65);* the Buxtehude–Bruhns device – perhaps once familiar in the canzonetta – of a 'harmonic pedal point' against a moving bass (b70). The toccata scales and the pedal line (for alternate-foot pedalling) are more typical of the north German toccata than of many other types. The sequences generally have great energy and develop without strain (e.g. bb41–5), so that the obsessive passage before the F♯ pedal note is the more striking and leads the more naturally to a toccata close. The exact point at which the subject re-enters is often a surprise to the ear (e.g. bb47–8, 58–9). The tailpiece or final bar of the fugue subject is generally harmonized with variety and imagination (bb39–40, 54–5). Figuration and tessitura – the latter varied and wide-ranging – are typical of the composer's harpsichord toccatas, although many details of the figuration are common to both harpsichord and organ, such as the broken chords of bb7–8, 20, 26, 60 etc. It is the quick chord-changing of such bars as 26 that is unfamiliar in the composer's maturer organ music, rather than the broken-chord figuration itself. Most indebted to tradition is the final toccata section, with its dactyl rhythms, scales, pedal line, sixths, clear perfect cadences and – not least – the new key of b66 (G minor not C minor).

---

* F♯ not f♯ in P 213 and P 247 (*BG* 38); there is only a doubtful justification for the middle voice of b66 (Peters IV).

576   Fugue in G major

Copy formerly in possession of F. Hauser (Schelble, according to Peters IX and *BG* 38).

Various doubts have been voiced about the authenticity of BWV 576 (Keller, Peters IX rev. edn). While the exposition may be authentic, the pedal entry in b68 does not suggest J. S. Bach any more than the long, unified shape suggests any previous composer (Keller *BJ* 1937); yet the 'melodic beauty and charm of the theme' make it possible to believe it the work of J. S. Bach (Keller 1948 p51).

The theme conforms to the canzona kind of subject familiar in various guises, such as keyboard fugues (Buxtehude in G major BUXWV 175), Italian sonatas (e.g. Corelli Op III) or Italianate concertos (e.g. Handel Op III); the very key and the treble compass are evocative. The composer has followed a type rather than borrowing a theme, and the type brings with it decorated 7–6 progressions in the countersubject (bb4–6, 8–11) and a tendency toward homophonic phrase endings (bb20–1). As is usual in such fugues, most attention is directed to the subject; but a few independent episodes are introduced and help to extend the movement to almost 100 bars:

1–23	exposition of five entries in four parts
23–8	statements of subject (all but complete) serving as episode
28–40	entries and answers in the relative
41–4	episode, new
45–50	entry and answer in subdominant
51–6	episode, with reference to subject
57–9	entry in supertonic
60–8	episode, partly new, partly derived, partly direct from older material
68–74	entries in tonic
74–96	development of subject-motifs sequentially or antiphonally, broken up, finally above a tonic pedal point

Such fugal treatment gives the impression of an experiment, with irregular entries and answers, often strictly incomplete. The entries are characterized by a common harmony, not sufficiently elaborated to be called a permutation fugue, but within an organ idiom not dissimilar to (e.g.) J. K. F. Fischer. The episodes are more characteristic of German keyboard music than of the canzona tradition in general. The same is true of the solo pedal passages towards the end, clearly written for the alternate-foot pedalling technique. Other passages are perhaps enough like 'later' music (b51, cf. the concerto transcriptions; bb42–3, cf. the end of the D major Fugue, *The 48* Bk I) to suggest that the composer was a pupil of J. S. Bach. The non-thematic pedal entry of b68 is hardly conclusive of authorship either way, since it supports a thematic complexity in the manuals, i.e. stretto. Similarly, conclusions are difficult to draw from the square bar-by-bar figuration – the only suspensions are those associated with the countersubject – which could characterize many an immature composer.

577 Fugue in G major

No Autograph MS; copy formerly in possession of F. W. Rust and 'another old copy inscribed "da J S Bach"' according to Peters IX and *BG* 38; also Brussels Cons. Roy. MS XY.15.42.

Questions concerning BWV 577 are: Who wrote it? Who authorized the *p* and *f* signs and the pedal part? Is the movement complete? The composer was usually assumed to be J. S. Bach (Peters IX, *BG* 38, Spitta I p320) until doubts were raised more recently, probably because the poor sources aroused suspicion; the *p* and *f* signs and the pedal part have been thought sufficiently authentic to justify adding further *p/f* signs. The third question is rarely asked. All three questions, however, are integral to the special quality of this movement and deserve further consideration.

Ex. 220

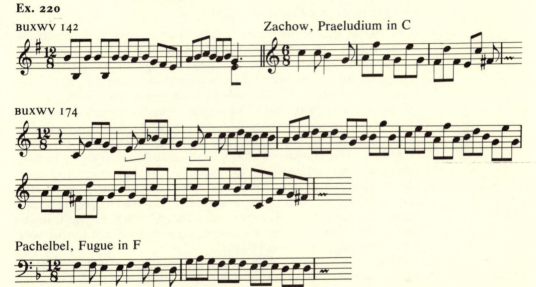

Although the fugue has no direct parallel amongst the keyboard or non-keyboard works of J. S. Bach, it belongs to a recognizable *genre*, at least in subject: Ex. 220. Spitta, who pointed out the similar Buxtehude subjects (I p320), heard in BWV 577 'a bolder verve' ('ein kühnerer Schwung') that precluded Buxtehude, 'who otherwise could well have written it'. Buxtehude's E minor Fugue BUXWV 142 does include pedal (unlike the others by that composer) but is nevertheless no close parallel: its forty or so bars are the final section of a praeludium in which the jig subject is a variant on a fugue subject heard earlier (b17). Similar points could be made about many jig subjects by Zachow, Pachelbel, Lübeck, Böhm and others; in some cases, the new subject is arguably 'better' than the original ⁴/₄ version (e.g. Böhm Praeludium in D minor, in the Möller MS). So familiar were jig variants or jig themes in large-scale works (e.g. BUXWV 166, 170, 171, 176) that

Spitta thought the C major Canzona BUXWV 174 part of a larger composition – a suggestion more recently rejected, though only on account of the length of the theme and the thoroughness of its working-out (Pauly 1964 pp93–5). However, if Buxtehude's C major Canzona were demonstrably part of a larger composition, so could BWV 577 be, for they have many features in common, and in both cases it would be possible to suggest what form the first $^4/_4$ version of the theme had taken. It may also be significant that the extant source for Buxtehude's jig fugue is the Andreas-Bach-Buch. The Buxtehude and BWV 577 themes are similar: the opening bar (Ex. 221), the overall length

Ex. 221

BUXWV 174

BWV 577 (transposed from G major)

(six bars), several of the motifs, and the sudden move to the dominant at the end, a detail not particularly typical of J. S. Bach's subjects. Spitta sees the theme of BWV 577 as having 'figuration contrived with special regard for the pedal' (I p320) which can 'easily play it' (!); but Buxtehude's canzona makes no demand for pedal.* Nor are the iambic chords of BWV 577 typical of jig fugues, whether variant sections in larger compositions or not; and there is a confidence of idiom – however simple the sequences – that is difficult to ascribe to any other composer. This confidence shows itself in such a passage as bb26–7 where the four-part sequence exploits a well-spaced series of seventh chords above the subject, provides an unusual but obviously useful texture for keyboard practice, and is again referred to only two bars later. That the latter is no empty repetition, however, is clear from its thinner figuration and the turn towards the mediant, not for the only time in the fugue (see also bb73ff).

On two occasions only (bb12, 40), the repetition within the subject itself is specified as an echo and in turn seems to lead to another echo in one of the fugal episodes (b16); it is not known how far these reflect the wishes of the composer or how far they justify the *p*/*f* signs added in *BG* 38† and other editions. There cannot be many precedents for incorporating echo devices within a fugue subject itself; normally they appear in other contexts, whether episodes (e.g. Bruhns's Praeludium in E minor) or cadences (e.g. Lübeck's Praeambulum in G major). However, at least one commentator has been able to find examples in André Raison of fugal episodes played on two manuals (Grace *c*1922 pp36–8). As to the pedal, not only is it required because of the spacing, but the subject seems altered for its sake (b28 etc); nevertheless, limitations of compass make it unlikely that the pedal enters

---

* The spacing in the final bars of BUXWV 174 would cause no inconvenience on a keyboard with short octave.

† In *BG* 38, the additional *f* signs should be placed – judging by the precedent in b12 – at b6 (halfway) not b7, at b44 (halfway) not b47, and presumably somewhere in bb24, 68 and 75.

in b57 (*BG* 38 but not Peters IX). A non-thematic entry (in b63) is not out of character in 'early' fugues.

Considered as a fugue, BWV 577 has some unusual features:

1–29 exposition, with long modulatory codetta after first answer, and a shortened fourth part (pedal) merging into:

29–34 episode, sustaining the texture of the exposition

35–40 entry (mediant), disguised or distributed over tenor and soprano, settling on to the tenor and passing to:

40–7 episode, reducing the texture to one part

47–86 series of entries (relative, tonic, dominant) interspersed with short episodes: alto (b47), bass (b57), soprano (b63), tenor (b70 halfway, eventually towards mediant), bass (b77 halfway)

Only the episodes contain motifs not found in the subject; such a passage as bb78–86 is a thematic complex based on two chief motifs of the subject, motifs that can equally fall or rise in sequence. A similar motif is also used in BUXWV 174, but not at all to the same exhaustive degree; nor does BUXWV 174 contain regular entries for the last third of the piece, or such gravitation towards four parts as BWV 577. That the episodes of BWV 577 contain simple sequences is no argument against J. S. Bach's authorship, since they throw the entries into relief and also suggest that the composer was consciously adopting conventional figures. However, it is difficult to imagine J. S. Bach during the Weimar period writing such passages as bb55–6; but such a poor progression could suggest a corrupt source.

578

Fugue in G minor

No Autograph MS; copies in Lpz MB III.8.4 (Andreas-Bach-Buch), P 803 (J. L. Krebs), P 288 and P 501 (2nd half of 18th century), P 320 (Kittel), BB 11544 (J. C. Vogler), P 541, P 279 (c1800), three Scholz MSS, 'Schubring MS', unnumbered Oxford Bodleian MS, unnumbered MS in Göttingen Bach-Institut, BB 30377 and other late sources (P 313, P 557, LM 4842g, LM 4941, Lpz MB III.8.22, Lpz Poel 20), some of which are after Kittel; in G♯ minor in one Scholz MS.

Two staves; headed 'Fuga' (Andreas-Bach-Buch, P 803), 'Fuga pro organo' (P 288), 'Fuga pro Organo pleno' (P 557).

The form may be expressed:

1–22 exposition; theme in three phrases bb1–2, 3, 4–5; codetta at end of b5; real answers bb6, 17; persistent countersubject

22–4 episode

25–30 'false' entry (tenor, then soprano), tonic

30–2 episode

33–45 entry in relative (alto complete with codetta as at b11, then pedal)

45–50 episode as b22

50–5 entry, subdominant

55–63 episode

63–8 final entry, shortened for cadence

This clear pattern – sectional, and independent of learned effects (augmentation, diminution, stretto etc) – is that of the canzona fugue (Bullivant 1959 pp115ff), while the dance-like subject itself has a somewhat violin-like nature (Krey 1956 p177) springing from the open d′ string. That the subject contains distinct motifs – triadic crotchets, a quaver line, leaping quavers, semiquaver dactyls, a semiquaver line – has encouraged organists and commentators (e.g. Keller 1948 p74) to produce complex phrasings, none of which are based on more than conjecture.

While no doubt it is the charm of its subject that has given the fugue its popularity, the movement has other qualities. Neither the canzona element nor the violinistic is particularly striking; rather, the subject belongs to a north German tradition of subjects springing from figures idiomatic to the keyboard (the so-called *Spielthema*), but now given a melodious turn not familiar to Weckmann, Bruhns, Reincken and others. Comparison with (e.g.) Reincken's G minor fugue shows similar semiquaver figures, a tendency towards broken chords, simple sequences and a succinct close etc; BWV 578 has clearer entries (always well prepared and timed) and more consistent counterpoint. The counterpoint itself has been described as 'mostly only one-part', and the fugue has thus been allotted an inferior position 'behind those of the following years' (Spitta 1 p400); but in fact the three-part texture of bb17–21 is that of a regular permutation fugue in which the counterpoint – however simple its semibreves – returns in different keys and in different inversions. The three parts of bb27–30, for example, are a complete inversion of bb18–21, largely explaining why the pedal enters without theme in b26, for by the next bar it takes up a role in the inverted three parts.

The subject has other points of interest. Some have though that the countersubjects are 'derived from the second and third part of the subject' itself (Frotscher 1935 p878), though the *figurae* do not exert a unifying force like that in (e.g.) BWV 537.ii. The entry at b25, because it is answered in a decorated form in the following bar, is not so much a 'false' entry as a quasi-stretto – as perhaps are the right-hand quavers of bb18–19 and the semiquaver paraphrase of the subject-*caput* in bb58–9. The alterations, in the bass part, of both the subject (bb44–5) and the countersubject (bb51–4) argue that this bass line was meant for pedal. Codetta scales and episode sequences are conventional; the sequences from b22, for example, are based on the trio-sonata texture of two violins and cello and will be found in many guises as episodes in fugues, sonatas or concerti grossi. In addition, the semiquaver lines verge on simple *figurae*: the motif in Ex. 222 appears in both subject

Ex. 222

(b5) and countersubject (b6), and in *rectus* or *inversus* form the motif is found in about half of the bars, including the line rising to the final entry (bb58–60). That this group of notes is not merely an accident of the style is suggested by the alternation between sections that contain it and those that do not, e.g.

37–41   with
42–7   without
48–51   with

But there is as yet no rigorous application of the *figurae* – the motif slips into b45 (inner part) as if unnoticed. Characteristic of the composer is a fluency that is both distinct from more static fugues such as BWV 579 and free from the repetitive or motoric rhythms typical of fugues by Buttstedt, Vetter and others.

---

579   Fugue in B minor ('on a Theme of Corelli')

No Autograph MS; copies by W. F. Bach, now lost (? Peters IV), and in P 804 (J. N. Mempell? 1st half of 18th century), Lpz MB MS I (middle of 18th century), Lpz MB III.8.18 (J. A. Dröbs, early 19th century).

Two staves; headed 'Fuga' in Lpz MB MS I, 'Thema con Suggeto Sigre. Correlli elabor. Ped. J. S. Bach' in P 804.

The subjects are those of the second movement (Vivace) of Sonata IV in Corelli's *Sonate da Chiesa a Tre* Op III (Rome 1689). The movements correspond as follows:

Corelli Op III no. 4.ii		BWV 579	
1–3		1–3	octave lower
9–12	top part	6–9	top part
15	cadence to D	?10	cadence to B minor
16–19	B minor	?11–14	(F♯ minor) or 23–4 (B minor) or 32–4 (B minor)
30–1	bass	?90–1	bass

As can be seen, the correspondences are slight and uncertain; 39 bars have become 102, a fourth part has been added and pedal is required. Two difficult questions are: Was the 1689 Rome edition the one used by the composer of BWV 579? and Was that composer J. S. Bach? Both are assumed to be so by more recent commentators (Braun 1972) as they were by Spitta (I p423), but at least the second has already been doubted (Blume 1968). In the light of discoveries concerning sources for the Vivaldi concerto BWV 594, the first may also be challenged; however, it should be noted that BWV 579 has no claims to be a transcription as such and that Corelli's Op III, in its many editions (Rome 1689, Modena 1689, Bologna 1689 etc, Amsterdam 1700 etc), had been in circulation longer than Vivaldi's concertos.

The B minor Fugue is of the so-called canzona type, in which interest centres on the subjects (Bullivant 1959 p710), which in BWV 579 – but not in Corelli – always appear together.

1–24	exposition of double fugue subjects, entry and answer in 1–24 tonic (the second shortened – a♮″ not a♯″in b8, etc); first (see dominant answer (11/13); further tonic answer (21/23) below)
24–31	episode; new semiquaver figure, descending minims 25–34 derived from *c* (see Ex. 223), 'rich in invention' according to Spitta (I p423)
31–41	entry and answer, each double; new countersubject material 37-61
41–9	episode extending the quaver line, with derived minims
49–58	tonic entries, each double
58–73	episode, first based on extended minim suspensions (derived), then new motif (b62: derived from tenor 62–71 countersubject of b6?); from b67, main subjects combined with previous episode motifs
73–7	tonic entry, with countersubject newly treated (tenor b75 73–102 in D, and b76 B minor)
78–90	episode, at first developing material similar to 43ff and 58ff
90–102	stretto final entries; underived close

Ex. 223

As has been pointed out (Schöneich 1947 pp198ff), the form of BWV 579 is none too clear, and the episodes produce a more developed fugue than would be required in a sectional toccata. (Schöneich's divisions are shown in the right-hand column above.)

While it may be true that 'Corelli's six theme-complexes have become ten' (Braun 1972), the two composers – judging by the 1689 edition of the one and the MS P 804 of the other – had a quite different conception of the double subject, and the idea of a 'theme-complex' means different things for each composer. In BWV 579 the two subjects always appear together, so that b67 is no true entry, and it is thus the *third* voice in the stretto of bb90off that is strictly the subject. In Corelli, both the fugue subjects are treated to single stretto, though not together in stretto, and appear as a true double subject only four times. Both fugues keep to the tonic and closely related keys (dominant in BWV 579, subdominant in Op III). BWV 579, omitting Corelli's regular strettos, both at the bar and at the half-bar (bb6/7 and 16 respectively), concentrates its stretto entries on the fourfold tonic–dominant half-bar stretto in bb90–1. This stretto too has been anticipated by Corelli, though only in three parts (bb35–6). It somewhat resembles other strettos based on falling fifths/fourths (e.g. B flat minor Fugue, *The 48* Bk I, from b67). Two particular effects result from the treatment in

BWV 579; the harmony is naturally richer (e.g. bb90–4), and the shape is more sectionalized, with clear difference between entry and episode. Largely reserving semiquavers for episodes is untypical of the maturer Bach.

As it has come down to us, BWV 579 has many points of interest. The double theme itself – beginning in an ambiguous major–minor – is typical of the Italianate fugue subject as adopted by Handel (e.g. Concerto Op III no. 2.ii, or fugues in B flat and G minor from *Six Fugues or Voluntarys for the Organ or Harpsichord*, 1735), although it also resembles other organ fugues of German composers: Ex. 224.

Ex. 224

Bruhns, Praeludium in E minor
b74

BUXWV 151 (Möller MS)
b23

The closeness of Buxtehude's countersubject to Corelli's has already been pointed out (Keller 1948 p73); the question-and-answer nature of such double subjects is bound to lead to similarities. But the Italianate nature of BWV 579 goes further than its subjects. There are no passages familiar from German toccatas – final flouishes, pedal-point coda, etc – and the style behind such sections as bb79–90 is basically as Corellian as the theme, despite the rich four-part harmony (cf. BWV 532.i) and the sudden melodic flare at bb82–3, which is more typical of a Buxtehude or Bruhns. Even the 'German' episodes from b25 or b65 are not unlike the solo sections of a concerto, or the episodes of a trio-sonata fugue (e.g. Corelli Op III no. 12.v). Also, despite some play with such derived motifs as Ex. 225 – which come as much from parts

Ex. 225

b54   b62

of Corelli's fugue that are not included in BWV 579* as from parts that are – the prevailing style remains non-motivic. It is based, rather, on harmonic treatment of suspensions and sequences (like BWV 532), all within a few keys and a general Corellian vocabulary. The final cadence is unusually modest for a single fugue movement (cf. BWV 578, 577, 574) and may reflect the influence of – or even the wish to imitate

* E.g. Corelli's b5; or the previous movement in Op III no. 4.

– the string fugue. Instructive for the later development of fugue, however, is the tendency for material to issue in sequence, to extend itself not merely in circles of fifths but with a sense of urgency and invention (bb16ff, 35ff, 75ff, 93–4).

It is surely right to see the Corelli movement as more energetic and hence faster than BWV 579 (Braun 1972); its tense series of strettos suggests this as much as do its tempo indication or the presence in BWV 579 of semiquaver figures and a pedal line. However, although it is much less succinct, BWV 579 makes conscious attempts at continuity: episodes (as at b24) and entries (as at b30) are not preceded by clean breaks, and there is no clear demand for changes of manual.

---

580   Fugue in D major

No Autograph MS; copies in Am.B. 606 (last third of 18th century), P 784 (2nd half of 18th century).

As has been pointed out (*BG* 38 p. xiv), the subject of the fugue is virtually the same as the countersubject to the Allabreve subject BWV 589, in notes, key and pitch; either J. S. Bach used it by chance or intentionally when he later wrote the Allabreve, or a less expert hand adopted it from the Allabreve and wrote a fugue on it. Obviously, BWV 580 could be the work 'of a not very advanced pupil of Bach' (Keller 1937) or of an older composer such as Johann Christoph Bach (1692–1703), whose fugue BWV Anh.77 is also found in Am.B. 606. But in any case, it should be noted that the subject is not exactly the same as the countersubject to BWV 589 (it begins without syncopation and the answer is later), and that it has conventional features typical of a certain subject type. Plain rhythm, a line half scale-like and half leaping, with a simple suspension: these are typical of subjects producing the simple Italianate counterpoint on which even the polished Allabreve is founded.

Despite the ordinariness of its musical language – which is not characteristic of J. S. Bach after he became familiar with Italian counterpoint – there are some features suggesting what he or other composers of the early eighteenth century saw as belonging to this style. Thus, far from its being a permutation fugue of the kind known in such early works as BWV 131.v (1707; see BWV 131a), the subject has a succession of countersubjects, all formula-ridden but in principle different from each other: bb5, 28, 44 (counterpoint inverted in 49), 86 and 102. While the part-writing is often of scant interest, there is some attempt to develop such figures as the rising fourths of the theme or the quaver groups of the countersubject.

---

581   Fugue in G major

No Autograph MS; copy in Lpz Poel 18 (K. H. L. Pölitz c1790).

Headed 'Fuga di J. Sebast. Bach'; two staves.

The MS Poel 18 (a single sheet) contains two three-part fugues competently composed on somewhat angular themes: BWV 581 and the chorale 'Wir glauben all' BWV Anh.70, the latter of which is anonymous. Neither requires pedal, and in neither does the fugal technique lead to more than an exposition, a middle entry, a derivative episode and a coda or final entry. It is possible that BWV 581 is also a chorale-fugue: for the first five notes, see also the E flat Fugue BWV 552. Neither BWV 581 nor BWV Anh.70 shows form, texture, motif, invention or scoring characteristic of J. S. Bach at any period.

---

582   Passacaglia in C minor

No Autograph MS (MS once owned by C. W. F. Guhr, said to be Autograph by Griepenkerl in Peters 1, 1844); copies in Lpz MB III.8.4 (Andreas-Bach-Buch), Lpz MB MS R 16, 9 (fragment (last 59½ bars), chief copyist of the Andreas-Bach-Buch), P 803 (J. T. Krebs), P 320 (Kittel) and late copies (MS in Rust's collection, two Scholz MSS (shortened versions), P 274, P 277, P 279, P 286, P 290, P 557, Vienna S.m. 5014), some of which belong to the Kittel group.

Two staves in Andreas-Bach-Buch and P 803 etc; headed in Andreas-Bach-Buch 'Passacalia. ex C♭ con Pedale'; fugue in P 803 headed 'Fuga cum Subjectis'.

(i) Instrument and purpose. Whether or not the MS owned by Guhr and used by Griepenkerl was indeed autograph is not now known.* A copy by Hauser (of the autograph? – see Kinsky 1936 p160) was headed 'Passacaglio con Pedale pro Organo pleno'; but·most copies are called simply 'Passacalia', and even P 803 omits such phrases as 'pro Organo' or 'con Pedale', which are found in other pieces copied in other gatherings of the MS (e.g. BWV 537, 540). There is no authority for the rubric 'Cembalo ossia Organo' in BG 15, despite Forkel's famous phrase about the Passacaglia (Forkel 1802 ch.IX) – 'die aber mehr für zwey Claviere und Pedal als für die Orgel ist' ('which however is more for two keyboards and pedal than for organ') – by which he seems to be suggesting two-manual harpsichord or clavichord. From the layout of Var. 17 (b140) it has also been argued that two manuals are intended (e.g. Grace c1922 p92), whatever the kind of keyboard instrument

---

* According to Mendelssohn's letter of 18 June 1839 to his sister, he had been offered an autograph of the 'Passecaille' as a present by Guhr in Frankfurt. From Mendelssohn's remarks it seems the copy also contained the Legrenzi Fugue in the same key (BWV 574), as does the Andreas-Bach-Buch.

required. Griepenkerl had already thought that the Passacaglia, like the Six Sonatas, was for 'a clavichord of two manuals and pedal' (Peters I), while Schweitzer later opted for harpsichord with pedals (1905 p258); it is very doubtful that either writer had ever heard either instrument. Yet the work hardly has a place in the church service even as a postlude, for which Mattheson notes that organists were free to use their fantasy in such movements as *ciacone* (1739 p477); he seems to have had in mind a different kind of dance, at a later date, in a church province with different traditions.

Both the Andreas-Bach-Buch and the Möller MS may be dated as early as 1707/8 or even earlier (Kilian 1962), in which case the Passacaglia is one of the composer's earliest and most advanced masterpieces in sustained form. However, research in progress on the Andreas-Bach-Buch (H.-J. Schulze, S. Daw) makes such conclusions very questionable. The copyist of BWV 582 (and of BWV 563, 574, 911 and 916) probably belongs to a 'third phase' in the writing of the album, perhaps around the middle of the century. The Andreas-Bach-Buch therefore cannot be used as evidence for an early date of composition, which besides would go against musical details in the work as a whole – for example, it is difficult to believe that the fugue could have been composed before J. S. Bach got to know ritornello concerto movements in 1713 or so. In any event, however, it can be said that the earlier the Passacaglia was composed, the more it can be seen as a deliberate essay in *genre*-composition, very likely under the influence of Buxtehude.* The Andreas-Bach-Buch itself – whoever compiled it, and for whatever reason – contains several categories of works which suggest that it was compiled to reflect a range of styles at the hands of various composers. Several keyboard works of Bach copied in that MS are composed in clearly distinct types, though contributed by some five or six different scribes (scribes 1, 3, 6, 7, 8):

> Toccata in F sharp minor BWV 910 (scribe 1)
> Ouverture in F BWV 820 (6)
> Passacaglia in C minor BWV 582 (3)
> Fugue in G minor BWV 578 (1)
> Chorale prelude BWV 724 (?)
> Aria variata all. man. Italiana BWV 989 (7)
> Legrenzi Fugue BWV 574 (3)
> three kinds of fantasia: BWV 570, 563, 944 (1, 3, 8)

Quite such a miscellany of French, Italian and north German elements in contrasting keyboard idioms is striking. Moreover, in addition to the Variations BWV 989 and the *Mayerin* Partita of Reincken, there is a distinct group of ostinato works, perhaps all but the first copied by the same scribe:

> Buxtehude: Ciacona in C minor BUXWV 159 ⎫
> Ciacona in E minor BUXWV 160 ⎪ unique extant
> Passacalia in D minor BUXWV 161 ⎬ source
> Praeludium (with Ciacona) BUXWV 137 ⎭

* Even perhaps as a result of the Lübeck visit of 1705–6. Certainly BWV 582 is most unlikely to have been composed during the Leipzig period, as is still sometimes maintained (e.g. Klotz 1975 p375).

Pachelbel: Ciacona in D minor
Böhm: Suite in D major (with Chaconne)
J. S. Bach: Passacaglia in C minor BWV 582

Although this survey of styles (by one composer) and exploration of one particular *genre* (by several composers) do not prove the volume to have had a purely didactic aim, its usefulness in this direction is certain. Nor is this element weakened by the doubtful authenticity of some of the Bach works concerned (BWV 820, 563); rather, it supports their claim to be genuine works composed in specific and somewhat experimental styles. Moreover, that the Andreas-Bach-Buch is now the unique source for the Buxtehude pieces may well suggest that the copyist or owner had some particular interest in ostinato works; even if the assembling by a central German organist of so many ostinato works was in some way done 'according to French taste', as has been tentatively suggested (Riedel 1960 p206), the Passacaglia BWV 582 is still related to Buxtehude's chaconnes by their juxtaposition in this source. Ostinatos appear not to have been common in north German organ music, and the selection in the Andreas-Bach-Buch is remarkable on these grounds alone.

It is even possible to think that BWV 582 was composed to bear some or all of these pieces company in a broad selection, or to adopt some of their devices as the basis of a more extended composition, or to serve as a demonstration of ostinato technique, not always realized in strict keyboard terms. The Andreas-Bach-Buch as a whole cannot be adduced as evidence for this, since it was not written out by the same copyist at the same time. But until more is known for certain about the book's provenance, it cannot be held to contradict such an interpretation, which is supported by further points: there are moments in BWV 582 that require an unusual kind of manual dexterity; it has many elements in common with Buxtehude (see below); and, moreover, a series of conventional *figurae* are used (one after the other) in a texture varying from one to five parts. There is even little correspondence between BWV 582 and ostinatos in the earlier cantatas, which are more modest and less thoroughly, less demonstratively worked out (e.g. the ostinato aria BWV 131.iv, 1707).

(ii) Influences. Perhaps no other organ work of J. S. Bach is open to so many direct comparisons as the Passacaglia. The theme, the development of variations on it, and the details of the fugue that follows all have a history stretching back to the works of older organists. It is probably the rarity of passacaglias compared with preludes and fugues of various other kinds that encouraged both the composer and his commentators to seek influences from elsewhere.

The fugue theme and the first half of the passacaglia theme were shown by Guilmant & Pirro (*Archives des Maîtres de l'Orgue* II, 1899) to be the same as the theme of the Christe – subtitled 'Trio en passacaille' – in the second mass of André Raison's *Premier Livre d'Orgue* (Paris 1688): Ex. 226. Whether or not either Raison or J. S. Bach knew that this theme closely resembles the opening of the

Ex. 226

Raison, *Premier Livre d'Orgue*: second mass, Christe

Gregorian Communio for the tenth Sunday after Pentecost is not known (Radulescu 1979), nor indeed whether it is more likely that Raison knew it than that Bach did. In the preface to the *Livre*, Raison notes that each piece in his masses corresponds to 'a Sarabande, Gigue, Bourrée, Canaris, Passacaille and Chaconne', played more slowly 'à cause de la Sainteté du Lieu'. The 27-bar *passacaille* is not the only piece of its kind: in Raison's sixth mass the Christe is another 'Trio en Chaconne' with a four-bar bass resembling the second half of the Passacaglia theme – a curious coincidence, if that is what it is. Such movements are not otherwise familiar in the organ works of the 'old French masters' whom Carl Philipp told Forkel his father admired (*Dok* III p288), although a 104-bar chaconne appears in Chaumont's *Pièces d'Orgue* (Liège 1695). Nor are such ostinato passacaglias at all common in French keyboard music, the usual *passacaille* being a rondo like the 'Chacone en Rondeaux' of Dandrieu's suite copied by J. G. Walther in P 802. The imitative opening of Raison's little movement in Ex. 226 is unexpected for a *passacaille* and gives the impression that the ostinato repetition was an afterthought.

That the fugue theme of Bach's Passacaglia quotes exactly the first four bars as they appear in Raison may perhaps be a coincidence, a 'superficial resemblance' (Buchmayer *SIMG* 1900–1 p270) arising from their archetypal character. Moreover, the theme of BWV 582 is less exceptional in its German context than Raison's is in French music. Similar (though less consistent) rhythms, lines, intervals (especially the semitone), cadences and sometimes lengths can be found in other German sources – Ex. 227. None of these has the sustained melody and logic of BWV 582, but they do contain its elements and demonstrate its tradition. An important element in the make-up of almost all these themes is that they appear to be newly conceived and not mere variants

Ex. 227

BUXWV 159

BUXWV 161

BUXWV 160

J. Krieger, Ciacona (*Clavierübung*, 1698)

on seventeenth-century ostinato basses – such as the descending tetrachord still found in (e.g.) Pachelbel's Ciacona in F minor, Böhm's D major Suite in the Andreas-Bach-Buch, the first four bars of the *Goldberg Variations*, and even (in ornate form) the Chaconne of the Partita in D minor for Violin. The descending tetrachord, like other ostinato themes, produces a four-bar phrase which later composers varied in their own versions of it (e.g. eight bars in Chaumont; five, seven and eight bars in Purcell). That such four-bar themes remained common in German keyboard music (e.g. the Buxtehude examples just cited) and vocal–instrumental music (e.g. Cantata BWV 12.ii, 1714) led some earlier commentators to claim the eight-bar theme of BWV 582 to be more uncommon than it is. An unusual element in BWV 582 is the playing-over of the theme at the beginning, though that too is known elsewhere (e.g. Schmelzer's Violin Sonata in D (1664), the Lament in Purcell's *Dido*). Moreover, it is scarcely an accident that this playing-over introduces a theme which 'contains all the characteristic intervals...and chords of the C minor tonal centre' (Wolff 1972), and which already introduces 'the three dimensions of the following composition: the harmonic, the melodic and the figurative–ornamental' (Radulescu 1979).

The development of variations in BWV 582 has distinctive features, quite apart from the hidden symmetries, the sustained tension and the gradual evolution from homophony to polyphony. Thus, (i) the theme ends with a clear perfect cadence each time; (ii) the theme does not pass to other keys or appear in them; (iii) the theme moves out of the bass into the treble, and then (iv) out of the treble, jumping octave from beat to beat (Var. 15, bb121ff); (v) the bass varies the theme, including a staccato version; (vi) variations with similar figures come either in pairs or in groups; (vii) a fugue follows, beginning as a Variation 21. While this last feature can be found in no other known passacaglia, it is striking that in his C major Praeludium BUXWV 137 Buxtehude employs his *ciacona* as a variation on the fugue subject, not vice versa. The Passacaglia BWV 582 is also unique in the organ works of J. S. Bach in the obvious relationship between the 'prelude' and the fugue – almost leading to the speculation that the fugue was written first, perhaps as a 'Fugue on a Theme of Raison' corresponding to the Fugue on a Theme of Legrenzi BWV 574 (also in C minor). The other features listed above can be found elsewhere: (i) is found in Buxtehude's E minor Ciacona, (ii) there and in the C minor Ciacona (but not the D minor Passacaglia); the clear demarcation between (iii) and (iv) is not familiar in other chaconnes, but many basses drop the theme (e.g. Pachelbel's Passacaglia in F minor) whilst its notes and harmonies are incorporated in the manual figures; (v) is found in Buxtehude's E minor Ciacona, (vi) in Buxtehude's C minor Ciacona (not merely the four-bar repetitions of Pachelbel and other central and southern composers). It is scarcely possible to argue from J. S. Bach's unique organ passacaglia and violin chaconne that the term 'passacaglia' indicated a movement with repeated bass theme and 'chaconne' one with a recurring harmony, any more than for Buxtehude 'passacaglia' indicated a $^3/_2$ movement with modulating variations and 'chaconne' a $^3/_4$ movement without modulation.

Many of the patterns in both the passacaglia and the fugue of BWV 582 are familiar in the *genre* as left in particular by Buxtehude, Pachelbel, Kerll, Kuhnau, C. F. Witt and Muffat. There can be no doubt that BWV 582 is a conscious acknowledgement of these patterns. Converting the bass theme into short, detached notes has already been referred to – see b80 of BWV 582 and b53 of BUXWV 160; to take further examples, Muffat's Passacaglia in *Apparatus musico-organisticus* (1690) uses a similar strategy to BWV 582 – first quaver lines, then anapaests, semiquavers (right hand, then left hand, then together),

Ex. 228

BUXWV 160 b53

(variation repeated)

BWV 582 b80

arpeggios, leaping semiquavers, and quaver triplets. The most remarkable demonstration of how traditional these figures are was given by R. Buchmayer (*SIMG* 1900–1 pp265ff), who not only proved the attribution of the Passacaglia in D minor BWV Anh.182 to C. F. Witt (composer of a Capriccio in the Andreas-Bach-Buch) but also showed that the similarity of these figures to the Passacaille from Lully's *Acis et Galatée* (1686) argues a close dependence on the latter. Assuming Buxtehude's BUXWV 160 to be earlier than BWV 582, it can be seen that J. S. Bach clarifies and regulates the figuration yet further; for although (as in BUXWV 160) the right hand plays semiquavers, it does so in a more systematic, scale-like way: Ex. 228. In this sense, BWV 582 is more 'doctrinaire' than some other passacaglias. Its extraordinary invention lies in the exact form of these figures, given the relentless nature of the eight-bar theme and its inevitable diatonic gravitation. Comparison with (e.g.) Pachelbel's D minor Chaconne shows that while both themes have such a 'diatonic gravitation', BWV 582 is more advanced in two specific ways: the greater length of its theme enables a motif to be more fully developed (and not merely repeated), and its careful four-part harmonies produce an obviously more intense counterpoint – Ex. 229.

Ex. 229
Pachelbel, Chaconne in D minor   b9

BWV 582   b32

That in the process something of the seventeenth-century chaconne/passacaglia has been lost – a light, dance-like tempo and phrasing – is not the foregone conclusion it might seem to be, for Pachelbel's and Buxtehude's D minor ostinato pieces have already become distinct keyboard passacaglias of a serious cast. Buxtehude's in particular has a degree of restlessness occasioned by its short bass theme – its strong dominants are constantly being brought to the surface by the repetition – and this is no longer felt in BWV 582, where each eight-bar unit is a resolved entity.

As the last examples show, the *figurae* behind the variation in BWV 582 belong to tradition, but the composer's inventiveness has given the *figurae* new shapes. The up-beat semiquaver *suspirans* figure takes various forms (ascending, descending, extended, leaping), each one of which can be compared to figures in other organ works of the Weimar period, most notably the *Orgelbüchlein*: Ex. 230. The leaping figure

Ex. 230

b48

BWV 630

b56

BWV 638

b65

BWV 644 b2

b72

BWV 601

(*figura corta*) of Var. 5 (bb40ff) gives new colour to the anapaest –
Ex. 231 – just as the prevailing melodiousness gives new life to the
simple arpeggio of Var. 15 (bb120ff), compared to a similar variation in
Pachelbel's D minor Chaconne. It could be said, too, that the leaping

Ex. 231

b40

anapaest of Var. 5 is more direct and thorough-going than the similar
figure in 'In dich hab' ich gehoffet' BWV 640.

Certain traditional influences are more subtle than mere resemblances
between figures. Thus, while the triplet thirds and sixths of Var. 17
(bb136ff) recall a variation in the C minor Chaconne BUXWV 159,
Buxtehude's influence on the last two variations of BWV 582 is less
superficial. The insistent figure Ex. 232 that runs through these

Ex. 232

b153

variations (bb153–68) is not only found in simpler form in the D minor
Passacaglia BUXWV 161 but is the kind of obsessive idea known in other
works of Buxtehude, e.g. the F sharp minor Praeludium BUXWV 146 at
b67 and b74. It is likely that such insistent, obsessive figures – all
basically embroidered pedal points in the top part – derive ultimately
from what may be regarded as the seminal passacaglia of the
seventeenth century, Frescobaldi's 'Cento partite sopra passacagli'
(*Toccate d'intavolatura*, 1615): Ex. 233.

Ex. 233

Frescobaldi, 'Cento partite sopra passacagli'

b253

see also Ex. 162

Although BWV 582 lends itself to such general observations, it does
seem to have a particular relationship to Buxtehude's C minor
Chaconne BUXWV 159. The very opening must be a salute to it, and
Spitta heard in the opening of Bach's variations the 'painful longing'

characteristic of the older master (1 p580). It even looks, in bb16–17, as if BWV 582 is going to pair the variations in the same way, but the greater length of its theme permits a more complex form (see below). Both form and figuration in BWV 582 are more systematically worked than in BUXWV 159, where the opening four-part harmonies are only fitfully sustained, and the patterns exploited in the variations are not used towards such points of climax as the two in BWV 582. None of the passacaglias before BWV 582 has quite a comparable sense of climax, itself an eighteenth-century feature; some have an air of finality, some are tentative, some achieve roundness of form by a rondo-like return of the opening. BWV 582 not only uses a repertory of figures found complete in no other single passacaglia but uses it towards secondary (Var. 12) and primary (Var. 20) climaxes of a kind not traditionally within the character of a passacaglia. In this sense, it could be that Bach deliberately set out from the standpoint of BUXWV 159 to create a new structure of planned tension and relaxation, achieved through carefully and inventively written harmony.

Crucial to this tension structure is the fugue itself. Beginning as a kind of Variation 21,* it has certain formal features of traditional interest (see below); but it also incorporates a set of keyboard patterns or *figurae* as conventional as the variations themselves. The semiquaver countersubject of bb174–8,† for instance, produces similarities to manual variations in Pachelbel's F minor Chaconne: Ex. 234. Whether

Ex. 234

Pachelbel, Chaconne in F minor

b65

or not the fugue was composed before the rest of the Passacaglia, it rises to a parallel sense of tension or climax – but now more as the result of fugal treatment and a fugal order of events than through increase in the number of parts or intricacy in the development of motif. This different method of achieving a climax is itself an important parallel between the two sections of BWV 582: the coupling of a passacaglia and a fugue is not merely a matter of formal neatness but is a means of presenting the main theme in two guises. Throughout the fugue, the four-bar theme appears as a kind of reiterated cantus firmus and is itself scarcely developed. This process, though it may be obvious, in fact

* Schumann described the work as having twenty-one variations (David & Mendel 1945 p372). Why it has been argued that the fugue does not follow on immediately but breaks from Var. 20 and then begins *attacca* (Wolff 1969) is not clear; compared to the usual prelude and fugue, the close of Var. 20 is lacking in finality – e.g. in closing on a weak beat and in rising to the mediant of a tonic minor chord.
† Numbering the bars in one sequence through the whole of BWV 582.

suggests a radical re-thinking of conventional ostinato techniques. Thus, for Buxtehude, the C major Praeludium BUXWV 137 has a fugue subject later transformed into an ostinato bass* which creates a kind of chaconne-coda. The obstinate quality of the reiterated bass in BUXWV 137 produces a simple sense of climax not possible with the longer theme of BWV 582, which therefore uses a more strategically planned, symphonic means.

(iii) **Form of the passacaglia.** What exactly the strategic plan of BWV 582 is has been the subject of some disagreement amongst the commentators. Two points of tension are usually heard in the work: Var. 12 (bb97–104) after which there is an 'intermezzo' of three variations (bb105–52), then a rise towards a second climax with the soprano 'pedal point' of the final two variations (bb153–68) (Keller 1948 pp96–7). But further groupings of the twenty variations are problematic: schemes have been suggested, as shown in the table on the next page. Geiringer implies important breaks in the flow: at Var. 6 (bb48ff) is the first unbroken semiquaver motion, at Var. 11 (bb88ff) the theme leaves the bass, at Var. 16 (bb128ff) the theme returns to the bass, giving a decided finality to the last group of variations. According to the other schemes, manuals may be changed, but only on the basis of conjecture; nothing in the sources, and no documentary evidence concerned with the work, can serve as a guide on the changing of stops or manuals in either passacaglia or fugue.

Disagreements on the inner groupings of variations concern the choice of elements in the figuration. Is the semiquaver line that is shared by Vars. 10 and 11 (bb80–96) – they have the same countersubject – sufficient to unify them despite the changing position of the bass theme, the different number of parts and the contrast between textures? If Var. 13 (bb104–12) drops the pedal, to some extent conceals the theme, and (as the phrase-marks suggest) becomes more cantabile, does it herald a new section, despite the continuous semiquavers? A thoroughly methodical analysis of motifs, number of parts, use of pedal, position of the theme, degree to which the theme is varied, tessitura and compass, probable or possible manual changes, and other details (e.g. derivation of motif from the theme itself) is scarcely possible despite attempts sometimes made (e.g. Wolff 1969, 1972), since – as the *Figurenlehre* elements in the *Orgelbüchlein* also suggest – the composer is not preoccupied by any one particular factor. There is only an artificial connection between the shape of BWV 582 and the symmetries of the late published works, whether that shape is regarded as axial (Wolff 1969) or more subjectively based on inner tension (Keller 1948 p96). Similarly, it requires a personal commitment to a set plan to find a break or change of grouping at b72 between Var. 8 and Var. 9, or to claim that there is no break at b104 between Var. 12 and Var. 13.

---

* It is striking that Buxtehude gives his *ciacona* theme a distinctly more bass-like character than the original fugue theme; it could be that in BWV 582 Bach used only the first half of his passacaglia theme in order to prevent its bass-like quality from dominating the fugue.

	Geiringer 1966 p228	Wolff 1969	Vogelsänger 1972	Klotz 1972	Radulescu 1979
Theme					
1 syncopated four-part harmonies	1	1	1	1	1
2	2	2	2	2	2
3 quavers	3	3	3	3	3
4 smooth anapaests	4	4	4	4	4
5 leaping anapaests	5	5	5	5	5
6 rising *suspirans*	6	6	6	6	6
7 falling *suspirans*	7	7	7	7	7
8 extended *suspirans*	8	8	8	8	8
9 broken triads	9	9	9	9	9
10 scale countersubject above staccato	10	10	10	10	10
11 theme, then below legato theme	11	11	11	11	11
12 further semiquaver figures	12	12	12	12	12
13 further semiquaver figures (NB phrasing)	13	13	13	13	13
14 further semiquaver figures	14	14	14	14	14
15 further semiquaver figures	15	15	15	15	15
16 for harmonies, see Var. 1	16	16	16	16	16
17 triplets (thirds & sixths)	17 condensed	17	17	17	17
18 dactyls (thirds & sixths)	18 recapitulation	18	18	18	18
19 ostinato figure; C minor chords	19 of Vars. 1–10	19	19	19	19
20	20	20	20	20	20

In that case, however, all the groupings above are suspect. Rather, the composer has been guided by his skill in creating contrast on one hand and in ensuring continuity on the other; throughout the work there is a degree of caprice, an instinct for composition inimical to a clear dismembering either on the study-desk or on the different manuals of an organ.

(iv) **Form of the fugue.** Quite apart from its opening already referred to, the fugue has some features unusual in the corpus of Bach organ fugues. Each entry is accompanied by both countersubjects, and the movement thus belongs to the type of 'permutation fugue', known from some early vocal works, in which each theme follows regularly in each part. The full countersubjects are not used alone, and the fugue is not so much a double fugue as a fugue with two countersubjects: the three lines are combined not only continually but in different and varied permutations (a = subject; b = countersubject 1; c = countersubject 2):

bar	169	174	181	186	192	198	209	221	234	246	256	272
S		*a*	*b*	*c*		*c*	*b*	*c*		*a*		*a*
A	*a*	*b*	*c*		*a*	*b*	*a*	*b*	*c*		*b*	*b*
T	*b*	*c*		*a*	*b*	*a*	*c*		*a*	*b*	*c*	
B			*a*	*b*	*c*			*a*	*b*	*c*	*a*	*c*

As can be seen, no one permutation of themes and voices appears twice (quite apart from the question of key), and the invertibility exceeds even that in the Concerto in D minor BWV 596.ii. The interludes and episodes are never independent, being based instead on the counter-subjects; but these episodes increase in length and complexity as the fugue proceeds, creating a movement of broad sweep and uncommonly tense continuity. Each time the subject enters, it passes to a phrase based on conventional organ figures which in turn lead to a key whose first I–V progression or imperfect cadence comprises the first two notes of the next theme entry (bb195–7, 203–8, 212–20 etc). As with other Bach fugues (including such later examples as BWV 679), the twelve entries appear progressively less frequently – another way of saying that the episodes become longer. But the entries disguise the four-bar length of the subject by passing to different material each time (e.g. codetta in b172), harmonizing the countersubject (e.g. bb201–3) or even referring to the passacaglia theme (? pedal at bb184–5). The key-plan itself is a model of fugal structure based on contrasted but related keys, a structure in which the episodes contain crucial modulations:

168–9	tonic (with 'fifth' part, b192)
197–8	relative, then dominant of relative
220–1	dominant–tonic–dominant
255–6	subdominant
271–2	tonic, then coda

The passacaglia theme, with its basic intervals and motifs centring on the scale of C minor, has been described – though not convincingly – as underlying the two countersubjects and the final coda (Vogelsänger

1972). It is significant that the coda – which is longer than the eight bars it is usually described as comprising – does not even close with the perfect cadence of the theme, which each variation of the passacaglia does clearly and unambiguously. Rather, the composer seems to have been aiming at contrast between the movements, which only together form the full complement of treatment for this whole theme: neither passacaglia nor fugue alone can present its full aspect.

Just as the passacaglia sometimes presents textures known elsewhere – e.g., b97 is not unlike an *Orgelbüchlein* movement except in spacing – so the fugue carries familiar ideas, even possibly allusions. Some points were made above, section (ii). Such figures as b217 or b237 would be in place in a Buxtehude praeludium; the whole coda section (about bb281–92) belongs to the family of the G major Prelude BWV 541. The figure Ex. 235 can be heard in both BWV 541 and the G minor

Ex. 235

b267

Fugue BWV 542, while the trill over the same figure in the pedals (bb269–70) recalls the Fugue BWV 537.ii bb101–2 (in the same key as the Passacaglia). Other bars are reminiscent of other works, e.g. b262 with the opening of the F minor Prelude BWV 534. The Neapolitan sixth in b285 is matched by those towards the ends of the fugues in D major BWV 532 and G minor BWV 535, though – like the cadenza phrases in the closing stages of the D minor Toccata BWV 565 – these examples of the Neapolitan chord break the continuity in a manner foreign to that in the Passacaglia. A curious fact about the fugue is that although the composer keeps to figures known in other passacaglias, to details of style familiar in his other organ works, to a classic key-plan, to carefully derived episodes, and to a classic creation of three-part invertible counterpoint, there remains a sense of free, almost capricious invention throughout. The essential traditionalisms of the work have not stultified it. A proper *organo pleno* throughout will not only convey its combination of lyricism and invention but also sustain the *pleno* of Var. 20 that led immediately into the fugue.

583

'Trio in D minor'

No Autograph MS; copy in P 286 (C. P. E. Bach's copyist Anon 300), P 1115 (A. Kühnel?), Copenhagen Grönland MS (Emery 1957 p31); Peters IV used a MS belonging to C. A. Reichardt.

Headed in P 286 'Choralvorspiel auf der Orgel mit 2 Claviere und Pedal von Johann Sebastian Bach' (also advertised by Westphal in 1780 as '4 [sic] Choral-Vorspiele...'; see *Dok* III p269); in P 1115 one of 'Sammlung von 35 Orgeltrio's von Sebastian Bach', in Grönland MS one of 'VIII Trios...'; present title from *BG* 38 etc.

The form of the movement may be expressed as:

A	1–19	main subject supplying a motif imitated and extended in sequence; beginning and ending in D minor (13–17 = 1–5, upper parts exchanged), middle passage in relative
B	19–41	second subjects in similar imitation, also including motif from A; two sections (30–40 = 19–29 in dominant, upper parts exchanged)
A	41–51	shortened reprise: 41–4 = 3–6 down a fifth, and 45–51 = 7–13 down a fifth with parts exchanged
Coda	51–3	(inverted motif from A?)

While the movement, expressed in this manner, may appear to conform to the shapes characteristic of the Six Sonatas, the imitation is throughout shorter-phrased and in this respect alone untypical. All themes are answered at the half-bar, a structural element much to the fore even when the lines are extended (e.g. bb26ff). Such sequential and close imitation above a moving bass line as that of bb19ff is found in the Six Sonatas only in episodes or secondary material, e.g. D minor, BWV 527.i bb24ff. The short phrases, mostly half a bar long, may be a reference to French or other trio writing.

The subjects themselves could all be regarded as either 'early' or 'written in the style of the master' by a pupil, a fact which probably explains the resemblances heard by Keller (1948 p109) between two motifs and the G minor Fugue BWV 542: Ex. 236(i). Similar points could

Ex. 236

(i)   **(ii)**

b1 (cf. BWV 542.ii b1)   b24 (cf. BWV 542.ii b39) b24

be made about the pedal motif Ex. 236(ii), which is common to BWV 542.ii and many other pieces. The texture itself accords perfectly with the Six Sonatas, as a comparison of a pair of bars would show (e.g. bb39–40 with bb3–4 of BWV 526.i), and the motivic detail is equally ingenious. Motif *a* appears ten times in the first four bars, including its *inversus* form (*b*) and a decorated version (*c*): Ex. 237. In

Ex. 237   b1   b2   b3

comparison with the sonata movements, however, the juxtaposing of one subject with another is not always managed so as to appear natural (e.g. b41), nor is the linking effortless (e.g. b45). A curious detail is the coda which, while not even strictly necessary, could equally well become an imperfect cadence ending on the dominant; had this *adagio* Trio once been a slow movement, such a cadence would have been quite in keeping (compare BWV 526.ii). A further sign of the work's doubtful provenance is that though marked 'Adagio', the material itself (motifs, phrasing) would equally well suit 'Allegro' – an unusual quality.

As Spitta suggested (II p692), the trio is probably to be understood as one of the single movements referred to by Forkel in his list of unpublished works (Forkel 1802 ch.IX):

Mehrere einzelne, die noch hier und da verbreitet sind, können ebenfalls schön genannt werden, ob sie gleich nicht an die erstgenannten reichen.

Several single movements, dispersed here and there, can likewise be called fine, although they do not quite reach the level of those [trios and sonatas] first mentioned.

In this connection, it is instructive that the 1820 English translation of Forkel (probably made by A. F. C. Kollmann, editor of one of the Six Sonatas: see BWV 525) renders 'hier und da verbreitet' as 'in the hands of different persons' (David & Mendel 1945 p346). What the title in P 286 can mean is open to question; in the Grönland MS, the movement is one of several sonata movements (BWV 529.ii, 525.i, 583, 528.ii) which precede three chorales (BWV 653, 661, 664a). The trio on 'Allein Gott' BWV 664a is also to be found in P 1115, and the implication may be that BWV 583 is a trio working of a chorale melody; if so, however, a cantus-firmus statement of the melody at some point would be expected. The opening motif itself is chorale-like and can be found in (e.g.) 'Hier lief' ich nun' BWV 519 (twice in the first three bars), but no complete chorale melody is an obvious source for BWV 583. Rather, its details – such as the opening pedal notes or the progression C minor/A major in the penultimate bar – join with the technique of imitation by short phrases to suggest a separate trio movement composed by a gifted pupil.

584

Trio in G minor

No Autograph MS; pub. in G. W. Körner and A. G. Ritter, *Der Orgelfreund* VI (c1842), pp10–11; MS copy in Lpz Go.S.27 (19th century).

Headed in Körner 'Trio'.

The 30 bars are a version of the first section *A* of an *A B A* aria of 78 bars in Cantata 166 (BWV 166.ii, 1724):

    right hand = oboe part
    pedal   = basso-continuo part
    left hand = partly tenor vocal line; but mostly different from the parts of
                BWV 166, despite shared thematic material

While it was once thought that the trio was the earlier version of the two (R. Oppel *BJ* 1909 pp27–40), it is more likely that the true original is neither BWV 584 nor BWV 166.ii but rather a lost (i.e. incompletely preserved) aria with two obbligato instruments, and that BWV 584 is an arrangement not made by Bach himself, since some major thematic references are missing (Dürr *NBA* I/12 *KB* pp 18–20). By comparing the cantata parts with the Trio BWV 584, a second obbligato part has been reconstructed for the aria (Dürr *NBA* I/12).

Whoever arranged or transcribed BWV 584, the bass line remains a characteristic basso-continuo part, and the close-packed stretto technique of the upper parts (which do not require two manuals) is characteristic of episodes in the Six Sonatas, not of their opening themes. The arrangement accords with other Körner publications, e.g. the Sinfonia of Cantata 21, and is probably nineteenth-century in origin.

---

585 Trio in C minor

No Autograph MS (note in P 289 refers to a source said to be Autograph in possession of C. F. G. Schwenke); copies in Lpz MB MS 7, 1 (hand of J. N. Mempell? 1730–40?), P 289 (probably hand of J. C. Westphal (1773–1828); or 2nd half of 18th century) 2nd movement up to b54 only; a lost MS owned by Griepenkerl (Peters IX, see BWV 587). Transcription of movements by J. F. Fasch (see below).

Headed 'Adagio', 'Allegro' in Lpz MB MS 7, where it is entitled 'Trio. ex. C mol. di Bach' and the movements are reversed; 'Largo' and 'Allegro un poco' in the Fasch source (see below); 'Moderato' for both movements in the Krebs edition (see below).

While Spitta (II p692) thought the trio perhaps one of the separate works referred to by Forkel (see also BWV 583), Naumann (*BG* 38) thought it should rather be credited to J. L. Krebs: the present work appeared to conform to Krebs's two-movement trios and was included in a complete edition of his works by C. Geissler in the middle of the nineteenth century (Schulze 1973 p150), from an unknown source. But if comparison with the C minor Trio BWV Anh.46 (Keller 1948 p58) is justified by more than superficial resemblances, then the composer would be rather J. T. Krebs (Tittel 1966 pp 126–9). However, it has now been established (Schulze 1974) that BWV 585 is an arrangement on three staves of the first two movements of a Trio Sonata in C minor for two violins and continuo, preserved in parts in a Dresden MS and attributed there to J. F. Fasch (1688–1758), a competitor of J. S. Bach's for the cantorate of St Thomas, Leipzig in 1722 (sources in Schulze 1973 p151). Perhaps the transcription as it exists in Lpz MS 7 and P 289 is the work of Bach; at least, the fact that not all the grammatical faults of the original are eliminated there does not 'speak conclusively against Bach's authorship of the transcription' (Schulze 1974 p4). The order of events appears to be first the Fasch sonata, then the first two movements transcribed for organ, and thirdly a copy, now lost, made or owned by J. L. Krebs and incorporating minor 'improvements' (Schulze 1973 p153).

Since the pair of movements keeps a clear trio linearity, it was reasonable to credit the work to a composer of J. S. Bach's generation. But in overall form and in the detail there is little in common between BWV 585 and the Six Sonatas BWV 525–530. The subject of the Adagio is long (16 beats at slow tempo), with a doubly modulating codetta; the development emphasizes short motifs; the pedal point is an addendum to the previous phrase; the movement works towards an imperfect cadence and is therefore undeveloped in proportion to its subject. The Allegro subject has a unison answer despite a modulating codetta; the sequences are all of the same two kinds, one bar or one half-bar long; the pedal bass, though organ-like, is never more than an on-beat accompaniment. None of these features can be found in the Six Sonatas, nor is the simple ritornello form itself characteristic of them.

The simplicity of conception and detail is employed for material more typical of J. F. Fasch's later years than earlier. But detailed criteria for dating eighteenth-century trio sonatas are still very uncertain, and it is just possible that the work dates from the period 1708–11 when Fasch, a former choirboy at St Thomas, conducted a *collegium musicum* in Leipzig. On the whole, however, the sonata probably belongs to the period in the mid-1730s when the young Krebs and presumably other Bach pupils such as Gerber were playing and composing trios with such characteristics as those listed above.

---

586   Trio in G major

No Autograph MS; copy in Lpz MB MS 7, 2 (J. N. Mempell, probably before 1740), and another source used by G. W. Körner for an edition in 1850 (see Peters IX 1904 edn). Transcription of movement by G. P. Telemann (see below)?

Headed 'Trio. ex G.♯. 2. Clavier et Pedal. di J. S. Bach'.

Reported on by Seiffert in *Peters Jahrbuch* 1904, the movement was taken into the 1904 edition of Peters IX; K. Anton subsequently showed (*MuK* 1942 pp47ff) that it was a work of G. P. Telemann, 'arranged by Bach' from a harpsichord piece or from the theme of a harpsichord piece (Siegele 1975 p76). This probably dated from Telemann's Leipzig years; amongst other material belonging to the *collegium musicum*, it was destroyed in 1945 (*ibid*). Although it is possible to link such material directly with J. S. Bach himself, it is considered likely that the arrangement was made by somebody else (*MGG* 1 col.1014). The transcriber of all the first three trios now in Lpz MB MS 7 is uncertain, although the hand itself is thought to be that of J. N. Mempell (Krause 1964 p29, Schulze 1974a). The transcription of BWV 586 and 587 includes pedal e'.

Not conforming to the details of binary form familiar from Bach's instrumental and organ sonatas, the movement plays with its themes, and works towards cadences in various keys, in a manner typical of movements in Telemann's *Musique de Table* (1733). However, this conclusion is contradicted by the further suggestion that BWV 586 – though not in any case written by J. S. Bach – may have been an entirely new composition, based on a theme of Telemann (Schulze 1973 pp150, 154). Despite this, there is a sense of continuity well sustained if rarely 'tense'. All three parts show that at least some movement-types in chamber music of the period are not too far removed from the idiom of the Six Sonatas of J. S. Bach, although in details – simple imitation, passages in thirds, some basso-continuo figures in the pedal part, the idea of a binary Allegro, the absence of patent contrast between a subject (b1) and other material (b18) – BWV 586 has more in common with BWV 587 than with BWV 525–530.

587

'Aria in F major'

No Autograph MS; only source, a lost MS in the possession of Griepenkerl, later used in Peters IX (1881), not known in *BG* 38 (1891). Transcription of a movement by F. Couperin (see below).

Headed 'Aria' in Peters IX; only heading in Couperin 'Légérement'.

The 'Aria' BWV 587 is an almost literal transcription, omitting some ornaments, of section 4 of 'L'Impériale', the first of four movements from François Couperin's Troisième Ordre for two violins and continuo published in *Les Nations, sonades et suites de symphonies en Trio* (Paris 1726). The pedal compass is to e'.* It is not known exactly why Griepenkerl published it as a Bach work, whether in the source J. S. Bach was credited with either the composition or the transcription of the piece, or whether the transcription was made before or (as is generally assumed) after the publication of 1726. Nor is there any evidence from the sources of the toccata and Fugue in F BWV 540 that, as has sometimes been conjectured, the movement was included as interlude between the two movements of that work (all in F major) for performance on the long pedalboard at Weissenfels (Klotz 1950 p201). It is not even ascertainable that the transcription belongs to the Leipzig circle of c1726–50 and thus reflects the fitful currency of French styles there. That it is similar in compass to, and may have shared the same source as, the arrangement BWV 586 is scant evidence that J. S. Bach was involved in either work, despite suggestions to the contrary (Siegele 1975 pp76–7).

Apart from the basso continuo, the lines suit the organ as idiomatically as they do strings, and the details of thematic development in such a well-constructed *A B A* movement would have interested a player of BWV 527. However, 'Légérement' suggests a lively tempo, stylistically in keeping with string parts carefully articulated and

---

* Bar 59 (which contains the e') has an eb' in Couperin's original, as does the next bar in both versions.

ornamented in the original. It is also striking that this fourth section is the least contrapuntal or imitative in the original movement: a lively interlude only.

---

588   Canzona in D minor

No Autograph MS; copies in BB 40644 (Möller MS, last 16 bars only), Lpz MB MS 7, 21 (J. G. Preller), P 291 (2nd half of 18th century), P 320 (J. C. Kittel), P 837 (18th century), P 204 (C. F. G. Schwenke) and late sources (P 308, P 557, Lpz Go.S.26).

Two staves; heading in Lpz MB MS 7 'Canzona ex D mol à 4', similar headings in the other sources.

The fragment in the Möller MS is 'an early copy' (Dürr 1954), presumably well before 1714 (Kloppers 1966 p216). The closing cadence in Lpz MB MS 7 is highly ornamented (Ex. 238),* though it

Ex. 238   b168

is not known by whom. Griepenkerl reported that one unnamed copy had 'Adagio' above the start of the penultimate bar (Peters IV p. iv). In P 204 and P 291 the Canzona immediately precedes the D major Prelude and Fugue BWV 532; in P 320 and P 557 (Grasnick c1820, based on P 320?) there is also a copy of the D minor Fugue of Christian Flor (1626–97). The fugal opening for pedal alone, far from providing a unique authenticated example in the work of J. S. Bach, is very doubtful, both for this reason and in view of the spacing of the counterpoint; not even at the final pedal point or at the two cadences is the pedal necessary, unlike (e.g.) the Allabreve BWV 589.

Whether or not Pirro and others (e.g. Frotscher 1935 p880) are right to see in the theme of BWV 588 an allusion to the *Canzon dopo la pistola* of the Mass of the Blessed Virgin in Frescobaldi's *Fiori musicali* (1635) – Ex. 239 – it is known that J. S. Bach owned a copy

Ex. 239   Frescobaldi, *Canzon dopo la pistola*
 b5   (double subject)

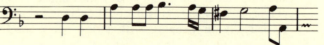

* The bar-numbering is in one sequence through the whole of BWV 588.

of the *Fiori musicali* by 1714 (*Dok* I p269). So in any case he will also have seen that the canzona is generally a lively piece, often with a repeated-note figure in the subject. This feature is if anything emphasized yet further in the usual $^3/_2$ second half of Italian canzona (as in the same *Canzon dopo la pistola* above) and was retained in the fantasy-like two-manual canzonas of certain north German composers (e.g. Canzona in G attributed to Scheidemann). Such *alla breve* characteristics in the counterpoint of BWV 588 as the dactyl figures (e.g. bb24–9) or the continuity that avoids cadences (e.g. bb35–40) would justify the terms 'ricercar-like and vocal–melodic' (Wolff 1968 p26) rather than 'canzona-like' in the most traditional sense. Further developments of this fugal idiom can be heard in such pieces as the D minor Fugue BWV 538. While terminology became flexible, and composers or copyists had their own habits in this respect, 'canzona' for such composers as Buxtehude always indicates a lively piece, generally with a triple-time second section, sometimes with a repeated-note subject not of the old vocal-canzona type but newly conceived in keyboard terms. Whether the function of such canzonas was the same as of those in the *Fiori musicali* – to serve as interludes after the Epistle or communion – is unknown, and the resemblance should not be overstated.

The form of the work may be expressed as follows:

A	1–31	exposition
	32–9	episode
	39–70	second exposition (first octave answer), towards imperfect cadence:
B	71–107	irregular exposition (with octave answers)
	107–14	episode
	114–29	second series of entries
	129–40	episode
	140–54	third series of entries
	154–62	episode
	162–9	final entry

No entries are in the relative or in any other major key. The ease with which the *B* entries extend to codettas or episodes contrasts with the strictness of the *A* entries. Clearly the *B* subject is derived from *A*, whilst its nature as a double fugue also depends on the original countersubject of *A*: Ex. 240. The chromatically descending fourth (see also BWV 131a, 625) was associated with fugues of the ricercar type, either as the subject of a chromatic fantasia (e.g. Sweelinck, Dowland) or as a countersubject to another theme (e.g. second Christe of Frescobaldi's *Messa delli Apostoli*, *Fiori musicali*). Inventive development of this fourth would also include an ascending version, as here at b111 (cf. the rising chromatic subjects in *Fiori musicali*): judging by fugues of W. F. Bach (F minor), C. P. E. Bach (D minor) and J. L. Krebs (F minor), this may have been a device taught by J. S. Bach. New countersubjects to both this and the main subject of BWV 588 are constantly being produced in the counterpoint, as can be seen by comparing such passages as bb15–22, 39–46, 46–54, 54–60, each of

Ex. 240

which adds a new third part to the combined subject and countersubject. In this respect *B* is rather less inventive than *A*, although Spitta saw the part-writing of *B* as 'bolder' (1 p420). But in any case the piece aims more at producing such new lines or melodies than at developing motifs themselves, which a chorale prelude might be expected to do. However, it is noticeable that the chief motifs of both *A* and *B* (Ex. 241) are taken from their respective subjects.

Ex. 241

The nature of the piece is somewhat elusive, since ricercar elements (⁴/₄ signature, chromatic countersubject) and an opening pedal solo are mingled with canzona elements (the triple-time section, freer texture). However, since neither the time-signature nor the use of pedal can be authenticated, it is possible to see the piece as a lively canzona or at least as something very different from the familiar dream-like fugue as usually interpreted today. Also, both cadences – particularly the link between sections *A* and *B* – are more dramatic than they are in the sectional canzonas of Frescobaldi or even those of such later composers as Buxtehude.

589

Allabreve in D major

No Autograph MS; copies in P 1106 (18th century, owned by J. C. Oley), P 316 (19th century), Stift Göttweig MS J. S. Bach 34 (dated 1839) and P 917 (19th century, only up to b172).

Headed in P 1106 and P 316 'Allabreve con Pedal pro Organo pleno'.

The 'ricercar-like and vocal–melodic' nature of *alla breve* counterpoint in general can be seen in BWV 589 even more clearly than in the

Canzona BWV 588. Some characteristics of this contrapuntal style are:

> ¢ signature, prevailing note-values minims and crotchets
> quasi-double subject (cf. quasi-strettos in exposition of the B flat minor Fugue, *The 48* Bk I)
> lines moving largely by step, but with conspicuous leaps (thirds, fourths)
> frequent minim suspensions (at least once every four beats)
> characteristic crotchet figures running through the movement: Ex. 242(i)
> characteristic quaver figures: Ex. 242(ii)

Ex. 242

(not found in BWV 589)

The result is a double counterpoint depending not on two independent melodies but on lines deliberately planned to counter each other: as one rises the other falls (*x*), as one moves the other is suspended (*y*), as one proceeds by step the other proceeds by leap (*z*), etc: Ex. 243. Within

Ex. 243

this generally Italianate counterpoint, there is in Bach's keyboard music considerable variety of tempo (BWV 589 faster than the Gratias agimus of the B minor Mass), of figure (no quaver figures in BWV 589 but many in *Goldberg Variation* 22), of subject (subject of the D minor Fugue BWV 538.ii longer than that of BWV 589), in addition to details of the working-out. In general, the *alla breve* style is more a result of the fugue or ricercar writing of keyboard composers after Frescobaldi (Froberger, Kerll etc) than of Frescobaldi and his contemporaries; it can be found in other contexts at the end of the seventeenth century and beyond – Ex. 244. The Corelli movement is similar in so many respects as to be sometimes regarded as the inspiration for BWV 589, but unnecessarily so, since similar idioms could be found in contemporary keyboard music, e.g. of J. K. F. Fischer and Gottlieb Muffat. Corelli's $^4/_2$ signature is a reminder of the origins of the *alla breve* style, a style that could lead to much variety of treatment. But it is highly questionable whether BWV 589 should be seen as an example of a 'south German harmony-type', or the G major Fantasia BWV 572 as an example of a

Ex. 244

Corelli, Concerto Op VI no. 1.iii (Allegro)

Strings · soli

Fischer, *Blumenstrauss*, Praeludium 7

b117

'north German' type (Frotscher 1935 p880). It can only be conjectured why BWV 589 has no prelude in the few extant sources.*

The form of the work can be expressed:

1–37	opening tonic section
37–90	further entries and episodes towards relative minor
90–158/9	episodes leading to two sets of tonic entries
158/9–197	final tonic entries, with stretto at one bar (174/5), chromatic preparation and closing pedal point

It is possible to see the divisions differently, since the piece has several manual episodes after which the pedal enters strikingly with the subject. The main subject often enters in stretto at two bars (at the fourth above or fifth below), and indeed it appears at first and sometimes later with a second or double subject. But this second or double subject is an extension of the first – i.e., it is the countersubject to the answer and does not produce a textbook double fugue: Ex. 245. The composer has been at pains to prepare an entry of the main theme

Ex. 245

subject · countersubject

---

* The sources are fewer than those for the fugues in F major (BWV 540.ii) and G minor (BWV 542.ii), which are also often found without preludes.

each time by a short or long rest, although, as Spitta pointed out (I p420), the counterpoint flows easily into the subject since the latter moves by such simple diatonic steps. The continuity of the work is very striking, depending as it does on the classical formulae produced by the motifs *a* and *b*. Other crotchet and minim motifs running through the fugue are already in evidence in the opening bars. That their treatment belongs to the eighteenth century and not to the seventeenth is clear from the dramatic extension of these smaller motifs into climaxes (e.g. *b* during bb119–26) and from the extension of the subject itself (e.g. alto, bb32–45). Moreover, each time the subject enters after an episode, it produces a kind of climax (e.g. b97).

Nevertheless, it is obvious that the fugal working has not yet produced the clear form of the maturer organ fugues, for the very continuity is a token of the ricercar–fugue, as are the non-structural use of key (returning tonics) and the array of subject entries (bb10, 18, 23...). Yet the composer's facility in manipulating motifs is already advanced and in such straightforward passages as bb57–9 or bb111–18 exceeds that of J. S. Bach's contemporaries, while the drive elsewhere almost disguises the movement's indebtedness to figures known to many other composers (e.g. bb164–75). Even the 'returning tonics' have the effect, and probably the pupose, of working against the aimlessness that can so easily arise in such styles; the archetypal quality of the main subjects gives the piece a sense of progression despite its easy continuity. As in the *alla breve* section of the Fantasia in G BWV 572, there seems no reason why the composer should not go on and on weaving this effortless counterpoint of whose formulas – including the chromatically descending fourth of bb180–5 running into a Neapolitan sixth – he is so clearly master.

---

590 'Pastorale in F major'

No Autograph MS; copies in P 290 (see List of Sources), P 287 (J. P. Kellner), P 277, two Scholz MSS (4th movement only), unnumbered Oxford Bodleian MS; Darmstadt Mus. MS 1322 (no 1st movement); early-19th-century copies of single movements in P 662 (3rd) and Lpz MB III.2.147 (1st).

Headed in P 290 and P 277 'Pastorella', in P 287 'Pastorella pro Organo di Johann Sebastian Bach'. No movement headings.

Questions about BWV 590 centre on three uncertainties: Are the four movements authentic Bach works? Do they belong together? Are they for organ? In overall plan and in many details BWV 590 not only resembles no other organ work but also is unlike any known keyboard suite; yet on the first question each movement can be shown to have features of one Bach idiom or another. On the second question, the sequence of keys suggests that of a sonata, particularly between the third and fourth movements; the imperfect cadence at the end of the first requires separate examination, however. The change from major to minor between the second and third is also typical less of the sonata than of the suite, though even there such a change normally occurs between two similar movements (e.g. the two Bourrées of the Cello Suite BWV 1009). If therefore the first movement was originally intended to be followed by the other three, on the analogy of an Italian sonata (Taesler 1969), the sequence of keys alone would be unique in the works of Bach. However, this is not to deny that at least the two central movements are similar in layout and texture or that the three so-called manual movements can form a sequence of their own. Whether they follow the first movement is a point that also bears on the final question above. They are all suitable for organ, according to some commentators (*BG* 38 p. xlii), and belong together even if in performance they are separated in the manner of – and perhaps for the same *alternatim* reasons as – Magnificat versets (Keller 1948 p76). But only the first movement requires, or was originally transcribed for, pedal: and that movement may well be incomplete in the sources.

It is possible that the four movements ought indeed to be grouped in the familiar way (Griepenkerl Peters 1) and that J. S. Bach wrote the whole work for some specific occasion now unknown (Frotscher 1935 p882). It is also possible that the three latter movements have nothing to do with the first (Spitta II p692), that the title 'Pastorella' applied only to the first movement (Naumann *BG* 38) – whoever it was that applied it – and that the first movement should have been – and perhaps was, in sources now unknown – completed to end in the tonic, with or without the other movements. Such distinct movements as this resemble not so much the north German toccata as that of a different school, in particular Georg Muffat's *Apparatus musico-organicus* (1690) where (e.g.) the F major Toccata Sesta has a series of movements featuring toccata pedal points and finally a $^{12}/_8$ fugue. Traditional organ pastorales had gradually encompassed several movements, from the merely sectional $^6/_4$ of Frescobaldi's *Capriccio pastorale* (*Toccate...libro primo*, Rome, 1637 edn) to the three movements of Zipoli's Pastorale (*A Third Collection of Toccates*, London, c1722 edn). In the last, a $^{12}/_8$ movement is followed by a contrasting section in binary time, after which a pedal point returns, making a shape of $A_1 B A_2$. It is possible that the composer or compiler of BWV 590, whoever he was, further extended this kind of plan by adding three movements to an organ pastorale that either had been left incomplete or was to have served as the prelude to another movement – even perhaps a (rejected?) interlude between a prelude and fugue in D minor.* Since no MS copies of the three manual movements as a group are known to exist, it is possible that they were indeed added later to an original organ pastorale, each of the three showing a confident technique and manipulation of its material. Moreover, they each show elements of the pastorale drone: BWV 590.ii begins with and later returns to a held bass

---

* In both P 290 and P 277, the work appears immediately before the Toccata and Fugue in D minor BWV 538; P 287, on the other hand, is made up of MSS from different sources.

note, and 590.iii uses a repeated bass quaver figure in the same way, while 590.iv has a fugue subject which itself incorporates a tonic *point d'orgue*.

Each movement also includes a dominant statement or 'answer' to an opening tonic phrase:

590.i   tonic b1, dominant b11
  ii   tonic b1, dominant b9
  iii   tonic b1, dominant b25
  iv   tonic b1, dominant b4 (and *inversus* b25)

which follows the pastorale tradition as demonstrated or laid down in the first movement. However, it is also typical of both binary and fugal structures, as too it is of organ preludes where sooner or later a dominant pedal point follows the tonic (e.g. A major BWV 536). It is this element that gives some toccatas a superficial resemblance to the true pastorale (e.g. Pachelbel's Toccata in F major).

First Movement

Despite its opening simplicity, the movement has a series of motifs and details not customary in the Frescobaldi-inspired pastorales of Kerll and other south German composers. Important and distinct motifs are heard in bb1, 3, 5 and 7. That such figures are close to the Italian idiom is clear from b10: similar figures to these can be found in (e.g.) Handel's *Messiah* pastorale.

A dominant 'answer' follows as in other pastorales (e.g. Corelli's Concerto Op VI no. 8) and continues with conspicuously new motifs in bb21 (left hand), 25–6 (left hand – cf. 'In dulci jubilo' BWV 608) and 28, after which a D minor pedal point returns to some of the ideas heard in the first section. The chromatic motif in b28 is in keeping with the style of Italian pastorales, in which such tones are probably meant to recall the doubtful intonation of the bagpipe-players (e.g. Zipoli's Pastorale). But the dominant-seventh sequence of bb21ff seems more typical of Bach (cf. bb33ff of the Pastoral Symphony of the *Christmas Oratorio*). Like other pastorales of Corelli, Locatelli (Op I) and others, the movement lacks the dotted siciliano rhythm often found in latter-day $^{12}/_8$ pastorales. Smooth $^{12}/_8$ figures on a pedal point produce quasi-pastoral idioms in many different contexts, such as vocal pieces concerned with Jesus the Shepherd (e.g. Cantata 104.v) or organ toccatas lacking any such association (e.g. Buxtehude's Toccata in F BUXWV 156).

The imperfect cadence at the end certainly suggests either that an F major/D minor movement follows or that a *da capo* is intended, as indeed at least one nineteenth-century edition attempted to show (*BG* 38 p. xli). Judging by such sonatas as that in E for Violin (BWV 1016.iii) or in G for Viola da Gamba (BWV 1027.iii), the following movement would be a third down from the final cadence (i.e. F major in BWV 590), though normally in such sonata movements the imperfect cadence is to the dominant, not (as here) the mediant. However, the same mediant cadence is to be heard at the end of *B* in the *A₁ B A₂* of Corelli's

Pastorale, Op VI no. 8. If a *da capo* had been intended, it is more likely to have drawn to a close in F some bars after the dominant entry (i.e. around b20) than before it (i.e. around b10).

Second Movement

Despite suggestions in *BG* 38 that BWV 590.ii is to be seen as an allemande, there is no characteristic up-beat, nor are such long-held bass notes normal for such movements – particularly since the result is that b3 is a variation on b1. Yet the two- and three-part figuration is allemande-like, and such bars as (e.g.) 5–6 are not unlike the style of the Allemande of the G major French Suite BWV 816. On the other hand, the melodiousness of both the main cadences (bb7–8, 21–2) is sufficiently striking almost to suggest a violin line or a phrase from a cantata aria.

Quite apart from such lines as bb15–16 and the harmonic counterpoint of bb19–22 (left hand), the formal details of the movement also resemble those of J. S. Bach's binary movements. While it is not common for the second half both to begin like the first (in the dominant) and to include a shortened recapitulation of it (in the tonic) – it is usually a question of one or the other – further examples can certainly be found, e.g. the Sarabande of the C minor French Suite BWV 813.

Third Movement

The shape of the movement resembles such sonata movements as the Largo of the F minor Violin Sonata BWV 1018: i.e., tonic and dominant statements of the melody are followed by a section leading to some kind of imperfect cadence. In BWV 590.iii, the final cadence appears to be in the opening key, but in fact its nature and purpose are to serve as an imperfect cadence (perhaps a phrygian cadence, over bb57–64) after the full cadence of bb56–7. The modulations of the penultimate section are well managed, giving the impression of an improvised fantasia; on the other hand, the dominant modulation at bb24–5 is a shade abrupt. In general, the texture and the melodies would be more in place in an aria with violin obbligato than in an organ movement; on the other hand, both would be equally at home in the middle movement of a harpsichord sonata of the 1740s or 1750s.

Fourth Movement

The fugal finale has more in common with fully-fledged suite gigues – regular fugal exposition, sequences and entries to halfway, then inverted subject, modulatory second half, final return to subject – than with any other kind of movement, despite some superficial resemblances sometimes found elsewhere (e.g. finale of Third Brandenburg Concerto). Other details conform to those of suite gigues, such as the low tessitura at the beginning of the second half (cf. Gigue of the A minor Partita BWV 827), and the texture seems to call for harpsichord even more clearly than in the second movement.

---

591   Kleines harmonisches Labyrinth

Copies in P 1107 and P 303 (18th century), and late sources (a late Schelble source used in Peters IX).

Two staves; headed in P 1107 (only) 'Kleines harmonisches Labyrinth. Joh. Seb. Bach'.

Since movements incorporating chromatic and enharmonic devices used for demonstrations of harmony (particularly with reference to questions of temperament) are known to have interested such composers as Heinichen, Sorge and Kirnberger, BWV 591 has long been credited to one or another of these – in particular J. D. Heinichen (Spitta I p654; *BG* 38 p. lii). The term 'labyrinth' is also to be found on the title-page of J. K. F. Fischer's *Ariadne musica* (1715), in which preludes and fugues in different keys are claimed to help in 'difficultatum [!] labyrintho educens' ('leading out of the difficulty of the labyrinth'), though at this stage there was no question of using all twenty-four keys. 'Le Labyrinthe' in Marin Marais's *Pièces de Viole* IV (Paris 1717) is a rondo in which the main theme returns in different keys, passing through A, F♯ minor, B, C♯, D♯ (*sic*), C minor, F, D minor and back to A for a chaconne; a writer of 1732 describes it as the 'uncertainty of a man confused in a maze; at last he comes out of it happily, and finishes with a chaconne gracious and natural in key' (Titon du Tillet, *Le Parnasse françois* 1732, pp626–7). Locatelli's 'Laberinto armonico', Caprice no. 23 from *L'arte del violino*, Op III (Amsterdam, 1733), exploits no harmonic or tuning complexity but is an exercise in violin technique, mostly on tonic and dominant drones. Its motto 'facilis aditus difficilis exitus' provides a curious reminder of the title of the last section in BWV 591. Mozart possessed a copy of BWV 591 also attributed to J. S. Bach, though what MS this was is now uncertain (*Dok* III pp512–3). The word 'Ped' in P 1107 and in the Schelble source (?) eight bars from the end – perhaps merely an indication of the pedal point? – justified Peters IX and *BG* 38 in including the movement amongst the organ works.

The influence of J. S. Bach can be argued in each of the three movements: the appoggiatura chords after the arpeggios recall the close of the Chromatic Fantasia BWV 903; the fugue subject recalls those of the B minor fugue, *The 48* Bk I, and of the doubtful B flat Fugue BWV 898; the part-writing in the *Exitus* (bb41–3)* is in a Bach idiom. The 'programme' – Ouverture, then a lost direction, entry into labyrinth, discovery of C major, exit beneath the 'sun of clear harmony' (Keller 1948 p57) – is scarcely evidence of authorship. There are some

---

* Numbering the bars in one sequence through the whole of BWV 591.

competent harmonic progressions that seem to result from their composer's being versed in Bach keyboard idioms, for example bb38–41. But such flaccid moments as the final pedal point and close are difficult to attribute to J. S. Bach, as is the working-out of the fugue, which is little more than a set of harmonized statements. The B-A-C-H spelt out in retrograde within the first six notes of the subject is, if anything, more a salute than a sign of authorship.

592-596   Concertos

No complete Autograph MS or album copy.

Questions concerning the sources, origin and style of the concertos can be summarized as follows.

(i) Sources. It is not known whether there was ever a group of concertos copied out as a set either by the composer (like the set of harpsichord concerto transcriptions with strings BWV 1052–1059, in P 234) or by any other copyist (like the set of solo harpsichord concerto transcriptions BWV 972–982, in P 280). That the number of extant copies of the individual concertos varies widely from concerto to concerto speaks against this; so does the fact that two harpsichord versions of the organ concertos concerned (BWV 592/592a and BWV 595/984) appear in different MS collections. But neither fact is conclusive; the organ version BWV 592 appears in one of the same sources as the Harpsichord Concerto BWV 984 (P 804), and no certain origin is known for BWV 592a. While most of the harpsichord transcriptions exist in only one or two copies, neither they (except for BWV 981) nor the organ concertos exist in albums that appear to be based on early sources. The autograph MS of the D minor Organ Concerto BWV 596 is by far the oldest extant copy of any of the organ transcriptions, and for that reason alone it may be considered likely that there were once more than the five concertos known today.

(ii) Origin. An argument has recently been put forward to explain the origin of these works (Schulze 1972 p10):   ·

Despite the complex picture given by the sources, Bach's organ and harpsichord transcriptions BWV 592–596 and 972–987 belong to the year July 1713 to July 1714, were made at the request of Prince Johann Ernst von Sachsen-Weimar, and imply a definite connection with the concert repertory played in Weimar and enlarged by the Prince's recent purchases of music. Since the court concerts gave Bach an opportunity to know the works in their original form, the transcriptions are not so much study-works as practical versions and virtuoso 'commissioned' music.

The youthful Prince Johann Ernst (1696–1715) was at Utrecht from February 1711 to July 1713, studying in the university, and from there he probably improved his knowledge of music (with visits to Düsseldorf and Amsterdam) and even had Italian music sent back to Weimar; after the Prince's return from Holland, the organist at the town church, J. G. Walther, gave him lessons in composition, specifically of concertos (Schulze 1972 pp6–7). Walther later noted that he himself had transcribed no fewer than seventy-eight concertos, 'aufs Clavier applicirte Stücke' ('pieces applied to the keyboard' – *ibid* p12), and no doubt a good many of them were elaborated beyond the originals (Tagliavini 1969). Other German transcriptions from Vivaldi's Op III (represented in BWV 593 and 596) are found in various sources. Quantz later remarked on the impression that Vivaldi's violin concertos made on him when he first got to know them at exactly this period, i.e. *c*1714 (quoted in Schering 1902). The Prince's departure from Weimar in July 1714 to seek a cure for his fatal illness may have ended the call for such transcriptions, at least for their use in the court chapel.

It is possible that neither the Prince's return to Weimar in 1713 nor his final departure from there in 1714 actually did circumscribe Bach's activity in this field quite so completely as appearances suggest; but any further opportunity or desire for such works is nevertheless difficult to find. Forkel thought that the composer transcribed the concertos in order to give himself tuition in musical form (Forkel 1802 ch.V). He would have been able to see there

dass Ordnung, Zusammenhang und Verhältnis in die Gedanken gebracht werden müsse, und dass man zur Erreichung solcher Zwecke irgend einer Art von Anleitung bedürfe. Als eine solche Anleitung dienten ihm die damahls neu herausgekommenen Violinconcerte von Vivaldi. Er hörte sie so häufig als vortreffliche Musikstücke rühmen, dass er dadurch auf den glücklichen Einfall kam, sie sämmtlich für sein Clavier einzurichten.

that order, continuity and proportion must be brought to bear on ideas, and that to such an end some kind of guide was necessary. The then newly published violin concertos of Vivaldi served him for such a guide. He heard them so often praised as excellent compositions that he hit on the happy idea of arranging them complete for his keyboard.

While Forkel can be expected to have known little about such background details as Walther's activity in this field, and has been criticized for his oversimplification of the circumstances (see Schulze 1978 p93), it is striking that he thought Bach had transcribed Vivaldi concertos 'complete'. The whole passage suggests inspired conjecture on Forkel's part. If self-education were the composer's intention, it is difficult to see why he should transcribe the works of Johann Ernst; if 'order, continuity and proportion' came to Bach only from the Vivaldi violin concertos, he must have known them before composing such potential ritornello movements as Cantata 196.iv some years earlier (1708?). Nor could such qualities have been easily learnt from (e.g.) the C major Concerto BWV 594, where the circle-of-fifths sequences would teach only by negative example. Equally conjectural is Schering's view that the composer made such arrangements 'for the refreshment of the souls of music-lovers', as the engraved title-pages of some later keyboard works were to claim; the concertos were not published or publicized, and such verbal formulae were not of interest to professional organ-players as they were to at least the more learned among the buyers of *Clavierübung III* a quarter of a century later. It is not certain that Bach and Walther competed with or emulated each other in their transcribing, as has been suggested (Besseler 1950 p108), not least since the style of some concertos transcribed by Walther and found in BB 22541/4 suggest that the originals themselves belong to a later decade. And insofar as the later copies of Bach transcriptions suggest that his later pupils and friends used them for practice purposes, this too was unlikely to have happened in the 'middle Weimar period'. Nor does the Weimar liturgy give any evidence that such concertos were used in the course of the service; the claim that they are Communion music – on the analogy of instrumental sonatas or concertos for the Elevation – is conjectural, as it is in the case of the Six Sonatas. However, it is not out of the question that J. S. Bach used them during the service, thus providing for the court chapel what Walther may have been providing for the town church over the same period. But if that was the practice, Weimar was exceptional.

Schulze's suggestion that the transcriptions were in some sense 'commissioned' is open to some of the same objections. Also, since the G major Concerto differs from Ernst's original in ways that suggest Bach to have been 'improving' it (see BWV 592), it is difficult to believe that Ernst had requested straight transcription. Nevertheless, the suggestion that they were 'commissioned' does tie in closely with what is known in detail about musical life at the Weimar court in c1713. Thus, in April 1713 a Bach pupil, P. D. Kräuter, asked his school board for an extension of leave to study in Weimar specifically on the grounds that the Prince,

welcher...selbst eine unvergleichliche Violin spilen soll, nach Ostern aus Holland nach Weimar kommen und den Sommer über da verbleiben wird, kunte also noch manche schöne Italienische und Frantzösische Music hören, welches mir dann absonderlich in Componirung der Concerten und Ouverturen sehr profitabel seyn würde... Nun weiss ich auch, dass Herr Bach nach Verfertigung dieser neuen Orgel in Weimar absonderlich anfänglich gwiss unvergleichliche Sachen darauf spilen wird (*Dok* III pp649–50).

who himself plays the violin incomparably, will return to Weimar from Holland after Easter and spend the summer here; I could then hear much fine Italian and French music, which would be particularly profitable to me in composing concertos and French Overtures...I know too that when the new organ in Weimar is ready Herr Bach will play incomparable things on it, especially at the beginning...

This is still some way from suggesting that Bach or Prince Johann Ernst was attempting to establish in the court chapel organ concerts of the kind the Prince may well have heard in the Netherlands; but it does suggest more than that 'musicians of the prince's entourage' merely 'had to interest themselves' in Italian concertos (Spitta I p409). The Prince's interest in concertos, his possible purchases of scores abroad, the court organist's interest in a variety of styles and forms,* the potential and versatility of the newly rebuilt organ, the apparent willingness of the town organist to join in transcribing such works: these conditions help to form a background as clear and certain as any to the

* The period 1713–14 also saw work on the *Orgelbüchlein* and possibly the longer organ chorales of 'The Seventeen' (BWV 651–667).

various *genres* of organ music in which J. S. Bach worked. In any case, the sources for BWV 592–596 and 972–987 suggest that the Bach circle maintained its interest in such works throughout the Leipzig period (Schulze 1978 p93).

(iii) Style and influence. According to Forkel – who in this has been more or less echoed by Spitta and later writers – J. S. Bach learnt from such concertos of Vivaldi two particular arts (Forkel 1802 ch.v):

Er studirte die Führung der Gedanken, das Verhältniss derselben unter einander, die Abwechselungen der Modulation und mancherley andere Dinge mehr. Die Umänderung der für die Violine eingerichteten, dem Clavier aber nicht angemessenen Gedanken und Passagen, lehrte ihn auch musikalisch denken, so dass er nach vollbrachter Arbeit seine Gedanken nicht mehr von seinen Fingern zu erwarten brauchte, sondern sie schon aus eigener Fantasie nehmen konnte.

He studied the way ideas were developed, the relationships they had to each other, the changes brought about by modulation, and many other things. The adaptation of musical ideas and passage-work conceived for violin but not suited to the keyboard also taught him how to think musically, so that when [such] work was completed he no longer needed to wait for ideas to come from his fingers but could take them from his own imagination.

Although Forkel's 'musical ideas' is a loaded phrase, since it belongs to his conception of the composer as 'a poet' who 'considered music entirely as a language' (*ibid*), it is clear that he saw the concertos as giving the composer technical instruction in two directions: experience in organizing musical form and encouragement towards composing 'from his own imagination' and not merely 'from his fingers'.* As a comparison between the first movements of the Concerto BWV 592 and the Toccata in C BWV 564 shows, however, form and content are bound together. The length of the main theme of the concerto movement and the simple contrast between it and the episode material sustain a movement of comparable length to that produced by the toccata, which is much more broken up at the beginning. In each movement, form is closely related to content. The scale of the main themes, the alternation of ideas (and probably of manuals), the vigour of the overall drive are in each case conceived in terms of respectively a concerto movement and a toccata. It is arguable which has the 'better-developed' form; the short motifs of the toccata should not disguise their skilful handling and inspired development.

While the concertos are obviously similar to the Six Sonatas with respect to number of movements and general ritornello elements – if little else – J. S. Bach's more traditional organ works from the E/C

* Forkel's second idea is somewhat confused, or at least the sentence is elliptical. He seems to be saying that in re-writing violin figuration for keyboard, Bach learnt not to be dependent as a composer on mere finger technique. Forkel implies an intermediate step in the argument: the composer learnt to appreciate that the idiom suitable for one particular instrument was distinct from the thematic or formal content, and in transcribing violinistic passages would learn to distinguish between one and the other. The maturing composer, after such experience in transcribing, would be able to work from form to idiom, not merely from idiom to form.

major Toccata BWV 566 to the E flat Prelude and Fugue BWV 552 follow their own line of development, in form and content. Though they frequently refer to other instrumental forms, they cannot be seen to be based on, derived from, or even paralleled by particular concerto movements of Vivaldi. The concerto transcriptions remain somewhat isolated. In this respect BWV 592 is particularly interesting, since it presents a German composer's idea of Italian ritornello form: as such it is clearer, less whimsical, more controlled and – though Johann Ernst was scarcely comparable in stature to Vivaldi – more open to further sophistication than a Vivaldi first movement, which stands or falls by the strengths of its caprice. From such a simple ritornello idea as that of BWV 592.i – and not directly from Vivaldi – would develop the first movement of the G major Organ Sonata BWV 530. Otherwise, the effects of the concerto transcriptions on the other organ music are open to disagreement. Frequently mentioned 'concerto elements' in the greater organ preludes – in particular, the change of material after the opening exposition – are characteristic of too many kinds of music for much direct influence of the concerto transcriptions to be traceable there. More instructive is the crucial device of 'partial returns' of the main subject, shown typically and skilfully in the A minor Concerto BWV 593.i; the idea should be compared with the 'partial returns' in the C minor Prelude BWV 546. In these cases, parallels seem close because a particular method is involved. But in general, J. S. Bach's forms cannot easily be traced to this or that influence, since they seem rather to evolve gradually. Even as late as 1715, as Cantata 31 shows, either the ritornello elements seem to arise naturally through the nature of the material, or else the tendency is for the movement to end as it began, i.e. with a short *da capo* reprise (BWV 31.i, iv, vi, viii). From BWV 31 to the first movement of the Third or Fourth Brandenburg Concerto there must have been a gradual evolution of highly intricate ritornello form, not one jerking along or changing course under specific influences, however true it might be that Vivaldi's concertos of 1710 'excel other instrumental forms of the period' in their 'many-sided use of motif' and their 'tendency to thematic contrast' (Eller 1958).

As the first part of Forkel's comment therefore needs careful examination, so does the second – that the composer no longer had to compose 'from his fingers'. It is certainly true that the transcriptions introduce new figuration. As has been pointed out before (Grace c1922 p249), 'in these transcriptions Bach employs some keyboard methods used nowhere else in his organ music'. Thus the alternating-hand patterns in the concertos seem by nature more transcription-like than those in *Goldberg Variation* 29: Ex. 246. Other figures and textures appear frequently in the concertos* but rarely outside them, such as fast repeated pedal notes or ritornello octaves. Max Seiffert, who compared some of J. G. Walter's arrangements with their originals (*DDT* 26/27 p. xxi), noted that Walther 'remains true to the original' and

---

* 'Many manuscripts' of BWV 592 do not include the lowest notes of the right-hand chords in the first part of Ex. 246, according to *BG* 38 p. xlv; nor does that of the harpsichord version BWV 592a (*BG* 42 p287).

Ex. 246

BWV 592.iii   BWV 593.iii   *Goldberg Variation* 29
b41   b75

Ex. 247

J. G. Walther (*DDT* 26/7 p297)   BWV 593.i
b99   b56

introduces only a few freedoms in such details as the decoration of the main theme. But both composers produce, in their transcriptions, textures uncharacteristic of their other organ music: Ex. 247. The very nature of such conventional string sequences as Ex. 248 is alien to the

Ex. 248

J. G. Walther (*DDT* 26/7 p286)
b47

organ, and to keyboard instruments in general. It may itself suggest why such organ composers as Bruhns and Buxtehude write sequences generally somewhat less conventional than those of the Italian string composers: the natural vivacity of string music sustains interest in sequential formulae better than organ music.

    In general, although the main themes themselves introduce textures rare outside the concerto transcriptions, it is noticeable that the least conventional use of the organ in the transcriptions is found in the solo violin episodes. Such episodes spring 'from the fingers' in Forkel's sense quite as much as do the idiomatic runs of the organ praeludium known to the young Bach; there are many passages in (e.g.) BWV 594 that must have been composed 'from the fingers', although the fingers were those of Vivaldi on a violin, not of Bach on an organ. By its nature, a solo or duo concerto would be more likely than a *concerto grosso* to have such finger music developed at length in episodes, and in this respect the Vivaldi concertos have a somewhat exceptional position in the complete repertory of works transcribed by Bach and Walther. In the case of Bach, the finger music of the episodes in the C major Concerto BWV 594 (even in its shortened form) introduced nothing new to the finger music of (e.g.) the G minor Prelude BWV 535, except that the concerto lines are rather less organ-like.

It must be for such passage-work as in BWV 594 that the concertos have often attracted adverse criticism ('not much of musical value...' – Grace *c*1922 p248). But the opening paragraph of BWV 593 in particular could have taught the composer much, with its five clearcut sentences – continuous, despite several perfect cadences – and its subordination of keyboard convenience to structure and thematic drive. Despite what may have been Bach's deliberate alterations of Vivaldi's original score (see BWV 593) in the matter of figuration and placing, there is a faint clumsiness in the writing that results from the music's very concerto style; its quasi-homophony produces a good string ritornello but not particularly convenient keyboard writing. Here, if anywhere, could be found an illustration of Forkel's claim that the concertos taught the composer how 'he no longer needed to wait for ideas to come from his fingers but could take them from his own imagination'. Neither in Walther's extant set of transcriptions nor in J. S. Bach's harpsichord transcriptions is there another such musical paragraph as the opening of BWV 593.

The significance of the concertos for J. S. Bach's use of two manuals and of alternating organ choruses is clear from the commentary on each concerto, below. Judging by the published originals – which, however, are not always relevant – Vivaldi laid out schemes of *forte*, *piano* and in particular *pianissimo* that have not been carried over to the organ transcriptions. Yet the *pp* signs that are apparently ignored in BWV 593 and 596 would not require outlandish ingenuity if, as is commonly supposed, the composer was assuming that a registrant would be at hand. The various and changing choruses of string instruments in the concertos are suggested not in great detail at all but by blanket *Oberwerk/Rückpositiv* directions which, whether or not they were written or authorized by Bach himself, offer simple contrast and rely for true variety not on changes in dynamic but on changes in texture. A further point concerns the direction 'organo pleno'. Most commentators on the concertos have assumed that because operating the push-coupler between the manuals 'would have been impossible in the course of a piece', the direction 'organo pleno' 'must therefore indicate an increase in the number of stops' (Williams 1972 pp22–3) rather than the coupling of the two manuals concerned. Two factors argue against this: it is not always difficult to operate push-couplers while playing (depending on the manual being played and the direction of the coupling or uncoupling); and even when it is difficult, a small gap in the music is not always inappropriate.* However, such pragmatic considerations are probably unnecessary if 'organo pleno' is regarded more as a structural indication, showing that *both* hands are playing on the main manual (Kloppers 1966 pp211–14), and playing there the main theme or a part of it.

---

592   Concerto in G major

No Autograph MS; copies in P 280 (with BWV 972–982, dated 'J. E. Bach, Lipsiens. 1739' – owner or copyist?), Lpz MB MS 11 (dated 1739), P 804 (J. P. Kellner), P 320 (Kittel), P 289 (2nd half of 18th century), P 400a (ditto), LM 4838 and late sources. Transcription of concerto by Prince Johann Ernst von Sachsen-Weimar (see below).

Headed in Lpz MB MS 11 'Concerto. di Giov. Ernest: appropriato. all'Organo. di Joh: Seb: Bach:', in P 280 (general title) 'XII Concerto di Vivaldi elabor: di J. S. Bach' (*sic*), in P 804 'Concerto in G♯. di J: S: Bach', in P 320 'Concerto à 2 Clavier con Pedale di J. S. Bach', in Westphal catalogue of 1774 'Concerto a 2 Cemb. con Pedale. G dur' (*sic: Dok* III p271). Second movement 'Grave' in P 280 only, 'Adagio' in P 804 only; third movement 'Presto' in P 280 only. In the string version (see below), the movements are headed 'Allegro assai', 'Adagio' and 'Presto è staccato'.

The heading in Lpz MB MS 11† makes the origin of the concerto clear, though unlike the harpsichord arrangements of Johann Ernst's concertos (BWV 982, 987) the original does not belong to the set edited by Telemann and published in 1718. MS parts of the string version of the concerto were found in 1906 at Rostock, headed 'N[umber] 1' (Praetorius 1906); the harpsichord continuo part is headed 'Concerto a 6 Violini e Violoncello col Basso per l'organo fatto del Illustrissimo Principe G[iovanni] E[rnesto] D[uca] di S[achsen-] W[eimar]'. The scoring, however, is principal violin, two obbligato violins, two ripieno violins, viola, cello and figured bass. Keller's remark that the work 'shows features more in the Walther than the Vivaldi manner' (Keller 1948 p67) requires modification, since Walther's only known original concerto, published in 1741, is different in all major respects – movements, structures, melodic construction, texture – and shows him deliberately taking account of Corelli's various concerto techniques.

* It cannot be assumed that unbroken continuity is an ideal always respected in all periods of music and in all idioms. The expressive keyboard instruments of the nineteenth century (both organ and piano) were able to produce continuity and dynamic change in a manner unknown to the player of the several two-manual movements in *Clavierübung II*.
† 'Appropriato' is also the term used by J. G. Walther for his organ transcriptions in BB 22541/4.

General comments on the ritornello conception of BWV 592 were made above. The three-movement plan, with clear ritornello outer movements and a lyrical slow middle section, is one of the chief Italian concerto forms and the main (though not the only) type found in the arrangements by Walther and by J. S. Bach.

First Movement

In texture, rhythm, registration (or change of manual) and at times choice of key, the ritornello principle of the movement is not only clear but is more sharply drawn than in many Italian concertos (e.g. BWV 593.i). The transcription is also so managed that the change of manual is neither inconvenient nor disruptive to the phrasing (see bb22, 54 etc); indeed, the transcription looks as if it has simplified the tutti/solo contents. But that the main sections and the episodes keep entirely to their own theme is also a simplification of the ritornello principle: the whole movement could serve as a model of simple ritornello shape. Both subjects are open to development as the movement proceeds, and it says much for the native sparkle and even originality of the movement that the development sections of the main theme (bb73ff, 121ff) sustain interest through repetition and sequence although perfect cadences abound in both passages.

  Although the unusual texture and style of the sequences that begin at bb5, 26, 74, 113, 121 and 123 almost suggest as their original a concerto for two violins – perhaps with the second violin an octave lower – the parts discovered by Praetorius show that this was not the case. That the upper pedal part is not strictly necessary is clear from the harmony and from the fact that in P 804 it is mostly omitted (*BG* 38 p. xliv).* Even in bb3–4, it is possible to imagine that two violins played in the same register and were pitted against each other (Ex. 249);

Ex. 249

bb144–5 would provide a similar opportunity. In addition, the possibilities of string crescendos in the final ritornello section are lost, as are any antiphonal effects in the sequence from b74 onwards. The organ transcription may therefore appear to lose much of the original. But the original string scoring is not so inventive as such remarks

* Keller's suggestion that the upper pedal part may have been written on this stave only for scribal convenience (Keller 1948 p67) is in itself plausible; but eighteenth-century fingering would make it unlikely that the left hand played both this line and the semiquavers.

Ex. 250

Johann Ernst
b4

Strings

suggest. The sequence of bb5ff is established with a simple figure –
Ex. 250 – and the solo episodes are simple duos for violin and continuo.
For the greater interest that is necessary in a keyboard arrangement,
extra figures have been introduced into BWV 592.i by the arranger –
notably the semiquavers of bb38ff and 48ff and the striding bass of
bb48ff – while a degree of musical excitement has been added to a line
originally less tense, and in its lyricism more suited to the violin:
Ex. 251. Since the bracketed bar seems to be an addition by J. S. Bach,

Ex. 251

b59
Johann Ernst

BWV 592

it is tempting to see in this simple example a significant pointer: that Bach
writes a sequence not necessarily more idiomatic for keyboard but one
with more momentum – a momentum not always sought by earlier
Italian composers. The cadence bb70–2 is also simpler and plainer in
the original, as throughout is the bass line of the solo episodes.

As is clear also from the transcriptions by Walther, such concertos
make a distinctive contribution to the repertory of organ effects
accepted in the second decade of the century. The homophonic
melody-with-accompaniment of the opening, the broken-chord figuration in the left hand, similar effects for both hands together: these are
new elements in themselves, in their extent, and in the frequency with
which they recur in the course of the movement. The kind of melody
in the main theme is also new, for repeated-note themes are usually
reserved for fugue subjects. The *Rückpositiv**** episodes are in their

* Whether J. S. Bach wrote 'Positiv' ('Pos' etc) or 'Rückpositiv' is unknown; probably
the former, since it is more general and inclusive, and since there was no Chair Organ
in the court chapel.

different way atypical of organ music, in their texture (the *Rückpositiv* lines in the Dorian Toccata BWV 538.i are closer and more varied) and figuration (more typical of harpsichord gigues).

Second Movement

The shape – tutti *piano* framework around a solo middle section – is even more immediate than in the Vivaldi Concerto BWV 593, since the tutti theme appears only at the beginning and end. Again the *Rückpositiv* parts may suggest two violins, with the ripieno basses entering for the *jeu en trio* of b28, but the original is not so clearcut:

1   opening dotted-note theme is accompanied by a (simple) bass line
6   solo enters with simple accompaniment, not canonic
18 original bass line (Ex. 252) has no repeated motif requiring change of manual
25 middle parts added in BWV 592.ii, melody made more continuous (with ties etc); final five-part passage added in BWV 592.ii

Ex. 252   b18

etc

The contrast between the framework and the solo passages has therefore been made more stark, just as the cadence of the solo passage has become more of a climax. Although its counterpoint is reminiscent of such chorales as BWV 654, the five-part passage has unusual scoring: two upper parts solo, two parts accompaniment, one bass – as distinct from such five-part pieces as BWV 678 (two cantus-firmus lines), 682 (interspersed cantus-firmus lines), 653b (two pedal lines), 768.xi (*organo pleno*) and 562 (four fugal parts above a bass).

    Though short, the movement thus has much of interest. The dotted-note theme looks at first like an ostinato bass (cf. Cantata 31.iv, 1715), though such empty octave lines are known in other Italian concerto movements, both slow (BWV 593) and fast (e.g. Handel Op VI no. 3). Melodic details throughout the movement are familiar from other (later) German imitations of Italian concertos, and the whole movement is a web of Italianate allusion. Thus the octave imitation for the solo theme at b6 is known not only in Corelli and Handel but also in the D minor Concerto for Three Harpsichords BWV 1063.i, while the whole cast of the melody from b12 onwards anticipates Handel's sequences derived from Corelli. Similarly, the antiphonal imitation of the two phrases beginning at b22 (as for one violin answered by continuo?) and b28 (as for two violins?) was a staple of Italian works, as are the cadences at the end of those phrases. Such passages give an impression of antiphonal contrast between solo and tutti that is different from the dialogue technique of the Dorian Toccata: in the concertos it is a question of soloist *versus* ripieno, in the Dorian Toccata more the technique of statement and counter-statement.

Third Movement

Adapting the violin writing in the finale called for much new figuration – Ex. 253. While it may once have been thought that the 'third movement has gained most by the arrangement' (Praetorius 1906 p100),

Ex. 253
Johann Ernst

Bach's alterations when viewed more objectively do seem to introduce several anachronistic elements. For instance, in the original ritornello the bass line – Ex. 254 – certainly lacks the poise and momentum of

Ex. 254
Johann Ernst

BWV 592, but with its simple dominant sevenths and first inversions it is far closer to a bass line of Vivaldi. On the other hand, Bach has been able to conform to the Italian concerto idiom in the bars he has added (bb12, 81–6), even when, as in bb81–6, they replace something equally idiomatic (cadence on the violins' open g string). That Bach was fully aware of the string idiom is clear from (e.g.) his use of the device *a* from Ex. 253 in the first movement of the E major Violin Concerto BWV 1042.

The *perpetuum mobile* element is less characteristic of Italian concertos than may be imagined, certainly in the case of such regular ritornello movements. The ritornello shape itself is as clear as in the first movement (even to the sequential development in the second tutti section bb23–39), but the distribution between the two manuals is ambiguous throughout the following section. If the whole passage is solo (*Positiv*), do the hands move to *Oberwerk* for the pedal sections? Even the first entry of the solo is uncertain: judging by the final bars, the scale in b12 is tutti not solo, which is then delayed until b13. The changeover of hands is nowhere so easily managed as in the first two movements; or at least its notation is not so clear.* Other problems are

* E.g., the first note of b13 (lh) could have double tails, like the rh of b35 in the slow movement.

the uncharacteristic nimbleness required for manual-changing across bb41–2;* the possibility that the left hand remains on the *Oberwerk* throughout; and the inconsistency of the notation, perhaps relevant to the use of two manuals (compare b47 with b65 as printed in *BG* 38).

There are several possible reasons for the absence of manual indications in each source: (i) the composer did not distinguish tutti from solo; (ii) the transcriber did not wish to distinguish; (iii) the transcriber did not wish to specify whether the player should distinguish; (iv) the transcriber did distinguish along the lines suggested, but the (or an) original copyist rejected or ignored the indications; (v) the transcriber distinguished in none of the movements; (vi) the copyist or copyists added indications for the first two movements but was or were uncertain for the last. Answers i and iv are less likely than any of the others. Comparison with Walther's transcriptions may suggest that, for one reason or another, the transcriber himself did not indicate manual changes in this movement.

With the exception of bb41 etc, the hands play only in two parts, and the string tuttis are indicated both by pedals and by simultaneous semiquavers in both hands. Such changes of 'scoring' may be thought to contribute enough contrast in the movement. In the event, neither 'tutti' nor 'solo' figuration is characteristic of organ music, except that the episodes from b13 suggest textures to be found in later organ concertos of other composers, as they were in Bach's own harpsichord concertos. The organ writing, though unusual, is fully idiomatic; its lack of scope for further development should not disguise the fact that even the Sonata BWV 530.i may owe something to it.

592a   Concerto in G major

No Autograph MS; source Lpz Poel 39 (c1780/90).

Headed 'IV. Concerto per il Cembalo Solo del Sigr: Giov: Seb: Bach'.

Judging by its agreement with BWV 592 in those details in which J. S. Bach's arrangement differs from Johann Ernst's original (bass line of ritornello in third movement, bare octaves in middle movement, etc), BWV 592a is not an independent transcription but an arrangement of the organ transcription for manuals only. Since BWV 592 resembles the string original in details not found in BWV 592a (e.g. b3 of the first movement), it is more likely that 592a is arranged from 592 than vice versa. It is possible, however, that they are quite independent of each other and both derive directly from an unknown copy of Johann Ernst's concertos.

Although BWV 592a is not certainly authentic, it offers interesting examples for a comparison between organ and harpsichord transcriptions. Some general points are: the harpsichord writing is usually thinner; a sense of tutti writing is given in the ripieno sections both by

* But see the first footnote on p. 290.

bigger chords and, more often, by much activity between the two hands; no manual changes are indicated; figures found in the harpsichord version but not in the organ version are unsuitable for organ (which however has its own kind of figures not found in other types of music); and, in general, lines and textures are re-composed for the particular medium. The final bars of each version (BWV 592a is a bar shorter) typify these points: Ex. 255.

Ex. 255

b81

BWV 592a.iii

BWV 592.iii

Ped.

---

593 Concerto in A minor

No Autograph MS; copies in P 288 and P 599 (2nd half of 18th century), P 400b (J. F. Agricola 1720–74), and late sources. Transcription of concerto by Vivaldi (see below).

Headed in P 400b 'Concerto del Sigre Ant. Vivaldi accommodato per l'Organo a 2 Clav. e Ped. del Sigre Giovanni Sebastiano Bach'; second movement 'Adagio', third movement 'Allegro' in P 288.

The concerto is a transcription of Vivaldi's Concerto in A minor for Two Violins, Op III no. 8 (Amsterdam [1711]); the reasonable assumption made by Naumann in *BG* 38 and by later commentators is that the work as transcribed by J. S. Bach takes the same form as that published, and therefore that any differences between the two versions are the result of deliberate changes by the transcriber. However, as Schering already suspected (1902 p236), such a string concerto might well circulate in manuscript copies (with variant readings) before being published in the version now familiar (see also BWV 596). In the case of BWV 593 it is probable that J. S. Bach had the published version in front of him (Eller 1956); but the question cannot be regarded as settled beyond doubt. Op III itself is likely to have been composed between 1700 and 1710; concertos whose first solo entry includes important thematic and not merely episodic material (such as Op III no. 8) were perhaps the latest to be written (Eller 1958).

Points that can be made about the three-movement form and about the use of two manuals in BWV 593 (such as the careful two-manual notation at b16 of the first movement) are similar to those made above concerning BWV 592. The significance of the opening ritornello paragraph of this concerto has already been pointed out (p. 287). In its free, almost capricious use of ritornello structure, the work naturally served the transcriber as a more sophisticated model of what a concerto is than would any of Johann Ernst's, as too the counterpoint of the middle movement showed a genuine and new art of combining themes (ostinato and solo melody). Once again, in the transcribing of violin figuration for the organ, new textures and figures are introduced; and particularly in the finale the two manuals are used to distinguish not only tutti from solo, but solo I from solo II. In its sustained tension and originality of melody, the concerto is perhaps the most important of the three-movement transcriptions made by J. S. Bach.

First Movement

The ritornello principle centres on returns of one or another of the five sections of the main theme:

		1–3	a
		4–5	b
A	{	6–8	c
		9–13	d
		13–16	e
		22–5	e
		39–42	c
		52–4	a
partial returns	{	62–5	d
		68–71	a
		78–86	b, c, e
		90–3	e

The episodes not only refer to each other but use material from the main ritornello melodies. Four of the last five episodes develop the single motif Ex. 256, which comes from *b*. Moreover, the manual indications

Ex. 256

b4

in *BG* 38 introduce the *Oberwerk* during the second episode, thus furthering Vivaldi's merging of solo and tutti in the next section (*c* in bb39–42 is shared between solo and tutti in the 1711 Amsterdam edition, unlike its first appearance at b6).

The melodic material of the movement is very diverse, from the full pleno* sound of bb9–16 to the slender two-part episodes. Neither is characteristic of organ music; the episode figures in two parts (e.g. bb48ff) are clearly derived from violin lines, while the fuller held chords in the tutti sections, judging by the 1711 Amsterdam edition, have been filled out by the transcriber. The differences between BWV 593 and the 1711 Amsterdam edition can be further summarized as follows:

> tuttis with filled-in harmonies in BWV 593
> imitation introduced in bb6–7, bb40–2, bb81–3 of BWV 593
> original momentary gaps filled (bb19ff, 46, 47) in BWV 593
> original bass in bb30–3 enlivened and rewritten in BWV 593
> scales in bb42–4 were originally more varied in scoring and took in the bass line, with no climax on c‴ in b44
> octaves in bb51ff originally harmonized
> bb71ff pedal in BWV 593 takes a line originally found in viola part

The original solo violin figuration in the episodes did not have to be completely changed. But the string passages that produce the organ textures of bb55ff and bb71ff were less similar to each other in the original than the transcription suggests; Bach's transference technique – with its atypical pedal line – has reduced the original difference in scoring between these two episodes, curbing the variety. Some other differences remain uncertain. Was the transcriber responsible for putting the semiquavers of bb28–9 down an octave, for writing a new bass to bb30off, for omitting the harmonies of bb51ff? The changing of a violin figure to a keyboard figure in b71 – Ex. 257 – is straightforward,

Ex. 257

b71 Vivaldi   BWV 593.i

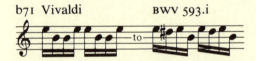

but the continuation of the scale figure in b44 is not and is thus more creative and more original. Particularly interesting is that Bach partly filled in the gaps of the original sequence in bb19ff – Ex. 258 – as he did that at the beginning of b46, although in b46 natural reverberation would make a break very dramatic; discontinuity in bb19ff would be more serious, perhaps. (A fuller example of Bach reducing the gaps – less suitable for organ than string ensemble? – occurs in the last movement.) Important too is that at one moment of tension, at b45, BWV 593 retains a violin figure that is not particularly idiomatic on the organ; indeed, the whole passage bb43–7 is instructive for under-

---

* For a note on *organo pleno*, see p. 289. Bar 51 does seem to require additional stops to compensate for losing the original harmonies of this passage: but if so, one would expect to find a similar difference between the two appearances of another theme, at b9 (registered 'Oberwerk') and b62 (registered 'organo pleno' in P 400b), and this does not seem likely. Moreover, the sources are ambiguous: P 288 has 'Oberwerk' at b62 but 'organo pleno' at b68 (the latter is perhaps due to a copyist's confusion); according to *BG* 38 p. xlvi, only in b51 are the sources agreed on specifying 'organo pleno', and if this means 'add stops' or even 'couple manuals' there must be a gap before the theme in that bar. Were the copyists attempting to counteract what they thought a weakness in the *Oberwerk* octaves?

standing the transcriber's priorities, for he simplifies the string writing into lines possible on the organ but still involving that element of strain found at this point in the original concerto.

The impression given by the movement, from whatever Vivaldi source it sprang, is that Bach was engaged in no mere simplification for organ, nor was he content to transcribe according to fixed or general rules, but wrote each passage in itself, responding to Vivaldi's variety in texture and scoring. While the transcription irons out some of the scoring distinctions, at other times it introduces distinctions not found in the original. The result is an unusually lively movement from the point of view of texture, as it is in its melody and drive.

Second Movement

Although the division into *Oberwerk* ostinato and *Rückpositiv* solo (including the solo duet for two violins from b14 onwards) is not specified in the sources of BWV 593, it is clear enough from the layout and by analogy with BWV 592.ii.

The strong and unusual personality of the movement is pronounced, and is due not only to the unusual spacing and tessitura but to the 'disintegrating' ostinato theme (the movement is scarcely an ostinato once both violins play in duet) and to the tendency of the two hands to lilt together (b5 etc, b31 etc). By the standards of the Six Sonatas the exchange of parts between the soloists is elementary:

    13–18 = 25–30
    31   = 32
    33–7 = 37–41

But such exchange was a characteristic – and perhaps a purpose – of the Italian concerto for two violins, two oboes, or the like. Indeed, the sudden return to the tonic in b24 seems to have been made for the sake of such an exchange. Yet none of this exchange of parts is in the 1711 Amsterdam edition: there bb13ff and 25ff are the same, and from b30 to the end of the solos the two violins play in thirds throughout. Also characteristic of the Italian duet tradition, from at least c1610 onwards, are the singing thirds, particularly after a passage of imitative counterpoint as at bb16–19. In later concertos Bach himself retained the idea of a theme in bare octaves framing a slow movement of lyrical solo embroideries, in (e.g.) the D minor Concerto for Harpsichord BWV 1052.

The transcription differs from the 1711 Amsterdam edition as follows:

1	original heading 'Larghetto e spiritoso'
9–12	violin II down an octave in BWV 593
16–17	original imitative phrase altered in BWV 593 to avoid d''' (see bb28–9)
26–31	violin I down an octave in BWV 593, becoming the alto
31–41	two solos originally in thirds throughout (but exchanging parts)
41	original ripieno marked 'forte e spiritoso', not '*piano*'

Third Movement

In such a ritornello movement, the weight of interest is thrown on to the episodes; the main theme itself may well be conspicuous with its rather bare scales and octaves but is less multi-limbed and versatile than that of the first movement:

A	1–13
A	25–37
A	82–6
A	114–18
A	142–8

The transcription differs from the 1711 Amsterdam edition as follows:

13ff	original bass line less active
42ff	string semiquavers altered (pattern varied, compass narrowed) in BWV 593
51ff	left-hand line an octave lower in BWV 593
59–63	pedal phrases of BWV 593 fill in original tutti rests
66–74	pedals and manuals exploit a motif heard only in bb69, 72 of the original version
83ff, 115ff	original bare octaves coloured by the same motif in BWV 593
86–113	original repeated quavers on e'', a', d' and g (i.e. open strings in descending order): e'' and a' dropped an octave in BWV 593, and their clear falling progression thus disguised
104	d''' in melody avoided in BWV 593
118–27	simple alto sequence varied and put in pedal (an octave lower) in BWV 593
128–31	originally tutti
132ff	string semiquavers altered in BWV 593 (same as bb42ff in the original)
142–4	originally octaves only

The chief differences concern the figuration (i.e. the colourfully varied episodes in BWV 593) and the avoidance of silence (the filling of gaps in BWV 593); there are also other incidental changes (melody avoiding d''' in b104, harmonies added to bb142–3, etc). The *f/p* marks as they appear in the 1711 Amsterdam edition are absent from the transcription, and textural or dynamic change is produced instead by differences in figuration and by the use of two manuals.

As Spitta observed (I p414), in the Vivaldi concerto new sound effects are produced by the interaction of the two soloists; the transcription achieves comparable effects through a repertory of keyboard devices, as shown in Ex. 259:

(i)   trio
(ii)   2 manuals for simultaneous lines
(iii)   2 manuals for antiphonal effect
(iv)   2 manuals for alternation
(v)   2 manuals for melody with accompaniment

Ex. 259

As in BWV 592.i, the double pedal permits a richer harmony, whilst the repeated pedal e's also contribute motion – a device unusual for organ and more characteristic of the string concerto.* Perhaps the most signficant feature in the re-writing – if BWV 593 was dependent on the 1711 Amsterdam edition – concerns the passage bb59–75. The pedal not only fills in rests and gaps found in the original (Ex. 260) but does so with a motif both convenient for pedal and neatly derived from a figure in the original Vivaldi concerto (bb69, 72) – Ex. 261(i). The whole

---

* It is uncertain whether the pedal e' (bb86, 27, 133 etc) was playable at the Weimar court chapel, but it seems unlikely; yet it can hardly be a later addition by either transcriber or copyist. BWV 593.iii is the only concerto movement to go above d': others (e.g. BWV 593.i b5) perhaps intentionally avoid the higher bass notes found in the original string concertos.

Ex. 260

Vivaldi
b59

Violin I
Violin II
Viola

Cello,
Violine,
Continuo

passage, therefore, comes to concentrate on a motif that was given only *en passant* in the original; since this motif appears to refer to, or arise from, the main ritornello theme – Ex. 261(ii) – the organ version of the

Ex. 261
(i) b69   (ii) b115

movement goes some way towards a 'motif unity' that is rare in Vivaldi's own works. The use of this motif in bb66–74 makes it necessary to change the harmony on the weak beats, though its appearance decorating the ritornello entry in b115 and b117 is less startling. Elsewhere Bach seems also to have altered the bare octaves of the ritornello theme: the final entry begins in thirds and sixths, unlike the 1711 Amsterdam version. However, again Vivaldi has supplied this material in another part of the movement (bb3–4). Perhaps, in view of this, it may be questioned whether the Amsterdam print respresents the original or an authorized version of the concerto; Bach may have been using a MS version that already included the thirds and sixths.

Ex. 262
b13
Vivaldi

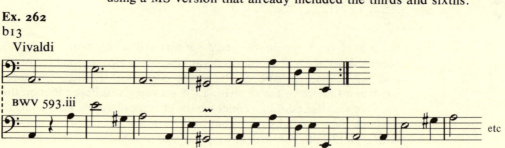

BWV 593.iii

etc

Perhaps more indicative of Bach's desire to add momentum is the simple alteration of the bass in the first episode: Ex. 262. Whether he felt that an organ adaptation would require more notes or whether he regarded the Italian simplicity as undesirable in itself can only be conjectured; the larger-scale alterations elsewhere in the movement could support either interpretation. Equally striking in the transcription, however, is that the episodes of bb75ff and 118ff scarcely depart from the original as regards the notes themselves: the important new element in these places lies in introducing a more organ-based scoring (through the distribution between two hands) rather than in making the figuration as such more suitable for keyboard.

---

594   Concerto in C major

No autograph MS; copies in Lpz Inst. f. Musikwiss. MS (W. F. Bach *c*1727, complete with 'cadenzas' of 1st and 3rd movements), P 286 (18th century, 'cadenzas' shortened or absent), P 400c (J. F. Agricola 1720–74), P 600 (2nd half of 18th century), and late sources. Transcription of a concerto by Vivaldi (see below).

Heading in P 400c as for BWV 593 (P 400b); in P 286, 'Concerto à 2 Clavier et Pedal di Johann Sebastian Bach. (C dur Nr. 1)'; in W. F. Bach's MS, attributed to J. S. Bach (Schulze 1966 p270); in P 286, second movement 'Recitativo. Adagio', third movement 'Allegro'.

The concerto is a transcription of Vivaldi's Concerto in D for Violin in the version now found in the autograph MS Turin, Collection Renzo Giordano V 21 (score) and in the MS Schwerin 5565 (parts); in another version it was published as Op VII, Bk II no. 5 (Amsterdam [1716–21]). For general remarks on the versions of Vivaldi concertos as transcribed by J. S. Bach, see BWV 593. A recent study of BWV 594 (Ryom 1966 p96) has shown, first, that its middle movement is that of the Turin autograph, not of the Amsterdam edition, and thus was not newly composed by J. S. Bach as was once thought (Waldersee 1885); secondly, that the cadenzas in the outer movements of BWV 594 resemble those of the Schwerin MS, not of the Amsterdam edition; and thirdly, that the sources are therefore not clear enough for it to be determined 'in what bars J. S. Bach transformed the musical text' (Ryom 1966 p109) despite previous assumptions. From the extant sources, BWV 594 can be said to be a transcription of the original version preserved in an autograph copy, complete with the cadenzas – authorized or not – as found in the Schwerin MS; the cadenzas are not found in Vivaldi's own score, which instead gives the direction 'qui si ferma a piacimento' ('here one comes to a close however one wishes'), a wording also used elsewhere by Vivaldi (Ryom 1977 p245). Also, a new or different middle movement was – not untypically in Vivaldi's publications – substituted when the work was published in Op VII (Ryom 1973 p52).

In this instance, the transposition down to C seems to have been made in order to avoid notes above c''', although apparently the first of the high passages (bb8–10) is not in Vivaldi's original. While it is possible that the concerto once existed in yet another form, Spitta's suggestion

(I p414) that the original concerto may have been for viola da gamba cannot now be sustained, despite the eminent reasonableness of the idea: the episodes of bb26ff, which lie rather low for the organ, are an octave higher in the published Op VII. Whatever freedom of opinion commentators may allow themselves on the long solo episodes of BWV 594 as now known, their presence in the Schwerin MS gives them authority; but the Schwerin MS cannot be proved to be the direct source of BWV 594, nor vice versa.

First Movement

In this movement a greater emphasis falls on the solo episodes than in the first Allegro of the A minor Concerto.

1–26	tutti, two particular motifs running throughout; preparatory chromaticism (including Neapolitan sixth) before the (reiterated) final cadence
26–58	solo, non-thematic, gradually working to dominant
58–63	tutti, return to opening motif
63–81	solo, non-thematic, more modulatory
81–93	tutti, return to opening motifs, with a tutti sequence
93–111	solo, non-thematic, modulatory
111–17	tutti, return to opening motifs
117–73	solo, non-thematic, mostly *non accompagnato*
174–8	tutti, opening motifs (cf. b25)

Neither the fourth tutti nor the fifth is a reprise in the usual sense (Klein 1970 p24). The emphasis on the episodes seems to presuppose an *allegro* or *vivace* style of performance with the *Rückpositiv* registered in lively colours. Moreover (while the transcriber's point of view can only be guessed at) it is reasonable to suppose that the organist can best sustain interest in the movement if he carries in his head a memory of the original concerto; in this way, the principle of transcription in BWV 594 may be different from that in BWV 593, where the solo passages are brief enough and thematic enough to be less dependent on the particular medium.

The main differences between BWV 594 and other versions are as follows:*

3ff	unison imitation of scales and motifs altered in BWV 594 to octave imitation
5ff	original harmonies filled in BWV 594
15–26	half-bar *f*/*p* contrasts ignored in BWV 594; broken chords and scales added to lh in BWV 594
26ff	solo episodes down an octave in BWV 594, lh parts added bb28, 31, 33, 35, 37, 39; rh change to *Oberwerk* in b28, an element of contrast introduced by the transcriber (*Ow* for rh also in bb31, 33, 35, 37, 39?)
77	original *pp* marks in the string parts, for the passage bb77–80 ignored in BWV 594

* Changes probably brought about by Vivaldi himself in the evolution of the concerto are listed by Ryom (1966 pp96–101).

105ff lh figure in BWV 594 replaces original continuo bass line
118–20 lh scales added in BWV 594
137–73 BWV 594 has a modified version of cadenza as it appears in the
Schwerin MS, conforming in style with other known Vivaldi MS
cadenzas (Eller 1956); in Op VII, five bars for violin alone link
the episode (ending b137) with the final tutti; in Turin autograph,
the direction 'qui si ferma a piacimento' only

In general, the transcription technique is more literal than that in BWV
593. In the string versions, too, the solo part requires realization by the
player, and Bach's version is simple: Ex. 263. The simplistic moments

Ex. 263
b26

are left loose – Ex. 264 – while such figures as those of bb65ff and 93ff
are straight transcriptions, except that the left hand is put down an
octave and the implied staccato is now specified. The transcription,
however, is more individual in its constant reference to the full
compass of the organ: neither the bottom C of bb1, 17, 26, 117, 178
nor the top c‴ of bb8ff are called for in the originals.

Ex. 264
b45

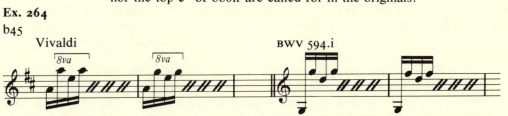

In general, the first movement of BWV 594 can be seen to be adding
to the repertory of organ effects in two particular areas: the unaccompanied solo line for manual, and the chord accompaniments of
bb65ff. Other effects, such as the repeated pedal quavers of bb86ff, are
known elsewhere. The final episode, often described as a 'cadenza',
is as violin-like as the episode at bb40ff; but the repeated notes and

left-hand pedal point of the earlier episode provide a different kind of manual exercise from the right-hand pedal-point effects and quick alteration of hands in the later episode. Also, the final episode prepares its eventual cadence more explicitly – it seems to be caught in the trap of 'the extended cadential phrase' (pedal-point harmonies requiring ever more space to resolve) – whereas the return to the tutti in the other episode (bb57–8) is almost abrupt.

Second Movement

The Grave of BWV 594, of the Turin autograph and of the Schwerin MS is a 23-bar recitative for solo with accompaniment, marked 'Adagio' in BWV 594; the Grave of the Amsterdam edition is a more conventional 11-bar melody for solo violin above repeated thirds for violins I and II. In the Schwerin MS the movement is in score for solo violin and basso continuo with the accompaniment chords notated in long notes (minims, semibreves; see Ryom 1977 p338).

Two significant details of the recitative as transcribed are that it provides a further example of the single-line organ solo also found in the episodes of the outer movements, and that the short chords of the recitative accompaniment no doubt reflect current performance practice in northern Italy, of the kind that may have influenced German composers to whom Italian recitative was still a novelty. That such an idiom is unusual in solo organ music – the *durezze e ligature* at the close of the middle movement of the C major Toccata BWV 564 are more common – is emphasized by the redundant directions given in the *BG* 38 edition of the work: 'Rückpositiv *forte*' and 'Oberwerk *piano*'. On the other hand, the movement is also unlike any conventional recitative idiom, as is clear from the compass and tessitura (an octave lower than the original) and the quasi-obbligato chromatic tenor line at the close. The melody is decidedly instrumental and not vocal, depending as it does on rising and falling scale patterns; and though it includes harmonic progressions familiar in recitative (bb5, 20 etc), it more than once produces a texture not far removed from the *tierce en taille* (bb15–19), though neither the melody nor the detached chords are French in idiom. Also uncharacteristic of vocal recitative is the apparently clear distinction between note-values, from minims (b4) to fast runs (b7).

Thus the movement is not only unique in the concerto corpus of Vivaldi (Ryom 1966 p97) but highly unusual in the keyboard music of J. S. Bach, only faintly suggestive of textures in other works, e.g. the opening of the G minor Fantasia BWV 542. For Bach, the movement must have offered a model for 'instrumental recitative' more expansive and even more dramatic than most vocal recitative but nevertheless more Italianate and vocally inspired than the unaccompanied flourishes characteristic of the old organ toccata or even of the new (e.g. BWV 572).

Third Movement

As in the first movement, the tutti ritornello has several repetitive limbs based on a pair of motifs and making way for solo entries which then dominate the simple returns of the tutti.

1–32	tutti, depending on one particular quaver motif
32–64	solo, new theme, into and out of dominant
64–76	tutti, on quaver motif (contraction of opening tutti)
76–112	solo, initially less thematic; to dominant
112–26	tutti, on quaver motif
126–64	solo, some slight development of ritornello quaver motif; to minor (bb151–2 repeated in P 286 and in the string versions)
164–79	tutti, beginning as in second tutti, ending as in first
180–283	solo, long sectional episodes; two sections missing in P 286 (186–97, 219–83)
284–90	tutti, contraction in octaves of opening tutti

For remarks on the transcription of such a ritornello form, see the first movement. BWV 594 differs from the other versions as follows:

1ff	unison imitation of motifs altered to octave imitation in BWV 594
24 etc	such bars filled in with scales in BWV 594
32ff	solo (*Rückpositiv*) lines down an octave in BWV 594; lh runs etc substituted for original basso-continuo accompaniment
81ff	original *pp* chords filled in and written staccato in BWV 594
90ff	new points of imitation attempted in BWV 594
106–11	as in 1st movement, original abbreviated notation for the violin now expanded (here in the manner of bb104–5); lh quaver line replaces original dominant pedal point
126ff	further references to quaver motif added in BWV 594
180–283	in Turin autograph, these bars are absent and are replaced by the direction 'qui si ferma a piacimento'; in Amsterdam edition, movement ends at b179; Schwerin MS version is similar to BWV 594

A passage from the first episode – Ex. 265 – can be taken as an example of how an original basso-continuo episode is realized in the Bach concertos. Like the finale of the A minor Concerto BWV 593, the movement provides what seems a greater variety of textures than are in the original version for strings. Thus, the first episode gives a two-part texture on *Rückpositiv*, the second a lively *Rückpositiv* line accompanied by *Oberwerk* chords, the third triplets, the fourth a solo line. The second episode is a rewriting of a passage originally conceived in terms of the violin and not amenable to direct keyboard transcription: Ex. 266. The final episode begins not as an Italian concerto episode but as a north German organ toccata – an element emphasized by the change to ₵. The sequences are more than usually Italianate, however, as is the thematic passage bb198–210. Much of the figuration can be seen to be a direct keyboard transcription of violin figures, such as the slow-moving harmonies of bb235–83. The dissonances (bb247ff) and minor-key colouring – characteristic of the final episodes of such concertos (e.g. C major Concerto for Three

Ex. 265

b56

Vivaldi

BWV 594.iii

Rückpositiv

f tutti

Oberwerk

Harpsichords BWV 1064.iii) – have appeared earlier, in chromatic form, at b159. From at least b210 onwards, the episode is unusually close to the original and suggests an experiment in violinistic keyboard writing. The copyist of P 286 either did not care for much of it or copied an alternative and shorter transcription. Much of the *Rückpositiv* figuration of the other episodes suggests an idiom familiar in the harpsichord concertos – an idiom which the C major Concerto for Two Harpsichords BWV 1061 (an original concerto) shows to have been typical of keyboard concertos rather than of transcriptions as such. It is possible, however, that such keyboard styles as bb32ff of bb81ff originated in transcriptions like BWV 594, and

Ex. 266
b96

that the composer from then on associated them with the keyboard concerto. Whatever its problems of performance may be, the whole concerto gave the composer a series of organ effects and idioms rather more versatile and open to personal development than were the already perfected devices found in the A minor Concerto BWV 593.

595   Concerto in C major

No Autograph MS; copies in P 286 (18th century) and P 832 (J. Ringk, before c1784?). Partial transcription of a concerto by Prince Johann Ernst von Sachsen-Weimar (see below).

Headed in P 286 'Concerto del Illustrissimo Principe Giov. Ernesto Duca di Sassonia, appropriato all'Organo à 2 Clavier et pedal (Nr. 2 C dur) da Giov. Seb. Bach'; in a catalogue of 1785 'Concerto für 2 Clav. et Pedal C dur No. 1' (*Dok* III p273).

Like the Concerto in G BWV 592, the original does not belong to the set of Johann Ernst's concertos edited by Telemann and published in 1718. Its attribution is based only on the title in P 286, and the original concerto has not been found. The first movement of the Concerto BWV 984 – a three-movement concerto found amongst the harpsichord transcriptions in J. P. Kellner's P 804 – is similar to BWV 595, but shorter; it is not known which version came first or whether both are equally authentic. (For a note comparing organ and harpsichord transcriptions in general, see BWV 592a.) There is no clear reason, with respect to keyboard technique, why the second and third movements of BWV 984 are not found in the organ version, though the second movement might have been unusual in texture; nor does either P 286 or P 832 suggest that BWV 595 ever had more than one movement.

Although the striking half-bar phraseology of BWV 595 may help to justify the usual opinion that Vivaldi and Johann Ernst had 'widely separated talents' (Schulze 1972 p6), the movement has a significant place in the repertory of Italian concerto shapes. The opening theme returns as a classic ritornello (bb1, 16, 25, 31, 50, 63, 72) but also repeats itself within those paragraphs (b1 also at bb7, 9; b16 also at b18; etc). Thus it lacks the clean formal lines of (e.g.) BWV 592.i, despite the fact that the last section is very like the first. While the theme may be thought to have much the same melodic charm as BWV 592.i, such a repetitive form puts it at a disadvantage. The danger is increased by the much-repeated solo/tutti sequence that is expected to serve both as part of the main ritornello paragraph and as episode material (bb3–6, 11–15, 20–3, 27–30, 35–9 . . .); it is also repeated on a larger scale (e.g. bb63–8 = 18–23). Links and cadences between the ritornello theme and the sequence are often suggestive of other organ works of strong character: for the figure in b9 compare the Dorian Toccata BWV 538, for the cadence in b7 and b31 compare those in the Concerto BWV 593.i. Other details show that Johann Ernst had grasped at least the letter of the Italian concerto (e.g. the sequences from b52) and at times its spirit (e.g. the Neapolitan sixth of b56). Moreover, although the entry of the soloist so soon after the opening is unlike Vivaldi's usual practice (as in Op III no. 7) the idea behind the sequence of bb3–6 is obviously well

Ex. 267

BWV 595 b58

BWV 538.i b43

within the general concerto style, even to such details as the bass line. Another Vivaldian passage is the non-modulating episode bb44–9.

That the sequences contain the germ of maturer music is clear from one typical comparison – Ex. 267. If the half-bar and two-bar phraseology is managed with less variety and sense of diatonic impulse here than in BWV 538, it should not disguise the fact that the latter work shares certain details with this concerto movement, such as the square phrase-lengths, the use of two manuals, and the semiquaver thread running through the several sections and themes. That thread provides an important element throughout BWV 595, particularly where one section leads into another (e.g. bb7–9, 31–3, 41–3, 56–8, 78–81). It is

Ex. 268

BWV 984 b25

BWV 595 b38

Ped.

such formal considerations, rather than the melodies or textures, that provide the interest of this movement amongst Bach's Weimar works.

The movement is shorter in the harpsichord version:

BWV 984 (harpsichord)	BWV 595 (organ)
1–6	1–6
7–21	12(2nd ½)–27
22–34	35(2nd ½)–48
35–6	49
37–8	50–1
39–42	52–7
43–66	58–81

As may be seen, the harpsichord version 'loses' an occasional half-bar and at one point two whole bars, though it 'gains' a bar elsewhere. The versions also differ in melodic detail, as well as in texture and the use of manuals. A characteristic passage is Ex. 268. It may well have been the strong characterization possible on two organ manuals that persuaded the transcriber to keep the longer movement for the organ version, although in neither case are the sources known certainly to be reliable. That the static episode sequence in bb3–9 of the harpsichord version is replaced by a more varied section in the organ version (bb3–15) implies neither which came first nor which is closer to Johann Ernst's original. In both cases it could be argued either way – e.g., that more thematic interest was added to BWV 595, or that the episode material was reduced for BWV 984 because no manual changes were possible. As it stands, BWV 595 is the organ work of Bach that specifies the most numerous changes of manual, and does so for simple phrases in 'question-and-answer' like much of the Dorian Toccata.

---

596 Concerto in D minor

Autograph MS P 330; later copies P 289 (2nd half of 18th century, middle movement written by Forkel), LM 4842h (fragment). Transcription of a concerto by Vivaldi (see below).

Headed in P 330 'Concerto a 2 Clav: e Pedale di W. F. Bach manu mei Patris descript' (the words 'by W. F. Bach, written in the hand of my father' added by W. F. Bach in c1770–80); for movement headings, see below.

The concerto is a transcription of Vivaldi's Concerto in D minor for Two Violins and Cello obbligato, Op III no. 11 (Amsterdam [1711]). Until 1911, the work was taken to be a concerto of W. F. Bach, as he claimed in the heading of P 330 (Schneider 1911), and it was published as such by Griepenkerl in 1844 (Peters edn 3002). However, the handwriting of P 330 has been declared to be autograph, and dated to 1714/17 (Dadelsen 1958 p79),* which agrees with Schulze's hypothesis

* The watermark of P 330 is found in the vocal and instrumental parts of cantatas performed in 1714 and 1715 (Dürr 1977 p233).

on the dating and purpose of the concertos (see pp. 283–6 above); W. F. Bach was therefore about five years old when the transcription was made or copied into P 330.

The first movement in particular has become celebrated as an example of J. S. Bach's registration practice, since the clear directions in P 330 –

b1	rh	'Octava 4 F' / 'Oberw.'
	lh	'Octava 4 F' / 'Brustpos.'
		'Princip. 8 F' / 'Pedale'
b21	rh	'Brustp.'
	lh	'Obw Princip. 8 F & Octav. 4 F.'
		'Pedal Subb. 32 F.'

– establish (or confirm) important principles –

(i)   manuals were not necessarily based on 8' nor pedals on 16'
(ii)   in transcriptions, the two manuals were used to replace several kinds of scoring, not only solo-with-accompaniment
(iii)   hands could exchange manuals in the course of a piece
(iv)   a stop (or stops) could be added to manual or pedal in the course of a piece

The last point is particularly important, since the music provides no clear opportunity for the organist himself to add stops to either manual or pedal without some hiatus. In b21, the first four semiquavers in the left hand are divided 𝄾♫♫ , which may indicate a change of manual as in the autograph chorale BWV 739 (P 488); there is no such break in the pedal quavers, which may therefore indicate that the 32' at the beginning of the bar is a later addition. In the *grave* section following, 'pleno' is directed; in the Largo, '*forte*' and '*piano*'; in the finale, 'Rückp.' and 'Obw.'. While these several directions do not contradict each other – they suggest a three-manual organ complete with pedal 32' – they could not have been carried out at the Weimar court chapel, nor are they matched by copyists' directions in the other concertos. Despite one rebuiling scheme at Weimar, there seems never to have been a *Rückpositiv* there, and this registration is therefore doubtful, as it is in the other concerto copies.* But nor is it certain that any of the directions in the first movement, except 'Octava 4 F, Octava 4 F, Princip. 8 F', were written in at the moment of copying; the manual indications of b1 and the registrations of b21 may have been subsequent additions by the composer. Even the semiquaver grouping of b21, mentioned above, corresponds as much to the change from violin to cello in Vivaldi's original movement as it does to a manual change in the transcription. Perhaps Bach began a short score of Vivaldi's concerto, beginning with violin I down an octave to avoid d''', and added

---

* Throughout the concertos, 'Rückpositiv' may be a copyist's reading for 'Pos' or 'Positiv', indicating a (or any) solo manual. The term offers no light on whether the Weimar court chapel was to have had a *Rückpositiv* for which J. S. Bach prematurely registered his transcriptions, whether the concertos are in any case to be associated specifically with the Weimar court chapel organ, or whether the composer intended that only *Rückpositiv* and nothing else be used for those passages.

directions afterwards. There seems no reason why each hand could not have begun on the other manual: this would avoid having to add stops and having to exchange manuals in b21. Certainly the right-hand contrary-motion scale of the last three bars (not a feature of Vivaldi's original) was written after the left-hand part, perhaps as an afterthought.

First Movement

Headed 'Allegro' in the Amsterdam edition, the movement begins as an unaccompanied duo for violins, followed by a duo for cello and continuo. Four sample bars serve to show the scoring in the Amsterdam edition and the version in BWV 596: Ex. 269. The movement is highly

Ex. 269
(i) Vivaldi b18

(ii) BWV 596 b18

unusual for a Vivaldi concerto, forming a 32-bar prelude more than half of which is based on a tonic pedal point; in turn, the organ texture of BWV 596.i is also unique, though the repeated pedal quavers are to be found in other concertos, both for organ (e.g. BWV 593.i, iii) and for strings (Sixth Brandenburg Concerto). Also unusual is the unison imitation between the two manuals, from which it follows that the first twenty bars produce a unique trio idiom.

Lowering the violins' part an octave and registering it for 4' stop, presumably to enable it to avoid d''', is paralleled by the organ solo version (Cantata 146.i) of the D minor Harpsichord Concerto, according to one commentator (Klotz 1975 p385). However, while it is true that in most of BWV 146.i the solo part is an octave lower than in the harpsichord version, it should be remembered that the harpsichord version was most certainly made later and not earlier, that there is no registration given in BWV 146.i for 4' stop or anything else, and that the organ part apparently avoids not only d''' but even c''' (e.g. b39). This can hardly be for reasons of compass: perhaps it is to provide a sombre tessitura, or to avoid the risk that high lines on an organ *plenum* would jar in intonation with the violins in BWV 146.i. The cantata version and BWV 596.i are therefore of slight relevance to each other, however attractive the idea of a parallel between them may be.

Second Movement

The two sections of this movement, headed 'Grave' and 'Fuga' in sources of BWV 596, have more specific tempo directions in the Amsterdam edition: 'Adagio e spiccato' and 'Allegro'. The transcription differs from the Amsterdam edition in the scoring and layout of the parts:

in BWV 596, the pedal takes a practicable bass line rather than the original bass, which comprises both the solo cello and the basso continuo; e.g., the original bass was uninterrupted in bb1–20*

in BWV 596, no distinction in texture or in manual/registration is made between tutti and solo (ripieno/concertino), i.e. despite the original solo passages in bb20–8, 45–52. Perhaps the transcriber did not feel it necessary to specify change of manual, since the fugue is so short; perhaps he did not come to add them later in the way he may have done for the first movement. Either way, the episodes could conceivably be played on the (*Rück*)*positiv*.

in BWV 596, the parts are frequently exchanged, not always merely in order to avoid d'''

The last point is the most surprising but perhaps can be seen as a reflection on Vivaldi's striking counterpoint – i.e., the movement carefully develops a four-part invertible counterpoint in which any line may become the bass line: Ex. 270. The thoroughness with which this is conceived is unusual for Vivaldi, who seems to be offering here a

---

* Bar numbers from the beginning of the fugue.

Ex. 270
b14   b17

distillation of Italian contrapuntal teaching. In view of this characteristic, the invertibility of parts in such bars as 45–6 – reversing
the original two upper parts – conforms to the contrapuntal nature of
the movement. This factor also enabled the transcriber to alter less of the
original than is usual if the right hand is to avoid notes above c‴; thus
in bb53–4 the two upper parts were the other way round in the
Amsterdam edition.

Although its fugal form distinguishes this movement from any other
in the concertos, some of the transcriber's additions are familiar from
elsewhere, such as the continuous semiquaver line in the tenor above
the closing dominant pedal point. The pedal point itself is of a kind
unusual in the organ works of J. S. Bach in its repetition of alternating
tonic and dominant harmonies, as distinct from the changing and
evolving harmonies above such pedal points as those in the Fantasia
BWV 572. Details of the fugue are also characteristic of Bach only when
he is writing under Italian influence: the long sequence in the subject
(following upon a traditional *caput* or head motif) returns to produce
passages much more typical of a Bach episode than of a fugal entry
itself (e.g. bb21–4). Despite good cadential passages which the
transcriber has modified to produce the desired impetus (e.g. bb10–12),
the fugue has a sectionality uncharacteristic of a Bach fugue of any
period, with constant sequences and cadences depending on invertible
counterpoint rather than on thematic development (e.g. the five tonic
cadences at bb33–4, 39, 42, 46–7, 52–3). That Bach has softened the
repetitive element in the fugue, and thus made its character less
dependent on lively string-playing, is clear from the semiquaver lines:
in the original, almost all semiquaver groups begin with a dactyl figure
♪ ♬, which is not the case in the transcription.

Third Movement

Headed in both versions 'Largo e spiccato'; in b1 '*piano*' (BWV 596
only); in b3, accompaniment '*pp*' (Amsterdam edition), '*piano*' with
'*forte*' melody (BWV 596). The form is that of a tutti framework around
an accompanied solo (cf. BWV 592, 593), in which the tutti has a
distinct and unmistakable siciliano character. The transcription differs
from the Amsterdam edition not only in the spacing of the accompaniment for the convenience of one hand but also at times in the

Ex. 271

harmony itself, as in Ex. 271. It is fruitless to speculate whether such alteration represents J. S. Bach's 'improvement' of Italian harmony or the unreliability of the Amsterdam engravers. The movement type exemplified by BWV 596.iii is far less common in organ music than might be expected; neither the tuttis nor the solo passages have close parallels in Bach organ works, where indeed exceptional scoring or textures are often associated with Italianate idioms, such as the Adagio of the C major Toccata BWV 564. What is exceptional in both movements is not so much the melody or even the bass line but the homophonic accompaniment.

Fourth Movement

Headed 'Allegro' in Amsterdam edition only. Though basically a ritornello movement, the finale has unusual features: the soloists provide not only the multi-limbed ritornello theme but also the episodes alternating with it. Shape and finality are given by a tutti passage with chromatic bass line, which appears at regular points (bb11, 27, 68). These formal elements are blurred in the transcription by the use of two manuals:

	Op III no. 11		BWV 596
	1–6	two violins	Rp
A_1	7–11	solo cello	Ow
	11–14	tutti	Ow

A_2	12–22	trio	*Rp*
	23–7	solo violin	*Ow*
	27–30	tutti	*Ow*
B	30–43	solo violins accompanied	*Ow*, then *Ow* + *Rp*
	43–6	tutti	*Ow*
	46–50	trio	*Rp*
	50–3	tutti with echoes	*Ow/Rp*
A_3	53–68	trio	*Rp*, then *Rp* + *Ow*
	69–73	tutti with echo	*Ow*

Although the material itself yields some organ textures that are unusual outside the concerto transcriptions, it has many allusions to the conventional Italian string writing of a previous generation:

> suspension style for two violins (bb1ff)
> paired quavers (b4)
> falling chromatic fourth, with Neapolitan sixth (bb44–6)
> a version of the tutti tremolo effect (b12)
> characteristic solo cello figures (b7)
> tutti violin suspensions (b12)
> parallel thirds for two violins (b14)
> repeated-note figure for solo violin with accompaniment (b35)
> punctuating cadences (bb45–6, 50–3)

The unusual organ textures result partly from finding equivalents for idiomatic string music (b7, b59), partly from keeping the idiomatic string figurations more or less unaltered (b35, b44). On the other hand, the tremolo tutti statements have been replaced by a new* semiquaver line: Ex. 272. As often in the concerto transcriptions, a few minor 'gaps'

Ex. 272

in the string writing have been filled in (e.g. first beat of b68), but perhaps fewer than usual (e.g. solo lines of b33, b43). It is possible, if unlikely, that the left-hand accompaniment of bb59–67 was not added by Bach, as is usually assumed (e.g. Schneider 1911), but was transcribed from an unknown version of the concerto; although it does not appear in the Amsterdam edition, it is by no means alien to Vivaldi's style. The original rise in bb63–4 of Vivaldi's original solo line

---

* The four-part writing in Vivaldi turns the traditionally three-part sequence $\begin{smallmatrix}7&6\\3&3\end{smallmatrix}$ into $\begin{smallmatrix}7&6\\5&3\\3&\end{smallmatrix}$; Bach further enriches the sequence in five parts: $\begin{smallmatrix}7&6\\5&4\\3&3\end{smallmatrix}$.

– from a up to d″′ – has been destroyed by what seems to have been the need to avoid d″′ in BWV 596, a factor which in other transcriptions (notably BWV 594) apparently led the transcriber to write the whole passage an octave lower in order to preserve the melodic feature.

597 Concerto in E flat major

Only source: Lpz MB MS 7, 15 (hand of J. G. Preller).

Heading 'Concerto, in Dis dur à 2 Clavier con Pedal. di Mons: Bach' (the only such attribution in Lpz MB MS 7).

Keller is no doubt correct to see in BWV 597 neither a concerto (in the sense of BWV 592–596) nor a composition/transcription of J. S. Bach, but rather a trio sonata by a composer in (e.g.) W. F. Bach's circle (Keller 1937 p66). The repetitive and partially decorated use of the material resembles that of no known work of J. S. Bach, quite apart from the nature of the material and of its decoration. Like many other doubtful works in the same MS, it may have originated at the hands of a Bach pupil, although there is little indication that the composer in his later years worked in such idioms with his pupils.

598 'Pedal-Exercitium'

No Autograph MS; only source, P 491 (C. P. E. Bach, early).

Heading, 'Pedal Exercitium Bach' (heading written by C. A. Thieme).

The incomplete movement has several possible origins: a fragment of a lost toccata; an independent pedal exercise by J. S. (or C. P. E.) Bach, incomplete (with a *da capo* and new close intended?), possibly written for C. P. E. Bach or for C. A. Thieme (who also wrote the title-page to J. S. Bach's figured-bass instruction of 1738; see Schulze *BJ* 1978 p40); a prelude to (e.g.) a fugue or even a suite; a composition exercise in solo bass lines, whether for organ or for cello. That the last is not out of the question can be seen by comparing figures in BWV 598 with those in the Prélude of the Cello Suite in G major BWV 1007: Ex. 273.

Ex. 273

BWV 1007.i b31   BWV 598 b9

BWV 1007.i b38   BWV 598 b32

319

Bars 19–23 read as much like a string-crossing exercise for cello as like a leaping exercise for pedal. As has been pointed out (Bruggaier 1959 p151), such figures encapsulate a two-part counterpoint, often working in contrary motion.

It is unlikely that the movement is a cello prelude on the one hand or simply the bass line of a fuller instrumental piece on the other, since in either case both compass and figuration would be less limited. Moreover, the opening figure belongs to the same *genre* as many a north German toccata or prelude, as shown in Ex. 274. The 33 bars provide

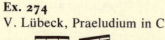

Ex. 274
V. Lübeck, Praeludium in C

etc

a repertory of pedal techniques: alternate-foot pedalling, leaps, the same foot for adjacent notes (b19), different feet for repeated notes (b17), probably off-beat slurs (bb28, 31). The structure itself places the movement amongst the preludes of the violin and cello suites: i.e., it begins with repeated passages (bb1–5) and goes on to a sequence (bb7–9), as in (e.g.) the preludio of the E major Partita for Violin BWV 1006. BWV 598 has elements of shape in its modulations which are not familiar in the pedal solos of north German toccatas: the rhetorical rests and the constant returns to the tonic in the pedal solo of the C major Toccata BWV 564 show this Pedal Exercise to be more in the line of the violin and cello suites. The 'hasty copy' may perhaps have been made by C. P. E. Bach from an improvisation by his father (Dadelsen 1957 p39).

---

790 Trio in B minor

No Autograph MS; only source Lpz MB MS 1, 10 (L. Frischmuth? d. 1764).

Headed 'Trio ex H mol di J: S: Bach'.

Not in Schmieder *BWV* as an organ trio in B minor (see *NBA* IV/3 *KB* p30), the movement is a transposed version, of doubtful authenticity, of the Three-part Invention (Sinfonia) in D minor BWV 790.

802–805   Four Duets (*Clavierübung III*)

Published 1739, no Autograph MS. Later copies only, either with other pieces from *Clavierübung III* or without (e.g. P 1010, 2nd half of 18th century).

Several problems surround the Four Duets, both in themselves and in their position within *Clavierübung III*.

(i) **'Duetto'.** Some uncertainty as to a suitable name for two- and three-part pieces of more or less strict imitative character is suggested by the use of the terms 'Praeambula' and 'Fantasie' in the *Klavier-büchlein für W. F. Bach* (late 1722/early 1723 – Dadelsen 1958 p 102) for the pieces that are more familiarly called 'Inventionen' and 'Sinfonien' respectively in the composer's fair copy of 1723. German theorists understood the term 'duetto' in several ways: (i) a 'petit duo' for two parts (above a bass) as defined in (e.g.) Brossard's *Dictionaire* (Paris 1703) and Walther's *Lexicon* (Leipzig 1732); (ii) an aria arranged in dialogue form with an 'opportunity to introduce and develop two *subjecta opposita*' (Mattheson, *Critica musica* vol. II (1725) p28); (iii) an instrumental or vocal piece (above a bass) 'skilfully fugued, more than in a four-part Contrapunct or Allabreve' (*ibid* vol. I (1722) p131); (iv) a two-part piece incorporating stricter contrapuntal techniques than mere 'imitation at the unison and octave' (*ibid* (1722) pp305, 360). Although the last comes closest to BWV 802–805, Mattheson was referring less to self-contained pieces of music than to the idiomatic technique behind them.

In the cantatas, 'duetto' is the composer's own term for a dialogue or duet aria, e.g. BWV 140.iii (dialogue between the Soul and Jesus, labelled 'duetto' in the parts: see *NBA* I/2 *KB*), or BWV 110.v (labelled 'duetto à soprano e tenore' in the score: *NBA* I/27 *KB*). The possibility that in BWV 802–805 the composer was in some way alluding to the art of duo writing in French organ masses (de Grigny, Raison etc) is attractive but doubtful, since the French duos are primarily melodic and, though imitative, only loosely organized as two-part counterpoint. They are often composed in a certain metre and rhythm (particularly dotted figures in triple time); they also span a wider tessitura and spacing and serve as only one of several genre-pieces scattered throughout the organ mass concerned.

(ii) **The instrument.** Both the figuration and the texture frequently suggest that the Four Duets were not written for church organ: for example, the countersubject of BWV 802, the figuration (e.g. bb26–9)

321

and spacing (e.g. bb29ff) of BWV 803, the opening bass of BWV 804, etc. The two-part sections of the E flat Fugue BWV 552 suggest more conventional organ texture, as often do the Two-part Inventions themselves. Of the four, the A minor Duet BWV 805 shows the closest affinity to the Leipzig harpsichord music. However, none is particularly suite-like, and it is outside the scope of the E minor Duet to show the same idiomatic harpsichord figures as in (e.g.) the Courante of the E minor Partita BWV 830. J. E. Bach's remark that *Clavierübung III* was 'mainly' for organists ('hauptsächlich' – *Dok* II p335) may suggest that some of the pieces were not; but it would be an over-simplification to see the four Duets as harpsichord music. By 1792, a Berlin reviewer thought the Duets an example of the '*Orgel-Duo* oder *Duetto*'; yet he referred to the Two-part Inventions in the same way, pointing out that all these pieces were 'only for the palates of a few initiates' ('nur für den Gaumen weniger Eingeweihten' – *Dok* III p517). Forkel (1802) is more certain that the Duets are not music for organ but for 'Clavier' (David & Mendel 1945 p338). The compass (CDE–c‴) suggests the organ but is also an 'ideal' counterpoint compass.

(iii) Relevance. Although in performance the Four Duets can be 'integrated' and interspersed with the chorales (Albrecht 1969), it is doubtful if they are in any sense 'Communion music' as has been suggested (Keller 1948 p198), since hymn-singing was the usual music during the distribution of communion. Nor is it certain that *Clavier-übung III* was liturgical. Even less certain is the claim that the Duets have thematic connections with some of the melodies used in *Clavierübung III* (Ehricht 1949–50). What is the significance of the fact that both Duet III and the fughetta 'Diess sind die heil'gen zehn Gebot' BWV 679 are in G major and in $^{12}/_8$ metre, or that selective sieving can produce the notes of the melody *Allein Gott in der Höh'* from the theme (and counter-theme) of the same duet (Ex. 275)?

Ex. 275

The tonalities – E minor for the first (after the F minor of the previous chorale BWV 689), A minor for the last (before the b♭ (dominant of E♭ major) that begins the following fugue BWV 552.ii) – suggest an attempt to make the contrast as conspicuous as possible. On the other hand, along with the six Lesser Catechism chorales (BWV 679, 681, 683, 685, 687, 689) the Duets make ten pieces of music for manuals, perhaps reflecting the ten relevant sections of Vopelius' *Gesangbuch*:

Commandments
Credo
Lord's Prayer
Baptism
Confession
Communion
morning prayer
evening prayer
prayer before eating
prayer after eating

The Four Duets may 'represent' the four Prayers already contained in Luther's Small Catechism, the last duet appropriately beginning with a cross motif (Leaver 1975); but such allusion would not invalidate points made in sections iv and v below.

(iv) Purpose. Perhaps the Four Duets were slipped into *Clavierübung III* for the convenience of the printer (to make a round number of pages), or to make the number of pieces 27 ($3 \times 3 \times 3$). The first is unlikely, since the duets take up exactly eight pages (pp63–70);* the second is possible, but organists would have found more useful two further pairs of organ chorales on Luther texts such as *Christ lag in Todesbanden* or *Ach Gott, vom Himmel sieh darein*. That the duets are four in number has also suggested to some writers that in one way or another – unclear to other writers – they 'symbolize' the Four Gospels (e.g. J. M. Ross *MT* 1974 p331) or the Four Elements (Steglich 1935 pp146–7). In any case, such species of symbolism would not correspond to that of the chorales in the collection, e.g. that divine Law is represented by musical Canon in BWV 678, 682 and 686. Another insupportable guess is that the two contrapuntal parts themselves mark the dualities of Bread/Wine and Saviour/Grace operating at the Communion (Chailley 1974 p267). More likely is that the duets were included as contrapuntal models of various kinds gathered within the framework of a pious composer's faith in the the Lord and giver of life. Contrapuntal ingenuity is offered *ad majorem gloriam Dei*. The variety of duet techniques speaks for this. As Forkel said, they are a 'model of duets admitting of no third part' ('die als Muster von Duetten keine dritte Stimme zu lassen', 1802 ch.IX).

(v) Techniques. The duets include the techniques of regular fugue, double fugue, *A B A* fugue, fugue with bass (the so-called invention fugue), strict invertibility, canon, inversion, motivic derivation (motifs from scale figures, broken chords and chromatic lines) and motivic imitation, all against a background of different modes (major/minor),

---

* Side 1 = title-page, sides 2 – 3 = blank, sides 4–80 = the 77 pages of music. The 78 printed pages are described in *NBA* IV/4 *KB*.

rhythms and metres (duple/triple/compound). It is possible that they have a common pulse.* The invertibility of the two duet parts becomes a further facet of Bach's apparently growing interest in canon and in a genuine melodic counterpoint free of Italianate formulae. Moreover, the techniques result in elements well outside Fuxian counterpoint: such details as the falling augmented octaves resulting from the chromatic bass in Duet I (b3 etc) and the effect of an augmented triad given by the canonic stretto of Duet II (bb46–7) contrast with the *stile antico* of the following and final movement of *Clavierübung III* (BWV 552.ii).

802   Duetto I

The formal characteristics are:

E minor, $^3/_8$: double fugue, 73 bars

all material invertible; chromatic, scale-like, angular and syncopated elements; one-bar phrases

The double fugue subject, answered in b7, is said to be the only double subject in Bach to modulate to the dominant (Souchay 1927); but the modulating bar is b6, which is not strictly part of the subject (e.g., it is absent after the tonic entry in b21). The main sections are tonic–tonic–relative–dominant. The row of parallel major thirds produced by the stretto scales gives an effect comparable to the 'augmented triad' referred to above in section v: Ex. 276. With the false

Ex. 276   b19

relation between minor and major sixths the composer is creating an original effect from the two forms of the melodic minor scale.†

    The two subjects (bb1–5) are contrasted in their chromaticism: the lower part has a traditional descending 'chromatic fourth', the upper a more modern melodic-appoggiatura chromaticism. The extension in b6 of the upper subject is developed in a highly original way in bb12ff and 40ff, the first time for a simple dominant–tonic modulation (B

---

* I.e. $^3_8$ ♪ = $^2_4$ ♩ = $^{12}_8$ ♩· = ¢ ♩. Such a relationship requires that Duet III be played quite quickly. For comparison with other proportional tempos in *Clavierübung III*, see notes to BWV 552.ii, and to BWV 674 in Volume II.

† A clear distinction between the two forms of the minor scale (sixth and seventh degrees sharpened when rising, flattened when falling) was first drawn in books on keyboard harmony, where as bass lines they required different harmonies (e.g. J. F. Dandrieu, *Principes de l'Accompagnement du Clavecin*, Paris c1719). Keyboard-players at this period did not practise scales *per se*.

minor/E minor) and the second for a remoter modulation (D minor/B minor). The two tonic final entries (bb61, 66) are unusual: the first appears in the course of the overlapping scales, the second in place of the original b6, and their invertibility is exact, unlike the two tonic final entries of (e.g.) the E flat Two-part Invention BWV 776.

---

803 Duetto II

The formal characteristics are:

F major, $^2/_4$: *A B A* fugue, 149 bars*

A regular exposition; most material invertible; triadic and broken chords; little syncopation; various phrase-lengths
B canonic second theme; canonic treatment and inversion of first theme; shifting tonality, minor, chromatic; syncopation
A *da capo*

The middle section itself serves as contrast to the first and last, in its stretto, mode, chromatics, and phrase-lengths. Typical of late Bach canonic phrases is (e.g.) the right-hand phrase bb57–60. From the shifting tonality of the second theme a new, chromatic countersubject to the first theme is produced (bb69–72), putting new light on its conventionality and propelling it to a minor inversion in b74. The middle section is extensive, containing exactly twice the number of bars as the outer sections (cf. the E minor Fugue BWV 548). This section itself goes some way towards symmetry in that its opening and closing strettos are introduced by the right hand and its middle stretto by the left, and the minor/inverted version of the first theme enters at almost exactly the halfway point (b74).

---

804 Duetto III

The formal characteristics are:

G major, $^{12}/_8$: invention fugue, 39 bars

non-chromatic, non-modulatory subject; rolling sequential figures; staccato elements; non-invertible bass

Although in form and melodic/harmonic detail, Duet III is the simplest of the four, its conception is as unusual as that of the others. The detached bass to the fugue subject is not a theme, is not found in the right hand, and does not lead to clearly developed passages, although the bass of bb6, 13–15 and elsewhere is presumably a derivative. The fugal answer plus countersubject in bb3–4 could conceivably be accompanied by a third part of the same kind; but there is nothing to suggest that the duet is a trio *manqué*. As a kind of invention fugue,

* 116 bars plus *da capo* of bb5–37.

the piece it is most similar to is the B minor Two-part Invention BWV 786, which in turn more closely resembles some of the Three-part Sinfonias (e.g. A major BWV 798) than it does the other Two-part Inventions.

As b3 compared with b9 shows, one version of the invertible counterpoint is more successful than others; but where the piece is most successful is, rather, in exploiting the development of rolling semiquaver figures in $^{12}/_8$ (particularly the need for a group of six semiquavers to introduce notes outside the implied triad), of sequences (short as in b11, long as in bb20–1; falling in bb31–2, rising in bb32–3), and of regular fugal entries (regular in bb16–18, stretto in bb28–30). Like Duets IV and II, Duet III also presents an example of a tonal answer (b3); but unlike Duet II the tonal answer is not strictly 'necessary', and here it results in a much-altered subject.

805

Duetto IV

The formal characteristics are:

A minor, $^2/_2$: fugue, 108 bars

fugue subject with minim head and quaver tail; chromatic element in subject and episodes; almost total invertibility

Like Duets II and III, Duet IV presents a tonal answer which may or may not be considered 'necessary'; all four duets give a demonstration of how to treat *dux* and *comes*, and the treatment varies from one to another. The real *comes* or answer in Duet I is fully dominant; the tonal *comes* in each of the other duets begins in the tonic and establishes the dominant only some way through.

Although sometimes called a 'regular fugue', Duet IV shows certain aspects of tight symmetry: two-, four- and eight-bar phrases; all counterpoint invertible except the link to the final entry (bb93–4) and the last five bars; all entries (*dux* or *comes*) in either tonic or dominant. The initial stretto at bb31–5 is not developed but returns inverted at bb94–7. Various symmetries can be seen in the overall form:

b1	A_1 (lh), b9 A_1 (rh), b11 A_2 (lh), tonic to dominant
b17	B_1 (rh), B_2 (lh), sequence subdominant to relative (C major)
b26	C_1 (rh), C_2 (lh), sequence relative (C) to tonic
b31 (end)	A_1 (stretto begins in lh) tonic; then b33 A_1 (rh), b35 A_2 (lh), b41 A_1 (lh), b43 A_2 (rh), tonic to dominant
b49	B_2 (rh), B_1 (lh), sequence dominant to relative (or G major)
b58	C_2 (rh), C_1 (lh), sequence relative (or G major) to dominant
b64	A_3 (rh), A_4 (lh), sequence to tonic
b70	A_1 (rh), b72 A_2 (lh), section identical to bb9–17
b78	B_2 (rh), B_1 (lh), sequence subdominant to relative (C), bb79–85 very similar to 18–24 (with partial inversion)
b86	A_4 (rh), A_3 (lh), sequence to subdominant

b93   link
b94 (end) A_1 (stretto begins in rh) tonic; then b96 A_1 (lh, 1st 2 notes taken
           from end b94, now augmented), b98 A_2 (rh)
b104   coda

The chromaticism takes the form of flattening certain notes for
harmonic/melodic purposes, not for modulation: supertonic (Bb in b4),
submediant (Ab in C major in bb21–3), Neapolitan sixth (b105). The
modulatory passages (bb64ff, 87ff) also incorporate extra rising chromatic notes.

1027a   Trio in G major

No Autograph MS; copy in Lpz MB MS 7, 3 (J. N. Mempell, before 1740?). Transcription of a chamber-sonata movement; see below, also BWV 1039.i, ii.

Headed 'Trio. ex. G.♯. 2. Clavier et Pedal. di Bach'.

The movement is a version for 'two manuals and pedal' of the Allegro Moderato either from the Sonata in G for Viola da Gamba and Harpsichord BWV 1027.iv (Autograph MS P 226) or from another version of the same work, a Sonata for Two Flutes and Continuo BWV 1039.iv known in late copies. It is not certain which of the two complete versions (BWV 1027 or 1039) is the earlier; both may derive from an original trio sonata for two violins (Eppstein 1966 p157). But BWV 1027a seems to have been made from BWV 1027 or 1039 (Eppstein 1965), probably the latter (Siegele 1975 p69), though it is very doubtful whether J. S. Bach himself made the 'arrangement' (*MGG* i col. 1014). Concerning the Mempell manuscripts as a source for trios, see also BWV 585, 586.

The arrangement of the part-writing –

BWV 1027a	BWV 1027	BWV 1039
rh (d'–c''')	harpsichord rh	flute I
lh (G–d'')*	gamba, octave lower than	flute II
pedal (C–c♯')	harpsichord lh	continuo

– may suggest that BWV 1027a is a straightforward transcription of BWV 1027 rather than of BWV 1039, as does the form of the melody itself. Also suggestive is that (e.g.) the gamba entry in b89 of BWV 1027 crosses the bass line. The bass line of BWV 1039 is something between BWV 1027 and 1027a, in general more like the former. A comparison of the bass lines of BWV 1027 and 1027a does support the idea that the pedal version is a 'clever simplification of the bass' of the instrumental sonata (Keller 1948 p109), i.e. was made from it. This seems more likely than that the instrumental bass was a more fluid and continuo-like re-working of the pedal line. Moreover, Lpz MB MS 7 not only has this simplified bass for pedal but avoids notes above c♯', as perhaps pedals would.

Of all the separate trio movements, BWV 1027a is the one which most conforms to the various melodic, harmonic and formal elements familiar in the Six Sonatas BWV 525–530. Quite apart from the similar charm of melody and length of phrase in the manual lines, the pedal goes some way towards variety of motif, and the fugal ritornello introduces simple episode material very much *sui generis* (compare bb26ff with BWV 530.i bb37ff). On the other hand, there is not the same careful interchange of parts (e.g., the episode at b26 has the same arrangement as b111, which would be unlikely in one of the Six

* I.e. extending below tenor c, unlike any movement in the Six Sonatas BWV 525–530.

Sonatas). Because of the 'pedal simplification', the motivic drive of the central section of the gamba version (bb49ff) is lost, and the bass becomes somewhat clumsy. Indeed, the arranger reduced the weight of bb66ff even further and at b115 gave up altogether the attempt to translate the sequence into organ terms, omitting eleven bars in his organ version (between b114 and b115). Not the least surprising 'simplification', however, is that the bass line no longer has the fugal entries (bb16, b97) which could certainly have been modified for pedal in the manner of BWV 530.iii to produce a fuller fugal texture of the kind found in so many chamber-sonata finales. In the event, the pedal part is from time to time very like the bass of the flute trio and more like an organ bass than the continuo line of the gamba sonata, as the opening bars show: Ex. 277. But the bass of the flute trio includes the

Ex. 277

long phrases of running quavers found in the gamba-sonata bass, and considered as a whole the organ pedal part is much less thematic than either instrumental bass part.

1029.iii   (Trio in G minor)

No Autograph MS; only source, London RCM MS 814 (Benjamin Cooke, c1770).

Headed 'Trio a 2 Clav: e Pedal', second subject 'cantabile'.

The work is a version of the movement known as the finale of the Sonata in G minor for Viola da Gamba and Harpsichord BWV 1029, itself possibly an arrangement by the composer of a three-movement concerto for unknown forces (Siegele 1975 p97ff). In RCM 814, the trio is placed between the Prelude and the Fugue in B flat major BWV 545b, and separated from them by a short interlude on either side: see BWV 545b. The history of this version will probably remain uncertain, but it is at least possible that the composer himself was responsible for the order and key of the three main movements, including BWV 1029.iii (Emery 1959 p. viii).

The versions differ in figuration, in length (only the gamba version has two final coda bars) and in other details; two-part passages may suggest that the organ trio is 'an arrangement of a string trio of some kind' (Emery 1958 p. iii), while the gamba sonata itself is also very likely an arrangement (Eppstein 1966 p119). While neither version (gamba or organ) can be shown to be arranged from the other, it is difficult to believe that in such a passage as Ex. 278 both are equally 'authentic'.

Ex. 278

That the second is indeed for organ is certain: its pedal takes a line of the kind known in BWV 1027a (also an organ version of a gamba-sonata movement). But the left-hand semiquaver line is less interestingly motivated in BWV 545b.ii than in the gamba version BWV 1029.iii and

– though this could otherwise be taken as a sign that it was early rather than spurious – leads to a spacing and compass alien to the Six Sonatas. Moreover, in the course of being transcribed, the repeated quavers of the upper parts have lost their line of suspensions at this point.

On the whole, the organ arrangement has been made with careful consideration of the medium and in particular of what is suitable for pedals. The absence of careful exchange of parts (bb85ff = bb61ff) and inconsistencies in scoring (compare bb19ff with bb69ff) suggest that the arrangement was made somewhat *ad hoc*, perhaps by a pupil or another organist familiar with some but not all details of J. S. Bach's organ-trio medium. Thus the alternate-foot motif for pedal is applied indiscriminately when motion is required, unlike its timed appearances in the development sections of (e.g.) the first movement of the G major Sonata BWV 530. However, that the arrangement was of an authentic movement differing in its own right from the (later?) gamba version is suggested by such a passage as Ex. 279, where the organ version may be lacking the motivic unity and drive of the gamba version but has its own logic of line.

Ex. 279

1039.i, ii   (Trios in G major)

No Autograph MS; copy of 1039.i in P 804 (J. P. Kellner), of 1039.ii in P 288 (2nd half of 18th century).

Heading in P 804 'Trio in G♮, Adagio', at end 'Sequi Allegro' (but no 2nd movement follows).

The movements appear to be keyboard versions of the Adagio and the

Allegro ma non Presto of the Sonata for Two Flutes and Continuo BWV 1039 (*NBA* IV/3 *KB* pp50–1), itself known in a version for gamba and harpsichord BWV 1027. (On the chamber-music versions, see also BWV 1027a.) Three of the four movements of this sonata thus exist in keyboard versions, scattered in three different sources. That in layout and other details such as melodic forms they resemble not BWV 1027 but BWV 1039 is not conclusive; the versions for organ and for two flutes may derive from a common source, for these media have much in common in texture and style.* Although the basso continuo of BWV 1039 would need simplification or re-styling for organ pedal (as happens in both P 804 and P 288), it is already closer to an organ idiom than BWV 1027. So is its spacing, although in P 804 the second part is written an octave lower. The thematic material of BWV 1039.ii is also more amenable to organ than that of other fast movements such as the D major Gamba Sonata. Although BWV 1039.i and ii might be said to display certain parallels with BWV 526.ii and iii – a preparatory slow movement with modified *A B A B* structure, followed by a fugue-like ritornello with a second or middle subject – the pairing is not known to have been made in any complete organ version. Less certain still is whether the whole sonata BWV 1039 ever existed in a version for organ, made by the composer or anybody else.

Ex. 280

A further point emerges from these organ arrangements of chamber sonatas. P 288 simplifies the bass line in order to make it more practical for pedals, and to avoid notes above c′ (Ex. 280). But in the Six Sonatas (e.g. BWV 525.ii, 529.iii, 530.iii) the simplified pedal version of a theme first heard in the manuals is made use of as a compositional device: sequences are based on it, and it is – or is made to appear – no mere simplification for the sake of convenience.

---

* There seems no reason why flute I is predominantly lower than flute II over bb1–13 of BWV 1039.ii; perhaps this scoring indicates that the flute trio too is a transcription?

1079.v   Six-part Ricercar from *Musical Offering*

Organ score: no Autograph MS; copies in P 667 (?J. F. Agricola 1720–74) and P 565 (18th century), Lpz MB MS R 16, 3 (c1800), P 289, Lpz Go . S . 318a (1819).

Three staves (in first three sources); title in P 667 'Ricercata a 6 Voci . . . sonabile sull'Organo col Pedale obligato'.

Despite the similarities between the *alla breve* counterpoint of BWV 1079.v and the middle section of the Fantasia in G major BWV 572, and despite the tradition of open-score music played or studied by organists from at least the sixteenth century onwards, there is no evidence that the six-part Ricercar from the *Musical Offering* was (like the three-part Ricercar and the Canons in Lpz Go . S . 318a) composed as an independent work for organ with pedals. This is so despite the value of the sources for the organ version – near-contemporary arrangements, made perhaps with the composer's tacit approval (see H. Lohmann, B & H edn 6584). Moreover, although the engraved open-score presentation of the organ works BWV 769 and 645–650 also suggests that such presentation was known to and presumably played from by practical performers, comparison with the *Art of Fugue* on the other hand would suggest, if anything, that ornate contrapuntal works presented in open score were conceived for manual alone. Playing contrapuntal works on organ or harpsichord was obviously possible; the crucial question is whether there was authority for converting the bass line into a pedal part. 'Adding' pedals (and presumably 16' tone) to the bass line of BWV 1079.v distorts the nature of the original distribution of the counterpoint in six equally important lines. Moreover, Agricola had to simplify the bass line for the sake of pedals by omitting certain quavers etc – Ex. 281 – and in the process weakened the freedom of the line in that particular episode of the Ricercar.

Ex. 281
b65

Anh.46   Trio in C minor

No Autograph MS; copy in BB 12011 (J. L. Krebs), P 833 (2nd half of 18th century, dependent on 12011).

Headed by J. L. Krebs 'Trio a 2 Clav: e Ped: di J. T. K.'.

Although P 833 ascribes the movement to J. S. Bach and more recent authors to J. L. Krebs (Keller 1948 p58), the title in BB 12011 seems to point conclusively to Johann Tobias Krebs (Tittel 1962). The supposed resemblance to the subject of BWV 585.i leads to no firm conclusion on the authorship, as the history of BWV 585 clearly confirms. Despite trio-sonata-like elements in BWV Anh.46 reminiscent of movements in the Six Sonatas BWV 525–530 – the dominant answer to a tonic melody, the motivic imitation, the shortened reprise – other features can be attributed rather to the various groups of Bach pupils, in particular the plaintive quality of the melody and the curious avoidance of strong cadences.

Glossary

acciaccatura: a 'delicate and admirable secret' (F. Geminiani, *A Treatise of Good Taste*, London 1749 p4) enabling a keyboard-player to enrich the harmony by adding (short) notes outside the chord itself: Ex. 282. See also BWV 572.

Ex. 282   F. Gasparini, *L'armonico pratico al cimbalo* (Venice 1708)

Affekt: a term used particularly by modern writers to denote the overall mood of a piece of music or its characteristics in the 'sensitive style' of C. P. E. Bach, the Mannheim school, the Berlin School etc, chiefly after the death of J. S. Bach. However, in 1746 J. G. Ziegler noted that J. S. Bach had taught him to play chorales 'not simply indifferently but according to the *Affekt* of the words' ('nicht nur so oben hin, sondern nach dem Affect der Wortte', *Dok* II p423). *Affekt* was presumably a germanized form of *affetto*, a term much used by supporters of the *seconda prattica* or new expressive style of composition in Italy c1600. See also BWV 534.

alla breve: strictly, a term from late medieval mensural notation denoting music in which the beat is a breve, not (as usual) a semibreve – in effect $^2/_2$ not $^4/_4$, i.e. quick duple time. However, by at least 1700 the term denoted in practice a certain contrapuntal style, vocal or instrumental, characterized by a lively minim pulse, certain rhythmic elements (quaver dactyls, crotchet counter-subjects etc) and particular linear/melodic details, all eventually derived (at least in theory) from the late-sixteenth-century counter-point celebrated by J. J. Fux in *Gradus ad Parnassum* (Vienna 1725). See also BWV 589.

alla stretta: in stretto or 'tight' imitation. In modern usage, 'stretto' refers to several related devices, some of which are climactic: incomplete imitation of one and the same theme (e.g. BWV 543.ii), pseudo-canon (e.g. subject altered in stretto at end of BWV 541.ii), and close or canonic imitation of either subject or episode (e.g.

335

BWV 538.ii). At the close of BWV 769.v, 'alla stretta' signals a combination of four themes and at least three derivatives.

alternate-foot pedalling: a phrase denoting the pedal technique (old-fashioned by 1750) in which the feet alternate in characteristic figuration; see e.g. BWV 531.i. In such 'early' pieces, the alternate-foot pedalling suggests two important factors: (i) the toes or front of the foot but not the heel are engaged in such playing; (ii) bass lines not obviously playable in this manner may well not have been intended originally by the composer as pedal parts (e.g. BWV 531.ii b36 as compared with b23), however they may have been understood by later copyists or editors.

anapaest: see *figura corta*

appoggiatura: a note outside the harmony 'leaning on' (down or up to) the following note. While theorists on ornamentation have, since around 1675, paid ample attention to the melodic attributes of this device – its nature and purpose, its notation and interpretation – its harmonic significance, particularly as a token of musical evolution, is not often demonstrated. The frenchified melodic appoggiaturas of BWV 562.i already lead to four-and five-part harmonies far in advance of Buxtehude–Bruhns triadism, while the chordal appoggiaturas of BWV 546.i or 552.i (simple effects which look like 'repeated suspensions') form a chief feature of the main themes. 'Appoggiatura harmony' may be an appropriate term for such harmonies as those of BWV 562.i, as distinct from the yet more significant 'accented-passing-note harmony' typical of many *Orgelbüchlein* preludes (e.g. BWV 600).

basso continuo: see continuo

brisé: a (probably modern) term with several meanings: a detached ('broken') bowing technique in eighteenth-century violin-playing; an ornament (turn), and more particularly a seventeenth-century manner of 'breaking' chords on the harpsichord or organ in imitation of the gentle arpeggiation (incorporating non-harmonic notes) practised by lutenists and guitarists when improvising preludes or playing suite movements. For an example, see BWV 599; the sectional cadence points in (e.g.) BWV 538.i also use this device very conventionally (adding to the already 'antique' flavour of that Toccata).

broken chord: a term to denote such figures as Ex. 283 in distinction to arpeggiated or spread chords, all of which were called 'arpeggio' by many theorists (e.g. Heinichen, *Der Generalbass*, Dresden 1728; Mattheson, *Grosse General-Bass-Schule*, Hamburg 1731).

Ex. 283

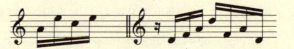

Brustwerk (*Bw*): the small organ chest (played by its own manual) encased compactly above the keyboards and below the *Hauptwerk*, 'in the breast' of the organ. Although it may have had a penetrating solo stop or two, it was always the smallest department when present in any two-, three- or four-manual organ.

cantus firmus: a pre-existent melody on which a contrapuntal movement is based by the creating of new voices. Although in both the organ and the vocal music of J. S. Bach there is normally a clear distinction between those pieces that are based on or include a cantus firmus and those that do not, some fugues of the *Art of Fugue* include the subject augmented in a manner recalling a cantus firmus.

caput: the 'head' of a fugue subject; a term coined for the opening motif, conspicuous or at least distinct from the rest of the subject. In late Italian theory (e.g. G. B. Martini, *Esemplare o Saggio fondamentale pratico*, Bologna 1774–5), the livelier sections of a fugue subject were called the 'andamento' as distinct from the 'attacco' (subsidiary motif open to imitation). In some cases, 'soggetto' ('subject') seems to denote the 'head' of the theme or 'tema' as distinct from the livelier 'tail'.

circle of fifths: a common sequence, gradually standardized during the seventeenth century, based on harmonies in a succession of dominant–tonic or tonic–dominant relationships: Ex. 284. Of the two, the falling sequence (in which each pair of chords is dominant–tonic, not vice versa) is the more common.

Ex. 284

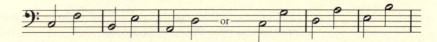

continuo or basso continuo: a bass line which may or may not be figured but which implies that the keyboard-player in ensemble music is to play harmonies with, and above, that bass line. As such, the bass line is characterized by certain details – e.g., it will include or even be totally given over to a simple bass foundation below lines played by other instruments; in most cases it will be more or less non-imitative, however lively it may be. Thus, in solo organ music it is usually possible to distinguish between a thematic pedal line and a 'continuo pedal line'. In one and the same set of pieces (e.g. BWV 645 and 647) or even within the same movement (e.g. BWV 769.v), the pedal line might be variously 'organ-like' and 'continuo-like', particularly in such exceptional late pieces.

dactyl: see *figura corta*

durezza: a term used by Italian composers (e.g. G. M. Trabaci, *Ricercate...durezze, ligature...*, Naples 1603) to denote keyboard music that makes a point of incorporating dissonances, e.g.

Ex. 285
Capriccio di durezza (Frescobaldi, *Capricci*, 1626)

etc

suspensions involving seconds and ninths: Ex. 285. The style became widespread in the later seventeenth century, particularly amongst German composers familiar with the Frescobaldi legacy. The difference between a *durezza* and a non-*durezza* piece is often only one of degree, but in most cases it is clear whether (e.g.) Buxtehude or Pachelbel is consciously adopting the style. See also BWV 555.

en ravalement: an eighteenth-century term which in modern parlance denotes the 'lowering' of an organ compass below C, usually for the pedal reeds of a French classical organ (e.g. to FF at St Quentin, 1697). 'Clavecin à grand ravalement' is an eighteenth-century term for a five-octave harpsichord (FF-f‴), as distinct from the older compass of C-c‴ or C-d‴. 'Ravalement' probably first arose as a term in organ contracts and other documents; it is not always clear whether it means there 'complete bass octave' (i.e. with C♯, D♯ etc) or 'further notes below C' (BB, AA etc). See also BWV 572.

en taille: phrase signifying that the solo or melody is 'in the tenor part'; in classical French organ music, the most characteristic tenor solos are played by the left hand with a Tierce or Cromorne registration (N. Lebègue, 1676). Some typical French *en taille* figuration (scales, ornaments, lively run-ins to the cadence etc) is to be found in BWV 663.

figura: a 'figure' or short group of notes in one of the patterns recognized and catalogued by such theorists as Printz (*Satyrischer Componist* 1696) and J. G. Walther (*Praecepta* 1708), and patently the basis of many works of J. S. Bach; see also *figura corta* and *suspirans*. Even so familiar a figure as the eight-note pattern of Ex. 286 – woven into so many types of movement (see BWV 537.ii, 546.ii) that it serves almost as a *signum* of J. S. Bach – had a name of its own in the seventeenth century: it is the *minuta* which decorates (e.g.) Sweelinck's *Fantasia chromatica*.

Ex. 286   Sweelinck, *Fantasia chromatica*

b112

figura corta: one of the most important figures or melodic formulae, distinguished in (e.g.) Walther's *Lexicon* (Leipzig 1732) as having two forms – ♩♪♪ and ♪♪♩ – i.e. the dactyl and anapaest. The *Orgelbüchlein* uses such figures with great variety: anapaest on the beat (BWV 610), dactyl on the beat (BWV 616), and an ambiguous rhythm that looks like a dactyl but seems to require a different phrasing: ♩♪|♪ ♩♪♪ ♩♪|♪. The very array of figures systematically applied in Bach organ works may suggest that they require systematically varied performance.

galant: a term belonging to the eighteenth century (see a note on the Trios, page 17), but applied today – apparently with more specific meaning than at that period – to light, elegant music of the middle of the eighteenth century, often reflecting a turn towards new kinds of public performance outside the Church, for whose music even C. P. E. Bach continued to employ *alla breve* and other old styles.

grand jeu: a characteristic French organ registration, known from at least the early seventeenth century, consisting of the chorus reeds with Cornet, Prestant 4', Tierce and other ranks which were not (once the practice was standardized) used in the *plein jeu*, which was made up of the Diapason chorus including Mixtures. While the theorists from Mersenne (c1625) to Bedos (c1775) were rarely unanimous in their description of or requirements for the *grand jeu* and the *plein jeu*, they agreed in general on the kinds of music served by or written for these registrations: fugues and contrapuntal music on the *grand jeu*, more massive homophony (usually with some or other degree of *durezze e ligature*) on the *plein jeu*, whether that of the Grand Orgue or the Positif (*petit plein jeu*). See also BWV 532.

Hauptwerk (*Hw*): the main chest and manual of an organ, as distinct from *Rückpositiv* etc. Although the term was known in the early seventeenth century, many eighteenth-century German sources (musical, theoretical, archival) still used 'Oberwerk' to denote this manual; this is the meaning in BWV 720 and in the other registrations of J. S. Bach and/or his copyists. From at least Praetorius (1619) onwards, 'Oberwerk' referred to the main manual, which was placed *above* the player (unlike the *Rückpositiv*). However, earlier Dutch builders and a few successors in Hanseatic cities kept the term 'Oberwerk' to distinguish a second *Hauptwerk* which was placed above the *Hauptwerk* proper in order to avoid too deep a chest. In north German organ music, the *Oberwerk* was used as the echo manual to the *Rückpositiv* and not vice versa, presumably because it was more distant from the listeners in the body of the church; in central Germany by c1710, 'Oberwerk' began to mean, for such builders as G. Silbermann, a secondary manual replacing the old-fashioned *Rückpositiv*.

hexachord: a scale-like progression of six diatonic notes, usually with the semitone between the middle pair (c–d–e–f–g–a). In the eighteenth century the hexachord was no longer a tool of theory and practice; but keyboard-players, not yet being taught to practise or think in octave and multi-octave scales, would be the more likely to perceive hexachord allusions in (e.g.) the opening bar of BWV 769.

inversus: a term denoting a melody or figure whose original ('right', *rectus*) intervals have been inverted, producing a new line that rises where the *rectus* fell and falls where the *rectus* rose. The coincidence of terms in English between 'inversion' of intervals in a single melody (*inversus*) and 'inversion' of two or more lines of a contrapuntal complex (*invertible* counterpoint) has led to a confusion not entirely obviated by using – as some dictionaries have done – the terms 'melodic inversion' for the first and 'harmonic inversion' for the second.

invertible counterpoint: counterpoint so written that each part may be the lower or higher of two, or the lowest or highest of more than two. Such exchanging of voices is achieved by one or the other being transposed an octave (or two octaves) up or down as the case requires.

motoric subject: a term used by some twentieth-century writers for those long or fairly long fugue subjects of the seventeenth century which are built up from lively semiquaver figures (repeated notes, broken chords, repeated motifs, sequential arpeggios etc). The subjects of BWV 532.ii and 575 have such motoric elements broken up by rests. Though motoric figures create a characteristic fugue subject associated with the north German organists – 'perhaps introduced by Weckmann' (Apel 1967 p599) – they are also typical of contemporary Italian harpsichord toccatas.

Neapolitan sixth: a term coined after the event to denote a cadential progression associated with Neapolitan composers from at least c1675 onwards – Ex. 287 – and distinguished from 'French' and other sixths. While it probably orginated in chromatic passages developing the more traditional *passus duriusculus* harmonies for the sake of some special effect or mood for word-settings, it was applied by J. S. Bach in his earlier keyboard music as a habit perhaps picked up from Böhm (see BWV 564.ii).

Ex. 287

notes inégales: an 'unequal' way of playing equally notated quavers (or semiquavers in a leisurely movement) arising as an articulation or playing method during the late sixteenth century and associated with the highly codified practice of the classical French composers from Lully onwards. The degree to which selected movements of J. S. Bach 'ought' to be treated in this manner is controversial; but it is in any case probable that *notes inégales* arose from the manner of – or even as a method for – playing the instrument concerned, rather than from a desire for jerky rhythms as such. See also BWV 539.i.

Oberwerk (Ow): see *Hauptwerk*

Orgelpunkttokkata: a modern term to denote those organ toccatas associated in particular with central and south German composers (probably based ultimately on the type of *toccata sopra i pedali* found in Frescobaldi's *Secondo Libro di Toccate*, Rome 1637), in which the hands weave motifs above a series of pedal points which themselves often follow a clear and to some extent standardized pattern of harmonies (tonic–dominant–subdominant–tonic, etc). Frescobaldi's own pedal points do not usually follow each other in such straightforward diatonic order.

ostinato: an 'obstinate' phrase, usually but not necessarily in the bass, which recurs persistently throughout the piece of music concerned; for typical phrases, see BWV 582. The term is also often used to designate a piece of music with such a phrase. 'Harmonic ostinato' signifies a chord or a group of harmonies so repeated or re-introduced; if the group were repeated on another degree of the scale (e.g. penultimate passage in BWV 544.ii), the effect would be that of a sequence, harmonic rather than melodic.

paraphrase technique: a modern term referring to the ornate treatment of a theme or cantus firmus in such a way as to produce a new melody within which, at least on paper, the original theme can be discerned. While examples by (e.g.) Böhm or Buxtehude tend to leave the notes of the original theme on the main beats – i.e., the theme is still recognizable, being not dispersed but merely separated by embellishments – those of J. S. Bach in *Clavierübung III* and elsewhere apply varying degrees of sophistication; see BWV 675–677, 681–682.

passus duriusculus: the term ('somewhat hard transition') found in the seventeenth century (C. Bernhard) for the descending chromatic tetrachord, i.e. the basic four-note tonic–dominant scale or group of adjacent notes 'coloured' by semitone passing-notes: Ex. 288. (For examples, see also BWV 131a, 537.ii, 588, 614.) Its frequent

Ex. 288

association with D dorian or D minor – related to the *tonus primus*, a survivor of the medieval modes – may reflect the traditionalism of the *passus duriusculus* in the seventeenth and eighteenth centuries.

per giusti intervalli: strictly, a term applied only to an inverted canon accomplished 'through exact intervals', i.e. one in which the *inversus* form moves by exactly the same intervals as the *rectus*, only inverted (e.g., when the *rectus* rises by a minor third the *inversus* falls by a minor third, not minor or major depending on harmonic convenience). Examples occur in late works (BWV 769.v bb1–27, *Musical Offering* BWV 1079.ix), but in freer movements, the canonic or imitative *inversus* is usually not exact (e.g. BWV 547.ii bb34–8 – it seems to be the approximate *inversus* form of this subject that suggested its chromatic metamorphosis later in the fugue).

permutation fugue: a modern term for a fugue in which all the parts at the close of the exposition are to reappear together on all subsequent entries of the subject, combined in different ways in invertible counterpoint. In a four-part fugue, it is as if there were three countersubjects, all clearly distinct and all able to function as the bass line when the permutation requires it. See also BWV 131a, 582.ii and 596.ii.

perpetuum mobile: a nineteenth-century phrase denoting a piece of music with non-stop motion in a lively tempo (e.g. unbroken semiquavers in *allegro* or *presto*); by analogy, the phrase is applied to one of the distinct fugue-subject types standardized by late-seventeenth-century composers (see 'motoric subject'). Non-stop motion obviously suits harpsichord fugues well; see BWV 855.ii and 944.ii.

phrygian cadence: a modern term for the cadence in which the bass falls a semitone, analogous to the church mode on E ('phrygian'): Ex. 289. While by 1700 such a cadence had become an Italianate

Ex. 289

formula for a half close before a lively movement in chamber sonatas and elsewhere (see also BWV 537.i), its appearance in *Clavierübung III* movements (BWV 671, 672) is more final and 'modal'.

plein jeu: see *grand jeu*

Positiv (*Pos*): the manual or *Werk* of an organ that resembles (and perhaps originated in) small movable or 'chamber' organs. Strictly it applies to any lesser manual of the organ (*Brustpositiv*,

Rückpositiv, Echo/Unter/Seiten-Positiv), and it cannot be assumed that copyists registering organ works meant by 'Pos' the *Rückpositiv* itself, which was found in few new organs in central Germany after 1700. In general, the term denotes a secondary manual.

rectus: see *inversus*

Rückpositiv (Rp): the 'back positive' or little organ placed behind the organist, usually in the front of the gallery, from which it speaks to a congregation more directly, immediately and sharply than the *Hauptwerk* or *Oberwerk*. By the early eighteenth century, such central German builders as Silbermann dispensed with it, handing over its functions as the solo, continuo, colourful and contrasting manual to the *Oberwerk*, whose key-action was lighter.

signum congruentiae: 'sign of agreement', a small graphic sign first found in the separate vocal parts of certain late medieval sources to indicate some point of coincidence between the various parts at that moment (e.g., that another voice answers in canon or drops out); by extension, a sign to warn the performer that 'something is happening here'.

Spielthema: modern term for the 'playful subject', one of the recognizable families of fugue themes standardized to some extent by the end of the seventeenth century, particularly at the hands of the north Germans. Such subjects as BWV 575, 577, 578 have *Spielthema* elements (broken chords, lively rhythms, spacious length).

suspirans: one of the most common of all *figurae*, beginning with a rest or 'sigh': Ex. 290(i). Although such theorists as Printz and Walther are not always clear in their terms and demarcations, it seems that the *suspirans* and the *figura corta* (q.v.) have each an essential shape, different in principle from the *tirata*, *circolo*, *tremolo*, *groppo* and *messanza*: Ex. 290(ii).

Ex. 290

(i)

(ii)

tetrachord (diatonic and chromatic): see *passus duriusculus*

Calendar

Phrases in quotation marks are taken from the Obituary or from contemporary documents, all to be found in *Dok* I–III.

1685–1700	(i) Eisenach. Possibly learnt organ from Johann Christoph Bach (1st cousin once removed), organist of the Georgenkirche. (ii) Ohrdruf. Possibly taught by brother Johann Christoph Bach (a pupil of Pachelbel).
Mar. 1700	Lüneburg, chorister of St Michaelskirche; possibly organ lessons there or in the Nikolaikirche or Johanniskirche (where Böhm organist). While there, said to have travelled 'occasionally' to Hamburg and to have heard Reincken there.
*c*1700	Perhaps learnt 'French taste' at the court of Celle (orchestra of the Duke of Braunschweig–Lüneburg).
1702–3	Applied for post of organist at the Jakobikirche, Sangerhausen.
1703	Few months at Weimar. May have studied Italian string music there. Received commission to test organ in the New Church, Arnstadt (Bonifatiuskirche, organ by F. Wender).
9 Aug. 1703 – 29 June 1707	Organist at Bonifatiuskirche, Arnstadt. Criticized for long interludes in chorales and for too bold and chromatic harmonization. At Arnstadt 'revealed the first fruits of his industriousness in the art of organ-playing and composition'.
1705–6	Winter journey to hear Buxtehude; probably heard special *Abendmusiken* performances (Dec. 1705).
1707 – 25 June 1708	Organist at Divi-Blasii-Kirche, Mühlhausen (organ by Wender, new contract 15 June 1707); possibly tested organ (Reformation Day 1709?).
July 1708 – Dec. 1717	Organist to the court of Weimar, a position enabling Bach to perform 'well-ordered church music'; 'here too he wrote most of his organ works'.
14 Dec. 1713	Invited to post of organist at Liebfrauenkirche, Halle.
2 Mar. 1714	Promoted at Weimar to *Konzertmeister*.
1 May 1716	With Kuhnau and C. F. Rolle, reported on new organ of the Liebfrauenkirche, Halle.
Aug. 1717	On payroll of Prince Leopold of Anhalt–Cöthen as Kapellmeister; allowed to leave Weimar 2 Dec. 1717.
Sept. (?) 1717	Visit to Dresden; extempore competition with Louis Marchand called off.
1717–23	Kapellmeister to the court of Cöthen.
17 Dec. 1717	Reported on the rebuilt organ of the Paulinerkirche, Leipzig.
Oct.–Nov. 1720	Played to Reincken at the Katharinenkirche, Hamburg; 23 Nov. 1720 leaves Hamburg after unsuccessful candidature for post of organist at the Jakobikirche (organ by Arp Schnitger).

1 June 1723	'Entered upon the cantorate' at Thomaskirche, Leipzig.
2 Nov. 1723	Inaugurates small new organ at Störmthal (by Z. Hildebrandt, still extant).
25 June 1724	New organ at Johanniskirche, Gera, tested and dedicated by the 'famous Cantor and Kapellmeister Bach' (organ by J. G. Finke).
Sept. 1725	Plays organ of Sophienkirche, Dresden (by G. Silbermann).
14 Sept. 1731	Plays organ of Sophienkirche, Dresden, where eldest son (W. F. Bach) is appointed organist 1733.
Sept. 1732	Examines rebuilt organ of the Martinikirche, Kassel (by H. Scherer, rebuilt by N. Becker).
1 Dec. 1736	Plays large new organ in the Frauenkirche, Dresden (by G. Silbermann), for two hours in the presence of 'many persons of rank'.
Michaelmas 1739	*Clavierübung III* published by the author.
1739	Visits the large new organ of Altenburg Schlosskapelle (by G. H. Trost).
26 Sept. 1746	With G. Silbermann, examines the large new organ of the Wenzels-kirche, Naumburg (by Z. Hildebrandt).
1746 or later	*Six Chorales* published by J. G. Schübler (Zella).
c1748	*Canonic Variations on Vom Himmel hoch* published by B. Schmid (Nuremberg).
8 May 1747	Plays organ of the Heiligegeistkirche, Potsdam (by J. J. Wagner).
28 July 1750	Dies in Leipzig, 'mourned by all true connoisseurs of music'.
1751	*Art of Fugue* published.

List of Musical Sources

These notes accompany only the more important MSS referred to in the main text and are designed to give a summary of the origin and contents of those sources. They do not describe every source that is necessary for a complete edition of Bach's organ works, nor do they give details beyond those of a summary. The dispersal of German manuscripts during and after the last war has also meant that some present locations are uncertain or temporary: this summary therefore identifies MSS only by the more familiarly used catalogue numbers. Further information on most of the sources can be found in *NBA* IV/2 *KB*, *NBA* IV/3 *KB*, Kast 1958, Krause 1964, Blechschmidt 1965 and Zietz 1969 (see List of References).

Abbreviations

Am.B. Amalien-Bibliothek (Berlin, Musikbibliothek der Prinzessin Anna Amalia von Preussen)

BB Berlin, Deutsche Staatsbibliothek, Mus. MSS (previously Preussische Staatsbibliothek (formerly Königliche Bibliothek), Musikabteilung)

Brussels Brussels, Bibliothèque Royale de Belgique

LM New Haven, Connecticut, Yale University Music Library

Lpz Leipzig

Lpz Go . S. Lpz Sammlung Manfred Gorke

Lpz MB Leipzig, Musikbibliothek (including former Musikbibliothek Peters)
Note: references in the text to 'Lpz MB MS 1, 5' etc indicate MB MS 1, section 5.

Lpz Poel Lpz MB Poelchau Mus. MSS

P P-signatures [for 'Partituren', scores] of BB – dispersed

St St-signatures [for 'Stimmen', parts] of BB – dispersed

Vienna Vienna, Österreichische Nationalbibliothek

Am.B. 45: Copy made for Anna Amalia's library of the print of *Clavierübung III*, entitled '. . . Catechismus Gesänge vor die Orgel / Opus 3'.

Am.B. 51, Am.B. 51a: Two complete copies of the Six Sonatas BWV 525–530, the first made by an unknown scribe, the second said (erroneously – see Am.B. 60) to be by J. F. Agricola; the first derives from P 271, the second from Am.B. 51 (Emery 1957 p22).

Am.B. 54: Album of three fascicles made by one unknown copyist: (i) BWV 572; (ii) music by C. P. E. Bach; (iii) BWV 545–548, 543, 544, the last fascicle a copy of Am.B. 60.

Am.B. 60: Copy by the scribe of Am.B. 51a (*BJ* 1970 pp6of), i.e. not J. F. Agricola as previously thought but an unknown copyist in the Berlin circle, working after 1754. MS includes BWV 545, 546, 547, 548, 543, 544.

Am.B. 543, Am.B. 544: Copies of BWV 541 and 566 respectively, made by the same unknown scribe.

Am.B. 606: Album of 'Seven Fugues' written by several copyists of the last third of the 18th century; includes BWV 733, 535.ii, 539.ii and 580.

Andreas-Bach-Buch (Lpz MB III.8.4): Important album of over 50 pieces by several composers (including Böhm, Buxtehude, Buttstedt, Kuhnau, Pachelbel, Reincken), made by unknown copyists from about 1710/15 (perhaps mostly J. Bernhard Bach – cf. Möller MS below); provides a unique source for certain pieces. Mostly free keyboard works including several in ostinato form; see notes to BWV 582. Work in progress on the MS suggests that the copies of BWV 582, 574 and 563 belong to a later, third phase in the make-up of the MS, BWV 578 and 570 to a second.

BB 40644: see Möller MS.

Brussels Fétis 2960 (Brussels, Bibliothèque Royale de Belgique; now MS II.4093): Late-18th-century copy of miscellaneous works (BWV 564, 910, 913, 915, 992, 911, 912, 571, 574, 993, 916, 922, 550, 990, 832, 989, 532.ii); once described as early and autograph (Dart *AM* 1970 pp326–8) but subsequently shown to be neither (*AM* 1971 pp108–9).

LM 4718: 'Preludio con fuga e Trio' BWV 545 with 529.ii, copy in the hand of J. G. Walther.

LM 4720: Copy dated August 1840 made for J. C. H. Rinck 'von J. P. Kellern, Organist in Frankfurt a/M'.

LM 4838: Album of free organ works made in first half of 19th century (?), owned and probably written by J. C. H. Rinck; includes BUXWV 148.

LM 4839a–i: Collection of nine MSS, perhaps of similar provenance to LM 4838, written in part by M. G. Fischer and in part by J. C. H. Rinck.

LM 4842a–h: Collection of eight MSS, with free organ works as follows: BWV 525 (4842a), 569 (4842e), 578 (4842g), 596 fragment, also 538.ii and 572.i (4842h); owned by J. C. H. Rinck.

LM 4941: Copies of BWV 578 and 948, made by the scribes of LM 4838 and LM 4839.

LM 5056: One of the most important tablature-books of the second half of the 17th century, dated 1688; bought by J. Becker in 1776 and acquired by J. C. H. Rinck in 1836. Becker added BWV 547 and 548, perhaps directly or indirectly from J. P. Kellner sources (Riedel 1960 pp100, 102).

Lpz Go.S.26 (Leipzig, Bach-Archiv MS Go.S.26): Early-19th-century copies by one Hohlstein, a copyist with access to MSS of the Kittel circle.

Lpz Go.S.318a Album of pieces copied and signed E. Grell, 1819; includes BWV 131a, 549, 550, the ricercars and five canons from the *Musical Offering*, and BWV 539.ii.

Lpz MB MS 1 (Scheibner MS 1): Album of nineteen fascicles, each one devoted to a separate work (mostly of J. S. Bach), copied by J. A. G. Wechmar in the second half of the 18th century: BWV 612, 562.i, 529, 527, 547, 548, 917, 946, 544. Works copied in unknown hands are BWV 718, 790, 579 and 574.

Lpz MB MS 3 (Scheibner MS 3): Album of five fascicles, of which two are organ works of J. S. Bach: BWV 639 and 540.ii, the latter copied by J. A. G. Wechmar.

Lpz MB MS 7 (Mempell–Preller MS x 7): Album of thirty-eight fascicles, of which some are devoted to free organ works copied either by J. N. Mempell and his scribe (before 1747: BWV 585, 586, 1027a, 527.i, 548; perhaps 532.i, 552, 550 in the same hand?) or by J. G. Preller (between 1743 and 1753: BWV 597, 541, 533a, 588, 569). See also notes to this MS in vol. II.

Lpz MB III.8.4: see Andreas-Bach-Buch.

Lpz MB III.8.14, 16, 18: Single copies, made early in the 19th century, of (respectively) BWV 543; 538 and 569; and 579.

Lpz MB III.8.20: Copies, made by Dröbs early in the 19th century, of BWV

532.ii, 565, 551 and 542.i. These four pieces are also found in copies made by late scribes: P 595 (mostly J. Ringk) and P 924 (Grasnick).

Lpz MB III.8.21: Copies, made by Dröbs, of BWV 544, 534, 545 and 548.

Lpz MB III.8.22: Early-19th-century copies of BWV 549, 578, 131a and 546.

Lpz MB III.8.29: Copies, made by Dröbs, of BWV 574 and 540.ii.

Lpz MB MS a 1: Autograph MS: see BWV 541.

Lpz MB MS R 16: Album of nine fascicles, containing two free organ works – BWV 552.ii (end of 18th century) and the last section of BWV 582.ii (from last beat of b233 to end), copied by the chief scribe of the Andreas-Bach-Buch.

Lpz Poel 12: Single copy of BWV 545a, made c1780/90.

Lpz Poel 14, 15, 19, 20, 21, 24: Single copies of BWV 548.ii, 548.i–ii, 535, 578, 542.ii and 544 respectively, made c1815/20, probably from Kittel sources, by J. G. Weigand.

Lpz Poel 16, 18: Early-19th-century copies of BWV 540.i and 580 (with Anh.70) respectively.

Lpz Poel 28: Late-18th-century copies of BWV 540.ii, 875a and 571.

Lpz Poel 32: Copy of BWV 547, made by C. F. Penzel c1755/60.

Lpz Poel 39: Album devoted to some 60 organ chorales of J. S. Bach, possibly based on copies by J. C. Kittel; perhaps in the hand of J. N. Gebhardi (from c1803?) or another copyist in the 'Kittel circle'.

Lpz Poel 355: Like Lpz Poel 14 etc, copies made by J. G. Weigand of a group of fugues: BWV 574, 552, Anh.44, 867.ii, 680.

Möller MS (BB 40644): Album of copies of over 50 pieces (by Albinoni, Böhm, Bruhns, Buxtehude, Flor, Lebègue, Reincken and others), made by several copyists around 1705/10; mostly free keyboard works. Both this MS and the Andreas-Bach-Buch have more pieces by J. S. Bach than by any other single composer.

Oxford Bodleian MSS (Oxford, Bodleian Library, unnumbered MSS): Late copies owned by Mendelssohn.

P 203, 204, 207: Large albums made towards the end of the 18th century, copied by C. F. G. Schwenke amongst others (with dates '1783' in P 203 and '1781' in P 204), containing pieces from *Das Wohltemperirte Clavier* I–II, and including certain free organ works: BWV 542.ii (J. S. Borsch), 566, 542.ii, 532 and 588 (Schwenke), 574a (anon).

P 213, 218: Albums of several fascicles, including free organ works (BWV 575, 539.ii, 549), copied by unknown scribes of the later 18th century.

P 224: *Klavierbüchlein für Anna Magdalena Bach*, a partly autograph album of music copied c1722–5.

P 228: Album of several fascicles, containing the arrangements of BWV 527.ii, 526.ii, 526.iii (early 19th century), and from the same period a copy of BWV 548.ii, 'newer' than the autograph MS according to *BG* 15 p. xxxiii, and inscribed 'copy from the B & H shop' ('aus der B & H-Handlung').

P 271: Largely autograph album containing groups of works perhaps not originally bound together: the organ sonatas, the first 15 of 'The Eighteen' ('revised' version), the *Canonic Variations* BWV 769a and (in earlier handwriting, but bound in later) BWV 660a. Two pieces were added by Altnikol (BWV 666, 667), and another by an unknown copyist (BWV 668). The sonata copies are dated c1730 (Dadelsen 1958 p104), the rest variously dated c1744–8 or later. Eventually owned by C. P. E. Bach, though perhaps originally passed to W. F. Bach (Wolff 1974).

P 272: Complete copy of the Six Sonatas, made by W. F. Bach and Anna Magdalena Bach; see introduction to BWV 525–530.

P 274: Album made up of copies of BWV 886.ii (autograph), 548 (part autograph, part J. P. Kellner), 547 and 531.i (J. P. Kellner), 582 and 813 (unknown copyists); 886.ii dated c1735–44/6 (Dadelsen 1958 p113).

P 276, 277: Albums copied by 'Anon 401' (Kast 1958 p18): (i) BWV 545, 546, 547, 548, 543 and 544 in the same order as (e.g.) Am.B. 60; and (ii) BWV 540, 582, 562.i, 590, 538, 566.

P 279: Copy, after 1820, of 12 keyboard works from the Andreas-Bach-Buch, including BWV 578, 570, 574b, 563, 582.

P 282: 19th-century copy of BWV 542.ii, 540.ii, 538, 545.i + 529.ii + 545.ii, 533, 549, 539.ii; a 'later, poor' source for BWV 538, 539 (*BG* 15 p. xxiv).

P 286, 287: Two collections of 18th-century MS copies, including amongst the free organ works BWV 545.i + 529.ii + 545.ii, 566, 564, 546, 590, 571 (all by J. P. Kellner), and 531, 547, 595, 594, 582, 538, 583, 532.i, 548, 552.i, 533, 549, 540.ii; also 542.ii (J. S. Borsch) and 550 (Michel).

P 288, 289: Two collections of MS copies, including amongst the free organ works three copies of BWV 572 (one by J. P. Kellner, two of the second half of the 18th century), other copies by Kellner (BWV 542.ii, 541, 562.i, 569, 543 (the last not certainly by Kellner)) and by unknown hands of the second half of the 18th century (BWV 1039.ii, 578, 535, 528.iii, 542, 593, 585, 540.i, 533, 549, 592, 596, 1079.v).

P 290: Album of pieces copied by 'Anon 303' (Kast 1958 p20), the copyist of many C. P. E. Bach compositions: BWV 545a.i, 545, 546, 543, 541, 540, 542.ii, 582, 562.i, 590, 538, 548, 544, 547.

P 291: Album of several fascicles of organ music by various composers, made by several copyists of the late 18th century; free organ works are BWV 588 and 532.

P 301, 303, 304, 308, 313, 316: Copies made by several copyists working in Vienna at the end of the 18th century and the beginning of the 19th; free organ works include BWV 568, 533.i, 549.i, 591, 568, 539.ii, 570, 563, 131a, 578 and 579 (the last four by A. Werner?). P 313 headed 'Four fugues from the MS of Kittel'.

P 319: Album including copies, made by J. C Westphal, of BWV 541, 528.iii, 538, 533 and 549; and a 19th-century copy of BWV 131a.

P 320: Important album probably written by L. E. Gebhardi (Kittel circle) and including BWV 533, 549, 542.ii, 572, 592, 562.i, 131a, 546, 541, 547, 578, 535, 582, 566 and 588, and a Fugue in D minor by C. Flor.

P 400a–c: Separate copies of BWV 592 (second half of 18th century), 593 and 594 (the last two by J. F. Agricola 1738–41: Dürr 1970 p49).

P 414, 416: copies of (i) BWV 572.i (c1800) and (ii) 538, 566 (second half of 18th century), in albums of miscellaneous keyboard music, including pieces from *Das Wohltemperirte Clavier* (*The 48*) and the Two- and Three-part Inventions.

P 557: Volume by Grasnick containing a similar selection of works to P 320.

P 595: Album of nine separate MSS, including copies of BWV 542 (18th century), 532.ii, 541, 551 and 565 (the last four copied by J. Ringk).

P 596: Separate copies of BWV 538, 546 and 540, by one Kauffmann, probably a Berlin organist at the end of the 18th century.

P 642: Copy, by an unknown 19th-century hand, of BWV 551, 565 and 550.

P 658: Copies of BWV 545 and 566 following three of Handel's *Six Fugues* (pub. London and Paris c1735), all in the hand of M. G. Fischer, 1792.

P 801: Important album of several fascicles written chiefly by J. T. Krebs and J. G. Walther, presumably during J. S. Bach's Weimar period; about two-fifths of the contents are works of Bach, the rest by Bustyn, Buxtehude, Kauffmann, J. L. Krebs, Lübeck, Telemann and an important group of French composers (d'Andrieu, d'Anglebert, Clérambault,

Dieupart, Lebègue, Laroux, Marchand, Neufville and Nivers), copied mostly by Walther. The album contains a particularly important collection of organ chorales (see notes to this MS in vol. II); free organ works are BWV 572 and 569.

P 802: Important album of several fascicles and possibly of several phases, written chiefly by J. T. Krebs (responsible to some extent for copying the music of J. S. Bach?) and J. G. Walther (music of other composers). P 802 seems to be the oldest of the three albums P 801, P 802 and P 803, and about three-fifths of its contents are devoted to organ chorales of J. S. Bach (see notes to this MS in vol. II); for the free organ works, see P 803.

P 803: Important album of several fascicles devoted to free pieces (except for the chorale BWV 663a) which may be for organ or other keyboard instrument; copied mostly by J. T. Krebs, J. G. Walther and J. L. Krebs, but including also some later music. The works of J. S. Bach are BWV 540, 543, 564, 542.ii, 578, 537, 582, 566, and 538, of which BWV 543 and 564 were copied by unknown scribes of the second half of the 18th century.

P 804: Album of copies by J. P. Kellner and several other copyists and containing free pieces for organ and other keyboard instruments. The works of J. S. Bach are BWV 579, 570.i, 563.i, 536.i, 536.ii, 592, 563.ii, 535.1 and 533.ii.

P 837: Early-19th-century album written by several copyists (BWV 567 inscribed 'Wien...1829') and including BWV 545, 546, 547, 548, 543, 538, 541, 544, 542.ii, 566, 552.i, 552.ii, 567, 536, 569, 572 and 588.

P 840: Copy by C. A. Klein of the Six Sonatas (companion MS to P 839 (Two- and Three-part Inventions)).

P 924, 925: Two early-19th-century groups of organ works: (i) BWV 542, 532, 551, 565, 550 (by Grasnick); (ii) BWV 543–548 arranged for piano four hands (unknown copyist; date 1832).

P 1071: Album made *c*1800 and including BWV 567, 542.ii, 542.i, 564.i (incomplete).

P 1115: Album probably copied chiefly by A. Kühnel and containing miscellaneous trio pieces, entitled 'No. 41 / 35 / Orgeltrio's / von / Sebastian Bach': BWV 645, 648, 646, 647, 649, 650, 529.ii, 583, 525.i, 664a, 769, 528.ii, 759, Anh.74.

Scholz MSS: Copies made by one Scholz, organist in Nuremberg in the eighteenth century. Kept at present in the Johann-Sebastian-Bach-Institut, Göttingen.

Schubring MSS: Copies made by or for J. Schubring and used in the *BG* edition. The identity and whereabouts of MSS in this group are now mostly unknown.

List of references

A few sources cited only once or twice in the text (where they are fully identified) are omitted from the following list.

Albrecht 1969 | C. Albrecht, 'J. S. Bachs *Clavierübung Dritter Theil*: Versuch einer Deutung', *BJ* 55 (1969) 46–66

AM | *Acta Musicologica*

Apel 1967 | W. Apel, *Geschichte der Orgel- und Klaviermusik bis 1700* (Kassel, 1967); English trans. H. Tischler, *The History of Keyboard Music to 1700* (Bloomington, Indiana, 1972)

BG | *Johann Sebastian Bachs Werke*, Bach-Gesellschaft edition (46 vols., Leipzig, 1851–99)

B & H | *Joh. Seb. Bach: Sämtliche Orgelwerke*, Breitkopf & Härtel edition, ed. Heinz Lohmann (Wiesbaden, 1968– , in progress)

BJ | *Bach-Jahrbuch*

Bernhard | J. Müller-Blattau, *Die Kompositionslehre Heinrich Schützens in der Fassung seines Schülers Christoph Bernhard* (Kassel, 2nd edn 1963); English trans. W. Hilse, 'The Treatises of Christoph Bernhard', *Music Forum* 3 (1973) 1–196

Besseler 1950 | H. Besseler and G. Kraft, *Johann Sebastian Bach in Thüringen* (Weimar, 1950)

Besseler 1955 | H. Besseler, 'J. S. Bach als Wegbereiter', *Archiv für Musikwissenschaft* 12 (1955) 1–39

Blechschmidt 1965 | E. R. Blechschmidt, *Die Amalien-Bibliothek: Musikbibliothek der Prinzessin Anna Amalia von Preussen (1723–1787) . . .* (Berlin, 1965)

Blume 1968 | F. Blume, 'J. S. Bach's Youth', *MQ* 54 (1968) 1–30

Braun 1972 | H. Braun, 'Eine Gegenüberstellung von Original und Bearbeitung, dargestellt an der Entlehnung eines Corellischen Fugenthemas durch J. S. Bach', *BJ* 58 (1972) 5–11

Bruggaier 1959 | E. Bruggaier, *Studien zur Geschichte des Orgelpedalspiels in Deutschland bis zur Zeit Johann Sebastian Bachs* (Frankfurt, 1959)

Bullivant 1959 | R. Bullivant, 'The Fugal Technique of J. S. Bach' (unpublished diss., Oxford, 1959–60)

BUXWV | G. Karstädt, *Thematisch–systematisches Verzeichnis der musikalischen Werke von Dietrich Buxtehude* (Wiesbaden, 1974)

Chailley 1974 | J. Chailley, *Les Chorals pour Orgue de J.-S. Bach* (Paris, 1974)

DDT | *Denkmäler deutscher Tonkunst*

DTÖ | *Denkmäler der Tonkunst in Österreich*

Dadelsen 1957 | G. von Dadelsen, *Bemerkungen zur Handschrift Johann Sebastian Bachs, seiner Familie und seines Kreises*, Tübinger Bach-Studien 1 (Trossingen, 1957)

Dadelsen 1958 | G. von Dadelsen, *Beiträge zur Chronologie der Werke Johann Sebastian Bachs*, Tübinger Bach-Studien 4/5 (Trossingen, 1958)

Dalton 1966 | J. Dalton, 'Bach Interpretation', *MT* 107 (1966) 341, 440, 536ff

David & Mendel 1945 | H. T. David and A. Mendel, *The Bach Reader* (New York, 1945; revised edn with supplement, 1966)

Dietrich 1931 | F. Dietrich, 'Analogieformen in Bachs Tokkaten und Präludien für die Orgel', *BJ* 28 (1931) 51–71

Dok I | *Bach-Dokumente* I, ed. W. Neumann and H.-J. Schulze (Leipzig/Kassel, 1963)

Dok II | *Bach-Dokumente* II, ed. W. Neumann and H.-J. Schulze (Leipzig/Kassel, 1969)

Dok III | *Bach-Dokumente* III, ed. H.-J. Schulze (Leipzig/Kassel, 1972)

Dufourcq 1948 | N. Dufourcq, *J. S. Bach, Le Maître de l'Orgue* (Paris, 1948)

Dürr 1951 | A. Dürr, *Studien über die frühen Kantaten J. S. Bachs* (Leipzig, 1951) (cf. Dürr 1977)

Dürr 1954 | A. Dürr, 'Neues über die Möllersche handschrift', *BJ* 41 (1954) 75–9

Dürr 1970 | A. Dürr, 'Zur Chronologie der Handschrift Johann Christoph Altnickols und Johann Friedrich Agricolas', *BJ* 56 (1970) 44–63

Dürr 1977 | A. Dürr, *Studien über die frühen Kantaten J. S. Bachs* (2nd, enlarged edn, Wiesbaden, 1977)

Ehricht 1949–50 | K. Ehricht, 'Die zyklische Gestalt und die Aufführungsmöglichkeit des III. Teiles der Klavierübung von Joh. Seb. Bach', *BJ 51* (1949–50) 40–56

Einstein 1936 | A. Einstein, 'Mozart's Four String Trio Preludes to Fugues of Bach', *MT* 77 (1936) 209–16

Eller 1956 | R. Eller, 'Zur Frage Bach–Vivaldi', in *Bericht über den internationalen musikwissenschaftlichen Kongress Hamburg 1956* (Kassel, 1956) 80–5

Eller 1958 | R. Eller, 'Geschichtliche Stellung und Wandlung der Vivaldischen Konzertform', in *Kongress-Bericht Wien 1956* (Graz, 1958) 150–5

Emery 1952 | W. Emery, *Notes on Bach's Organ Works*, I: *Eight Short Preludes and Fugues* (London, 1952)

Emery 1957 | W. Emery, *Notes on Bach's Organ Works*, IV–V: *Six Sonatas for Two Manuals and Pedal* (London, 1957)

Emery 1957–8 | W. Emery, 'The Dating of Bach's Organ Works', *The Organ* 37 (1957–8) 181–7

Emery 1959 | W. Emery (ed.), *J. S. Bach: Prelude, Trio and Fugue in B flat*, Novello Early Organ Music, vol 12 (London, 1959)

Emery 1966 | W. Emery, 'Some Speculations on the Development of Bach's Organ Style', *MT* 107 (1966) 596–603

Emery 1974 | W. Emery, 'Cadence and Chronology', in *Studies in Renaissance and Baroque Music in Honor of Arthur Mendel* (Kassel, 1974) 156–64

Eppstein 1965 | H. Eppstein, 'J. S. Bachs Triosonate G dur (BWV 1039) und ihre Beziehungen zur Sonate für Gambe und Cembalo G dur (BWV 1027)', *Mf* 18 (1965) 126–37

Eppstein 1966 | H. Eppstein, *Studien über J. S. Bachs Sonaten für ein Melodieinstrument und obligates Cembalo* (Uppsala, 1966)

Eppstein 1969 | H. Eppstein, 'Grundzüge in J. S. Bachs Sonatenschaffen', *BJ* 55 (1969) 5–30

Eppstein 1976 | H. Eppstein, 'Chronologieprobleme in Johann Sebastian Bachs Suiten für Soloinstrument', *BJ* 61 (1976) 35–57

Falck 1913 | M. Falck, *Wilhelm Friedemann Bach* (Leipzig, 1913)

Finke-Hecklinger 1970 | D. Finke-Hecklinger, *Tanzcharaktere in Johann Sebastian Bachs Vokalmusik*, Tübinger Bach-Studien 6 (Trossingen, 1970)

Fock 1974 | G. Fock, *Arp Schnitger und seine Schule* (Kassel, 1974)

Forkel 1802 | J. N. Forkel, *Ueber Johann Sebastian Bachs Leben, Kunst und Kunstwerke* (Leipzig, 1802). (References above to 'Forkel's Catalogue 1802' are to the thematic index included in this publication.)

Frotscher 1935 | G. Frotscher, *Geschichte des Orgelspiels und der Orgelkomposition*, 2 vols. (Berlin, 1934–5)

Geck 1968 | M. Geck, *Nicolaus Bruhns: Leben und Werk* (Cologne, 1968)

Geiringer 1966 | K. Geiringer, *Johann Sebastian Bach: The Culmination of an Era* (London, 1966)

Grace c1922 | Harvey Grace, *The Organ works of Bach* (London, c1922)

Gwinner 1968 | V. Gwinner, 'Bachs d-moll Tokkata als Credo-Vertonung', *MuK* 35 (1968) 240–2

Hammerschlag 1950 | J. Hammerschlag, 'Der weltliche Charakter in Bachs Orgelwerken', *Bach-Probleme* (Leipzig, 1950)

Hering 1974 | H. Hering, 'Spielerische Elemente in J. S. Bachs Klaviermusik', *BJ* 60 (1974) 44–69

Hoffmann-Erbrecht 1972 | L. Hoffmann-Erbrecht, 'J. S. Bach als Schöpfer des Klavierkonzerts', in *Quellenstudien zur Musik*, ed. K. Dorfmüller (Frankfurt, 1972) 69–77

Kast 1958 | P. Kast, *Die Bach-Handschriften der Berliner Staatsbibliothek*, Tübinger Bach-Studien 2/3 (Trossingen, 1958)

Keller 1937 | H. Keller, 'Unechte Orgelwerke Bachs', *BJ* 34 (1937) 59–82

Keller 1948 | H. Keller, *Die Orgelwerke Bachs* (Leipzig, 1948)

Kilian 1961 | D. Kilian, 'J. S. Bach, Praeludium und Fuge d-moll, BWV 539', *Mf* 14 (1961) 323–8

Kilian 1962 | D. Kilian, 'Studie über J. S. Bachs Fantasie und Fuge c-moll', in *Hans Albrecht in Memoriam* (Kassel, 1962) 127–35

Kilian 1969 | D. Kilian, 'Dreisätzige Fassungen Bachscher Orgelwerke', in *Bach-Interpretationen*, ed. M. Geck (Göttingen, 1969) 12–21

Kilian 1978 | D. Kilian, 'Über einige neue Aspekte zur Quellenüberlieferung von Klavier- und Orgelwerken Johann Sebastian Bachs', *BJ* 64 (1978) 61–72

Kinsky 1936 | G. Kinsky, 'Pedalklavier oder Orgel bei Bach?', *AM* 8 (1936) 158–61

Klein 1970 | H.-G. Klein, *Der Einfluss der Vivaldischen Konzertform im Instrumentalwerk Johann Sebastian Bachs* (Strasbourg/Baden-Baden, 1970)

Kloppers 1966 | J. Kloppers, *Die Interpretation und Wiedergabe der Orgelwerke Bachs* (Frankfurt, 1966)

Klotz 1950 | H. Klotz, 'Bachs Orgeln und seine Orgelmusik', *Mf* 3 (1950) 189–203

Klotz 1962 | H. Klotz, 'J. S. Bach und die Orgel', *MuK* 32 (1962) 49–55

Klotz 1969a | H. Klotz, 'Les Critères de l'interprétation française sont-ils applicables à la musique d'orgue de J.-S. Bach?', in *L'Interprétation de la musique française aux XVIIe et XVIIIe Siècles*, Colloques Internationaux du CNRS (Paris, 1969) 155–72

Klotz 1972 | H. Klotz, private communication

Klotz 1975 | H. Klotz, *Über die Orgelkunst der Gotik, der Renaissance und des Barock* (Kassel, 2nd edn 1975)

Krause 1964 | P. Krause, *Handschriften der Werke Johann Sebastian Bachs in der Musikbibliothek der Stadt Leipzig* (Leipzig, 1964)

Krey 1956 | J. Krey, 'Bachs Orgelmusik in der Weimarer Zeit' (unpublished diss., Jena, 1956)

Kolneder 1965 | W. Kolneder, *Antonio Vivaldi 1678–1741: Leben und Werke* (Wiesbaden, 1965)

Leaver 1975 | R. A. Leaver, 'Bach's "Clavierübung III": Some Historical and Theological Considerations', *Organ Yearbook* 6 (1975) 17–32

Löffler 1940–8 | H. Löffler, 'Johann Tobias Krebs und Matthias Sojka, zwei Schüler Johann Sebastian Bachs', *BJ* 37 (1940–8) 136–48

Mf | *Die Musikforschung*

MGG | *Die Musik in Geschichte und Gegenwart*, ed. F. Blume, 14 vols. (Kassel, 1949–68) plus Suppl. (Kassel, 1970–)

MQ | *Musical Quarterly*

MT | *Musical Times*

MuK | *Musik und Kirche*

Mattheson 1713 | J. Mattheson, *Das neu-eröffnete Orchestre* (Hamburg, 1713)

Mattheson 1739 | J. Mattheson, *Der vollkommene Capellmeister* (Hamburg, 1739)

May 1974 | E. May, 'J. G. Walther and the Lost Weimar Autographs of Bach's Organ works', in *Studies in Renaissance and Baroque Music in Honor of Arthur Mendel* (Kassel, 1974) 264–82

NBA | [J. S. Bach], *Neue Ausgabe sämtlicher Werke*, Neue Bach-Ausgabe (Leipzig/Kassel, 1954– , in progress)

NBA KB | Neue Bach-Ausgabe, *Kritischer Bericht* (Critical Commentary)

NZfM | *Neue Zeitschrift für Musik*

Neumann 1967 | W. Neumann, *Handbuch der Kantaten Johann Sebastian Bachs* (Leipzig, 3rd edn 1967)

Novello | *The Organ Works of Bach*, Novello edition, ed. W. Emery and others (18 vols., London, v.d., revisions in progress)

Oppel 1906 | R. Oppel, 'Die grosse A-moll-Fuge für Orgel und ihre Vorlage', *BJ* 3 (1906) 74–8

Oppel 1910 | R. Oppel, 'Über Joh. Kasp. Ferd. Fischers Einfluss auf Joh. Seb. Bach', *BJ* 7 (1910) 63–9

Pauly 1964 | H.-J. Pauly, *Die Fuge in den Orgelwerken Dietrich Buxtehudes* (Regensburg, 1964)

Peters | [J. S. Bach], *Compositionen für Orgel, kritisch–korrekte Ausgabe*, Peters edition: vols. 1–7, ed. F. G. Griepenkerl (Leipzig, 1844–7); vol. 8, ed. F. A. Roitzsch (Leipzig, 1852); vol. 9, ed. Roitzsch, rev. M. Seiffert, H. Keller (3rd edn, Leipzig, 1940); further revisions in progress

Plantinga 1967 | L. B. Plantinga, *Schumann as Critic* (New Haven, Conn., 1967)

Praetorius 1906 | E. Praetorius, 'Neues zur Bach-Forschung', *Sammelbände der internationalen Musikgesellschaft* 8 (1906–7) 95–101

Printz 1696 | W. C. Printz, *Phrynidis Mytilenaei oder des satyrischen Componisten anderer Theil* (Leipzig/Dresden, 2nd edn 1696)

Radulescu 1979 | M. Radulescu, 'On the Form of Johann Sebastian Bach's Passacaglia in C minor', *Organ Yearbook* 11 (1980)

Riedel 1960 | F. W. Riedel, *Quellenkundliche Beiträge zur Geschichte der Musik für Tasteninstrumente in der 2. Hälfte des 17. Jahrhunderts* (Kassel, 1960)

Ryom 1966 | P. Ryom, 'La Comparaison entre les versions différentes d'un Concerto d'Antonio Vivaldi transcrit par J. S. Bach', *Dansk Aarbog for Musikforskning* (1966–7) 92–111

Ryom 1973 | P. Ryom, *Antonio Vivaldi: Table des concordances des oeuvres* (Copenhagen, 1973)

Ryom 1977 | P. Ryom, *Les Manuscrits de Vivaldi* (Copenhagen, 1977)

Schering 1902 | A. Schering, 'Zur Bach-Forschung', *Sammelbände der internationalen Musikgesellschaft* 4 (1902–3) 234–43

Schmieder *BWV* | W. Schmieder, *Thematisch–Systematisches Verzeichnis der musikalischen Werke von Johann Sebastian Bach* (Leipzig, 1950)

Schneider 1911 | M. Schneider, 'Das sogenannte Orgelkonzert d-moll von Wilhelm Friedemann Bach', *BJ* 8 (1911) 23–36

Schneider 1914 | M. Schneider, 'Der Generalbass J. S. Bachs', *Peters Jahrbuch* 1914/15, 27–42

Schöneich 1947/8 | F. Schöneich, 'Untersuchungen zur Form der Orgelpräludien und Fugen des jungen Bach' (unpublished diss., Göttingen, 1947/8)

Schrammek 1954 | W. Schrammek, 'Die Musikgeschichtliche Stellung der Orgeltriosonaten von Joh. Seb. Bach', *BJ* 41 (1954) 7–28

Schrammek 1975 | W. Schrammek, 'Johann Sebastian Bach, Gottfried Silbermann, und die französische Orgelkunst', *Bach-Studien* 5 (Leipzig, 1975) 93–107

Schreyer 1911/13 | J. Schreyer, *Beiträge zur Bach-Kritik*, 2 vols. (Leipzig, 1911–13) II: 34–6

Schulze 1966 | H.-J. Schulze, 'Beiträge zur Bach-Quellenforschung', *Bericht über den internationalen musikwissenschaftlichen Kongress Leipzig 1966* (Leipzig, 1970) 269–75

Schulze 1966a | H.-J. Schulze, 'Wer intavoliert Johann Sebastian Bachs Lautenkompositionen?', *Mf* 19 (1966) 32–9

Schulze 1972 | H.-J. Schulze, 'J. S. Bach's Concerto-Arrangements for Organ – Studies or Commissioned Works?', *Organ Yearbook* 3 (1972) 4–13 (cf. Schulze 1978)

Schulze 1973 | H.-J. Schulze, 'Das c-moll-Trio BWV 585 – eine Orgeltranskription Johann Sebastian Bachs?', *Deutsches Jahrbuch der Musikwissenschaft* 16 (1973) 150–5

Schulze 1974 | H.-J. Schulze (ed.), *J. F. Fasch: Sonate C-moll für zwei Violinen und Cembalo*, Peters edn 9041 (Leipzig, 1974)

Schulze 1974a | H.-J. Schulze, 'Wie entstand die Bach-Sammlung Mempell–Preller?', *BJ* 60 (1974) 104–22

Schulze 1977 | H.-J. Schulze (ed.), *Katalog der Sammlung Manfred Gorke*, (Leipzig, 1977)

Schulze 1978 | H.-J. Schulze, 'Johann Sebastian Bachs Konzertbearbeitungen nach Vivaldi und Anderen – Studien oder Auftragswerke?', *Deutsches Jahrbuch der Musikwissenschaft für 1973–1977* 18 (Leipzig, 1978) 80–100

Schweitzer 1905 | A. Schweitzer, *J. S. Bach le Musicien–Poète* (Leipzig, 1905)

Seiffert 1907 | letter to editor, *BJ* 4 (1907) 180

Siegele 1975 | U. Siegele, *Kompositionsweise und Bearbeitungstechnik in der Instrumentalmusik Johann Sebastian Bachs* (Stuttgart, 1975)

SIMG | *Sammelbände der Internationalen Musikgesellschaft*

Souchay 1927 | M.-A. Souchay, 'Das Thema in der Fuge Bachs', *BJ* 24 (1927) 1–102

Spitta I, II | P. Spitta, *Johann Sebastian Bach*, 2 vols. (Leipzig, 1873–9)

Steglich 1935 | R. Steglich, *Johann Sebastian Bach* (Potsdam, 1935)

Taesler 1969 | W. M. Taesler, 'Von Zusammenhang in einigen zyklischen Orgelwerken Johann Sebastian Bachs – Beobachtungen eines Orgelspielers', *MuK* 39 (1969) 184–7

Tagliavini 1969 | L. F. Tagliavini, 'Johann Gottfried Walther transcrittore', *Analecta Musicologica* 7 (1969) 112–19

Tittel 1962 | K. Tittel (ed.), *J. L. Krebs: Ausgewählte Orgelwerke* I (Cologne, 1962)

References

Tittel 1966 | K. Tittel, 'Welche unter J. S. Bachs Namen geführten Orgel-werke sind Johann Tobias bzw. Johann Ludwig Krebs zuzuschreiben?', *BJ* 52 (1966) 102–37

Trumpff 1963 | G. A. Trumpff, 'Der Rahmen zu Bachs Dritten Teil der Klavierübung', *NZfM* 124 (1963) 466–70

Vogelsänger 1972 | S. Vogelsänger, 'Zur Architektonik der Passacaglia J. S. Bachs', *Mf* 25 (1972) 40–50

Waldersee 1885 | Paul Graf Waldersee, 'Antonio Vivaldi's Violinconcerte unter besonderer Berücksichtigung der von Johann Sebastian Bach Bear-beiteten', *Vierteljahresschrift für Musikwissenschaft* 1 (1885) 356–80

Walther *Praecepta* | J. G. Walther, *Praecepta der musicalischen Composi-tion* [1708], ed. P. Benary (Leipzig, 1955)

Williams 1968 | P. Williams, 'The Harpsichord Acciaccatura: Theory and Practice in Harmony, 1650–1750', *MQ* 54 (1968) 503–23

Williams 1972 | P. Williams, *Bach Organ Music* (London, 1972)

Wolff 1968 | C. Wolff, *Der Stile antico in der Musik Johann Sebastian Bachs* (Wiesbaden, 1968)

Wolff 1969 | C. Wolff, 'Die Architektur von Bachs Passacaglia', *Acta Organologica* 3 (1969) 183–94

Wolff 1972 | C. Wolff, 'Bemerkungen zu Siegfried Vogelsängers Aufsatz "Zur Architektonik der Passacaglia J. S. Bachs"', *Mf* 25 (1972) 488–90

Wolff 1974 | C. Wolff, 'Johann Sebastian Bachs *Sterbechoral*: Kritische Fragen zu einem Mythos', in *Studies in Renaissance and Baroque Music in Honor of Arthur Mendel* (Kassel, 1974) 283–97

Wustmann 1911 | R. Wustmann, 'Tonartensymbolik zu Bachs Zeit', *BJ* 8 (1911) 60–74

Zietz 1969 | H. Zietz, *Quellenkritische Untersuchungen an den Bach-Handschriften P 801, P 802 und P 803* (Hamburg, 1969)

Index of Names

Biographical details of composers, organists, copyists, organ-builders, editors and authors before the twentieth century have been collected from *MGG*, *Dok* I–III, *NBA KB*, etc. An organist's appointments ('appts') include his last major post. 'Author' indicates a twentieth-century author. 'Pupil of J. S. Bach', as defined by Hans Löffler (in Besseler 1950), implies those 'owing their musical education wholly or largely' to the composer, those only 'for a short time under his influence', and those 'strongly influenced by though not known to have taken instruction' from him.

Index of BWV Works Cited

This index excludes the main references to each organ work, certain simple cross-references, and the List of Sources (pp. 346–50).